VISUAL ORDER
the nature and development of pictorial representation

VISUAL ORDER

the nature and development of
pictorial representation

Edited by

N. H. FREEMAN
Department of Psychology,
University of Bristol

M. V. COX
Department of Psychology,
University of York

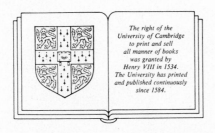

The right of the
University of Cambridge
to print and sell
all manner of books
was granted by
Henry VIII in 1534.
The University has printed
and published continuously
since 1584.

CAMBRIDGE UNIVERSITY PRESS

Cambridge
London   New York   New Rochelle
Melbourne   Sydney

Published by the Press Syndicate of the University of Cambridge
The Pitt Building, Trumpington Street, Cambridge CB2 1RP
32 East 57th Street, New York, NY 10022, USA
10 Stamford Road, Oakleigh, Melbourne 3166, Australia

First published 1985

Printed in Great Britain by the
University Press, Cambridge

Library of Congress catalogue card number: 85-5900

British Library cataloguing in publication data
Visual order: the nature and development of
pictorial representation.
    1. Drawing ability in children
I. Freeman, N. H.   II. Cox, M. V.
155.4   BF723.D7
ISBN 0 521 26668 8

68167109

CONTENTS

List of contributors   *page* xiii

Preface   xv

Introduction   1
N. H. FREEMAN and M. V. COX

1   **How meaning covers the traces**   17
ALAN COSTALL

    1 Introduction   17
    2 The projective model of pictures   18
    3 The picture theory of perception   22
    4 The 'picture theory' of pictures   24
    5 Conclusion   28
    References   28

Commentary   31
N. H. FREEMAN and M. V. COX

2   **A perspective on traditional artistic practices**   32
FRANCIS PRATT

    1 Introduction   32
    2 The *modus operandi* of the perspective frame   33
    3 Some propositions   35
    4 Knowledge and accuracy   40
    5 Aids and strategies used by artists   41
    6 Towards a theory of depiction   53
    7 Concluding comments   56
    References   57

3 **There is no development in art**   59
   MARGARET A. HAGEN

   1 Introduction   59
   2 Station-point assumptions and geometry   60
   3 Styles of painting and geometry   63
   4 Development in the geometry of art   67
   5 Development in children   69
   6 A perceptual interpretation of non-development   73
   7 A speculation   76
     References   77

4 **Drawing systems revisited: the role of denotation systems in
   children's figure drawings**   78
   JOHN WILLATS

   1 Projection systems: background   78
   2 Projection systems: definitions   80
   3 Projection-systems approach: validity   82
   4 The use of projection systems by children:
     implications   83
   5 Projection-systems approach: limitations   85
   6 Denotation systems: background   88
   7 Denotation systems: definitions   89
   8 Denotation systems: children's figure drawings   92
   9 Conclusions   98
     References   98

5 **The adolescent's point of view: studies of forms in conflict**   101
   R. K. DUTHIE

   Editorial note by Norman Freeman   101
   1 Introduction   101
   2 Space and depth   105
   3 The task of combining form with space   107
   4 Combining rectilinear forms   111
   5 Curvilinear space   116
   6 Reconciliation   119

   Commentary   121
   N. H. FREEMAN and M. V. COX

6 **On the discovery, storage and use of graphic descriptions**   122
   W. A. PHILLIPS, M. INALL and E. LAUDER

   1 Introduction: drawing as description-finding   122

2 Experiment 1: the effects of 'visual' and drawing
training 125
3 Experiment 2: the effects of four kinds of training 127
4 Learning to draw as learning appropriate
descriptions 130
5 Finding graphic descriptions 131
6 Remembering graphic descriptions 132
7 The use of graphic descriptions 133
8 Conclusion 133
References 134

7 **Anomalous drawing development: some clinical studies** 135
LORNA SELFE

1 Introduction 135
2 Mentally retarded children 135
3 Nadia 137
4 Drawing development 141
5 Stephen 143
6 Simon 143
7 Normal and anomalous drawing compared 147
8 Autism and realism 151
References 153

Commentary 155
N. H. FREEMAN and M. V. COX

8 **Young children's representational drawings of solid objects:
a comparison of drawing and copying** 157

MAY JANE CHEN

1 Introduction 157
2 Effect of models on drawing performance 158
3 Structural-directed *versus* content-directed
strategies in drawing 159
4 A developmental scale of depth-drawing devices 161
5 Experiment 1: comparison of drawing and
copying performance 164
6 Experiment 2: development of drawing and
copying skills 166
7 Experiment 3: comparison of copied drawing and
memory drawing 171
8 Discussion and conclusion 173
References 174

9   Some children do sometimes do what they have been told to do: task demands and verbal instructions in children's drawing   176
    M. D. BARRETT, A. V. BEAUMONT and M. S. JENNETT

    1 Introduction   176
    2 Making decisions   177
    3 Recent evidence   179
    4 How flexible are children?   185
    References   187

10 One object behind another: young children's use of array-specific or view-specific representations   188
    M. V. COX

    1 Introduction   188
    2 The problem of classification   189
    3 Freeman's model of the development of hidden-line elimination   191
    4 Explanations for the young child's response   192
    5 The 'cops and robbers' task   194
    6 Manipulating the task materials   196
    7 Conclusions   199
    References   200

11 The canonical bias: young children's drawings of familiar objects   202
    ALYSON M. DAVIS

    1 Introduction   202
    2 Canonicality: object-knowledge *versus* the encoding of viewpoint   204
    3 Drawing for a reason   208
    4 Summary   212
    References   213

12 The development of view-specific representation considered from a socio-cognitive standpoint   214
    PAUL LIGHT

    1 Introduction   214
    2 One thing behind another   216
    3 Communication games: a first attempt   218
    4 Communication games: a second attempt   221
    5 Overview and concluding comments   225
    References   229

13 **Three into two won't go: symbolic and spatial coding processes in young children's drawings** 231
NIGEL INGRAM

   1 Introduction 231
   2 Canonical orientation and stereotypic representations 233
   3 The experimental evidence 235
   4 Two codes 243
   References 246

14 **Knowledge and appearance** 248
CHARLES CROOK

   1 Introduction 248
   2 Drawings as messages 251
   3 The cognitive basis of early drawing 252
   4 Interpreting segregation 256
   5 Interpreting a transparency 258
   6 A note on production problems 261
   7 The promotion of view-specific drawing 263
   References 264

15 **The head is smaller than the body: but how does it join on?** 266
JÜRI ALLIK and TIIA LAAK

   1 Introduction 266
   2 Size stereotypy 269
   3 Stereotypy in connecting parts of the figure 271
   4 Experimental studies 273
   5 Re-evaluation of drawing performance 281
   6 In conclusion 284
   References 285

   Commentary 287
N. H. FREEMAN and M. V. COX

16 **Geometrical foundations of children's drawing** 289
MICHAEL C. MITCHELMORE

   1 Introduction 289
   2 Isographs and homographs 290
   3 The psychological primitivity of parallels and perpendiculars 292
   4 Drawing parallels in isographs 295
   5 Drawing parallels in homographs 299

6 Summary and conclusions   304
References   307

17 **Figural biases and young children's drawings**   310
J. GAVIN BREMNER

1 Introduction   310
2 The perpendicular error   314
3 A symmetry interpretation   318
4 Some complicating evidence   322
5 Further questions   326
6 Conclusion   328
References   331

18 **Cross-cultural analysis of drawing errors**   333
RÜVIDE BAYRAKTAR

1 Introduction   333
2 Experiment I (The standard paradigm)   336
3 Experiment IA (The red-line cue)   339
4 Experiment IB (The shortened baseline)   340
5 Experiment IC (Two quadrants)   342
6 Experiment ID (Four quadrants)   343
7 Experiment II (Drawing the angle from scratch:
matching-to-sample)   345
8 General conclusion and discussion   348
References   354

19 **The perceptual–motor skill of drawing**   356
JUDITH I. LASZLO and PIA A. BRODERICK

1 Introduction   356
2 Drawing skill considered within the closed-loop
theory of perceptual–motor function   357
3 A study of perceptual–motor development in
drawing   361
4 Individual differences   369
5 Concluding remarks   370
References   370

20 **The transition from construction to sketching in children's
drawings**   374
LARRY FENSON

1 Introduction   374
2 Early drawings   376

3 Picture construction   378
4 Copying simple forms   379
5 A hypothesis about copying   380
6 Spurs toward outlining   382
  References   384

Conclusions   385
N. H. FREEMAN and M. V. COX

Index of names   387
Subject index   392

CONTRIBUTORS

JÜRI ALLIK (and T. LAAK)
  Department of Psychology, University of Tartu, Lauristini 5–2, Tartu, Estonia 202400, U.S.S.R.
MARTYN D. BARRETT (and A. V. BEAUMONT and M. S. JENNETT)
  Psychology Department, Roehampton Institute, Digby Stuart College, Roehampton Lane, London SW15 5PH, U.K.
RÜVIDE BAYRAKTAR
  Department of Psychology, Hacettepe University, Beytepe Kampusu, Ankara, Turkey
J. GAVIN BREMNER
  Human Development Research Group, Fylde College, University of Lancaster, Bailrigg, Lancaster LA1 4YF, U.K.
MAY JANE CHEN
  Department of Psychology, Australian National University, P.O. Box 4, Canberra, ACT 2600, Australia
ALAN COSTALL
  Department of Psychology, University of Southampton, Southampton SO9 5NH, U.K.
CHARLES CROOK
  Department of Psychology, University of Durham, Science Site, South Road, Durham DH1 3LE, U.K.
MAUREEN V. COX
  Department of Psychology, University of York, Heslington, York YO1 5DD, U.K.
ALYSON M. DAVIS
  Department of Educational Psychology, University of Birmingham, P.O. Box 363, Birmingham B15 2TT, U.K.
ROBERT K. DUTHIE (deceased)
  Communication about his material may be addressed to Heide Duthie, Kinlochan, Gash of Philorth, Fraserburgh AB4 5UA, Scotland, or to N. H. Freeman (address below)
LARRY FENSON
  Psychology Clinic, San Diego State University, San Diego, Calif. 92182, U.S.A.
NORMAN H. FREEMAN
  Department of Psychology, University of Bristol, 8–10 Berkeley Square, Bristol BS8 1HH, U.K.

MARGARET A. HAGEN
  Department of Psychology, Boston University, 64 Cunningham Street, Boston, Mass. 02215, U.S.A.
NIGEL INGRAM
  La Sainte Union College of Higher Education, The Avenue, Southampton, U.K.
JUDITH I. LASZLO (and P. BRODERICK)
  Department of Physiology, University of Western Australia, Nedlands, Perth, W.A. 6009, Australia
PAUL H. LIGHT
  Department of Psychology, University of Southampton, Southampton SO9 5NH, U.K.
MICHAEL C. MITCHELMORE
  Department of Education, University of the West Indies, Kingston, Jamaica
BILL A. PHILLIPS (and M. INALL and E. LAUDER)
  Department of Psychology, University of Stirling, Stirling FK9 4LA, Scotland
FRANCIS PRATT
  Department of Psychology, University of Stirling, Stirling FK9 4LA, Scotland
LORNA SELFE
  'Brambledown', Lower Burton, Monkland, Leominster, Herefords., U.K.
JOHN WILLATS
  43 Newtown, Bradford-on-Avon, Wiltshire BA15 1NG, U.K.

PREFACE

There has been a vast amount of recent research in the field of picture production. Yet much of it seemed to us to be dispersed across a number of different topics and subject areas. The published work is in many different journals and books. We felt that the many ideas and studies should be gathered together in one place, so that picture production could be shown to be a major and fertile topic of research in its own right, and a most useful one. And so the idea of this book was born.

An open letter expounding some of the puzzles in the field of picture production was sent to a number of people who were either writing wide-ranging books which they might be willing to tell us about, or who had done a series of experiments on a specific topic and had come to novel and interesting conclusions. The response was marvellously encouraging. It would have been easy to gather twice as many authors as we actually did; but then the book would have been editorially uncontrollable!

As it was, to lessen the danger that the book would lack all coherence, a conference was held at York, organised by Maureen Cox, which half the book contributors managed to get to, as did an equal number of active researchers who were not planning to write chapters. It quickly became obvious that far more discovery was going on behind the scenes than one would possibly have guessed from reading the journals. From out of the exciting controversies which arose at the conference the book finally took shape in our minds. The book is intended both as a contribution to experimental psychology and as a contribution from psychologists to other practitioners and interested parties. Not all the authors are professional academic psychologists: the input from other teachers and educationists and from practising artists also played an important role in giving the book its shape. All that remains is for us to thank the contributors for their tact, patience and responsiveness, as we cajoled them to revise a passage yet again. They treated us better than we deserved.

We are particularly grateful to Kathleen Dixon, Barbara Levy, Anne Merriman, Mike Pugh and Jean Webber for their help in preparing the material, words and pictures. They gave their help willingly when it was most needed. So did Susan Milmoe and Penny Carter of Cambridge University Press: they were a pleasure to work with.

N.H.F. and M.V.C.

Introduction

N. H. FREEMAN and M. V. COX

After a very brave start, about a century ago the study of the development of pictorial representation seemed to have fallen into the doldrums. There was a minor upsurge of interest just before the mid-1970s, and then a sort of explosion in the number of active researchers towards the end of the seventies. In the past five years or so, immense gains in understanding have been made. A large number of cherished prejudices have let people down: one is that young children draw what they know rather than what they see; another is that perspective is a system of depiction superior to all other; yet another is that art imitates nature. It seems to us important that this new impetus in research should be collated, and that new evidence which is discussed in the bar at conferences becomes exposed to the cold glare of daylight.

It was not possible to cover all the areas of interest in this one book. There is very little cross-cultural psychology here, for example, or analysis of how children use drawing to discover new facts. But even within the confines set in the book, the range of phenomena and topics is vast.

The four themes which dominate the book are laid out in the next section. For the moment we take the liberty of commenting on the order in which the chapters have been put. The chapters have been so arranged that they can be read in succession from 1 to 20 with the minimum of strain in passing from one author to another. If the reader takes such a straight course, it will be necessary to change gear several times in negotiating changes in level of abstraction and ease of ploughing through different kinds of evidence, but that is no more than would be expected on any normal journey. A few chapters which contain particularly clear summaries have been dispersed so that they can act as high points, suitable both for looking back and looking forward. To put the matter more simply, there is a reason for the chapter-ordering, but it is the outcome of a whole set of compromises between putting type of argument and type of evidence in adjoining chapters. There is a price to be paid for such a straightforward way of reading. Since the majority of the chapters deal in depth with more than one issue, it becomes progressively harder to nip back, for comparative purposes, unerringly to the place where any one issue was last dealt with. We have accordingly placed editorial comments at what we judged to be places where such guidance might be welcome to those readers who either do not have a healthy contempt for editors or who are not as familiar with the area as they would wish.

We now go on to provide a bird's-eye view of how the order of chapters maps onto the relationships among four particularly important themes.

1. *How do we characterise the production of depictions?* One of the themes running through the book stems from the rather abstract problem 'what is a picture?' More usefully, what makes it possible for human beings to generate depictions and to respond to them evaluatively: *how do people use their perceptual apparatus to judge when they are in the presence of a successful depiction?* The first chapter, by Costall, is rooted in one of the major theories of perception which overtly attempted to determine relations between the rather specialised nature of picture perception and that of natural everyday perceptual activity. In the controversial work of James Gibson, one finds a resolute attack on notions of naïve photographic realism as any sort of criterion whence to judge the operation of perceptual systems. Costall argues that pictures are social artefacts, made to be informative by conforming to sets of agreed, non-arbitrary, conventions. There is not, presumably, a single end-point to development. There is no single induction ceremony to the social world of depictors to be held, at which the mysteries of linear perspective and the human camera are unveiled to universal applause.

Yet if many developmental psychologists have ignored perceptual theory to the impoverishment of their enterprise, it is also true that many perceptual theorists have rested content with analysing picture perception as though pictures did not have to be generated with a great deal of mental and physical effort. If pictures are unnatural sorts of things – the product of human labour rather than leaves torn from the book of nature – what sort of discipline must the depictor impose upon herself in order to generate the artefact? One answer is given in Chapter 2. Pratt argues that depictors cannot afford to let their normal perceptual habits run unbridled. After all, in normal perception, all current theories agree, the *separation* of figure from ground is not only at a premium, but is a basic process; yet in picture generation it may have to be figure–ground *integration* that has to be achieved. Such points are important but, by themselves, would run to no more than a minor aesthetic critique. Pratt's signal achievement is to demonstrate precisely how depictors' practices work in curbing the richness of normal perception. The laboratory experiments which Gibson found so pathetically constraining and unnatural provide precisely the recipes discovered by depictors in their efforts to constrain natural perception in the interests of picture production. A neglected area of developmental psychology is the study of how children discover for themselves, or become inducted into, this corpus of tactics.

Hagen, in Chapter 3, maintains a Gibsonian emphasis, but she is concerned rather less with the labour of production and more with the characterisation of the products. Like Costall, she is concerned to demolish the notion of a Long March to the goal of depicting faithfully what we see. Since, she argues, it does not get one anywhere to suppose that adults are characterised by drawing what they see, it is vacuous to use that nonfact to accuse children, by contrast, of drawing what they know. That would be to underestimate both the social character of adult depiction (cf. Costall) and the room for manoeuvre which any depictor has. She argues that there are only four options available to choose from in depicting a projection of a three-dimensional scene. Linear perspective is but one of these options, one particular *projective drawing system*. Each drawing system is simply the necessary geometrical consequence of taking a certain station point relative to the subject to be drawn. True, no art style is simply an exercise in geometry, but geometry imposes constraints on the depictor. There is, she avers, no compelling reason to think that children chase through the systems, in order, in pursuit of the elusive perspective mode.

Hagen's case is an important one, and the necessity for being informed about the geometry of drawing systems is affirmed by Willats in the early pages of Chapter 4. However, then comes the crunch. Willats clearly prefers the computational approach to perception, Marr rather than Gibson, and argues that there is indeed a logic of development in the progressive discovery of systems. But an account of projective systems will not catch the detail of the children's efforts to generate pictures. At least as much development consists in the discovery of what Willats terms *denotation systems*. These operate at a very fine level of pictorial decision: when to use a single line to represent a person's limb, or a single contour to represent not an edge but a region where a surface smoothly curves away from the viewer. Willats argues that development consists of the progressive discovery of rules for regulating the relationships between projective systems and denotation systems in the mind of the depictor. Such rules give us the key to understanding both how a picture works and what work a depictor has to do in order to generate a picture which will work.

Thus far, it is clear that there is a need for an analysis which will relate perceptual habits and geometrical rules which map between scene and picture plane, but different authors take different rules as the basis for their accounts. In Chapter 16, Mitchelmore goes straight for this problem. He argues that since so many of the authors in this book have found themselves impelled to take geometry seriously, it is perfectly proper to turn to mathematicians who have specialised in such problems, and to ask them what geometrical primitives may be. The answer is that for rectilinear scenes, parallels and perpendiculars are fundamental relationships. This has immediate consequences for the characterisation of depictions, for one can, and ought to, divide depictions into those in which such primitives can be used in direct mapping between scene and picture and those in which they may or may not be. The former case obtains where a one-to-one mapping between scene and picture is required, as in copying a letter H for example. The latter obtains where a many-to-one mapping is entailed, as when drawing a three-dimensional cube on two-dimensional paper. The distinction between two-dimensional *isographic* and three-dimensional *homographic* depictions enables one to refine one's criteria for a successful depiction across a range of tasks. It also helps clarify some of the connections between perceiving a relationship and realising its depictive significance, as Mitchelmore demonstrates in his experiments.

Duthie, in Chapter 5, is also concerned with the problem of how a two-dimensional shape can successfully depict a three-dimensional scene, and he too rejects the traditional answer that perspective works basically because it captures what we see. Indeed, he shows that people may actively *resist* a perspective system in favour of other systems. His solution to the problem of what is a successful homographic depiction is very different from that advanced by the other authors considered so far. He puts forward two important propositions. One is that depictions are not discrete solutions to a projective problem but take their place within a *range of credibility*. What determines the credibility of a shape on the page depends both upon features integral to the three-dimensional form to be depicted and upon the relations which such a form would normally contract with other forms in the real world. Thus real-world knowledge has a part to play in the depictors' choice of geometrical relations. It follows from this that depictors may be concerned much more with the depiction of space than with the depiction of depth. This is his second important proposition, that our obsession with depth and perspective has led us to overlook the fact that whilst projective systems may be valid characterisations of pictures, it is not the job of a depictor to search out a particular system and to force the depiction into it. In generating a picture, there are many spatial problems to be solved, and there is little reason to think that the depictor always puts the problem of depth to the forefront, as it were. Duthie's experiments on combining forms in the frontal plane and on relating shapes to surfaces illustrate his thesis with particular clarity. Pictures may 'possess credibility', be convincing to the viewer, without falling neatly into a projective-system category.

In sum, the theme of what constitutes a successful depiction is probed very deeply in the six chapters outlined above. All are agreed that it is a mistake to oppose what we know to what we see and to measure development by the extent to which a depictor of any age whatsoever can churn out an imitation photograph replete with perspective cues. There is no comfort at all for traditional stage theories in the work done by these authors. The conclusion is that in the past (not to speak of the present) people have unwittingly operated a sleight-of-hand: by prejudging the criteria for successful depiction they have, *sensu strictu*, prejudiced their chances of explaining development. It may even be, as Hagen argues, that this has led developmental psychologists to whip up spurious excitement in their writings. Be that as it may, it is now clear that one needs a new characterisation of what depictors are trying to do. *If we knew what problems they are confronting, then we should be better able to judge what their depictions are solutions to.* This leads naturally to the second theme in the book.

2.   *What mental apparatus drives the production of depiction?* The contemplation of a picture is not a paradigm case of normal perception, and depictors may need to curb some of their normal perceptual habits when generating a picture. That much is clear from the chapters by Costall and Pratt (Chapters 1 and 2). But that is the negative side of the case; what then is the positive side? Duthie (Chapter 5) argues that depictors have in their minds a set of general-purpose descriptions of the normally most credible shapes. The problem for the depictor is in combining one with another: as he shows, it is easy to draw a cube and a pyramid separately, but very difficult to handle the join between them to represent a church tower plus spire. Duthie argues that adolescent depictors handle the problem by on-the-spot tactics, repairs that are made on the picture plane itself. How may these tactics be classified, and can depictors alter their mental descriptions in advance to suit a new drawing purpose?

Pratt argues that the acquisition of depiction skill consists precisely in learning to create new descriptions. This theme is formalised in Chapter 6 by Phillips, Inall and Lauder. They put forward five propositions which together define the workings of a general-purpose depictive mechanism. In connection with the present theme, three powerful points emerge from their propositions. One is that one's usual descriptions of objects are not dominated by projective relations, thus do not necessarily come in a form which will unambiguously map onto a flat piece of paper. Another point is that if a description can be generated which will serve the depictor's temporary interest, then it must be stored in working memory for as long as it is needed. If it is not, then the depictor will have to use, by default, the description held in long-term memory, with the attendant danger that that description will be inappropriate. The authors argue that children have precisely this problem, a point which is also argued through by Crook in Chapter 14: just as normal perceptual habits may have to be curbed, so may normal intellectual short-cuts. The experiments discussed by Phillips, Inall and Lauder show that children become more skilled at depiction by learning to build and store new descriptions and not by developing general strategies for looking at objects. The final point which follows is that a drawing may look very queer in its early stages. It will accord with the temporary description but will have very low credibility if it be inspected with a view to matching it against the scene. It is a familiar experience that marks on the paper may not look at all 'right' halfway through an excellent depiction. A characteristic of the skilled depictor must be the development of tenacity, the ability to ride over the rough stage of mapping out secondary geometry in the sequence of production.

Now it is known that some people do develop remarkable depiction skills very early in life, when nothing in their general mental profile would enable one to predict that flowering. No one would demand precise predictions at this stage, but nevertheless, it would be a great achievement for the chapters noted so far if such flowering proved retrodictable, that is, comprehensible in the light of previous knowledge once the new information has been provided. In Chapter 7, Selfe takes up the challenge. She analyses the productions of some autistic children whose marvellous depictions are certainly anomalous. It transpires that they do *not* have all-round drawing abilities. What they appear to do is to go straight for the building of descriptions based upon projective relations. This is precisely what normal children, fully thriving on social relations, do not do. The autistic children thus are not superbly accelerated normal children: they are ones who are quietly building their special descriptions from a frozen fixed viewpoint. As Selfe points out, this is necessarily asocial on their part. It effectively insulates them from the problems which normal children thrash about in with such undisciplined vigour.

In sum, one can take the step from puzzling out what may be involved in producing a successful depiction to identifying some of the mental characteristics of the successful depictor. This brings one face to face with another problem which cannot possibly be evaded at this point. In order to test one's theories about the mental work done by a depictor one has to have a clear set of criteria for identifying what the depictor is primarily trying to do. Only then can one judge whether the depictor has succeeded, failed or moved right out of one's sphere of judgement. This is the next theme to be dealt with. *The most pressing issue is to decide whether a depictor is confronting a problem or evading it.* After all, to take an extreme case, we have seen from Hagen (Chapter 3) that there are four possible options to take in projective geometry, and it would be utterly absurd to poke fun at a classical Indian drawing which adopts one option on the grounds that a linear-perspective drawer would have done it differently. It is perfectly permissible to *compare* options, but not permissible to transport criteria for the success of one over to the other. The classic ground for misjudgement is with the efforts of children. Accordingly, the next theme is the mentality of children as seen in the efforts they make, in the problems they set themselves.

3.   *What information do children normally try to catch in their depictions?* We already have several clues to the answer. Duthie (Chapter 5) argued that children typically do not try to capture depth-as-seen-by-that-particular-viewer, not, that is, unless they are one of that small band studied by Selfe (Chapter 7). It may well be that they cannot help but try to capture more general aspects of the scene, as argued by Phillips, Inall and Lauder (Chapter 6) and by Crook (Chapter 14). This seems to be reasonable enough, yet the poles of contrast are uncomfortably wide: how general is 'general' and how restrictive is a viewer's view? What one needs is an experimental design which will bring these rather stark alternatives to within striking distance over a unified set of materials spanning homographic and isographic tasks (Mitchelmore, Chapter 16).

This is presented by Chen in Chapter 8. Her approach is the following. If children do not readily depict a viewer's-eye projection of a real object when it is in front of them, what would be expected if the object were replaced with a photograph? Presumably this solves some of the projective problems for them, but still leaves a denotation problem (Willats, Chapter 4): it is not easy to decipher a photograph in order to choose the most appropriate places for transforming into contours. A line-drawing, made by tracing such contours on a transparency placed over the photograph at its points of maximal information, demonstrates the solution to both projective and denotation problems. Chen asked children to draw objects, photographs of the objects and line-drawings of the photographs. She found that many children below the age of 9 years did benefit from the pictorial solutions presented to them, in the sense of managing to capture some projective relations which eluded them when drawing the real objects. She describes the children as being able to adopt a 'structure-directed strategy' (rather akin to that identified by Selfe, Chapter 7). But, by the same token, many of the children in the youngest age groups, 5 and 6 years, failed to benefit from the photograph and manifested problems in identifying boundary lines. These children she describes as adopting a 'content-directed strategy' (they were presumably using the sort of knowledge-based descriptions discussed by Duthie in Chapter 5, Phillips, Inall and Lauder in Chapter 6 and Crook in Chapter 14). A longitudinal study, all too rare in this area of research, confirms the findings.

Thus it seems that some children are locked onto undertaking depiction as though the task were to portray a recognisable object, whilst others tackle the problem of capturing a particular view. Advance towards the latter is correlated with age, with a turning-point round about 7–8 years of age. The dichotomy is very reminiscent of Marr's distinction between object-centred and viewer-centred coordinate systems, outlined by Willats (Chapter 4). The question is what would happen if one overtly asked young children to shift their mode of drawing: at what age would they be capable of responding? Of course, one would have to put the requests into very simple language for them.

In Chapter 9, Barrett, Beaumont and Jennett report the outcome of such an experiment, asking children (a) to draw objects and (b) to draw them as they see them. The results lead the authors to argue that even 5-year-olds may have more than one mode of depiction available, but that it is not until age 6 that their flexibility arises in a reliable form with an accompanying sensitivity to verbal instruction. An important aspect of one of the tasks was that it involved one object partially occluding another in the child's line of sight. The proper projective device for depicting this is to use *hidden-line elimination*, to violate the integrity of the further object. The authors conclude that hidden-line elimination is an on-the-spot solution adopted by children *after* they register that a viewer-centred strategy is called for. This particular drawing device is of crucial importance in classifying children's efforts to deal with simple projective relationships, as is well known from the literature. It amply repays close study, and this is undertaken by Cox in Chapter 10.

Below the age of 8 years or so, children do not reliably use hidden-line elimination. Instead, they may draw the further object above or even beside the nearer one, but in either case the two objects are separated on the page. Why? Is segregation a basic tactic adopted to avoid having to do hidden-line elimination? In such a case, children would be thought of as avoiding a depiction problem. Or is it rather the case that segregation is a basic drawing device which amply fulfils the children's aims? Perhaps they aim to represent the integrity of the two objects, adopting an object-centred (or a content-centred) mode. In a series of experiments Cox probes young children's understanding of, and production of, hidden-line elimination. At one point in the series, she gives the children a theme to work with, a robber-trying-to-hide-from-the-cops explanation: this neatly explains both the structure and the appearance of the scene for the child. Under this condition, nearly half her 4-year-olds used hidden-line elimination: the best performance reported to date. So it is clear that young children have been underestimated: they have more advanced drawing devices up their sleeves than anyone had suspected.

It could be the case that the 'human sense' of the situation had released the children's expertise in some mysterious fashion. But that would hardly be an explanation, for it would merely shift the problem away from depiction towards human mentality in general. In her final experiments, Cox sets her sights firmly upon the depiction problem. She presents the child with *visual contrasts* in the array, and shows that the probability of the child using hidden-line elimination increases as the two objects become dissimilar. In her final experiment she provides the contrast, despite controlling the structure and appearance of the scene, by calling the nearer object by different names. This is enough to alert many of the children to using hidden-line elimination.

It is now clear that previous research has greatly underestimated the capabilities of children below the age of 7. It is quite unjust to regard them as being locked into an 'intellectual-realist stage' as the Piagetians would have it. Even 4-year-olds may be already equipped with more than one functioning depictive strategy. Yet there is a reason why one regards such young children as being rather primitive in their approach to depiction. The reason is that they seem to be locked into producing rather stereotyped depictions, locked into accessing customary general-purpose descriptions. How about trying out a rather different analysis? Suppose we regard them as prone to retreating into stereotypy? The challenge then becomes one of taking a drawing task which is known to trigger such a stereotypy, and seeing how far the manipulation of scene contrasts can encourage the children spontaneously to emerge. This is obviously a severe test of any line of research, to induce a strong bias and then to predict what conditions will modulate its strength, and it is heroically undertaken by Davis in Chapter 11.

The most extreme case of hidden-line elimination is when a discrete part of an integral object has to be omitted, as when a cup is to be drawn in such a position that its handle cannot be seen at all by the viewer. Young children, 5- and 6-year-olds, have a tendency to draw the non-visible handle in its canonical position, on the side of their cup drawing. This *'canonical bias'* can be very strong indeed in a large number of individuals. What will serve to encourage young depictors to break with this particular object-centred mode? Just providing more visual information, by making the cup transparent, is actually counter-productive, as Davis shows. Giving them a clearer perception of the structure of the cup, then, apparently makes the children respond by retreating into their bias. This is intriguing, for literally making the display clearer to the viewer drives the children away from a viewer-centred depiction. It acts as a visual puzzle for them. The key to the matter turns out not to reside in the characteristics of the individual cup so much as in its *context*. Davis shows that the more the cup's appearance contrasts with that of another cup, the higher the level of complete hidden-line elimination. This ties up very neatly with Cox's work (Chapter 10): 5-year-olds have been terribly underestimated in the standard literature.

So it is clear that children benefit from being given visual contrasts to work with. Yet one must be careful about that. When Davis turned the situation into a communication game, asking the children to draw the target cup so that the next child will be able to use the drawing as a guide to find that particular cup in the array, the manoeuvre was counter-productive. Again the children retreated into their canonical bias, despite showing clearly in their depiction that they were trying hard to draw that particular cup. Simply, they overdid it: they chose to draw the wrong aspects of the cup. Communication is not a magic key for unlocking depiction expertise.

At this point one wants to try out a unified account of young children's problems in deploying their expertise, an account which will classify competing explanations. In Chapter 12 Light provides a clear summary of some of the major features of the types of account we have been considering so far. He divides explanations into positive and negative ones. Negative ones are those which view children's depiction biases as faults to be overcome, and positive ones are those which see them as deliberate depiction strategies, maybe primitive, but nonetheless aimed for by the child. The issue as he states it, is central to the theme being outlined in this section: not so much how well children do, but what information they are trying to capture in their depictions. Light makes the excellent point that depictions *convey* rather than *contain* information (cf. Costall, Chapter 1).

As we know, the conveying of information is a social act, and it is fitting that children be given social drawing games, rather as we saw in Davis, Chapter 11. Indeed, this seems to pay off and, with commendable persistence, Light's work with 5- to 6-year-olds reveals an impressive adaptive flexibility in their modes of depiction. Yet again, as has happened twice before, the key to the controlling variables does not lie in communication *per se* but in the *contrasts* which one puts within the child's mental reach as raw material upon which she can exercise her battery of drawing devices. The conclusion is that the conscientious analysis of contrasts will illuminate the key feature of development: *the adaptive flexibility in what children try to accomplish is more important than what they actually succeed best in.* The literature is full of studies which have discussed the former through a prejudiced emphasis on the latter. Is this not reminiscent of the first theme with which we dealt, the problem of diagnosing what is a successful depiction?

If the line of argument of these authors is anywhere near correct, it ought to be possible to subject it to a severe test. How about pushing the age range down to the danger zone of 3 years of age, and simultaneously examining depiction of relations between objects (cf. Cox, Chapter 10; Light, Chapter 12) and within an object (cf. Davis, Chapter 11)? Ingram, in Chapter 13, spotted an elegant way of bringing the trick off. What he invented is a decomposable object. In one task, children have to draw a sort of doll, made up of two blocks with a face on one of them. This can be perceived as an integral form of rather familiar symbolic significance. Wipe the face off, and one has two blocks with an arbitrary spatial relationship between them. Put the doll/two-blocks in different orientations with respect to the viewer, and one can compare depictions of the two types of figure over a range of spatial problems.

The results vindicate Ingram's efforts. Putting a face on one block triggers a bias whereby the blocks are depicted as more doll-like than in reality; and without the face, the children struggle to portray the spatial relations between the blocks. As Light has told us, they do not draw very well, but by looking at the temporal sequence of production, Ingram shows clearly that the spatial arrangement of blocks has a real effect on what the children are trying to do. Often, looking at the order in which children choose to draw things tells one far more than the finished product possibly can. And, of course, the study of sequencing is a proper part of the study of picture production, as has been documented in the literature before now.

In sum, if one is sensitive enough about one's observations and materials, it is clear that even 3-year-olds often attempt to depict what they see. So once again, armed with a new insight into the flexibility of young depictors, we return to the question that has been raised in so many of the chapters so far: what, in general, is the relationship between what we know and what we see? How does the relationship manifest itself in depiction? These questions are tackled by Crook in Chapter 14.

His argument turns on a point which we have already met. It is that although recent theoretical advances have laid stress on the nature of depictions as conveying information (cf. children's use of contrasts discussed in Chapters 10, 11 and 12), the failure of overt demands for social informativeness to improve depictions means that one ought to question whether it is at all useful to infer a motivation to convey information on the part of the child. Yet what option do we have? Crook's answer is to take up the structural-description argument outlined above under the heading of the second theme (Chapters 2, 6 and 7) and to use it in the light of what has been learned from the research in the preceding few chapters. Crook's point is that how informative a picture is results from the temporary structural description which the child builds, so any variable which induces the child to change that description will induce a change in the information conveyed in the depiction. This is close to the analysis of Ingram (Chapter 13), and is here applied in a new way.

The novelty consists in specifying in advance what a structural description would be, and mapping between that and what is known of the young child's battery of drawing devices. The focus is on segregation and hidden-line elimination. One can study the former by literally pushing together segregated objects in the scene. One can study the latter by increasing or decreasing the precise information about what is hidden: the feature that is hidden in the scene could either be a meeting of two discrete objects or a mark on one discrete object. The results show that the drawing device adopted by the young child is not a single product of the amount of information to be conveyed but can be explained in terms of the mental model which the child holds. Naturally there is much more work to be done on the nature of structural descriptions, but at least the evidence is strategically placed where it is optimally challenging for current accounts.

Thus far, the evidence is all to the credit of the children: their abilities have been upgraded in the eyes of the analytic researcher. But much of the evidence bearing on the present theme, of *what mental apparatus drives successful depiction*, is confined to the setting of overt homographic puzzles in which they have to struggle with the problem of depth. Not all the evidence is so restricted, but a lot of it is; and we were warned by Duthie (Chapter 5) that a confrontation with the problem of depth is not of central concern even to very advanced children, adolescents. Indeed, we find Mitchelmore (Chapter 16) arguing that when young children draw a cube, those beautiful obliques are not generated to represent depth but are on-the-spot solutions. Accordingly, we now turn to the final one of the four themes in the book: where there is no specific problem of depth or object solidity to be confronted, what is it like for a child to bring visual order onto the flat page itself, and how well can they be expected to do with that medium?

4. *Organising the lines on the page.* The point was made by Duthie (Chapter 5) that one does not need a depth problem in order to puzzle an adolescent: fitting two shapes together in the frontal plane is problem enough. What one needs, in order to make an analytically rigorous story is a frontal-plane problem which demands the use of the same drawing devices as does a depth problem. At first sight this seems unattainable; but there is, in fact, a perfectly simple empirical solution. Consider the problem of drawing one discrete object partially occluded by another. As has been reported in the literature, the child has but a small battery of drawing devices from which to choose: *segregation* (the two objects kept separate), *line elimination* (part of the further object deleted), *overlap* (both objects drawn in their entirety with their boundaries crossing), *enclosure* (one drawn inside the other) and various forms of *bridged segregation* (an odd line put in to fill the gap between two discrete objects). One can observe some of these in the depiction of very young children when they try to organise human-figure drawings for themselves, at the junction between head and trunk. Thus *these drawing devices are plurifunctional*. Will very young children choose now one device, now another, with different drawing-completion games?

Allik and Laak, in Chapter 15, present their investigation of the problem, and conclude that such drawing devices are local, on-the-spot decisions taken by the child. They are not laid down in the child's structural description of the frontal projection of the human figure. In contrast, head–trunk relative size does appear to be. This is interesting, because it is well known that young children tend to draw the head too large in comparison with the trunk. It is even more interesting that Allik and Laak's data lead them to conclude that the truth is the converse of that: it is minification of the trunk that is the problem, not magnification of the head.

That chapter bridges the previous theme and the present one: *how well children can be expected to do*. Even very young ones tackle the problem of joining two parts in an inventive manner, and it is striking that they do so by on-the-spot decisions, just as, Duthie argues (Chapter 5), adolescents do. The use of an on-the-spot decision when trying to join two objects or two very distinct parts of an object seems to characterise children of all ages.

Yet human-figure drawing undeniably advances with age. What is its most dramatic manifestation? The answer given by Fenson in Chapter 20 is that the children shift gear: instead of constructing a complex figure out of discrete parts by a set of on-the-spot decisions, they go in for moulding the outlines of the whole figure.) In Willats' terms, by using a continuous line for the occluding contour of the figure, they solve some of the denotation problems over which they previously came to grief (Chapter 4). But, as the chapter number shows, we have placed Fenson's work at the end: it makes a nice, human note on which to finish, and reminds one of the formal analysis involved in the first theme, the question of what counts as a successful depiction.

However inspiring the evidence for young children's depiction flexibility, there is one problem that that cannot illuminate, and it is a most important one. It is one thing to show that a child will make a clever choice when faced with a problem of selecting a drawing device on the picture plane, quite another to find out whether that child has executed that device well or badly. That is because it is no easy matter to *scale* the efficacy of any particular device. Take segregation for example in drawing two touching objects: if one child draws two shapes with a one-centimetre gap, and another child makes a half-centimetre gap, which child is showing more expertise at depiction? Is it the child who manages to make the two objects quite close or the one who more resolutely sticks to segregation? Put that way, the question is probably an absurd one. But it is far from absurd whenever one knows in advance what the scale is. Then it seems mandatory to investigate the problem. It so happens that a very long-researched topic in young children's depiction prowess falls fair and square into this category, although it is only relatively recently that researchers awoke to the fact.

The scale in question is that of orientation. A great deal is known about children's perception of angles and inclinations, their accuracy of discrimination and the alignment cues they tend to rely on. In one small area, all four themes can be focused. In copying an angle or inclined line, one knows precisely how to measure a successful depiction, precisely what information the children are trying to catch, roughly what sort of mental apparatus is required; and now one can ask how good they are at it. In Chapter 16, Mitchelmore sums up several important points which relate to these themes. He discusses a series of new experiments in children's copying of parallels and angles. Children may be able to perceive parallels and to understand the use of parallelism for purposes of alignment but still be very bad indeed at isolating precisely which cue will best serve their interests in drawing. They find it difficult to parse a figure for the purpose of copying, sometimes relying upon length more than directional cues. The conclusion is clear: one must be very wary indeed about making inferences from children's poor performance in an orientation task to children's understanding of geometry. It is well known that, by the sheerest bad luck, Piaget came a cropper here with his 'water-level task'. From the fact that children couldn't draw the water level horizontal inside a tilted bottle, he inferred that either they did not possess sufficient deductive powers or that they did not have enough respect for the external framework of the display. Yet it is extraordinarily difficult for young children to draw the requisite acute angle even when they want to. Indeed, even adolescents can fall prey to the bias if the problem be challenging enough (Duthie, Chapter 5).

The study of children's efforts to construct an acute angle is thus strategically placed in the scale of things: it fulfils the criteria of rigour which one now expects in depiction research, and is of vital importance for geometry education and for Piagetian testing. What is the nature of children's persistent bias to widen an acute angle, *the perpendicular bias* as it has come to be called?

Bremner, in Chapter 17, shows how to decompose the bias. It is not a unitary phenomenon, but is entangled with a bias towards creating symmetry on the picture plane. It is Bremner's signal achievement to devise a task which pits one bias against the other. It transpires that each is controlled by a different type of alignment cue from the other. This illuminates the hard mental work which the young depictor is trying to do. There is little comfort for those who see in children a lack of respect for wide alignment cues; and a clear need for researchers to disentangle biases which may be a product of the integrality of the figure to be copied from biases which may be local ones based on children's analysis of a part of the figure.

But a problem remains, and it is the dual problem of the status and generality of the biases. Do the biases mask yet more subtle efforts on the part of the child; and can one infer from the existence of the biases that, whenever a depiction task triggers one, the children will always be tripped by the same variable? To put it more basically, is there nothing which the young child has in stock which can help her overcome the problem other than by growing older and letting it ride? Bayraktar, in Chapter 18, takes one instance of the perpendicular bias and tracks it though a variety of tasks over urban and rural children. The bias is a very stubborn one to defeat. Indeed, in one of her tasks, the provision of alignment cues which, theory tells us, should help the children backfired badly and increased the size of the bias. She comes to two important conclusions. One is that the standard Piagetian test of the child's conception of spatial orientation is, as we had suspected, the bluntest instrument that one could devise, and that is being charitable. But that is a bit negative. The positive conclusion is that as the depiction task becomes freer, giving the child more work to do and hence more scope for error, the bias does not necessarily alter in size, but the order of difficulty of different conditions may radically alter. It follows that one cannot mechanically rank copying tasks in order of difficulty and predict, whenever a depiction involves one of them, the level of error of the child's performance (this is a little vexing because so many of the two-dimensional isographic copying tasks studied in Chapters 16, 17 and 18 do form the early stages of the emerging depiction in many three-dimensional homographic tasks).

At this point, matters may seem to have taken a rather gloomy turn. After all, many of the previous chapters were engaged in upgrading our view of the child's expertise, and now we have been conspicuously refusing to do so. There are two answers to that. One is that one cannot go on upgrading for ever. The other answer is more useful: it is that if one can demonstrate that there is a perfectly good reason why one's scale of error should not start at zero for any age group, then in comparison with one's revised estimate, the children may objectively be doing very well indeed, and it may be pointless to badger, educate or cajole them differently. This is one of the points made by Laszlo and Broderick in Chapter 19.

They go straight for the most basic level of expertise: the hand moving over the page. They argue that 5- to 6-year-olds do rather badly at isographic copying tasks because they lack the requisite degree of kinaesthetic sensitivity, the requisite sensitivity to feedback from the moving hand. This is indeed a basic level of skill, but the account is by no means a reductionist one, for, as Laszlo and Broderick argue, the issue of kinaesthetic sensitivity is intimately bound up with the level and type of planning that the child can project. And, of course, it is at this sort of age that we expect children to write neatly. It is also the age at which it is normal for vigorous experimentation to occur in spontaneous drawing, as Fenson (Chapter 20) reminds us.

How do the four themes relate one to another? There are as many views on this as there are chapters in the book. There is also a wide diversity of issues upon which the authors focus their main themes, and a wide diversity in the number of themes and issues upon which different authors focus. Enough has been said about the huge range covered by the book (it is actually but a small part of the massive research area), and it is time to let the authors speak for themselves. The many issues which arise – what our basic categories are, what training can usefully be given when, and so on – will be found collated in the editorial comments at the end of the book, and noted in the editorial comments seeded at a few interstices in the lines of argument.

1

How meaning covers the traces

ALAN COSTALL

The eye has become a human eye when its object has
become a social, human object, produced by man and
destined for him. (Marx, 1844/1971)

1. Introduction

Developmental psychology, considered as a method, promises to shed light
upon the nature of the *adult* through an analysis of the process of development.
Yet while there can be no question that developmental psychology has yielded
a highly productive research programme in recent years, its very productivity
has perhaps helped mask some important underlying problems. On the one
hand, its methods are not always appropriate to its avowed aims, lacking any
obvious developmental dimension. On the other hand, many of its proponents
seem intent upon talking themselves out of a job. When they are not
attributing the most sophisticated resources to the new-born baby (such as
mental maps, rules, representations and scripts), they anticipate the very
results their enquiry promised to supply. Even the acknowledged pioneer of
the recent research was not exempt from criticism. As Merleau-Ponty (1962,
p. 355) complained, 'Piaget brings the child to a mature outlook as if the
thoughts of the adult were self-sufficient and disposed of all contradictions.'

Over the last 10 years, children's drawings have provided the topic of a
lively field of research within developmental psychology. Over this same
period, my interest has been mainly devoted to research on the perception of
pictures by adults, and the theoretical examination of James Gibson's attempt
to replace what he termed 'the picture theory' of natural perception (Gibson,
1979). As an outsider, therefore, I have been fascinated by the results of the
research on children's drawings, but also puzzled to find the investigators
themselves largely untouched by the radical debates occurring within perceptual theory. As I see it, they have left basic theoretical assumptions about
pictures and perception unexamined and uncriticised. The risk is greatest
among those psychologists who investigate children's drawings the way
Edmund Hillary climbed mountains – just because they are there. Others seek

to explain why children's drawings deviate from 'adult-style' drawings, yet take the efforts of adults as unproblematic and hence ignore two important facts. First of all, even adults produce pictures of varied competence and in various styles, not only between different cultures but within the self-same culture. Secondly, we adults have not been too successful in providing a coherent account of how our own pictures 'work'. If these facts are ignored, we may well arrive at developmental accounts of representation that are just too good to be true – as if the artistic endeavours of adults were self-sufficient and disposed of all contradictions.

In the research upon children's drawings, easy reference is made to the idea of 'adult-style representations' as if it provided a secure base from which to make excursions into children's art. It goes without saying (they say) that photographs and related perspective pictures are ideal as representations since they, and only they, show things as they really are, or really look. While this claim seems harmless enough, it is perhaps analogous to the old boast that English is surely the best of all possible languages. Other languages use the oddest terms to describe things: the French call a dog a 'chien', the Greeks call it a 'skeelo' yet we English call it a 'dog', which is, of course, exactly what it is. The latter claim is just a silly joke, yet the claim for perspective pictures does not strike us as obviously silly. That the traditional theory of perception nurtures such complacency is hardly surprising. The history of the theory of vision is intimately connected with the discovery of linear perspective, and indeed takes a spectator encountering an image as its paradigm of perception. It was James Gibson's contention that this connection between the theory of pictures and the theory of vision has been unfortunate in that psychologists and artists had managed to mislead one another: 'we have borrowed the so-called cues for depth from the painters, and they in turn have accepted a theory of perception we deduced from their techniques' (Gibson, 1967, p. 140).

James Gibson attempted to establish a new theory of vision which did not *start* with pictures, and as a result he has helped us to see that pictures may well pose special problems. But if Gibson's theory constitutes a kind of Copernican revolution, we should remember that even Copernicus did not get things entirely right (Gombrich, 1971, p. 195).

2. The projective model of pictures

Within any system of representation some relation must be supposed between the depiction and that which is depicted (Figure 1.1). In the system of linear perspective, the relation is supposed to be one of optical equivalence, a

Figure 1.1 Cartoon by Kevin Woodcock. (Reprinted, with permission, from *The Best of Private Eye*, London: Quartet Books, 1975.)

Figure 1.2 Leonardo's sketch of a 'perspectograph', a device for tracing onto a sheet of glass an image of any object placed beyond it. A peep-hole in a board is used to keep the artist's eye in a fixed position.

point-to-point correspondence between the structured light provided by the picture and the light projected to the artist's eye by the depicted scene itself. A whole range of optical devices have been constructed both to demonstrate this relation and to aid the production of perspective images, from perspective screens or windows to cameras as such (Figure 1.2). Leonardo, for example, gave the following advice to the aspiring artist:

Have a piece of glass as large as a half-sheet of royal folio paper and set this firmly in front of your eyes, that is, between your eye and the thing you want to draw; then place yourself at a distance of 2/3 of a braccio from the glass, fixing your head with a machine in such a way that you cannot move at all. Then shut or cover one eye and with a brush or drawing-chalk draw upon the glass that which you see beyond it. (Richter, 1970, p. 317)

The existence of an explicit and unified optical rationale for the production of perspective pictures would seem to confirm the status of linear perspective as a peculiarly 'natural' system of pictorial representation. That linear perspective is indeed no mere convention appears to be amply demonstrated by examples of *trompe l'oeil*: under rather special viewing conditions, at least, a perspective picture may be mistaken for the real thing.

Our enchantment with perspective is reinforced by a further aspect of cameras and related devices in the making of pictures. For they do not serve solely as vivid demonstrations of the optical-geometrical basis of linear perspective. By mechanising the process of image formation they seemed to guarantee the authenticity of the representation in terms of its intimate *causal* connection with the depicted scene. It is easy to forget the very long history of the use of cameras. In the 17th century, for example, Huygens was moved to describe the image formed by the *camera obscura* as 'the apotheosis of the optic image' (quoted in Hammond, 1981, p. 24). But it was only with the invention of photography that this causal process appeared complete. There was no longer the need for the artist to trace the image; it could be captured automatically – directly 'transcribed' from nature. As Sontag has noted, a photograph, unlike a drawing or painting, seems to be no mere copy, but an actual trace or fragment of reality: 'something directly stenciled off the real, like a footprint or a death mask' (Sontag, 1977, p. 154). Indeed, it seems that the excitement aroused by the invention of photography was largely centred upon this aspect of 'mechanisation'. After all, much 17th-century Dutch painting rivals the realism of the photographic image. Furthermore, *if* realism were the point, it is odd that the subsequent inventions of stereoscopic and colour photography, and, more recently, of holography have not had a greater impact.

Two problems were soon recognised concerning the supposedly intimate relation between a perspective picture and that which it represents. The first problem is that, according to the rationale of linear perspective, the optical equivalence between the picture and the depicted scene holds only for one particular point of observation, the 'station point'. Yet, as Leonardo and many since have noted, the theoretically ideal conditions for viewing a perspective picture are seldom if ever realised in practice, and some important complications arise under the more familiar conditions of viewing pictures (Goodman, 1978 and 1979; Pirenne, 1970). The second problem, however, has figured much more centrally in theoretical discussions, and concerns the ambiguity of perspective projections. For whilst the projection from a scene is uniquely defined, it would seem that a given projection is consistent with a limitless number of possible scenes (Figure 1.3). As a solution to this problem of projective ambiguity, Leonardo, among others, recommended that the painter should use a variety of pictorial clues to suggest depth relations in the picture.

The problem of projective ambiguity might have been confined to picture makers were it not for the persuasive analogy between the eye and the camera, and the more implicit and general notion of the psychological subject as a passive onlooker – a bemused and paralysed spectator. Pictures came to play

Figure 1.3 Gravestone or arch in the wall? An ambiguous photograph by Steve Forrester. (Courtesy of West Surrey College of Art and Design.)

a fundamental role in the theory of vision itself. Picture perception became, and has remained, the paradigm of visual perception.

3. The picture theory of perception

Over the course of many years, Gibson insisted that pictures should not be taken as the starting point for the explanation of our contact with the real environment. It is important to note that in the several definitions given by Gibson of his concept of direct perception, he each time relied upon the contrast with pictures (Gibson, 1979, pp. 10, 42, 147). Normal perception, he argued, does not depend upon the ambiguous pictorial depth cues of traditional theory. The structured light available to a perceiver in the natural environment (the 'optic array') contains information which completely *specifies* places, things, persons and events, as well as the perceiver's relation to that environment. In contrast to a picture, the optic array available in the natural environment not only surrounds the perceiver, but is subject to change when the perceiver moves in the environment. In Gibson's terms, the normal optic array allows not only *ambient* but also *ambulatory* vision. And ambulatory vision allows the detection of *invariants*. Within the changing array exist invariant structures specific to the unchanging properties of the environment. Perceptual constancies, therefore, may not depend upon assumptions or processes of compensation, but upon the detection of invariants in the optic array. According to Gibson, only in far-fetched situations, such as those devised by the experimental psychologist, *where the perceiver is forced into a position analogous to a spectator confronting a picture*, does perception become uncertain and unreliable:

The standard approach to vision begins with the eyes fixed and exposed to a momentary pattern of stimuli...The ecological approach to visual perception works from the opposite end. It begins with the flowing array of the observer who walks from one vista to another, moves around an object of interest, and can approach it for scrutiny, thus extracting the invariants that underlie the changing perspective structures and seeing the connections between hidden and unhidden surfaces. This approach next considers the fact of ambient awareness and explains it by the invariance of the sliding samples of the 360° array. Only then is the awareness of a single scene considered, the surfaces seen with the head fixed and the array frozen. The classical puzzles that arise with this kind of vision are resolved by recognizing that the invariants are weaker and the ambiguities stronger when the point of observation is motionless. Finally, the kind of visual awareness obtained with eye fixed and the retina either briefly exposed or made to stay fixed is considered for what it is, a peculiar result of trying to make the eye work as if it were a camera at the end of a nerve cable. The visual system continues to operate at this photographic level, but the constraints imposed on it are so severe that very little information can be picked up. (Gibson, 1979, pp. 303–4; see also p. 168)

In contrast to the natural environment, a pictorial display is unusual in several important respects. It presents an array which is static, curtailed, lacking in disparity information and in which the flatness of the picture surface is itself manifest. In marking these important differences, Gibson has served to alert us to the special status of pictures, and forced us to re-examine the very idea of what things 'look like'.

The view that the analysis of visual perception must begin with the retinal image considered as a picture still prevails (e.g. Frisby, 1979, p. 156; Sutherland, 1981, p. 711), but it seems to me that students of children's drawings should be alert to Gibson's challenge to this long-standing notion. For much of the work on 'visual' and 'intellectual' realism in children's drawings seems to be committed to the idea that 'a painter, if he wishes to be realistic, must learn to see the picture...presented to him by his eyes...rather than the field of objects, for he must reproduce the actual picture on his canvas' (Woodworth, 1950, p. 395). If only children would attend to what they can *see*, the argument runs, then they would no longer have trouble producing a realistic picture.

It is important for students of children's drawings to be clear that Gibson's ecological approach to perception undermines the kind of contrast between perception and knowledge that motivates the research on visual realism. If Gibson is correct, then the view of pictorial realism as the *transcription* of the artist's retinal image can no longer be sustained (Gibson, 1979, pp. 286–7; 1966, p. 236). According to Gibson, perception neither begins with, nor is confined to, an awareness of those unhidden surfaces which happen to be visible from one particular point at one particular moment. Such an attitude requires us to stop in mid-flight, as it were. Yet this unusual feat does not achieve the expected prize, the retinal transplant operation promised by traditional theory. We do not come to experience a flat retinal image ready for transfer onto paper:

The notion of a patchwork of colors comes from the art of painting, not from any unbiased description of visual experience. What one becomes aware of by holding still, closing one eye, and observing a frozen scene are not visual sensations but only the surfaces of the world that are viewed from now from here. They are not flat or depthless but simply unhidden. (Gibson, 1979, p. 286; see also 1950, Ch. 3, pp. 122, 174, 181; and 1966; p. 236)

Gibson's account here bears some resemblance to Marr's ideas on the 'immediate representation of visible surfaces' derived from the retinal image (Marr, 1982, Ch. 4). But the resemblance is merely superficial. For all his technical ingenuity, Marr promotes the image-based approach to perception with remarkable naivety, and, as his comments suggest, seems to have mistaken Gibson's crucial point. Gibson did not, as Marr claims, raise 'the critically important question, how does one obtain constant perceptions in everyday life *on the basis of* continuously changing sensations?' (Marr, 1982, p. 29; emphasis added). Rather he tried to show why such a question was a crucially important mistake. For Gibson, unlike Marr, our ability to notice how things appear 'from now from here' is incidental to the detection of invariant structure: it is in no sense a preliminary 'stage'.

As a theory of perception based upon the analysis of 'images', Marr's account has surely many insights to offer the student of picture perception and production. But we need to be clear that his account simply begs the question of the relation between picture perception and the perception of the real environment – the question Gibson considered to be so fundamental.

4. The 'picture theory' of pictures

Gibson's challenge to the 'picture theory' of the perception of the real environment should be of concern to students of children's drawings in so far as it unsettles a complacent attitude we might have to the curious efforts of our children. But Gibson, the critic of image-based theories of perception, was not content to concede even pictures to the opposition. As far as Gibson was concerned, pictures were not to be dismissed as a theoretical residue. He was also intent, as it were, upon displacing the picture theory of pictures.

Despite Gibson's emphasis upon the special status of pictures, he showed a surprising eagerness to subsume pictures under his current views of perception. His interest in pictorial communication was long-standing (Gibson, 1979, p. 273; Reed and Jones, 1982), and as his views on perception changed over the years, so he revised his account of pictures to reconcile them to his general scheme (Gibson, 1947, 1951, 1954, 1960, 1966, 1971, 1973, 1978, 1979, 1980, 1982; see Reed and Jones, 1982, for a comprehensive selection of Gibson's papers on picture perception). Although Gibson shifted his ground, three issues remained central. His first concern was to counter conventionalist accounts of pictorial communication; unlike symbolic systems such as language, pictures, he argued, are based upon an *intrinsic*, structural relation between the picture and the depicted scene. Secondly, despite his increasingly disparaging remarks about the poverty of a 'frozen' array, he insisted that pictures do contain structures which uniquely *specify* their content. A third concern is also expressed throughout his writings, yet is seldom referred to by commentators on his work. Gibson, in this theorising, was concerned to respect the special status of a picture as a *socially mediated* object: 'a thing with which men communicate with one another' (Gibson, 1951, p. 404).

Although Gibson's earliest accounts of pictures promote the traditional projective model, he later realised that this model could not account for either line-drawings or caricatures. In neither of these cases is there a point-to-point projective correspondence between the image and the depicted objects. He moved on to an information-based account: pictures, he claimed, make available higher-order stationary structures which are also present in the optic array of a real environment (Gibson, 1971).

Gibson's final attempt to provide an account of picture perception was presented in two papers in *Leonardo* (Gibson, 1973 and 1978) and in his last book (Gibson, 1979). As I have mentioned, in his later work on the perception of the environment Gibson came to lean very heavily on the concept of invariants which exist in the 'flowing' optic array. The problem he now confronted, therefore, was to reconcile his treatment of picture perception with his increasing emphasis upon 'timeless and formless invariants' which become available in our active dealings with the real environment. For the more Gibson came to insist upon the importance of invariants in optic flow, and relegate the frozen array to 'a myth' or 'a limiting case' (Gibson, 1979, p. 168), the more he threatened his information-based explanation of pictures. As he admitted,

The hypothesis of invariants has met with a certain incredulity from perceptionists and artists. It seems to contradict some of our deepest convictions about vision. Surely, they say, the perception of an object can be aroused by a *picture* of the object, a still picture, and, since it presents no transformation, it can display no invariants under transformation. (Gibson, 1973, p. 286) GRAPHICS.

Developments within his own theory of the perception of the real environment therefore confronted Gibson with the unpromising task of explaining how 'formless invariants' are effective in pictorially mediated perception. His final account of pictures attempts to stretch this idea to cover the case of a static or 'frozen' array in order to explain how pictures are so effective as a means of communication. He argued that the invariants that underlie transformations can also be detected as a limiting case in an unchanging structure.

In Gibson's treatment of pictures, his concept of information and then later his concept of pictorial invariants directly addressed two of his enduring concerns. Because, he argued, pictures 'capture' information of 'the same sort as in a natural array', then two of his claims could be sustained: that pictures are based on an *intrinsic* relation with what they depict, and that they also *specify* their content unambiguously, requiring no 'interpretation' (Gibson, 1982, p. 291). For Gibson, the existence of pictorial information could then explain the third issue emphasised in his writings, the use of pictures as a vehicle for social communication. Pictures can serve as 'a means of communication and a way of storing, accumulating and transmitting knowledge to successive generations of men' because they exploit 'some of the information in the structure of light' (Gibson, 1971, p. 34).

Gibson's own account of pictorial invariants is certainly incomplete. However, Sedgwick, in a very useful paper, has sought to clarify Gibson's intention: 'pictorial invariants are structures in the static array from a picture that *would* remain invariant *if* the optic array were from a real scene and were being transformed by a movement of the observer' (Sedgwick, 1980, p. 65). As an example, Sedgwick considers the case of optical continuity as specifying continuity of edges in the scene depicted. *If* the optic array were from a real scene, then the optical continuity would be preserved, or invariant, across different viewing positions. But, as Sedgwick is aware, there is no 'mathematical guarantee' that this condition will hold for a picture (Sedgwick, 1980, p. 66).

For, of course, optical continuity in a picture can arise from 'false attachment', the fortuitous alignment of projected edges.

Although Gibson wished to stress the special status of pictures as providing socially mediated perception, he denied the importance of convention (see, however, Gibson, 1962, p. 232). But this position can only be sustained if indeed we can treat a pictorial invariant as if it were 'mathematically guaranteed'; that is, if we could treat a *potential* invariant as a *kind* of invariant. Sedgwick does appreciate this problem, and makes the important move of identifying the crucial role of the human, social nature of pictures both in sustaining the relation between the depiction and what it depicts, and in ensuring that the relation is not ambiguous. As he points out, an artist can misuse a pictorial invariant, but the outcome simply would not count as a 'good picture'; it 'would misinform us' (Sedgwick, 1980, p. 66). But Sedgwick, having made this concession, fails to explore the implications. For it is not only communication by means of pictures but the very process of their *production* which must be understood as a social phenomenon (cf. Bartlett, 1923, pp. 11–12). People *agree* to abide by the rules. Certainly misleading and ambiguous pictures are possible in theory and practice, but a picture of this kind is either to be judged a failure, or else a deliberate falsification, a witty demonstration or an attempt by a rampant perceptionist to make a dubious theoretical point. Pictorial communication is possible because pictures are *made* to be informative. As the developmental evidence (Olson, Yonas and Cooper, 1981) and the more recent cross-cultural evidence (Hagen and Jones, 1978; Jones and Hagen, 1981) make clear, pictures are easy to see. On the other hand, effective pictures are far from easy to produce. And the problems of pictorial communication are not exclusive to the child draughtsman. We need to remember, for example, that even photographers need to pursue a long course of study to ensure that the camera tells the truth – or misinforms convincingly.

Gibson's failure to pursue his own important insight into the socially mediated status of picture perception derives, I suspect, from his wariness about the concept of 'conventionality', given the usual identification of the conventional with the arbitrary. But this usual identification is a profound mistake. The social practice of cooking, for example, shows great cultural diversity, and obviously depends upon tradition. It is clearly conventional, yet we do not regard the rules of cookery as arbitrary (Wittgenstein, 1974, p. 29). These rules reflect, and in turn perpetuate, human discoveries of the *lawfulness* of nutrition. The fact that pictorial communication may, as Gibson claims, be based upon laws of ecological optics does not imply that the question of convention is irrelevant to how such laws are utilised within a particular pictorial system. Different pictorial systems certainly exist (Dubery and Willats, 1983; Hagen, 1981), and a choice between these systems may be construed as conventional (see Perkins and Hagen, 1980, p. 283). But often this 'choice' is only in the mind of the theorist; many different systems have developed independently, without reference to existing alternatives. Convention is important to the 'conservation' and elaboration of a *particular* pictorial system. The normative distinction between 'good' and 'bad' pictures is essential to the logic of Gibson's account of pictures. His purpose was to show that the various human practices of pictorial *communication* are incomprehensible without reference to the laws of ecological optics. But these practices are by no means *deducible* from those laws. Convention intervenes, though not to displace lawfulness by caprice. If cultural practices transcend 'nature', they succeed only by respecting the constraints of ecological law.

5. Conclusion

If I have seemed overly zealous in my insistence that students of children's drawings should heed developments in perceptual theory, it is because I am aware that we perceptionists have, in turn, failed to consider the question of *production*. For if, as Gibson suggests, a picture projects a frozen array, we should be clear that it is one frozen in an *intentional* way: pictures convey *information* not merely thanks to the dictates of 'ecological law', but because pictures are made by people with people in mind. And if pictures are made to be easy to see, what is easy to see in them is what they depict, and for this very reason, what is difficult to see in them is how they are produced. And *here* lies the charm that pictures have held over our theorising. Their immediacy as objects for perception renders them obscure as crafted products, for the better crafted they are the more they *seem*, as one early commentator on photography remarked, not 'copies of nature, but portions of nature herself' (Morse, 1840, quoted in Rudisill, 1971, p. 57).

REFERENCES

Bartlett, F. C. (1923) *Psychology and primitive culture.* Cambridge: University Press.
Dubery, F. & Willats, J. (1983) *Perspective and other drawing systems.* London: Herbert Press.
Frisby, J. P. (1979) *Seeing: Illusion, brain and mind.* Oxford: University Press.
Gibson, J. J. (1947) Pictures as substitutes for visual realities. Ch. 8 of *Motion picture testing and research.* Aviation Psychology Research Reports, No. 7. Washington: Government Printing Office.

(1950) *The perception of the visual world.* Boston: Houghton Mifflin.

(1951) What is a form? *Psychological Review,* 58, 403–12.

(1954) A theory of picture perception. *Audio-Visual Communication Review,* 1(1), 3–23. Reprinted with additions in G. Kepes (ed.), *Sign, image, and symbol.* London: Studio Vista, 1966, pp. 92–107.

(1960) Pictures, perspective, and perception. *Daedalus,* 89, 216–27.

(1962) The survival value of sensory perception. *Biological Prototypes and Synthetic Systems,* 1, 230–2.

(1966) *The senses considered as perceptual systems.* Boston: Houghton Mifflin.

(1967) Autobiography. In E. G. Boring & G. Linzey (eds.), *A history of psychology in autobiography,* Vol. 5. New York: Appleton-Century-Crofts, pp. 127–43.

(1971) The information available in pictures. *Leonardo,* 4, 27–35.

(1973) On the concept of 'formless invariants' in visual perception. *Leonardo,* 6, 43–5.

(1978) The ecological approach to the visual perception of pictures. *Leonardo,* 11, 227–35.

(1979) *The ecological approach to visual perception.* Boston: Houghton Mifflin.

(1980) Foreword. In M. A. Hagen (ed.), *The perception of pictures,* Vol. 1. New York: Academic Press, pp. xxiii–xxvii.

(1982) Notes on direct perception and indirect perception, May 1977. In E. S. Reed & R. K. Jones (eds.), *Reasons for realism.* Hillsdale, N.J.: Lawrence Erlbaum, pp. 289–93.

Gombrich, E. H. (1971) On information available in pictures. *Leonardo,* 4, 195–7.

Goodman, N. (1978) *Languages of art.* (2nd ed.) Indianapolis: Hackett.

(1979) Letter. *Leonardo,* 12, 175.

Hagen, M. A. (1981) Generative theory: A perceptual theory of pictorial representation. In M. A. Hagen (ed.), *The perception of pictures,* Vol. 2. New York: Academic Press, pp. 3–46.

Hagen, M. A. & Jones, R. K. (1978) Cultural effects on pictorial perception: How many words is one picture really worth? In R. D. Walk & H. L. Pick (eds.), *Perception and experience.* New York: Academic Press, pp. 171–212.

Hammond, J. H. (1981) *The camera obscura.* Bristol: Adam Hilger.

Jones, R. & Hagen, M. (1981) A perspective on cross-cultural picture perception. In M. A. Hagen (ed.), *The perception of pictures,* Vol. 2. New York: Academic Press, pp. 193–226.

Marr, D. (1982) *Vision.* San Francisco: W. H. Freeman.

Marx, K. (1844) Economic and philosophic manuscripts. In D. McLellan, *Karl Marx Early Texts.* Oxford: Blackwell, 1971, pp. 130–83.

Merleau-Ponty, M. (1962) *The phenomenology of perception.* London: Routledge and Kegan Paul.

Olson, R., Yonas, A. & Cooper, R. (1981) Development of picture perception. In M. A. Hagen (ed.), *The perception of pictures,* Vol. 2. New York: Academic Press, pp. 155–90.

Perkins, D. N. & Hagen, M. A. (1980) Convention, context, and caricature. In M. A. Hagen (ed.), *The perception of pictures,* Vol. 1. New York: Academic Press, pp. 257–86.

Pirenne, M. H. (1970) *Optics, painting, and photography.* Cambridge: University Press.

Reed, E. S. & Jones, R. K. (eds.) (1982) *Reasons for realism*. Hillsdale, N.J.: Lawrence Erlbaum.

Richter, J. P. (1970) *The literary works of Leonardo da Vinci*, Vol. 1. New York: Phaidon.

Rudisill, R. (1971) *Mirror image: The influence of the Daguerrotype on American society*. Albuquerque: University of New Mexico Press.

Sedgwick, H. A. (1980) The geometry of spatial layout in pictorial representation. In M. A. Hagen (ed.), *The perception of pictures*, Vol. 1. New York: Academic Press, pp. 33–90.

Sontag, S. (1977) *On photography*. London: Allen Lane.

Sutherland, S. (1981) More sight than sound. *Nature, London, 289,* 711–12.

Wittgenstein, L. (1974) *Philosophical grammar*. Oxford: Blackwell.

Woodworth, R. S. (1950) *Experimental psychology*. London: Methuen.

Commentary

N. H. FREEMAN and M. V. COX

Gibson's theory is extremely controversial, but the basic points which concern us here are not. They are that normal perception is well adapted to the real, dynamic world of which the viewer is a part, and having a viewer standing transfixed before a small flat, frozen slice of something is not a paradigm case of that which is normal. But pictures can give extremely compelling perceptual experiences, and people do not find it queer to think of a picture as being 'convincing to the eye'. How, then, do pictures do their work of convincing, and do it in such a way that it appears normal to us?

The analysis given in the next few chapters takes two courses. One may be traced directly through Chapters 2, 3, 4, 5 and 16: the construction of pictures bears a lawful relation to the geometry of space. There is not a single lawful relation which towers over all the others in its transparent veridicality. Rather there is a set of drawing systems which map onto scenes in different ways. Some of these may suit the depictor's temporary purposes better than others. The other course may be traced most clearly through Chapters 2, 4, 5, 6, 7 and 14: the mental apparatus employed by the picture producer is one which is based upon a particular model of the world. Presumably, the immediacy of a depiction depends on the depictor's skill in persuading viewers to cooperate in deploying a similar model on their part. But that is not of central concern in the present book: the central concern for the moment is what mental apparatus is used by a picture producer, and how does it relate to that of a normal real-world perceiver?

2

A perspective on traditional artistic practices

FRANCIS PRATT

1. Introduction

There is a resemblance between traditional laboratory experiments and traditional artistic practices which indicates that Gibson (1979) may have been wrong to suggest that such experiments have no ecological validity. However, Gibson's ideas suggest a line of argument which is supported by evidence from traditional artistic practices and by evidence from my own experimental studies. As will be seen, this line of argument can help explain recurring characteristics of depictions, not only by adults, whether skilled or unskilled, but also by young children. In particular, it can help clarify the nature and role of the knowledge used in making depictions and how this knowledge can have both negative and positive influences. The negative influences are due to an inherent tendency to conservatism, and the positive ones include the capacity to initiate procedures that can circumvent this tendency.

Gibson (1979) criticised traditional laboratory experiments on the grounds that their experimental conditions excluded (i.e. controlled for) too many interactions of the kind that would naturally occur between people and their environment in everyday life. His contention, which received vigorous support from Neisser (1976, 1983), was that the exclusions undermined the 'ecological validity' of the experimental findings; they rendered them virtually meaningless with respect to advancing understanding of 'real life' perception.

The inspiration for this chapter stemmed from a recognition of similarities between traditional laboratory experiments and traditional artistic practices. The artistic practices, like the experiments, depend for their efficacy on excluding potential interactions with the environment. However, their *raison d'être* is to promote fruitful perceptual activity. In this way, they seem to demonstrate a role for exclusion in the ecology of artists and, by implication, in the ecology of others as well.

Let me give a better idea of what I mean by comparing Gibson's and Neisser's characterisation of traditional laboratory experiments with the *modus operandi* of an artistic aid which has proved its usefulness to artists of all levels of depicting skill.

2. The *modus operandi* of the perspective frame

Gibson and Neisser criticised traditional laboratory experiments on two main counts. They unnaturally constrained the viewing circumstances of the experimental subjects and they unnaturally impoverished the structure of visual input. Thus, the kind of experiment they would criticise might have the following description:

1. an *immobile* subject, possibly using a headrest or biteboard, who
2. looks with *one eye*, possibly using an artificial pupil, at
3. material that is *stationary* and
4. *highly abstract*, displayed on
5. a *two-dimensional* card or screen, which might be
6. presented tachistoscopically or by computer instruction for but a *fraction of a second*.

A very similar description could be applied to the *modus operandi* of the perspective frame.

The perspective frame consists of a rectangular frame, usually made of wood, across which are strung wires or strings, in such a way that they form a grid of rectangles. The artist looks through these rectangles at a model and uses them as frames of reference to aid judgements of relevant relations. The purpose of the exercise is to produce a drawing of the model on a piece of paper. This drawing can be described as a 'secondary model', for it is not intended as a finished work of art. Rather it is intended as a stage in the production of the finished work. It is the secondary model, not the model seen through the perspective frame grid, that is then copied onto the picture surface.

Before actually starting work on the secondary model, the artist draws a grid of lines on the paper upon which it is to be depicted. These lines form rectangles, the proportions of which correspond to the proportions of the rectangles made by the wires of the perspective grid. This correspondence facilitates judgements of angle, length and position.

For effective use of the perspective frame, artists must observe certain constraints. If they do not, the grid references will become unreliable. Thus, the artists must:

  1. remain *immobile*, possibly using a chinrest or an aligning device, and
  2. look with *one eye*, at
  3. a *stationary* model.

When using the perspective frame, artists construct their depictions one rectangle at a time. In this way, they are encouraged to look at the model in terms of a collection of parts that have an arbitrary relation to the whole. This arbitrary fragmentation will tend to encourage perception of the model in terms of parts and aspects that might escape the depictors' attention if the model were to be perceived as a whole. Relations between the model and the grid are brought to the artists' attention, and these can only be analysed in terms of abstract relations (i.e. of angle, length and position). Thus the artists make their models:

  4. as *abstract* as possible. The degree of abstraction is greatly increased in the secondary model, which is constructed from lines drawn on
  5. a *two-dimensional* surface.

Thus, the *modus operandi* of the perspective frame can be characterised in five of the six ways that might be used by Gibson or Neisser to describe their idea of the archetypal laboratory experiment. The reason why the sixth way is not included is that the constraints imposed by the other five make its formalised use redundant. However, what Gibson calls 'snapshot' vision (i.e. one-fixation glances) plays an important part in normal depicting practice, since accurate depiction depends on an analysis of the relations (e.g. of length, angle, size, shape, etc.) that tend to vary most with changing viewing circumstances. Such relations I shall be referring to as 'view-specific'.

The success of the perspective frame in the history of artistic endeavour demonstrates a potential for the formalised use in creative perception both of constrained viewing conditions and of the intentional reduction in the richness of visual stimulation. Its *modus operandi* illustrates a number of different ways in which artists have been able to control which parts and aspects of their visual environment contribute to the information used in their acts of depiction. The evidence to be presented in this chapter suggests that such selective filtering of visual input may be intrinsic to all creative perception. The body of this evidence will consist of a fairly comprehensive list of well-tried artistic aids and practices. The list of aids will not only include sophisticated contraptions like the perspective frame, but also the essential prerequisites of depiction (namely the depicting instrument and the depicting surface). The practices will include ways of doing things developed specifically to meet the needs of the depicting situation (such as half-closing the eyes to help gauge tonal values) and such integral parts of everyday perception as choosing a viewing distance, standing still while looking, using brief glances to access information and focusing attention on salient parts of objects.

The need for aids that either force or encourage restrictive perceptual activity so as to enable appropriate and creative visual analysis has implications that should be taken into account in any satisfactory theory of depiction. It is the main purpose of this chapter to elucidate some of these implications and to integrate them with ideas drawn from other sources. The fact that people as highly trained in the skills of visual analysis as professional artists should seek the help of aids at all is an indication of the complexity of the depicting task. The fact that they have often felt the need to use several different aids in the course of making one depiction, some of which, like the perspective frame, are *plurifunctional*, strengthens this implication. It is, therefore, to be expected that any adequate theory of depiction will also have to be complex. The propositions enumerated below are intended both to help progress towards such a theory and to make the subsequent list of aids and practices more meaningful.

3. Some propositions

1. *Most people are born with similar perceptual potentials.* People who become skilful depictors do so primarily because they learn to realise these potentials appropriately, not because they are born with superior ones. Nevertheless, the nature of the potentials determines what can be learnt, and therefore any theory of depiction must take into account the structure of the processing mechanisms that provide them. Important are the visual processing mechanisms, amongst which are:

(a) mechanisms that enable the automatic detection of what Marr (1982) terms 'primitives'. These provide the basis for the perception of colour, shape, form, figure/ground separation, extent, orientation, etc. In combination, they can provide information about the object-centred axes that Marr and others think to be vital to object perception. KING,

(b) mechanisms involved in the short-term storage of newly acquired visual information. These are used in comparative visual analysis of the kind necessary for building descriptions of unfamiliar relations between parts or aspects of objects and scenes. They severely limit the amount of information that can be held in mind at any one time, particularly if that information has to be maintained during ongoing visual analysis, graphic output or thought (cf. Phillips, 1983, for an analysis of the properties of visual short-term memory).

(c) mechanisms that enable the use of same/different judgements and can provide crude estimates of the direction of any difference (e.g. shorter/longer, more/less sloping or greener/yellower). Where comparisons are between simple, juxtaposed stimuli, both sensitivity to difference and ability to describe its direction are very great. As we shall see, many artists' aids and practices function by converting the task in hand into one which enables the exploitation of the powerful potential of these mechanisms.

2. *People differ in the nature and extent of their knowledge.* The main explanation for differences in skill lies in this well-known fact. The knowledge involved can be divided into two categories:

(a) knowledge that enables people to draw from memory, and

(b) knowledge that enables fruitful control over the information base of visual analysis.

My list of artistic practices can be regarded as a formalisation of knowledge in both these categories.

3. *Control over the information base of visual analysis can be exercised by means of (a) muscular activity and (b) changing the structure of the environment.* Thus:

(a) actions, such as body and head movement, closing an eye or briefly fixating a particular part of a scene, affect interactions with the visual environment upon which perception depends (cf. Gibson, 1979).

(b) the structure of the environment determines what information is available for use in visual perception (cf. Gibson, 1979). For example, a picture (i.e. a static, two-dimensional visual field) of a scene will draw attention to different aspects of the scene depicted than would the scene itself (i.e. a possibly dynamic, three-dimensional visual environment).

4. *Visual processing is predicated upon comparisons between inputs, which display both similarities and differences.* Visual perception depends on the 'abstraction' of the similarities with a view to using them in action and thought (cf. Gibson, 1979).

5. *The process of abstraction takes place in an hierarchical manner.* Thus, 'abstractions' can themselves be made the basis of other abstractions. This idea is illustrated schematically in Table 2.1. It can also be illustrated by reference to processes involved in colour perception. As Zeki (1980) showed, when a multicoloured display is illuminated by combining light from three projectors, each of which is projecting light of a different one of the three colour primaries, perception is dominated by 'colour-coded cells' (which can be considered as corresponding to the 3rd-order abstractions in Table 2.1).

Table 2.1. *A schematic representation of a simple abstraction hierarchy. My term for abstractions at the apex of the abstraction hierarchy is 'apex abstraction'*

3rd order		A3		
2nd order		A2		A2
1st order	A1	A1		A1

As a consequence, colour constancy obtains, and changes in the relative contribution of the different light sources do not change the appearance of the display. However, if any one of the light sources is switched off, perception is now dominated by 'wavelength-coded cells' (2nd-order abstractions) and the appearance of the multicoloured display changes if the relative contributions of the remaining light sources are varied. If only one primary light source is used, only 1st-order abstractions can be created.

The number of levels of abstraction illustrated in Table 2.1 is, of course, arbitrarily chosen. In everyday perception, the number would be determined by the nature of visual input. As proposed above (in proposition 3), this will be determined by a combination of the viewer's activity and the contents of the particular visual environment. In this way, abstractions relating to colour, shape, motion, figure/ground separation, etc., involving inputs from different spatial and/or temporal locations, can form the basis of high-order abstractions relating to complex objects and scenes which, in turn, could contribute to the creation of abstractions within the semantic domain.

Well-researched detail of the kind used for fleshing out the colour-perception example is also available for various other relatively low-level processes. However, there are many perceptual processes for which it is not, particularly those where more complex and, often, multi-modal inputs are involved. My proposal that the principle involved may be the same at all levels of processing is, therefore, highly speculative. However, this is the proposal that I would like the reader to entertain and relate to the evidence provided by the artistic practices.

6. *The operation of perceptual processing is automatic.* If input is available, it will be processed. This can be illustrated by reference to the colour-processing example referred to above. Thus, if anyone were looking at Zeki's multicoloured display, it would be impossible for them to stop the operation of colour constancy, so long as it continued to be illuminated by the trichromatic light

source. This automaticity means that the highest-order abstractions consistent with the structure of input are always created automatically whenever anyone looks at anything.

7. *The creation of any one abstraction is achieved at the cost of any information that is not common to all the abstractions that contribute to it.* For example, when colour constancy is in operation, sensitivity to the wavelength of light is lost.

The preceding two propositions provide the key to the ideas developed in this chapter. If true, what they mean is that any episode of perceptual processing will always involve the loss of all information, except that contained in the abstraction at the peak of the hierarchy (hereafter called the 'apex' abstraction; cf. Table 2.1). Thus, information about colour, movement, edges, surfaces and object identity would be lost in the process of creating any abstraction relating to the class of objects to which a particular object belongs; and this abstraction alone would be the primary product of the act of perception. On the face of it, the tendency to obliterate low-order abstractions seems as though it would be counter-productive. What possible practical use could the highest-order abstractions have? For example, what use would abstractions relating to a class of objects (e.g. furniture) be to depictors when depicting specific objects (e.g. chairs)? It is difficult to imagine. However, any perplexity about answers dissolves if the model is expanded: on the one hand, to include perceptual cycles (cf. Neisser, 1976) by means of which low-order abstractions could be reaccessed; and, on the other, to include mechanisms by means of which the operation of such cycles could lead to the imposition of constraints on visual input. Thus, access to apex abstractions could trigger constraining behavioural responses (cf. Gallistel, 1980, for mechanisms by means of which this might be done). For example, the response could involve standing still, closing one eye and/or using brief, one-fixation glances. By such means, access to former apex abstractions could be blocked. The greater the degree of constraint, the lower the order of the abstraction that would be favoured and that could now dominate perception. Thus, perception could involve a top-down, cyclical mode of information acquisition. It is of crucial significance to my model of perceptual processing that this perceptual cycle is by its very nature *dominated by high-order abstractions.*

8. *Abstractions are always simple.* This is inevitable because the more complex the visual input, the less of it remains invariant under varying viewing circumstances. It is not necessary to perplex our imaginations with wondering precisely what information an abstraction might embody. The crucial point is that, whatever its nature, it must have the potential of acting as a unifying

principle in relation to the lower-order abstractions from which it was created. However, for such a potential to be realised it is necessary for the higher-order abstraction to be accessed *before* the lower-order ones. This, of course, is what is made possible by the use of the kind of perceptual cycle just described. In this way, higher-order abstractions can provide a means of simplifying the task of making sense out of visual input. The kind of simplification involved can be illustrated by reference to Marr's (1982) ideas about the functional utility of establishing the 'principal axis' of an object as a preliminary to its perception; Minsky's (1975) ideas about the need for what he termed 'frames'; or, even, Gregory's (1970) ideas about the need for 'hypotheses'. Two examples can be cited which show perceptual correlates of these ideas. The first is a specific example and comes from the characteristics of the unilateral neglect syndrome, where patients with parietal damage cannot perceive the left half of objects in front of them (e.g. a clock or a plate of food). This phenomenon is only credible if a 'principal axis' (in these cases, axes of symmetry) has been established *prior* to conscious perception. The second example is a more general one and relates to foreknowledge (variously referred to as 'set', 'expectation', 'priming', etc.). There are innumerable experiments that demonstrate the facilitatory effects of foreknowledge on all aspects of perception, including identification and categorisation.

9.   *Abstractions form the basis of descriptions.* Here descriptions are defined as output instructions, such as those required to guide the looking and drawing behaviour used by depictors. The definition seems appropriate since such output instructions correspond closely to verbal and visual descriptions which are, after all, an example of their implementation. In terms of the scheme presented here, descriptions can be said to depend on the access of apex abstractions that can 'trigger' constraining behavioural responses and, thus, enable the access of lower-order abstractions of various kinds. For example, such a sequence could provide an object with a frame of reference, incorporating information defining its axis of symmetry and, in turn, its position, extent and orientation.

10.   *Descriptions can be of varying levels of complexity.* The degree of complexity will depend to an important extent on the number of levels of abstraction that have to be incorporated into them. Here the concept of nested frames of reference or nested schemas may be helpful. For example, the lack of sufficient nested frames may help explain why unskilled depictors have an almost invariant tendency to depict the front-facing human figure as more vertical, more symmetrical (about a central axis) and as displaying more horizontals (e.g. with respect to the eye axis or shoulder line) than is justified by

appearances. What seems to be lacking is a means of relating the frames of reference for the parts to those of other parts or of the whole.

11. *A system that is dominated by high-order abstractions will be inherently conservative.* The same apex abstractions will always trigger the same responses. Depictors will tend to look at their visual environment in the same way over and over again.

12. *Creative perception depends on a potential for escaping the dominance of high-order abstractions.* As we shall see, the means of escape available to depictors depend on either

(a) the use of aids and/or practices that alter the structure of visual input, or

(b) the use of a mechanism whereby small differences between similar things automatically attract attention.

In either case, the new ways of seeing that are enabled are fortuitous. It is necessarily a matter of *chance* what aids and practices reveal. This point is of crucial importance to my thesis and will be elaborated later. Aids and practices may constrain the domain within which chance will operate, but neither they nor the depictor can control which features within that domain attract attention.

The last two propositions sum up the practical implications of the preceding 10, and provide a convenient introduction to my list of artistic practices. These may be regarded as exemplifying means of using one kind of knowledge (i.e. knowledge of artistic practices) to inhibit the use of another kind of knowledge (i.e. the kind used for everyday skills of the kind that more normally dominate perception), thus enabling the use of a third kind of knowledge (i.e. knowledge of descriptions that are of use in the organisation of acts of accurate depiction). Before coming to my list, a few words about this third kind of knowledge may be helpful.

4. Knowledge and accuracy

That 'familiar' objects can be depicted from memory is one of the fundamental facts of depicting practice. The problem for the depictor is that, where the objects concerned have complex structures, dependence on memory is likely to lead to inaccuracy. Very possibly, the inaccuracy will be gross, since information in memory is bound to be schematic; is unlikely to enable view-specific descriptions; and may not even be visually derived. The kinds of 'errors' that result are typical of the kinds found in so-called 'intellectually realistic' drawings.

However, it is by no means necessarily the case that intellectual realism should be associated with inaccuracy. The reason why it has tended to be so is that it has usually been considered in the context of children's drawings of 'familiar' whole objects; a context in which gross errors in terms of accuracy can be expected. However, it is also possible to depict parts of objects and these can also be 'familiar'. Thus, the shapes that make up a cube could be familiar, or the straight edges that define those shapes. Furthermore, just as we can all draw cubes from memory, we can also all draw squares, diamonds and straight lines. This fact provides depictors with a potential strategy for using information in memory as a basis for more accurate depictions. They can construct the depictions from parts that do not change much with variations in viewpoint. For example, they could construct them from simple curves (of which a straight line would be the simplest) or, even, from points. If they did, the description in memory could produce accurate depiction.

However, depictors, when they depict whole objects, need to do more than depict parts, and when it comes to putting the parts together into wholes it becomes necessary to analyse relations between them. This requires comparative visual analysis and the building of task-specific descriptions, based on unifying schemas.

5. Aids and strategies used by artists

Space will not permit a detailed description of all the aids and strategies mentioned below. Further information can be found in artists' manuals, in histories of depiction and in how-to-depict books. A sample of such books is listed at the end of the chapter. However, in some cases books will not help. The reason is that the aids and strategies involved are so intrinsic to normal depicting practice that their significance seems to have been overlooked.

Preparations and behaviours

When artists prepare to make depictions, they make several decisions that will affect the nature of the visual information available for perceptual processing. First, a *subject* or 'primary model' has to be chosen. If, for example, this were to be a distant or misty scene, a still-life illuminated by a high, north-facing window (as found in the traditional studio) or a vertical, flat building (as depicted in Monet's Rouen Cathedral series), the structure of visual input would determine what visual processing systems could be called into play. Second, the *scale* of the depiction has to be decided upon. If the depiction is a sketch, it is likely that the scale will be small. The reason for this is that a small-scale depiction is easy to 'hold in the eye' (cf. Blake, 1951, who suggests that, 'efficient draughtsmen' should limit themselves to 'six inch drawings' because these have the 'advantage of lying completely within the field of vision'). Next, the *location* of the projected picture surface has to be chosen. The distance between picture and the scene being depicted will determine whether it is possible to hold the latter within the field of vision. It is also desirable to place the projected picture surface in such a way as to minimise the distance that will have to be travelled by the artist's eyes when looking back and forth from scene to depiction. The picture surface itself has to be within arm's length. However, in the course of depiction, artists will often *step back* from it, particularly if it is large. This can enable them to bring it within their field of vision and to perceive important whole-field relationships. The artists may also *lean forward* so as to bring their eyes nearer the picture surface, to look at details of the emerging depiction. Finally, the artists prepare to *settle* in one place for a long time (often providing themselves with a seat). In these ways artists can:

(a) selectively inhibit or facilitate the use of perceptual processing systems involved in close-up or distance vision;

(b) facilitate the use of same/different judgements;

(c) inhibit perceptual processing systems that depend on body movement.

Often artists will adopt other strategies which constrain their perceptual circumstances further. They may *align features* in the scene they are depicting as a device for ensuring a static viewpoint. They may *half-close their eyes* (or, alternatively, use either a diffusing glass or darkened mirror, such as a 'Claude Glass'). Or they may *close one eye* altogether. In these ways artists can:

(d) inhibit perceptual processing systems that depend on head movement;

(e) degrade the information entering the eye in such a way that 'confusing' detail is obscured, thereby inhibiting the use of perceptual processing systems that depend on focused vision;

(f) inhibit two-eyed perceptual processing systems.

Furthermore, when artists embark upon their depictions, they will adopt various looking strategies. These involve looking back and forth between scene and depiction. A high proportion of the looks will be in the form of *brief glances*, allowing time for no more than one or two fixations (for experimental details, see below). Thus:

(g) looks of highly constrained duration are extensively used in normal depicting practice.

Image degradation can occur, not only as a consequence of deliberate strategy, but also as a result of physical 'defects'. Such defects would include *malfunctions of the optical systems*, such as myopia (shortsightedness), hyperopia (longsightedness) and cataracts. Artists with such 'disabilities' do not necessarily want to be rid of them. This is evidenced by the refusal of certain well-known artists to wear spectacles (e.g. Renoir and Cézanne; cf. Trevor-Roper, 1970, for a review of evidence indicating potential advantages of optical defects for artists). Cerebral malfunction can also have felicitous outcomes in terms of the artistic merit of depictions. A much-cited example of an artist suffering from unilateral neglect is Lovis Corinth (e.g. Gardner, 1977).

Secondary models

Secondary models are two-dimensional images of three-dimensional scenes which are used as models for pictures. Their significance to artists can be judged by their widespread use and by the widespread use of aids to their production. Here is a list of sources of secondary models.

(a) The perspective frame (type A, sometimes called a 'reticule'). As described above, this uses a reference grid of wires stretched across a frame, through which the model is viewed. The reference grid is used to guide the production of a two-dimensional image on squared-up paper.

(b) The perspective frame (type B). This substitutes a piece of glass for the grid of wires used in type A. An image of a model, as seen through the glass, can be traced directly onto it as a means of creating a secondary model. A reference grid may be scored on the glass.

(c) The mirror. This can be used in several ways. Images seen in it can be traced; are conveniently framed; and are reversed (a transformation that has been much used as a means of providing depictors with 'unfamiliar' views of models). Also, concave mirrors can reduce the size of images, making them easier to 'hold in the eye'; and the images in mirrors will be degraded to some extent. In the early days of mirror technology this may have significantly affected the colour appearance of paintings produced with their aid.

(d) The *camera obscura*, the *camera lucida*, magic lanterns and slide projectors. These all produce transitory two-dimensional images which can be projected onto a picture surface.

(e) The photograph. A much used two-dimensional image (cf. Scharf, 1968, who provides extensive evidence for the use of photographs by a high proportion of famous artists).

(f) Sketches, studies and cartoons. Sketches are exploratory drawings. They are based on an analysis of highly selected aspects or parts of scenes.

They are consequently highly 'abstract'. Studies are a category of sketch. However, they are more specifically oriented towards the production of a particular work of art and tend to be less abstract. Cartoons are a category of study. They are drawn on the same scale as the projected work of art and can be traced, by various methods, onto the surface upon which it is to be painted.

(g) Works by other artists. Paintings, drawings and prints, either by or based on the work of artists, have been used extensively as two-dimensional models (cf. Maison, 1960 and Gombrich, 1960).

All the secondary models referred to above display severely limited visual information, as compared to 'real' three-dimensional scenes. They can all be used in one of three ways.

(a) For tracing. Tracing involves a process of continuous alignment between pencil tip and the line being traced. It thereby forces the use of those perceptual processing systems that mediate this kind of process.

(b) For squaring up. This is a technique used for making the scale transformations that are necessary if a small secondary model is to be depicted on a large picture surface. Analogous reference grids are drawn on both model and picture surface. These facilitate depicting accuracy.

(c) For copying. Here the word 'copying' is used in the sense adopted by Gibson, who distinguished between copying and depicting. He defined copying as equivalent to 'replicating' and used this definition to assert that copying on a flat surface is only possible if the model is also two-dimensional. Thus, copying can be done without interference from perceptual systems involved in three-dimensional perception (cf. Chen, this volume, for relevant research on children).

Frames of reference

Cross-reference is a fundamental part of normal depicting practice. Reliable referents are essential for accuracy. Thus, viewer movement or unobserved changes in the primary model can lead to error; as can the use of parts of the emerging depiction as referents, since these themselves are subject to error. The efficiency of cross-reference is increased with increasing proximity of the referents, whether they be within-scene or within-picture ones. It can also be increased by the use of aids, such as the five listed below:

(a) The edges of the picture support. This provides two verticals, two horizontals and four corner points as referents.

(b) The tip of the depicting instrument used as a 'marker' (i.e. as a moveable point of reference that can be used in conjunction with other reference points and that can be sited according to the needs of the moment).

(c) The plumbline (sometimes called a 'plummet'). This enables depictors to gauge elements in scenes in relation to an absolute vertical. The plumbline can be moved horizontally. This makes it possible to align it with selected parts of the scene.

(d) The depicting instrument, combined with the thumb acting as a moveable gauge, used as a measuring device. This has most of the advantages of a plumbline and others as well. In general, it is more flexible. Also, it is much used as an aid to visual measurement of geometric relations.

(e) The perspective frame grid, already mentioned.

Mechanical aids to measurement and image transformation
These imply a difficulty with unaided visual measurement. Examples would be the ruler and the pantograph (a mechanical device for scaling up). It is worth noting that rulers depend on converting the task in hand into one which uses alignment (i.e. one for which people are well adapted).

The emerging depiction
When making depictions, artists alternate between looking at the scene which they are depicting and the picture which they are making. Our videotape records of the looking behaviour of some art students we studied showed that they spent about half their time looking at the former and about half at the latter. How does looking at the emerging depiction help?

The main source of help is visual feedback, but it is by no means the only one. Below, I have listed six ways in which emerging depictions can help appropriate visual analysis.

(a) *The medium*. The choice of a medium for making a depiction implies a decision about what instrument(s) and what colour(s) will be used. This can influence visual behaviour in significant ways. Thus, the prospect of using a pencil or a pen would be likely to stimulate scene analysis in terms of edges. In contrast, the prospect of using a set of brushes in conjunction with a rich palette of colours would be more likely to stimulate analysis in terms of surfaces.

(b) *The 'completion' convention*. Convention predisposes artists to 'complete' pictures. The degree of completion required will vary according to circumstances. For example, it will not be the same for the sketch as for the highly finished painting. However, the completion requirement will always tend to encourage kinds of visual analysis that may well be very different from that used in 'everyday life'. For example, the apparent 'blindness' to complex curvatures that seems to bedevil many unskilled depictors when depicting the edges of 'familiar' objects is an indication that edge analysis of this kind may not play a large part in their normal lives. It is particularly important to note that in everyday perception figure/ground *separation* is given high priority, whereas in analysis of scenes for depiction, figure/ground *integration* is at a premium. The curbing of normal perceptual habits is vital here; even the most basic and immediate impression may have to be regulated severely.

(c) *The flat surface.* Pictures are produced on flat surfaces. This means that when they are looked at a number of perceptual processing systems cannot be used for analysis of their content. For example, none of the perceptual processing systems that depend on movement, binocular vision or focus can be used. A major role for these inhibited systems is figure/ground separation. In their absence the task of analysing figure/ground relations is eased. An extreme example of such task facilitation is provided by Gilchrist (1980). In an experiment done by him, a tab seen against a brightly illuminated background appeared to be 'white' when viewed with both eyes and 'black' when viewed with only one eye. The explanation for this striking change is that the operation of binocular vision enables viewers to perceive planar separation and, concurrently, to inhibit effects the 'ground' might have on the 'figure'. In this way, the absence of binocular vision can extend the area of the visual field involved in the creation of colour appearance. By implication, a comparable extension can be caused by the absence of any of the other non-colour/brightness perceptual processing systems. In these ways, pictures, on account of their flatness, can provide experiences of whole-field colour relations that are difficult to match in 'everyday' perception.

However, though the perceptual processing systems that depend on binocular vision and focus cannot be used for analysis of images in paintings, they can affect perceptions of the physicality of the picture surface. The closer the surface is viewed, the more likely its physical properties are to be perceived. Thus, close inspection will tend to encourage perceptions of abstract qualities and discourage perceptions of images. In this way it can help undermine the dominance of whole-object perceptions. This tendency will be further encouraged by the fact that close inspection automatically reduces the area of the picture surface that is subject to foveal vision, thus encouraging perceptions in terms of parts rather than in terms of wholes.

(d) *Fragmentation.* Pictures are produced a bit at a time. While the picture is in the process of being made, only the parts that have been drawn already can provide visual input. Consequently, only abstractions derived from those parts can dominate perception. This can have a dramatic effect on the growth of visual awareness. In an experiment (cf. Phillips *et al.*, this volume) we demonstrated the benefits of a growth of awareness, brought about in this way, with respect to 7-year-old children's depictions. By ensuring that the children saw how a cube could be constructed using a sequence of straight lines, dramatic improvement in future copies of cubes was achieved. The improvement was immediate, long-lasting and did not depend on the memorisation of any particular line-production sequence. Clearly, the experimental conditions had helped the children to analyse cubes in 'new' ways.

(e) *Reintegration.* Reintegration is achieved by means of analysis of relations. The relations may be intra-figural (i.e. amongst parts of figures) or extra-figural (i.e. either between referents on different figures or between referents on the figure and referents on the picture support). In either case, the mode of analysis used must necessarily militate against the domination of whole-object perceptions. This is because intra-figural relations are necessarily relations between parts and because extra-figural relations are necessarily extra-figural.

(f) *Comparisons.* The emerging depiction consists of a set of marks which can be compared with corresponding elements in the scene being depicted. To make such comparisons, the depictor has to look back and forth between scene and depiction, attending first to an aspect of the one and then to an aspect of the other. The purpose of this activity is to check the accuracy of aspects of the depiction by checking for similarities and differences.

It would be hard to exaggerate the importance of same/different judgements in depicting practice and, indeed, in the practice of creative perception of any kind. The reason why this is so is that detection of difference depends on a mechanism which is independent of control by apex abstractions, free from the domination of 'knowledge' and unaffected by experience. Differences can call attention to themselves in much the same way as unexpected 'events' can call attention to themselves. For example, attention is invariably drawn to the appearance or disappearance of any one dot amongst a constellation of many hundreds of dots (cf. Wilson, 1981). This is because people habituate to common parts of inputs, remaining sensitive to new events. As a result, new events are isolated and draw attention to themselves. For similar reasons, attention is likely to be drawn to small differences between any pair of sequential inputs. Thus, visual comparisons can activate perceptual cycles, which are controlled directly by the structure of visual input. These cycles inhibit access to invariant information and, thereby, constrain perceivers in such a way that they are forced to narrow the focus of their attention. Since such cycles are activated by differences between things, I call them 'variance cycles'.

Variance cycles play a crucial role in creative perception. However, their potential for usefulness will depend on the structure of the inputs compared. Their activation need not necessarily result in a narrowing of the focus of attention. One reason for this is that it is possible to look in only one direction at a time. Thus, if a large number of dots were suddenly added to an existing constellation, we would be aware of change, but might be at a loss to distinguish between new dots and old. We just wouldn't know where to look. The feeling must be only too familiar to all would-be depictors! When we have just made a very inaccurate depiction, we are only too aware that something is dreadfully wrong, but we are likely to remain perplexed as to precisely what it could be. This perplexity may help by initiating constraining search strategies. It may, however, lead only to confusion and, thus, pose a threat to the creation of visual order. It may be important for safeguards against the inappropriate activation of variance cycles to be built into everyday perceptual processing procedures. Top-down control by apex abstractions could provide the necessary mechanism, since high-order abstractions would be given precedence over low-order ones. Thus, advantage could be taken of the fact that two things that are very different in terms of a detailed description can be very similar in terms of a gross description (e.g. all people differ in detail, but still look like people).

Top-down control is intrinsically conservative in effect. If people want to use variance cycles creatively, they must learn to overcome this conservatism and access levels of description that provide useful degrees of difference between inputs. This might be done by means of a strategy of progressive constraint, involving a narrowing of focus of attention and/or a progressive reduction in the duration of abstraction-creating looking activity. The ultimate step in this process would involve looking at details with one-fixation glances. An alternative strategy would be to find or create whole scenes (e.g. experimental displays or minimal paintings) in which only useful degrees of difference are manifest (cf. Davis, this volume, who shows that a two-cup display can call attention to differences that remain obscure in a multiple-cup display).

The constraining looking strategies would themselves be under the control of apex abstractions, and these would need to have learnt the advantages of using them. The advantages would be in terms of an ability to detect errors at various levels of detail. If people could not detect errors at any particular level of description, they could not learn from mistakes made in terms of that level. This may be the predicament that faces children who make copies of cubes like those illustrated in Figure 2.1 and may explain why they tend to be so uncritical of their productions. Copy B illustrates an error of a kind that tends to be noticed at a relatively early stage. Copies C, D and E are corrections, but ones that are still based on a very gross level of description.

The necessary conditions for the activation of variance cycles are met whenever attempts are made to correct errors. If more than one attempt at

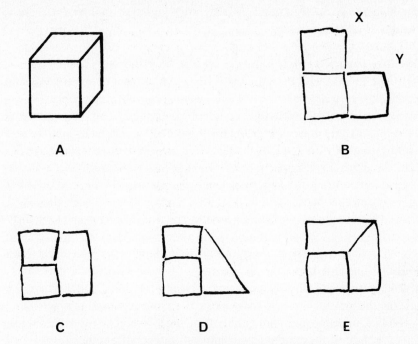

Figure 2.1 Some examples of 'intellectually realistic' copies of cubes (based on Phillips *et al.*, 1978). A is the model. C, D and E are copies that provide 'solutions' to the problem posed by the separation of X and Y in copy B.

depicting the same feature is left visible (i.e. if nothing is obscured or rubbed out), then comparison between them will be possible and, since error in the first attempt is the cause of the subsequent attempt(s), differences are inevitable. These differences, unlike the differences between a scene and a depiction, can be taken in at a glance. This is important because it means that any comparisons made cannot require between-glance storage. As a result, error correction provides a method of constraining perception so as to give control to apex abstractions that derive solely from view-specific information.

I have been discussing variance cycles in the context of comparisons involving the emerging depiction. However, other kinds of comparisons could also activate them. Thus, whenever people look at an object from a sequence of positions, they could be expected to find their attention drawn to parts of it that they might otherwise have overlooked. This is because small changes in position are bound to produce differences in visual input. In the drawing class, much advantage can be taken of this fact. Looking at the model from different positions can be very fruitful in terms of drawing attention to aspects of it that have hitherto been overlooked. Small changes in viewing position can help people to see 'new' details; larger changes can provide a new awareness of 'structure'.

Cognitive factors (1) their influence on looking behaviour

When we monitored the looking behaviour of a number of art students and psychology students while they were copying various types of models, we found both interesting differences and interesting similarities. When we asked them to copy line-drawings of 'familiar' objects (i.e. a cube, a tumbler and a human leg), the art students indulged in a great deal more looking activity than the psychology students. They also achieved significantly better levels of depiction accuracy. In contrast, when copying groups of separated straight lines of randomly determined length, orientation and position on the paper, there was no significant difference between art students and psychology students, either in the amount of looking activity or in terms of the levels of accuracy achieved. These results show that 'familiarity' can affect both looking behaviour and copying accuracy. They also suggest a correlation between number of looks and copying accuracy (cf. Pratt, 1984, where the case for the formulation 'the more looks, the more accurate' is argued).

The looking behaviour of our subjects included looks of various durations. About a third of them lasted less than half a second; another third lasted between half a second and one second; and the remaining third lasted more than one second and often as much as two, three or even more seconds. These different durations can be translated into terms of numbers of fixations per look (cf. Noton and Stark, 1971, and Campbell and Wurtz, 1978, whose work suggests that fixations last about 250 ms and that allowance should be made for 100 ms' 'lag'). Thus, the looking behaviour of our subjects can be classified in terms of one-fixation, two-fixation and multiple-fixation looks.

If my earlier speculations about the use of apex abstractions and variance cycles are correct, then a plausible explanation for this looking behaviour would be that the multiple-fixation looks are used to educate appropriate apex abstractions, enabling them to 'know' how to activate perceptual cycles that can be of use in the context of the task in hand. An alternative way of expressing this explanation would be to suggest that the multiple-fixation looks are used to create task-specific memory schemas which, in turn, can be used to help the efficiency of information pick-up.

We tested this explanation by means of a computer-controlled experiment. This involved subjects (psychology students) copying pairs of separated straight lines of randomised length, orientation and position, which were displayed on a VDU screen. We found that five seconds of preliminary looking at the model helped subjects to improve the efficiency of their subsequent

300 ms looks and 800 ms looks with respect to their capacity for mediating copying accuracy. This facilitation was not interfered with by intermediate drawing activity. Thus, the five seconds' preliminary visual analysis does seem to have enabled subjects to create task-specific memory schemas.

In another experiment, we found evidence that longer-established memory schemas could also have similar facilitatory effects on the efficiency of information pick-up. This led us to view the formulation 'the more looks, the more accurate' with some circumspection.

The experiment involved art students and psychology students copying line drawings of cubes. There were two conditions. The copies had to be made either 'normally' (i.e. without constraint) or from 'memory'. In the memory condition, subjects were allowed five seconds to analyse the model before drawing it. The surprising result of this experiment was that, in terms of the battery of measures used by us, there was no significant difference in accuracy between the copies made under the different conditions by either group (cf. Pratt, 1983, where other kinds of difference are alluded to). However, this finding contrasted strongly with the finding of another experiment in which different stimuli were copied under the same two conditions. This time the stimuli were our separated straight-line models. For these, the performance for the two conditions was very different. Accuracy for the memory condition was very much worse.

We concluded that the explanation for these contrasting results lay in the degree of 'familiarity' of the model used. In the case of the cube, the structural relations between the parts was familiar; in the case of the straight lines, they were not. Thus, taken together, our experiments demonstrated that well-established complex memory schemas could indeed facilitate information pick-up.

The experiment in which the students copied cubes also told us something about the kind of information picked up. As just mentioned, when we compared the results of the two subject groups, we found that the depictions of the art students were more accurate than those of the psychology students. This was no surprise, but it did demonstrate that familiarity could have different consequences for different people and that these consequences could be reflected in the degree of visual realism exhibited by depictions.

It is worth emphasising that the fact of 'familiarity' did not inhibit looking activity in skilled depictors but, on the contrary, stimulated it. When copying cubes, legs or tumblers, the art students engaged in a great deal more looking activity of all the categories we analysed. They looked more before starting to draw and more in preparation for each line; and they used more multiple-fixation looks and more brief glances. What is the purpose of all this looking activity? According to the speculations presented above, it is used in the creation and use of task-specific schemas, dedicated to the accessing of information that would otherwise be overlooked.

Depictors need not necessarily be aware of the perceptual information that triggers the acquisition of task-specific schemas. Indeed, it may be presumed that the information is often, if not always, unavailable to consciousness. However, artists' manuals are full of formulations of regularities in the structure of objects and appearances. Such regularities have traditionally been referred to as 'Laws of Nature' and have been enshrined in books on perspective (linear and aerial), on anatomy, on colour, etc. Their use has pervaded traditional depicting practice and they have provided the core of traditional academic instruction. In general, they have provided the knowledge base of artists' looking strategies.

However, the use of such 'knowledge' has its shortcomings. No matter how sophisticated, knowledge-based looking strategies are subject to the limitations of intrinsic conservatism (i.e. recurrent cycling of the same perceptual cycles). They will always dispose the depictor to look for information that is specified in memory schemas and, consequently, to overlook that which is not; and what is overlooked may well be essential to an advance of perceptual awareness.

The struggle to break free from the tyranny of memory schemas is reflected in all the aids and strategies listed previously. To these can be added others. Thus, it is common practice to attempt to perceive the 'familiar' as the 'unfamiliar'. Depictors try to do this by making use of upside-down images (cf. Edwards, 1979) and mirror images (cf. Doerner, 1949); they force themselves to look at objects in terms of 'negative shapes' (i.e. they attempt to regard the edges of a figure as the edges of the surrounding visual field); and they use production strategies that force attention to be given to aspects of appearances that would otherwise be overlooked. I have already mentioned the strategy implicit in the requirement that pictures should be 'completed' (cf. above, p. 45). Another forcing strategy is one we have termed CLAM (cf. Phillips et al.,1978). This involves the depictor drawing while continuously looking at the model (cf. Nicolaides, 1941, who gives good advice about implementing CLAM and, along with many others, advocates its merits as a technique both for depicting and for learning to 'see'). CLAM is also used unconsciously. My videotapes of subjects' coordinated eye and hand movements show that both adults and children use it spontaneously, particularly when depicting complex curvatures.

Cognitive factors (2) their role in drawing behaviour

As I have already emphasised, it is not necessary to look at familiar objects or familiar parts of objects in order to be able to draw them. They can always be constructed, however inadequately, on the basis of knowledge. Most how-to-draw books seem to depend largely on providing formulae and 'laws' intended to increase the knowledge base of such constructions. Formula drawing is used in the construction of standardised views (e.g. when collections of geometric forms are used as the bases for drawings of animals, birds and people: cf. Gombrich, 1960). Laws can also be used in the construction of 'novel' views (e.g. when they are laws of perspective, anatomical relations or colour relations). It can be hard to distinguish whether drawings by skilled artists owe their apparent accuracy to skilled visual analysis or to skilled construction (i.e. it is not necessarily at all easy to distinguish whether artists, or anyone else, including young children, have been drawing what they 'know' or what they 'see').

6. Towards a theory of depiction

A postal address can be described as a set of nested schemas that enable the Post Office to locate a specified individual by means of a homing-in process. The use of a sequence of sorting offices, going from the central, via the regional, to the local and, thence, to the particular address makes what might seem an almost impossible task relatively simple. According to the speculations presented in this chapter, the skilled use of perception also depends on the use of nested schema. However, the task performed by perception is more like that of locating a person who doesn't know where he is (imagine him as a kidnap victim). However, he is able to send out a sequence of envelopes on which he had written the word 'Help!' Imagine that, according to the normal practice of the sorting system, this letter would be channelled automatically and in sequence to the local, the regional and, finally, the central sorting office, where the message 'Help!' would be read for the first time. The search for the sender could now be initiated. The process of finding him would be made easy if only there were a way of establishing from which of the network of regional offices the missive had come. This would allow the central office to alert the regional office to look out for another similar letter and, when it came, to alert the local office, etc. At each stage, the official who has been alerted has only to wait until he sees the word 'Help!' on an envelope before initiating the next stage in the process. In this way, by a series of stages, the kidnap victim could be located and rescued. The whole process has much in common with the notion that access of apex abstractions can initiate perceptual cycles that enable the reaccess of visual input, which is, in turn, capable of initiating processes that involve the recreation of lower-order abstractions. However, here perception faces a difficulty. It cannot necessarily depend on there being an equivalent of the sorting official with knowledge of what to do. Without such an equivalent, capable of looking out for and stopping incoming messages, there is no reason why the same circumstances of perception should not lead to the same outcome; there is no reason why subsequent messages should not be sent all the way back to the central sorting office every time! To meet this difficulty, my model proposes the incorporation into the cycle of a means of inhibiting such reaccess. Amongst the ways that this might be done is the one indicated by my analysis of artistic practices. This is to tackle input at source, using a combination of alternative or complementary methods. These may involve:

1. using perceptual constraints which can be implemented by means of muscular control over body, head and eye movement (enabling the use of close inspection, alignment, the activation of variance cycles, etc.);

2. changing the structure of the visual environment so that it is likely either to stimulate the creation of unfamiliar sets of abstractions or to increase the chance that variance cycles will be activated.

However, that is not the end of the list of problems that have to be faced. The next problem stems from the nature of the information residing in an apex abstraction. Fundamental to my model is the proposition that access of higher-order abstractions incurs the loss of information residing in lower-order ones. If this is so, how could an 'ignorant' apex abstraction initiate purposive cycling? It seems to me that it could not unless it had acquired relevant knowledge.

How could the knowledge be acquired? My model suggests a method which helps explain both why *unaided* perceptual learning is such a long-drawn-out affair and why *aided* perceptual learning can be so rapid. It can also provide insights into the growth of personal style. The method depends on the use of *constrained chance*. The constraints are the ones I have been referring to so often: the ones that accompany everyday activity, imposed by every movement of body, head or eyes and by every cessation of movement. They are the ones that afford either close-up or distant views of the same object, small changes in the appearances of particular objects and similar views of different objects belonging to the same category. In these ways, high-order abstractions will be inhibited willy-nilly, allowing low-order ones to dominate perception in unpredictable ways. It is chance associations between such low-order abstractions and higher-order ones that form the basis of the kind of associative model of learning proposed by Hebb (1949) and Gibson (1966). The key to learning is the recurrent discovery that particular constraining actions initiated in particular circumstances result in the acquisition of information of use in ongoing activity. Functional utility can be reinforced. New conjunctions of abstractions, deriving from various modalities of input, create even higher-order abstractions. These provide the integrating principle of new action plans and new perceptual descriptions. Thus, learning to perceive is inevitably a haphazard and idiosyncratic process, which must tend to produce people who see in individualistic ways.

However, as Gibson (1966, 1979) has cogently argued, perceptual learning cannot be totally haphazard. Thus, the main thrust of his ideas about the operation of 'perceptual systems' in the visual environment is that their structure determines what can be perceived and, therefore, what is perceived. If this were wholly true, there would be no room for individuality. Nevertheless, it seems obvious that it must be partly true and, if so, we can conclude that factors which influence which constraints are actually used in any particular circumstances must critically affect the nature of a person's learning experience. Such factors might be cultural, as in the case of those that influence artists to use the traditional practices described in this chapter. When they are, they are likely to perpetuate ways of seeing things typical of that culture. Thus, artists who use traditional artistic practices are likely to perpetuate the artistic tradition to which they belong.

Perpetuation of tradition can be attributed to the intrinsic conservatism of those perceptual processes which depend on activation by apex abstractions. Thus, as a result of learning processes, apex abstractions become associated with particular perceptual cycling procedures, which come to dominate perceptual activity. In this way, the same apex abstractions tend to activate the same kind of perceptual activity whenever they are accessed. This tendency to conservatism inhibits the growth of perceptual awareness. An example of how it may do so can be suggested. It relates to the production of so-called 'intellectually realistic' drawings of cubes, such as the one illustrated in Figure 2.1B.

Children's experience of cubes is likely to relate, at least in part, to their experience of toy bricks. These they use for building, an activity which involves the operation of the various perceptual processes used in locating, manipulating and positioning the blocks. None of these processes depend on information deriving from view-specific appearance. Consequently, they will not help the children to learn how to see the building blocks in ways that might later help in making visually realistic depiction. According to my model, all view-specific information should be lost in the process of accessing the particular high-order abstractions which dominate children's building-block activity. It would not be reaccessed because previous experience had not demonstrated its usefulness. The only information specifying shape capable of reaccess would derive from tactile sources. This would relate to the physical rather than the visual properties of the building blocks. It would make no distinction between visible and invisible surfaces and would represent all corners as rectangular. These are, of course, well-known properties of many 'intellectually realistic' drawings of cubes. Perhaps such drawings would be better described as examples of 'visuo-tactile realism'!

7. Concluding comments

The main thrust of this chapter has been to show how traditional artistic practices help artists to overcome the problems posed by dominance of apex abstractions. However, these problems are not confined to artists. They also face people using other skills. For example, the difficulty of isolating parts of wholes also faces children learning to read and spell. These children can suffer because whole words tend to dominate and inhibit access to phonemes and graphemes. And the strategies used by artists to aid depiction are essentially the same as ones used by other people for innumerable other purposes. Thus, same/different judgements are used to identify unique aspects of things; close inspection is used for isolating detail; cross-reference is used for locating and relating; and alignment is used for visually guided targeting. All these strategies have provided inspiration for the invention of both aids to and substitutes for many different perceptually based skills. It is no coincidence that so many of these involve the display of information on a flat surface, using photographs, transparencies, maps and diagrams. In this way, people can be provided with view-specific information. Moreover, they can be provided with it in a manner that neither precludes the use of both eyes nor constrains movement in uncomfortable ways. All these examples could be used to undermine the argument that constrained perception can have but limited ecological validity. On the contrary, what they show is that the ability to formalise and extend the use of constrained perception has been one of man's most considerable assets.

ACKNOWLEDGEMENTS

The experiments referred to in this paper were mostly done with the help of an S.S.R.C. grant. My thanks are also due to Bill Phillips, to Lindsay Wilson and to Karel Gisbers.

REFERENCES

Some artist's manuals, histories of depiction and how-to-depict books
Blake, V. (1951) *The art and craft of drawing*. New York: Dover.
Constable, W. G. (1954) *The painter's workshop*. Oxford: University Press.
Doerner, M. (1949) *The materials of the artist*. London: Harrap.
Edwards, B. (1979) *Drawing with the right side of the brain*. Los Angeles: Tarcher.
Gombrich, E. H. (1960) *Art and illusion*. London: Phaidon.
Maison, K. E. (1960) *Themes and variations*. London: Thames and Hudson.
Nicolaides, K. (1941) *The natural way to draw*. Boston: Houghton Mifflin.
Shider, F. (1947) *An atlas of anatomy for artists*. New York: Dover.
Wright, L. (1983) *Perspective on perspective*. London: Routledge.

Other references
Campbell, F. W. & Wurtz, R. M. (1978) Saccadic omission: Why do we not see a grey-out during saccadic eye movement? *Vision Research, 18*, 1297–303.
Gallistel, C. R. (1980) *The organization of action*. Hillsdale, N.J.: Erlbaum.
Gardner, H. (1977) *The shattered mind*. New York: Knopf.
Gibson, J. J. (1966) *The senses considered as perceptual systems*. Boston: Houghton Mifflin.
 (1979) *The ecological approach to visual perception*. Boston: Houghton Mifflin.
Gilchrist, A. L. (1980) When does perceived lightness depend on perceived spatial arrangement? *Perception and Psychophysics, 28*, 527–38.
Gregory, R. L. (1970) *The intelligent eye*. London: Weidenfeld and Nicolson.
Hebb, D. O. (1949). *The organization of behaviour*. New York: Wiley.
Marr, D. (1982) *Vision*. San Francisco: Freeman.
Minsky, M. (1975) A framework for representing knowledge. In P. H. Winston (ed.), *The psychology of computer vision*. New York: McGraw-Hill.
Neisser, U. (1976) *Cognition and reality*. San Francisco: Freeman.
 (1983) Towards a skilful psychology. In D. Rogers & J. Sloboda (eds.), *The acquisition of symbolic skills*. New York: Plenum.
Noton, D. & Stark, L. (1971) Eye movements and visual perception. *Scientific American, 224*, 34–43.
Phillips, W. A. (1983) Short term visual memory. *Philosophical Transactions of the Royal Society, London*, ser. B, *302*, 295–309.
Phillips, W. A., Hobbs, S. B. & Pratt, F. R. (1978) Intellectual realism in children's drawings of cubes. *Cognition, 6*, 15–33.
Pratt, F. R. (1983) Intellectual realism in children's and adults' copies of cubes and straight lines. In D. Rogers & J. Sloboda (eds.), *The acquisition of symbolic skills*. New York: Plenum.
 (1984) A theoretical framework for thinking about depiction. In W. R. Crozier & A. J. Chapman (eds.), *Cognitive processes in the perception of art*. Amsterdam: North-Holland.
Scharf, A. (1968) *Art and photography*. London: Allen Lane.

Trevor-Roper, P. (1970) *The world through blunted sight.* London: Thames and Hudson.

Wilson, J. T. L. (1981) Visual persistence at both onset and offset of stimulation. *Perception and Psychophysics, 30,* 353–6.

Zeki, S. (1980) The representation of colours in the cerebral cortex. *Nature, London, 284,* 412–18.

3

There is no development in art

MARGARET A. HAGEN

1. Introduction

In the West, history is often thought of, and taught, as a grand evolutionary
march toward the pinnacle known as modern Western civilisation. In the
history of art, the path of the great march wends its way from Altamira to
Egypt, thence to Greece and Rome, through the darkened Middle Ages of
Europe with stops at lighted monasteries, to Italy for the Renaissance and back
again through an enlightened Europe, stopping finally but uncertainly at the
threshold of Cubism. Of course, many art writers take intellectual side trips;
some spend their entire professional lives in 'foreign' countries or even in the
20th century. But few such deviants attempt to integrate their special
interests into what was seen as the grand developmental march of art. It was
assumed, although usually only implicitly, that whatever the artistic value
of foreign or modern art, it is not relevant to the central developmental motif
of Western art. That motif, the integrating key, the fundamental moving force
in Western art, was assumed to be the attempt to mirror reality through
application of the principles of vision.

Development in art was thought to keep pace, albeit one step behind, with
development in visual science, philosophy and geometry. The more closely art
incorporated visual principles, the more closely did it mirror reality. By the
time of the Renaissance, the fundamental principles of visual perception were
clear, at least in terms of the geometry if not the neurology, and found
expression in painting. Many, many scholars from diverse fields have argued
that since the Renaissance, painters – at least Western painters – have known
how to paint what we really see. All other painters – primitive, non-Western
and amateur – are trapped, presumably, in the perceptual fallacy of painting
not what they see but what they know.

59

So the story goes. But is there substance to this story or is it a Western ethnic myth? Perhaps an appraisal of the world's art with a less vested interest in the outcome would suggest a different interpretation. The central aspect of painting dealt with in this history (and this chapter) is the problem of spatial layout, the problem of depicting the layout of surfaces in space on a two-dimensional plane. Arnheim (1954/1974) wrote that everyone, child or master painter, Eastern or Western, cave dweller or palace *habitué*, must solve the fundamental problem of transposing three dimensions into two, within the formal requirements of the medium – or at least they must try to do so. In the sparsest exposition, the projection of surface layout can be thought of as a problem in visual geometry. How can one project the surfaces of three-dimensional objects in space onto a flat surface? There are various geometrical solutions to this problem, but to understand them one must understand certain facts about representation itself.

2. Station-point assumptions and geometry

A representational picture is one that represents the objects of the world, real or imagined, on the image plane of the painting. Faced with the complexity of the representational task, let us start with its most elementary formulation. Every artist engaged in representational depiction of an object or scene must assume a stance, a station point, relative to that subject, even if the subject of the picture is only in the mind's eye. That is, the depictor has to stand somewhere and take a look at his subject. There are special tricks and aids (like the 'perspective frame') that depictors use in fixing the viewpoint, which Francis Pratt (this volume) analyses. But let us imagine someone simply standing and looking. Physically, the artist has only a limited number of options. He can assume one or many points of view for the subject of the picture – the single- or multiple-station-point assumption. The artist can stand frontal to the object to be depicted so that the subject and image planes are parallel, or he can stand at an angle to it. Last, the artist can stand close to the subject, at a moderate distance from it or at a distance known as optical infinity. Optical infinity is not nearly as far away as it sounds. It is the distance beyond which the decrease in visual angle with increasing distance is no longer apparent. As an example, consider a one-foot cube 10 feet away. At that distance the back of the cube subtends a visual angle about 10 per cent smaller than the front. At 20 feet, the angular size difference is only 5 per cent, and at 40 feet only about 2.5 per cent. A station point assumed at a distance of 40 times the size of the object is effectively at optical infinity. These

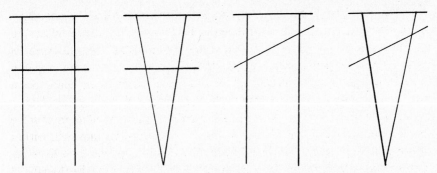

Figure 3.1 The four geometrical projection systems. From left to right, Orthogonal, Similarity, Affine and Projective.

three components of the station point – number, angle and distance – determine all the possible physical options.

Mechanically, too, the artist has only so many options. Consider the case where multiple objects are to be depicted. Compositional logistics are constrained in the following ways. First, all the objects can be arrayed in rows, one behind the other as in a classic 14th-century composition, or set in a non-planar composition. Second, all the objects depicted can be in uniform orientation relative to the depiction surface, or at varying angles. Third, the picture plane – canvas, paper, wall, etc. – can be parallel to the subject planes or intersect them. Fourth, the projection lines, the lines of sight, so called, can be parallel to each other or convergent to a centre of projection. This gives a total of eight physical, compositional options, determined by the physical logistics of the representational enterprise; this is a reassuringly small number. Even more heartening, however, for our understanding of the representation of surface layout in space is the realisation that all of these options can be categorised even more simply in terms of the geometry of the projection, in terms of the geometry that describes the spatial layout system employed.

Geometrically, if both the subject and picture planes are parallel to each other and also the projection lines are parallel to each other, the picture is an Orthogonal projection of subject to image. If the planes are parallel but the projection lines are convergent, then the picture is a Similarity projection. If the subject and image planes intersect one another, but the projection lines are parallel, then the picture is an Affine projection. If neither the planes nor the projection lines are parallel, then the picture is a Projective projection. These four types of projection are illustrated in Figure 3.1.

The most interesting fact about these different projection systems, the most

Figure 3.2 Prototypical house drawings. From left to right, Orthogonal, Affine and Projective.

basic fact and the most difficult to comprehend, is that together they comprise the whole of natural perspective. Natural perspective is nearly always thought of in the Western mode, as a construction formula like linear perspective, but it's not. Natural perspective is a comprehensive description of the structure of the light to the eye under all possible conditions of observation – in this case, *mutatis mutandis*, under all possible conditions of realistic representation. All possible conditions of realism are described by the four projection systems presented here.

What do pictures created by each of these four systems look like? A corner view of a prototypical house generated by each of the four systems is shown in Figure 3.2. In an Orthogonal projection, right angles remain right angles and parallel edges are drawn in parallel. Size remains invariant under the projection so there is no diminishing projected size with increasing distance. In a Similarity projection, shape is still invariant so both angle and parallelism are preserved, but size is not; the image size decreases as the distance of the subject increases. Otherwise, Orthogonal and Similarity projections of a *single* object are identical. In Similarity geometry, a large figure and a small one of the same shape are equivalent. In an Affine projection, shape as defined by angle is no longer invariant; that is, right angles are no longer depicted as right angles. Parallelism, however, is invariant, so parallel edges are depicted by parallel lines. In an Affine projection, a square and a parallelogram are equivalent to each other. In a Projective projection, not even parallelism is preserved. Parallel edges are depicted by lines converging to a point and angles undergo dramatic change in the projection. Projected size decreases with distance. The major Projective invariants are the cross-ratios of points and lines, the invariants that specify a rigid object. Of course, betweenness and collinearity and adjacency and such are also invariant in a Projective projection. An explication of the Projective invariants is beyond the scope of this paper, but it is important to note that perspective derives in part from the invariance of the cross-ratios, that a geometrical abstraction finds expression as a working tool in the hands of Western artists. (See Hagen, 1980, 1981 and in press for an extended treatment of this analysis.) In fact, each of these sets of geometrical abstractions, each of these formal projection systems, finds expression in the hands of some culture's artists. Because these four geometries describe all the physically consistent possibilities for projecting the layout of space onto a flat surface, every art style engaged in the representation of space can be categorised as exemplifying, at least predominantly, one of these geometries. We shall see below that sporadic attempts to ignore physical consistency which have occurred at different times in different cultures never comprised a coherent art style, although they appear with some frequency in the efforts of the untutored.

3. Styles of painting and geometry

To understand the reality of the relationship between formal geometric systems and actual styles of painting, it is useful to examine actually occurring styles and not the poor efforts of the present author, who is not an artist. Consider, for example, the art of ancient Egypt, which exemplifies an Orthogonal projection system (see Figure 3.3). The station-point assumption is multiple, a different station point for each object. For variously articulated objects like people and birds, there is a different station point for each major body part. The distance of the station point conventionally assumed is at optical infinity. At this distance the projection lines are parallel. There is no projected size decrease with increased distance between object and image plane. The image plane is parallel to the dominant plane of each object. The parallel planes and parallel lines create an Orthogonal projection system in which shape is the major invariant. Thus, parallel edges are parallel, right angles are right angles. All metric information, relative size and proportion, parallelism and perpendicularity, is preserved in this style. This is not to say, however, that there are no exceptions to the dominant geometry in the system. For example, for reasons not related to the simple representation of space, size relations among human beings are depicted not in terms of geometric consistency, but in terms of a social/political hierarchy. The dominant male is always larger than subservient males, women, children, slaves, captives and servants. But no art style is simply an exercise in geometry.

Traditional Japanese art, pre-16th-century, exemplifies an Affine projection system. Here the station-point assumption is single, at least for each scene, event or time frame. Since several events and the passage of time are often depicted in this style, it may appear to the Western observer to be a multiple-station-point system, but it is not in the sense that Egyptian art is. The distance of the station point is at optical infinity, so the projection lines, the lines of sight, from artist/observer to scene, are parallel. It can be seen

Figure 3.3 Egyptian painting from Thebes, XIX Dynasty, Tomb of Sennedjem (Vaulted Chamber). (Photograph by Egyptian Expedition. Metropolitan Museum of Art, New York.)

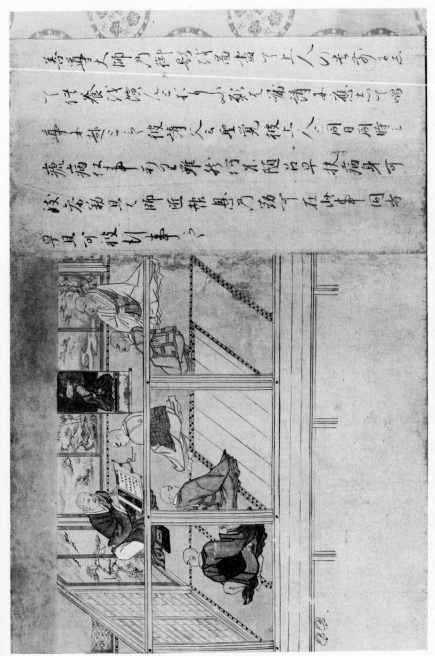

Figure 3.4 Japanese painting from the Kamakura Period, early 14th century. Hanging scroll. (Gift of Mrs Russell Sage (1980.221). Metropolitan Museum of Art, New York.)

in such paintings that parallel edges do not converge towards the horizon and there is no perspective compression with increasing distance of depicted objects. The most striking difference between the spatial treatment in Japanese art and that in Western painting is not the greater distance of the station point, but its greater height. In Western painting the conventional height of the station point is five to six feet above the ground. In Japanese painting, an aerial, or bird's-eye, view is common. Figure 3.4 illustrates one of the consequences of assuming a station point at such a great height – the rooflessness technique, common in narrative scrolls, used to display the indoor activities of the characters. It is sometimes argued that in traditional Japanese painting there is no point of view, no place where the observer really stands relative to the scene. But a moment's consideration of Figure 3.4 will reveal that this is not true. The artist and observer are clearly at one consistent angle relative to the objects, to the buildings and terraces in this example. The picture plane quite obviously intersects the front surfaces of the subjects. It is this combination of intersecting planes and parallel projection lines that makes this system of painting Affine. The Affine invariant of parallelism is clearly preserved, while angularity quite clearly is not. So we see that a rectangular terrace appears as a parallelogram, circular wheels are depicted as ellipses and there is no size diminution of projected images with greater and greater distance.

— The projective system with the fewest invariants, Projective projection, is best illustrated with Western post-Renaissance art, since it is the style with which people are the most familiar. In a Projective system, the subject and image planes intersect and the station point is relatively close so the projection lines are convergent to the station point. Size, shape, angle, parallelism all undergo major changes in this system. Nevertheless, there is sufficient information in paintings like that of Figure 3.5 to permit ready recognition of objects and events.

It is the Projective system of painting that is touted as the only truly visually valid system, as the only system that actually represents natural perspective. Natural perspective describes the world as seen, not the world as known. I hope that it is clear from the analysis presented above that each of the projection systems is simply the necessary geometrical consequence of taking a certain station-point stance relative to the subject. Physically, there are a limited number of options; the consequent geometry describes the structures in the light to the eye attendant on each of those options. Each geometry is as much a part of natural perspective as Projective geometry. Formally, Orthogonal, Similarity and Affine geometry are all nested in, are subsets of,

Figure 3.5 Western post-Renaissance painting by Raphael, *Madonna and Child Enthroned with Saints*. (Gift of J. Pierpont Morgan, 1916. Metropolitan Museum of Art, New York.)

Projective geometry, but a formal hierarchy need not imply a developmental order. Then again, it might.

4. Development in the geometry of art

Despite the equivalent visual validity of these different projection systems, it still might be the case that the Projective system *per se* represents the highest level of development of spatial representation. It might be true that the earliest art we know of is generally Orthogonal, that later-appearing styles tend to

Table 3.1. *Art styles by time and geographic area*

Date	Europe	Africa	Middle East	Far East	Americas
30,000	Ice Age Ⓟ-(M)				
3500					
		Old Egypt O-(M)			
2000					
		Mid Egypt O-(M)			
1500					
		New Egypt O-(M)			
1000			Assyrian O-(M)		
	Etruscan O-(M)				
	Greek vases O-(M)				
500					
	Greek vases A-(M)				
1	Roman murals A-(M)				
				Chinese caves A-(S)	
500	Medieval A-(M)				
	Irish O-(S)				
1000		Bushmen Ⓟ-(M)			
	Romanesque A-(M)			Chinese landscape Ⓟ-(S)	Inca, Aztec, Mayan A-(M)
	Italian A-(S)		Persian A-(S)	Japanese A-(S)	
1500	Renaissance Ⓟ-(S)				
					Plains Indians O-(S)
	Cubism A-(M)				Northwest Indians
2000					A-(M)

P = Projective; O = Orthogonal; A = Affine; (M) = multiple station points; (S) = single station point.

be Affine, and the most modern – but not too modern – are Projective. It might be true, but is it? Table 3.1 categorises many of the coherent art styles known through history. From the table it is clear that observation of the world's art reveals no universal developmental pattern across time of adoption of certain geometries in any fixed sequence. I do not find that Orthogonality and multiplicity of station point were necessarily present in the earliest known art in each region; some of the oldest styles, presumably the most 'primitive', were certainly not Orthogonal. I cannot find evidence that the art styles of different cultures have developed systematically in an Orthogonal to Affine to Projective progression. Even in Western art (including Egypt), one can make this case only by choosing stylistic ancestors with great care and by ignoring diversions such as Cubism.

5. Development in children

Still, it is possible to examine the question of development ontogenetically, with Western children whose cultural end-point is presumably Projective. Many writers have offered descriptions of the stages in the development of drawing. See, for example, Kellogg (1969), Lark-Horowitz, Lewis and Luca (1967) and Eng (1931/1964). These writers vary a bit one from the other, but generally they all conclude that the child is supposed to go through the following stages of pictorialism or spatial representation. Stage one is the complete absence of space or the setting of various objects alongside one another. Stage two is that of conscious but unsuccessful attempts to represent space, including map-like representations showing objects turned over in the plane of the paper, unsuccessful bird's-eye (aerial) views, representations from two or several points of view. Stage three is that of successful but incomplete spatial representation in which the child makes use of a strip of ground of some width, takes perspective foreshortening into account and does some masking of one figure by another. Stage four is that of the coherent pictorial representation of the whole space, in which stage the child finally grasps intuitively the laws of perspective, and takes pains to make use of them.

Is all that true? or some of it? or any? To examine this issue, drawings of children and adults were collected under constrained and similar conditions, and an attempt was made to identify the similarities and differences among them. In particular the geometry employed in the representation of spatial layout was examined. We asked college freshmen and children from first, third and fifth grades (6, 8 and 10 years old) to draw a picture of a model of a house. The model house was 10 inches square and 8 inches high with two identical fronts and two sides, and was placed in the centre of a round table. Subjects were seated at the table so that they faced a front, or a side, or a corner. They were asked to draw everything they could see from where they were sitting, and only what they could see from where they were sitting. We measured all the lines and angles in each of the corner drawings and classified the drawings as Orthogonal, Affine, Projective or Other. Again, Orthogonal meant that right angles were depicted by right angles and parallel edges by

Table 3.2. *Frequency of drawing styles produced with house model present*

| | Age | | | |
Drawing style	6	8	10	Adult
Orthogonal	83%	75%	55%	29%
Affine	17%	25%	30%	21%
Projective	0%	0%	10%	43%
Other	0%	0%	5%	7%
Drew two sides	6/24	12/28	20/28	28/28

parallel lines. Affine meant that right angles were not preserved, but the parallel edges were depicted as parallel in the drawings. Projective projections were those in which parallel edges converged and right angles were lost. 'Other' included unclassifiable drawings (there were almost none) and Divergent projections. Divergent meant that parallel edges were depicted by lines that diverged upward in the picture plane. It is not a system of drawing that falls under any of the geometrical categories described above; it exemplifies instead a projection system *manqué*, to be explained below. Previous research had indicated the necessity of including it as a category. We found the following.

The younger the children, the less likely they were to draw two faces of the house when seated at the corner. They said they could see both sides but it was too hard to draw them. Only 6 out of 24 first-grade children attempted to draw both sides. (Average age was 80 months.) People who drew only one side, whether seated at a corner or a face, drew it in Orthogonal projection with seemingly arbitrary roof shapes. It was not possible to distinguish the children's drawings from the adults' except by the relative firmness of the lines, and that was not always reliable. The group of people who did try to draw two sides produced all of the possible layout systems, usually singly but sometimes in combination. Among those asked to draw again for a reliability check, about half produced drawings in the same system as before and half did not.

Table 3.2 gives the percentages of Orthogonal, Affine, Projective and Other corner drawings for each of the age groups tested. From the table it is clear that over 50 per cent of the children at any age use Orthogonal perspective, while close to 30 per cent of the adults also do so. The frequency of Affine productions increases with age, as does that of Projective renderings. Data cited in Freeman (1980) also support the finding that Orthogonal drawings

Table 3.3. *Frequency of drawing styles produced with no model present (adults) (percentages). I: 'Draw a house'; II: 'Draw a house in perspective'*

	I	II
American		
Orthogonal	58	19
Affine	22	40
Projective	10	23
Divergent	10	18
Spanish		
Orthogonal	62	15
Affine	17	44
Projective	14	30
Divergent	7	11

occur over 50 per cent of the time in the works of children. The 50 per cent figure for Orthogonal drawings contradicts Willats (1977*a* and *b*), who found in his study of 108 children between the ages of 4 and 16 years that only a small minority of children used the Orthogonal system, and that only a bit over 20 per cent of the drawings were Affine. The differences may lie in the different methodologies and instructions employed.

It is true that the frequency of the Projective system increased with grade, but more than half the adults did not use it. Those 12 who did came nowhere near faultless photographic realism. The size of their angles, the height of the centre of projection, the amount of convergence, bear little discernible relationship to the model. Only 9 out of these 12 used a consistent degree of perspective across the whole picture, and that varied from 50 to 90 per cent. Only 3 out of 28 adults even depicted the sides as equal in length to the front, which they in fact were.

The house-drawing study was repeated with educated adults, both Spanish and American, under unconstrained conditions with no model present. This time the participants were simply told, 'Draw a house.' After the first effort they were asked to 'Draw a house in perspective.' Under the simple instruction, 58 per cent of the Americans drew in Orthogonal perspective, 22 per cent in Affine and 10 per cent in Projective. Of the 29 Spaniards, 62 per cent drew Orthogonally, 17 per cent in Affine perspective, 14 per cent Projectively and 7 per cent in Divergent perspective. Under the perspective instruction the

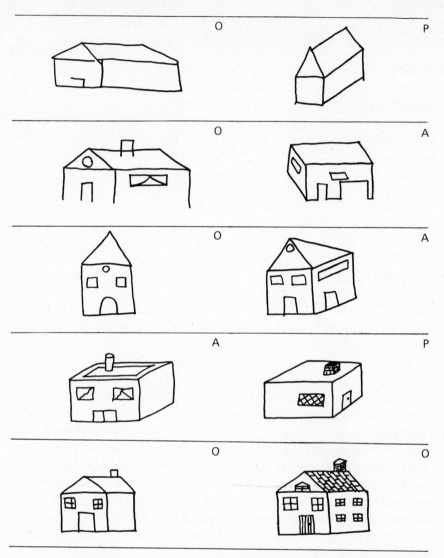

Figure 3.6 Pairs of drawings by educated adults created under the instructions (left) 'Draw a house'; (right) 'Draw a house in perspective'.

American percentages were: Orthogonal, 19 per cent; Affine, 40 per cent; Projective, 23 per cent; Divergent, 18 per cent (see Table 3.3). Figure 3.6 shows pairs of drawings under the two different sets of instructions. It is clear that the frequency of Affine drawings increases under the more demanding instruction. However, the frequency of drawings truly in perspective increases from very few to not quite so few. Again, the Projective drawings are 'in perspective' only by the most generous criteria.

In another, less formal study, two dozen adults were asked to draw a table and four chairs, a cube and a bed after they drew a house first under the free instruction and then under the perspective instruction. Of those adults, 10 per cent used one system for all four subjects, 50 per cent used two systems, and 40 per cent used three. Freeman and Hayton (1980) found a somewhat greater degree of individual consistency in their study of 20 10- to 11-year-old children.

This work provides no evidence that adults 'draw what they see' any more than children do, in the sense that 'seeing' is considered to be the making of a photographic record. All of these amateur artists simply attempt to draw what is visually possible and, age group by age group, everything that is possible in terms of the geometry of natural perspective in the broad sense explicated above. Neither the average adult nor the average child is an artist; the artist will generally create pictures in accord with the reigning canons for the representation of space. Ordinary people will try to reproduce all of the visual structures available in natural perspective from Orthogonal to Projective with the frequencies of each type perhaps influenced by the artistic preference of the culture.

6. A perceptual interpretation of non-development

Why do these amateurs, children and adults, draw so often in Orthogonal perspective when the artistic canon of their culture is clearly Projective? I think it is because seeing is not a photographic phenomenon; visual perception does not involve the making of tiny retinal snapshots. As long as we believed that vision was based on retinal photographs, then a photographic model of visual realism in art sufficed. However, once the metaphor of 'eye as camera' is dropped, then a different level of analysis of the stimulus in both ordinary perception and art is required. The primary proponent of an alternative stimulus analysis was James J. Gibson (1950, 1966, 1971, 1973, 1974, 1979). He argued that perception of the world is based on the pick-up of visual information about its more or less permanent properties. Visual information is invariant structure in the light to the eye that specifies the relatively constant size, shape, location and composition of objects. The momentary appearances of objects in frozen photographic slices of time have very little to do with the perception of a changing world by a moving observer. The pick-up of invariants takes place across change; we perceive the persistent properties of the world through the experience of transformations. Gibson argued that momentary perspective or photographic structures are available in the light to the eye, but are incidental to perception. If that is so, and I believe it is, it explains why Orthogonal projections make such frequent appearances in the artwork of amateurs. Orthogonal projections carry the greatest number of invariants. They show angle, parallelism, shape and relative size as they 'really' are, not as they appear at one moment in time from one fixed angle in space. (It is for this reason that Orthogonal projections are usually those called 'canonical' by traditional writers on art development. Where the canonical form of an object is not its Orthogonal projection, it is usually just the image that conforms to the cultural canons for drawing the object. Canons and canonical form in the latter sense are surely learned.)

This explains too why Projective (perspective) projections appear so infrequently. They are tied to single moments of time, accidental viewpoints, and not to the persistent properties of objects. Projective projections carry very few invariants. The ones carried are critical, to be sure, but they hardly express the same degree of 'sameness' (relative to their subjects) as do Orthogonal projections. In this sense, drawing is reproductive perception. All of our artists are drawing what they 'know' about their subjects – but it is what they know perceptually, not cognitively. They draw what they know from 'seeing', not from 'thinking'. It is drawing in perspective that may well be defined as drawing what one knows. It is the knowledge of momentary appearance and how to depict it that must be taught. We are quite capable of noticing, at least if we practise and only to some extent, the 'photographic' appearance of scenes, and can certainly be taught to reproduce, at least if we practise and only to some extent, photographic structures of scenes on paper. Almost no one ever does it spontaneously, although clearly the information is available visually to everyone. Still, drawing is not ever *simply* reproductive perception. It is a skill; it is learned and the artist gets better with practice. As Arnheim wrote so clearly in his discussion of the problem of growth,

Artistic representation is normally not based on a particular object watched from a fixed point of view at a given moment, but on the three-dimensional visual concept of a species of objects that have been observed from many different angles. As a rule perceptual experience does not contain the perspective changes of shape and size that are found in the retinal projection. Pictorial representation is not a mechanical replica of the percept, but renders its structural characteristics through the properties of a particular medium. (1954/1974)

Ordinary perception is not such a skill despite assertions to the contrary about the educated eye of an artist. The artist does not see more or differently from the non-artist; he selects what he wishes to draw and he knows how to draw it according to the canons of his artistic culture. Certainly that is a form of 'trained eye', but not the form usually associated with artistic vision. Artists, like the rest of us, are constrained by the geometries of natural perspective. They can select among them, and are free to mix and match, although they seldom do so, but they do not experience a visual spatial world uniquely artistic.

If all people who draw are constrained by the varieties of natural perspective, how do we account for the occasional occurrence of divergent perspective in the art of the world and in the art of present-day amateurs? Recall that in divergent perspective the parallel edges of a house, for example, are depicted by nonparallel lines diverging from each other upwards in the picture plane. There is no station point, no angle or distance, at which an artist can stand where such a projectively divergent structure would appear in the light to the eye. Divergent perspective is not a geometrical consequence of standing anywhere outside a perception laboratory. If representational drawing always reproduces what is seen and divergence in space of parallel edges is never seen, why does it make an appearance at all? In the art of *amateurs*, there are, no doubt, two reasons. One is that the untrained 'artist' knows he 'cannot draw'. He is aware of his inability to depict according to the canons of his culture parallel edges receding in space. This is the reason that many adults given a choice in the house-drawing study simply chose to draw a single front view of the house with no difficult corners or edges. When confronted with the perspective task, they reluctantly attempted to draw corners with receding edges. They do not know what to do; physically they have only three options. They can draw two lines parallel to each other, two lines converging toward one another upwards on the picture plane, or two lines diverging upwards. Adults draw all three. They know the divergent efforts 'don't look right', but they are so unaware of photographic realism as to be uncertain whether things are supposed to get bigger or smaller as they recede from the viewer in space. The second reason is simply error. Many adults and older children when questioned about the divergent parallels replied that they thought they were drawing parallel lines. Younger children did not understand the question. I have argued that representational art represents what actually is seen, that all the various coherent art styles of the world are components of natural perspective. Why, then, does divergent perspective occur among the *art styles* of the world? The simplest answer is that it doesn't, at least as a consistent, characteristic component of any style. It can be seen in some early Chinese art, some Japanese works and some Persian, among others, and with a great enough frequency to be notable in Western Gothic art. But even in the last case, a count of known works using it will prove to be a small percentage. Parallel and convergent systems,

systems that make sense in the geometrics of natural projection, were adopted by various cultures as consistently used systems; the system that does not make sense was not adopted.

7. A speculation

I have argued in this chapter that drawing, in terms of systems of spatial representation, does not develop across culture or with increasing age. Most readers of the present chapter cannot draw and know they cannot. When asked to draw they become embarrassed and say they cannot. They are quite correct. They cannot draw as the skilled artists of their culture can. But, for reasons that are no doubt of great psychological importance, these same readers believe that other ordinary, untrained adults *can* draw. Why do they believe that? The reader is invited to ask half a dozen artistically naïve friends to draw three or four objects or scenes. The inexplicable sense of uniqueness will disappear quickly. Certainly, drawing skills can be developed, they can be taught to children. There are many books available to teach drawing, and many teachers, and some of these are quite effective, whether the stylistic goal be Projective, Affine or Orthogonal. (There are books available to teach the drawing styles of non-Western European cultures, although they are generally overlooked in Western treatments of drawing development.) By drawing skills I mean something other than simple motor control; I mean cultural canons. Children's fine motor development improves with practice, just as does that of the adult learning a new skill like knitting or drawing. So one could plot the development of motor control in the creation of drawings if one wished. But neither the mastery of specifically taught canons nor the acquisition of motor skills is reason for the excitement generated by those who espouse the theory that drawing undergoes a developmental progression with ordered stages that differ qualitatively from each other. The assumption that drawing exhibits a truly developmental character implies significant age-related changes in the perceptual and cognitive components that underlie the understanding as well as the generation of representation. There may be such changes that occur in infancy, but the data do not provide evidence of their existence in childhood or later life. I cannot draw well; I trust it doesn't inhibit my understanding of the representational efforts of others more skilled.

That drawing develops is a basic assumption underlying the use of drawing tests to measure cognitive, perceptual, emotional and sexual development. Is it possible to measure developmental level with a tool that itself shows no development? Of course, representational drawing, like representational art, involves the depiction of many aspects of human experience other than that of spatial layout. It may be the case that these aspects permit the valid use of drawing tests to <u>measure developmental level</u>, but the issue invites some scepticism and considerable empirical work.

REFERENCES

Arnheim, R. (1954; 2nd ed., 1974) *Art and visual perception: A psychology of the creative eye.* Berkeley: University of California Press.

Eng, H. (1931; 2nd ed., 1964) *The psychology of children's drawings.* London: Routledge and Kegan Paul.

Freeman, N. H. (1980) *Strategies of representation in young children.* London: Academic Press.

Freeman, N. H. & Hayton, C. (1980) Gross failure to utilise alignment cues in children's drawing of three-dimensional relationships. *Perception, 9,* 353–90.

Gibson, J. J. (1950) *The perception of the visual world.* Boston: Houghton Mifflin.

(1966) *The senses considered as perceptual systems.* Boston: Houghton Mifflin.

(1971) The information available in pictures. *Leonardo, 4,* 27–35.

(1973) On the concept of formless invariants in visual perception. *Leonardo, 6,* 43–5.

(1974) Visualizing conceived as visual apprehending without any particular point of observation. *Leonardo, 7,* 41–2.

(1979) *The ecological approach to visual perception.* Boston: Houghton Mifflin.

Hagen, M. A. (in press) *Varieties of realism: Geometries of representational art.* Cambridge: University Press.

(ed.) (1980, 1981) *The perception of pictures,* 2 vols. New York: Academic Press.

Kellogg, R. (1969) *Analyzing children's art.* Palo Alto, Calif.: National Press Books.

Lark-Horowitz, B., Lewis, H. P. & Luca, M. (1967) *Understanding children's art for better teaching.* Columbus: Charles E. Merrill.

Willats, J. (1977*a*) How children learn to draw realistic pictures. *Quarterly Journal of Experimental Psychology, 29,* 367–82.

(1977*b*) How children learn to represent three-dimensional space in drawings. In G. Butterworth (ed.), *The child's representation of the world.* New York: Plenum, pp. 189–202.

4

Drawing systems revisited: the role of denotation systems in children's figure drawings

JOHN WILLATS

1. Projection systems: background

In any discussion of children's drawings the word 'perspective' is likely to make an early appearance, and at this point the intellectual level of the discussion usually begins to sag. The trouble with 'perspective' is that it means such different things to different people. At one extreme, almost any more or less realistic picture can be, and often is, described as being 'in perspective'. At the other extreme, definitions of perspective are hedged about with all sorts of technical jargon about picture planes, station points, lines of sight, visual angles and so on, and in this context pictures can be said to be in true perspective only if they conform to a rather strict set of rules involving the convergence of the projection rays as they intersect the picture plane. This effectively confines the occurrence of pictures in true perspective to photographs and to artists' pictures in the Western world from, roughly, the 15th to the mid 19th centuries. Very few children's drawings can be said to be 'in perspective' in this sense. In an attempt to overcome the problems arising from these two different ways of using the word perspective, Dubery and Willats (1972, 1983) introduced the general term 'drawing systems' to cover all the pictorial systems based on projective geometry. Some of these systems are illustrated in the next section. The range of available systems is wide, and the usage varies from one discipline, culture and even individual artist or illustrator to another. Among these drawing systems are orthographic projection (now mainly used by engineers), the oblique and isometric projections and their variants such as axonometric, dimetric and trimetric projections (now mainly used by architects and illustrators) and all the various kinds of linear perspective. The term 'perspective' proper is reserved here for those systems in which the projection rays converge to the eye (artificial and synthetic perspective) and a rather rare system (inverted perspective) in which the projection rays diverge. Dubery and Willats showed that all these projection systems belong to a mathematical family, that is, a group of systems (like the conic sections) based on a common formula whose parameters can vary. A member of a family is said to be 'special' if the parameters take a special value; for example, the circle is a special case of a conic section because its radius is constant, while the ellipse is a more general case because its radius varies within the confines of the figure.

As a consequence of this approach, Dubery and Willats were able to isolate two systems – horizontal oblique projection and vertical oblique projection – which had not previously been described. They also showed that periods and cultures other than our own had used systems other than true perspective, and, in particular, that the use of horizontal and vertical oblique projection was quite widespread.

A number of writers have discussed children's drawings in terms of projection systems or perspective or both. Clark (1897), in a pioneering work, discussed the child's attitude towards 'perspective problems' (in the sense of '*natural* perspective', or the appearance of objects as they are projected to the eye) in relation to both a smooth object (an apple) and a rectangular object (a book). In an important contribution to the topic, Lewis (1963) described five successive developmental levels in representation of 'spherical space' (a sphere), 'cubic space' (a rectangular object) and 'spatial depth'. These five levels were, Lewis says, 'based upon solutions reported in the literature' (p. 97), but were implicitly related to the various projection systems.

The approach used by Willats (1977*a, b*) was to assign children's drawings of a rectangular object (a table, with various objects on it), to classes based on the family of systems described by Dubery and Willats (1972). The systems included in this scheme were: orthographic projection, vertical oblique projection, oblique projection, naïve perspective (included because a number of drawings seemed to fall into this category, rather than as a true projection system) and true perspective. The results showed that there was a correlation between age and the complexity and mathematical generality of the systems used.

One surprise was that even by the age of 16 or 17 only a minority of children were using anything approaching true perspective. Even more surprising was that, overall, the most commonly used system was vertical oblique projection: a system which children would hardly ever have encountered in their pictorial environment. On the basis of the results of this experiment, Willats suggested that the acquisition of drawing ability was, like language, primarily a process of discovering increasingly complex and powerful rule systems, the 'rule systems' in the case of drawings of rectangular objects being those of projective geometry.

Since the mid seventies the study of children's drawings has had rapid progress. This revival of interest in developmental picture production as a research area contrasts with the relatively long period of stagnation which followed the early work of Sully, Bechterev and Luquet (Freeman, 1983), and forms the background to, and the occasion for, this present volume. It therefore seems timely to revisit the 'projection systems' approach, in order to see how well it has stood the test of the last few years. I shall consider first the validity, then the implications and then the scope of the projection-systems approach, and then introduce the idea of another kind of drawing system. To begin with, however, we need some definitions.

2. Projection systems: definitions

Projection systems in the abstract can be exhaustively defined in terms of two factors: (a) whether the projection rays converge, diverge or run parallel, and (b) the angles at which the rays intersect the picture plane (normally assumed to be a flat surface). Such a definition, in terms of what is called three-dimensional or 'primary' geometry, is very general, and can afford to ignore both the shapes of objects projected and their orientations. When it comes to analysing drawings, it is more usual and more convenient to define the projection systems in terms of the *effects* of varying these two factors on what happens to the image on the picture surface: what is called the 'secondary' geometry. Analysis of these effects involves two assumptions: (a) that the objects projected are rectangular, and (b) that they are oriented so that their principal faces lie parallel to the picture plane.

In *orthographic* projection objects are projected using parallel rays which strike the picture plane at right angles. In terms of secondary geometry (Figure 4.1a) this means that vertical lines in the picture represent vertical edges in the scene and side-to-side lines in the picture represent side-to-side edges in the scene. Edges or other features in the third (horizontal) dimension of the object or scene are simply ignored. Drawings in this system are clearly related to the object depicted, but give only a limited amount of information about it.

In *vertical oblique* projection objects are projected using parallel rays which strike the picture plane at right angles in the horizontal plane, but at an oblique angle in the vertical plane (hence the name). This means that for rectangular objects edges in the third dimension, instead of being ignored, are

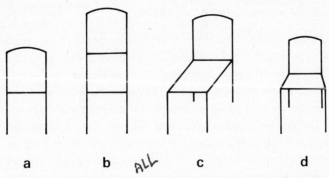

a   b   ALL   c   d

Figure 4.1 A chair drawn in various projection systems: (a) orthographic projection; (b) vertical oblique projection; (c) oblique projection; (d) perspective.

represented by vertical lines in the picture (Figure 4.1b). Drawings in this system are more 'realistic' than drawings in orthographic projection; but as vertical lines are also used to represent vertical edges in the scene, drawings in this system tend to be ambiguous (Willats, 1977*a*, Fig. 9; Freeman, 1980; Jahoda, 1981).

In *oblique* projection the projection rays are again parallel but can strike the picture plane at any angle. This means that in terms of secondary geometry, edges in the third dimension are represented by oblique lines in the picture, so that the front, side and top faces of a rectangular object can be seen together in a single drawing (Figure 1c). An undeniable impression of 'realism' is obvious from a glance at the picture.

Finally, in *perspective* the projection rays converge to the eye of the spectator. In terms of secondary geometry this means that lines representing edges in the third dimension converge to a vanishing point on the picture surface.

Illustrations showing the primary geometry of the projection systems, together with examples of pictures in all the systems, taken from a wide variety of disciplines and cultures, are to be found in Dubery and Willats (1983). The importance of the distinction between oblique projections and perspective depends very much on the nature of the object or scene. For small objects the two systems are often almost indistinguishable, whereas for large scenes, or relatively large objects seen close to, the distinction is an important one, so that the scale of the object drawn will affect the classification system chosen when analysing drawings. The importance of scale and distance is referred to in Hagen's chapter in this volume.

3. Projection-systems approach: validity

The strength of the drawing-systems approach is that the method of classification is based, not on an *ad hoc* division of drawings into classes on the basis of a subjective assessment of similarity, but on an abstract mathematical description of the various projection systems. This means that any experimentally determined correlation between age and systems is proof against the danger of circularity: the dangers that the correlation is there because that's how the classes were (covertly) chosen in the first place.

The corresponding weakness of the approach is that it cannot cope with drawings which do not appear to be based on *any* of the projection systems. Leaving this point on one side for the moment, for it will be discussed at greater length in the section headed 'Limitations', the experimental results connecting age with systems do appear to be fairly robust. Willats' work with British children has already been mentioned; this showed a developmental sequence which followed the order: no projection system, orthographic projection, vertical oblique projection, oblique projection, naïve perspective and perspective. Saenger (1981) found the same developmental sequence with North American children in production, but also asked the children about their picture preferences. Interestingly, the majority of children of all ages preferred drawings in oblique projection even when they could produce perspective drawings themselves. In many ways this makes good sense, since oblique projections show the front, side and top faces of an object together, and yet at the same time they are free from many of the distortions found in perspective. For example, drawings in oblique projection show parallel edges as parallel in the picture, and as true lengths. The only real advantage of perspective is in allowing a change of scale with distance: in pictures of landscapes, for instance, trees and mountains will swamp the picture if they are shown to the same scale as people. Children's readiness to adopt different systems in order to draw different kinds of scenes is an untapped research area which might well prove fruitful. In addition, Saenger's finding is a pointer to a crucial difference between production and perception: in drawing the developmental sequence in each seems to be quite distinct (Willats, 1981*a*, Ch. 2).

Jahoda (1981) replicated Willats' (1977*a*) study with adults in Ghana, partly in order to test Willats' suggestion that two distinct abilities were involved in the use of projection systems and the depiction of overlap, and partly because he was sceptical of Willats' claim that the 'development of at least the earlier stages of drawing development is independent of cultural influences' (Jahoda, 1981, p. 133). Jahoda opened the discussion of his results by saying, 'Given the radical disparities in cultural background and age between Willats' original and the present sample, the broad congruence of the findings is remarkable. Not only was it feasible to apply the analytical scheme to the drawings of Ghanaian subjects, but Willats' suggestion that the learning of drawing systems and the depiction of overlap may involve distinct abilities is supported by the Ghanaian evidence' (p. 140). As regards Willats' suggestion that the development of at least the earlier stages of drawing development is largely independent of cultural influences, this has been questioned by a number of writers, and will be discussed (briefly) in the next section.

Finally, Willats (1984) and Willats and Freeman (1984) carried out two further experiments in which children were asked to draw rectangular objects. In the first of these, children were asked to draw a number of made-up 'unfamiliar' rectangular objects, choosing their own viewpoints; in the second, children were asked to draw a cube (in the form of a die) in positions chosen by the experimenters. Both experiments confirmed the correlation between projection systems and age.

In view of all these results, the correlation between the formal sequence of projection systems and the child's ability to use different systems with increasing age may reasonably be regarded as fairly well established, so far as drawings of rectangular objects are concerned. One point needs emphasising: the importance of including the paired systems of horizontal and vertical oblique projection in the method of classification, if only because these systems are so widely used by children.

4. The use of projection systems by children: implications

The correlation found between age and projection systems tells us little in itself of how or why the various systems are acquired, only *when* they are acquired. Perhaps the most crucial question is the one raised by Freeman (1980, 1983): does the child's ability to use a particular system depend on the ability to perceive the scene correctly? or on the ability to get the lines in the right place on the paper? or on the ability to understand what the lines stand for? Here the acquisition of the oblique systems (oblique projection, allied systems like isometric projection, and perspective) provides an important test case. Most writers agree that children in the West do not acquire the ability to use one or other of these oblique systems until quite late on: perhaps 9 or 10 years, depending rather on the complexity of the task and whether or not the child or the experimenter chooses the viewpoint; and some children never acquire the ability at all. Is this because of the difficulty of perceiving oblique edges and similar features in the scene: what Freeman calls the 'scene-encoding' problem? Or is it because of the 'picture plane' problem of drawing oblique lines within a context of horizontal and vertical alignment cues on the picture surface? Or is it the symbolic difficulty of using oblique lines on the picture surface to stand for horizontal edges in the third dimension of the scene?

It is too early to give any definite answers to these questions, but we do have some pointers. Freeman's work suggests that, as between the first two questions, it is the structural geometry of the picture plane which provides most of the problems, rather than the difficulty of encoding the scene. As between the relative importance of mastering symbolic and structural skills, the two must surely be complementary. The important question is not whether a 'symbolic skills' or 'production bias' account of developmental picture production, taken in isolation, can give a satisfactory account of children's drawings, but just what part, in detail, each account has to play. To this extent the study of visual representation is beginning to come of age, just as the study of verbal language began to come of age with Chomsky's distinction between competence and performance.

In rather the same way, the vexed question of cultural influences *versus* innately determined development is best seen, not in terms of two mutually exclusive theories, but rather in terms of culturally determined variations on a common central model. Wilson and Wilson (1982) have shown that children's figure drawings in the West have changed remarkably in some respects since the end of the last century; and they ascribe this, quite plausibly, to changes in the child's pictorial environment. They also show (Wilson and Wilson, 1983) a very marked difference between the drawings of Egyptian village children and those of town children, due again, they argue, to the different groups drawing on different stylistic sources. Another recent study, again mainly concerned with figure drawing (Hartley, Somerville, Jensen and Eliefja, 1982), showed that different styles could be identified reliably in the drawings of 5-year-old children. However, as regards the development of the ability to use the projection systems, it seems likely that the main course of development for younger children must be largely independent of cultural influences. The rather simple optical and geometric constraints which govern the earlier projection systems, and the relative simplicity of the mechanisms of interaction between production and perception which leads the child from one system to the next (Willats, 1984), just do not allow the possibility of much cultural variation. For older children the situation is quite different. In the first place, there are quite a large number of varieties among the oblique systems, and the particular variety a child learns to use may well be the one he or she is taught, or sees most used in the pictorial environment.

Perhaps more important, the very *possibility* of transition to one of the oblique systems probably depends on the existence of suitable exemplars in the pictorial environment. As Gardner (1980) puts it, 'achievements by Leonardo do not ensure that every child will master perspective: but with those achievements in the background, there is a far greater chance that the average youngster can convert her naturally evolving skills into correct perspectival renditions' (p. 219). This fits exactly with Jahoda's conclusion from his results with adults in Ghana: 'the absence of any significant difference between unschooled and those with only limited schooling, coupled with the significant difference between these two groups and those with secondary schooling, strongly suggests that the boundary between Classes 3 and 4 [vertical oblique projection and oblique projection] represents a critical divide; in the absence of an environment rich in perspective drawings, it is not crossed' (p. 142). Thus, as Wilson and Wilson (1982) rightly say, 'in order to realize an adequate theory of graphic development, we will need to pay attention to both of the factors that appear to be operating in that sphere – the innate and the influence [of the pictorial environment]' (p. 30). This is true of every aspect of the acquisition of drawing ability, including the acquisition of the projection systems.

5. Projection-systems approach: limitations

The assignment of drawings to classes based on the projection systems is far from being a universal panacea for the analysis of children's drawings. To reiterate, one point that needs to be stressed is that it cannot be assumed that ability in production and ability in comprehension develop at the same rate. This is a difficult area to discuss, because, as Jahoda says, 'there just has not been adequate research done in this, one of the reasons probably being that we have no effective way of assessing comprehension except verbally, with all the drawbacks that entails' (private communication). Nevertheless, Saenger's (1981) results described above, and those of Willats (1981a, Ch. 2), suggest that young children both understand and prefer systems much in advance of those they use in production. Because the process of production seems to involve children's interpretation of their evolving drawings during the course of the drawing process (Willats, 1984) the question of how children *interpret* drawings in different drawing systems is an important one, and deserves more research, in spite of the difficulties Jahoda mentions. The point is raised in the chapter below by Phillips, Inall and Lauder.

A second limitation on the projection systems approach is that not all children's drawings, even of rectangular objects, can be described in terms of projection systems. These drawings, which I shall now discuss, seem to be of three quite different types, and appear at different ages; they have also received quite different kinds of interpretations.

_ Young children often draw rectangular objects using a single closed curve. Piaget and Inhelder (1956) have suggested that drawings of this kind are based on 'topological' rather than projective geometry. The argument is a persuasive one: because topological geometry precedes projective geometry in the hierarchy of transformation systems (Klein, 1939), we might well expect drawings based on topological geometry to precede drawings based on projective geometry in the developmental sequence. On the other hand, drawings of this kind might simply be the result of poor motor control (Olivier, 1974). That level of skill is analysed in the chapter below by Laszlo and Broderick.

The second type of drawings which cannot be fitted into the projection-systems approach are those which Kennedy (1978) has described as 'fold-out'. The characteristic feature of drawings of this kind is that they look like rectangular boxes which have been cut along the edges and flattened out. Minsky and Papert (1972) suggested that they reflect the nature of children's internal descriptions, a view hotly contested by Kosslyn, Heldmeyer and Locklear (1977), but taken up again by Hayes (1978). Another possible argument which immediately springs to mind is that they are again the result of difficulties with picture-plane geometry: the child would like to join the corners together with oblique lines, but is unable to do so because of the operation of the perpendicular bias (Ibbotson and Bryant, 1976). The chapters below by Bayraktar, Bremner and Mitchelmore demonstrate the strength of such biases.

Finally, there are drawings by older children which *do* contain oblique lines, but which are somehow wrong by the standards of projective geometry. One common type are drawings which Phillips, Hobbs and Pratt (1978) describe as containing a 'flat bottom error': drawings which resemble oblique or isometric projections but which have a characteristic straight line depicting the bottom edges of the object. Deręgowski (1977) has suggested that in drawings of this kind the child is trying to show the object resting on a flat surface, such as the top of a table. A somewhat similar argument is offered by Phillips et al. (1978), who suggest that the 'flat bottom' is intended to show the object's inherent stability. Alternatively, the straight line at the bottom might be seen as reflecting the child's difficulty with oblique lines as such, that is, in terms of picture-plane geometry.

A different kind of argument is suggested in Willats (1981b and 1984). Here, all three kinds of drawings are seen as representing successive stages in the acquisition of *denotation systems*. I shall define these in the next section. For the moment, an analysis of the three types of drawing which I have regarded as lying outside the projection-systems approach can be categorised as follows. In drawings of the first type, the child uses a *region* (that is, an enclosed area) to denote (or stand for) a *volume* (that is, the object as a whole). In drawings of the second type, the child uses *regions* to denote *faces* (hence the 'fold-out' appearance of the drawings). Drawings of the third type are seen as transitional: the child is beginning to use *lines* to denote *edges* (the only way to get the corners to join up properly in drawings of rectangular objects), but falls back on using regions to denote faces wherever the use of a more advanced system is unnecessary. Here we have a description of a new kind of drawing system, different from, but complementary to, the projection systems. The sequence of the developmental stages in which children acquire the denotation systems is seen as corresponding to the sequence of stages in the use of scene primitives which Marr (1982) uses to describe the human visual system.

The final, and probably the most important, limitation on the projection-systems approach is that it tells us little about children's drawings of smooth objects like people. Of course, people are not entirely composed of smooth shapes: that is, shapes without wrinkles, puckers, creases or other surface discontinuities (Huffman, 1971); but on the whole people are more smooth than they are rectangular. It is true that projection systems of a kind must underlie all representational drawings: in figure drawings, for example, top to bottom in the picture usually represents top to bottom in the real world (Goodnow and Friedman, 1972; Millar, 1975). But whereas a drawing of a rectangular object in, say, perspective or isometric projection looks quite different from a drawing of the same object in orthographic projection, there is not all that much to choose between drawings of people in these different systems. Moreover, it is hard to see how a rule like 'represent edges in the third (horizontal) direction by oblique lines' (the basis of oblique projection) can be applied to smooth objects which, by definition, do not have edges. In order to gain a useful insight into children's drawings of people we have to supplement an account in terms of projection systems with a parallel account in terms of denotation systems. The following section gives a brief sketch of a possible approach to analysis of children's figure drawing in terms of denotation systems.

6. Denotation systems: background

The history of perspective and the projection systems goes back to Euclid's *Optics* (*c.* 300 BC) and Alberti's *Della Pittura* (1436). In contrast, the formal description of denotation systems can hardly be said to have begun before the work of Clowes (1971) and Huffman (1971) in the field then known as Artificial Intelligence. Both these writers analysed line-drawings of rectangular objects, showing how elements in the picture were related to corresponding features in the real world. Huffman also gave an analysis of line-drawings of smooth objects. Perhaps the single most important breakthrough in this field, in contrast to earlier work (Guzman, 1968), was the realisation that it was vital to use *different sets of words* for picture elements and for features of the real world. Pictures are often so vivid that we are inclined to speak of them as actually containing features such as people and chairs, or edges and corners. The importance of the work of Clowes and Huffman was that they pointed out that pictures consist of elements like lines or line junctions which *stand for* or *denote* these features, a point subsequently emphasised in perceptual psychology by Kennedy (1974).

In the field of children's drawings, Olivier (1974) made an early attempt to describe how the marks in children's drawings become 'charged with meaning'. According to Olivier,

the development of children's drawings corresponds to the progressive differentiation of a limited number of stereotypes, easy to reproduce, and susceptible to the formation of relationships one with another according to simple rules so as to constitute the signifiers of an unlimited number of significates. This differentiation is the same among all children. Once achieved (between 4 and 6 years) it puts at their command for a prolonged period a system of graphical elements (EGs) from which spring all their drawings; it is this period which is generally defined as that of 'intellectual realism'. Between 7 and 9 years new rules are substituted for the previous ones, the system is lost and the elements from which it was composed disappear in favour of procedural means of another type. (My translation)

Olivier concludes that these elements are similar to linguistic phonemes. They are not created by the child but obtained from the cultural environment, being nothing but graphic substitutes for verbal knowledge; so that drawing is simply an apprenticeship for writing, a symbol system which takes over from drawing and eventually supersedes it. The following account differs from that of Olivier's in a number of respects, not least that the early denotation systems are seen as leading naturally to later ones, so that the development of the denotation systems, like that of the projection systems, forms a continuous whole.

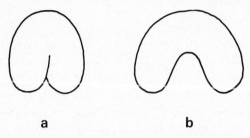

a   b

Figure 4.2 A drawing of a sausage: (a) including a line junction showing the point at which a nearer contour hides or occludes a contour which is further away, and (b) consisting of a single line which denotes an occluding contour.

7. Denotation systems: definitions

Denotation systems 'say what the marks in the picture stand for' (Willats, 1981 b). To put this more precisely, denotation systems map features of the real world, or *scene primitives*, onto corresponding elements in the picture, or *picture primitives*. According to Marr and Nishihara (1978, p. 274), 'the primitives of a representation are the most elementary units of shape information available in a representation'. In grown-up drawings of smooth objects the picture primitives are lines, and the scene primitives to which they refer are the 'smooth edges' of the objects they represent, seen from a particular point of view. The technical term usually used to describe these 'smooth edges' is *occluding contours* (Marr, 1977). Consider the drawings shown in Figure 4.2, which represent a sausage.

We *know* that the lines in drawing (a) represent occluding contours because the line junction represents the point at which a nearer contour occludes or hides a contour which is further away. In drawing (b) there is no line junction; but in the context of adult drawings we would assume that here too the line denotes an occluding contour, since this is the system normally used by adults. As Marr (1977) says, discussing the use of occluding contours in Picasso's *Rites of Spring*, 'such contours are an artist's principal means of conveying information about shape' (p. 441).

But do the lines in children's drawings of smooth shapes also represent occluding contours? Notice that the whole idea of an *occluding* contour depends on seeing the object from a particular point of view, from which the contour occludes the background or other objects; and everything we know about young children's drawings, including that venerable maxim that young children draw what they know rather than what they see, suggests that children do not pay attention in their drawings to what they see from a particular point of view until a comparatively late age (but see the chapters

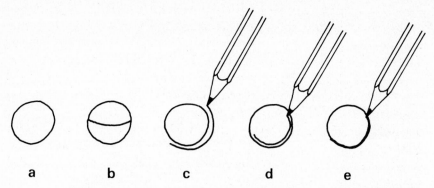

a   b   c   d   e

Figure 4.3 A child's attempts to draw the mould mark on a ball: (a) the child's drawing of a ball; (b) an adult drawing, including the mould mark; (c) 'I can't draw it here because it's not outside the ball'; (d) 'I can't draw it here because it's not inside the ball'; (e) 'And I can't draw it here because it won't show up. So I can't do it'.

below by Barrett, Cox, Davis and Light). Moreover, this is borne out in their drawings of smooth objects, which rarely, if ever, contain points of occlusion similar to that shown in Figure 4.2a, the drawings of Nadia (Selfe, 1977) being a notable and remarkable exception (Pariser, 1981, p. 23). In general, adult prejudices aside, unless a child's repertoire of drawings contains line junctions denoting points of occlusion, we have no warrant for supposing that the lines in their drawings denote occluding contours.

But if the lines in young children's drawings do not denote occluding contours, what do they denote? An anecdote (for which I am indebted to Dennie Wolf) may suggest an alternative. A young girl was asked to draw a ball, and responded by producing a drawing similar to that shown in Figure 4.3a. This drawing, in the form of a circle, hardly surprises us, and is just what an adult would have produced; so we naturally assume that the line in the child's drawing denotes the smooth edge or occluding contour of the ball. However, the child wanted to go on and draw the mould mark on the surface of the ball, produced by the meeting of the two halves of the mould when the ball was made. An adult would probably have produced a drawing similar to that shown in Figure 4.3b. However, the child first drew a line *outside* the first circle, saying as she did so, 'I can't draw it here because it's not outside the ball' (Figure 4.3c). She then drew a line *inside* the circle, saying, 'I can't draw it here because it's not inside the ball' (Figure 4.3d). Finally, she drew a line on top of the first circle, saying, 'And I can't draw it here because it won't show up. So I can't do it' (Figure 4.3e). It is hard to resist the conclusion that for this child the shape enclosed by the circle stood for the whole volume of the ball, while the circle itself stood for the surface of the ball, dividing the inside of the ball from the space outside. If this is correct, then it makes perfect good sense to draw the mould line where it belongs, on the line representing the surface of the ball – except that a line drawn there 'won't show up'. This explanation is, of course, in accord with Piaget and Inhelder's suggestion (1956) that a child's early drawings are based on topological rather than projective geometry; since there is no room in topological geometry for occluding contours or points of view, a closed curve separates inner from outer space. If this account is correct, we can say that in drawings of this type the region or enclosed space denotes a volume. Adopting the conventions suggested in Willats (1981 *b*, 1984):

In this convention the arrow indicates the 'denotes' relationship. The number 2 on the left of the diagram indicates that the region is a *two-dimensional picture primitive*, and the number 3 indicates that the volume is a *three-dimensional scene primitive*. Each number is thus the *dimensional index* of the primitive it qualifies.

Not all smooth forms take the shape of spheres. How can we qualify other, more complex, shapes? Marr and Nishihara (1978, p. 275), for example, discuss the possibility of 'pillow-shaped' volumetric primitives, extended in different degrees in the three dimensions of space. We can capture this general idea in formal terms by adding an *index of extension*, in the form of subscripts, to the dimensional index of a primitive.

Consider first two basic kinds of two-dimensional regions: roughly circular regions and regions which are rounded but long, that is, extended in one direction only. The subscript 1 will be used to indicate a 'marked' extension, and the subscript 0 to indicate an 'unmarked' extension. Thus a roughly circular region will be written as 2_{11}, indicating marked extension in the two possible dimensions of space, while a long region will be written as 2_{10}, indicating marked extension in one direction only (Figure 4.4). A 2_{00} region would, in this system, be a region having extension in neither of the two possible directions; but it is more economical to consider this kind of shape as a zero-dimensional or point primitive. Similarly, there is no reason to add subscripts to line primitives, which can be extended in only one direction.

The same approach can be used to qualify volumes. The three basic shapes

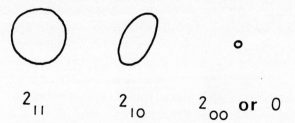

2_{11} 2_{10} 2_{00} or 0

Figure 4.4 Three kinds of rounded regions, showing the dimensional index of each, with subscripts showing marked extension in two, one and zero directions.

are: roughly spherical, like balls or people's heads; rounded but flat, like people's ears or hands; and rounded but long, like fingers or legs. Roughly spherical shapes are written as 3_{111}; the figure 3 indicates a three-dimensional or volumetric primitive, while the subscripts show that the shape is marked for extension (i.e. is roughly equally extended) in all three dimensions. Rounded but flat shapes are written as 3_{110}; that is, a volumetric primitive extended in two directions only. Finally, long shapes are written as 3_{100} because they are markedly extended in one direction only.

Notice that even this apparently rather elaborate formalisation is too simple to capture Marr and Nishihara's 'pillow-shaped' volumes, which are extended in different degrees in all three spatial directions. To capture shapes of this kind one would have to use parametric subscripts, something like $3_{x,y,z}$. However, the formalisation described above is sufficient for my immediate purpose, and will enable me to say something about children's figure drawings.

8. Denotation systems: children's figure drawings

Consider first a fairly typical 'tadpole' figure, taken from Freeman (1975). As Freeman points out, there has been a long-standing controversy as to whether the large, roughly circular region stands for the head alone, or the head and trunk; but in either case we can be fairly confident that this large region represents either a volume or volumes. Presumably the lines stand for the arms and legs, and the two smaller regions for eyes.

The analysis shown in Figure 4.5 suggests that even this apparently simple drawing is based on quite a complex denotation system. To begin with, the drawing seems to be based on three different kinds of systems: a rounded region denoting a rounded volume (the head, Figure 4.5a), lines denoting long volumes (the arms and legs, Figure 4.5b) and rounded regions denoting

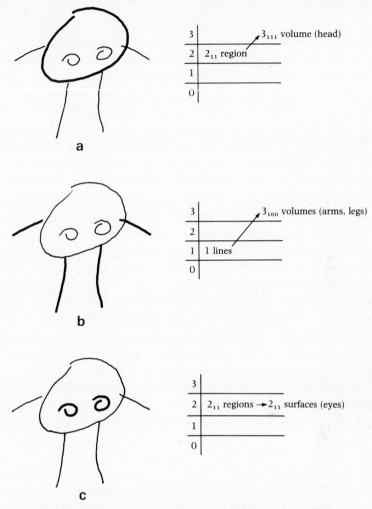

Figure 4.5 A tadpole figure, showing suggested denotation systems for the various parts. (a) and (b) are cross-dimensional systems; (c) is an intra-dimensional system. (Drawings taken from Freeman, 1975, Fig. 1b.)

rounded surfaces (the eyes, Figure 4.5c). Why have these systems been chosen?

Any answers must be regarded as very tentative at this stage, but the argument might go something like this. Three-dimensional volumes cannot be represented by three-dimensional picture primitives, because pictures are flat. So the thing to do is to use a picture primitive with the highest possible dimensional index, and this leads to the use of a region to denote a volume.

In other words, since heads are roughly equally extended in all possible directions, they are represented by regions which are equally extended in all possible directions. This leads to the use of a 2_{11} region to denote a 3_{111} volume.

Arms and legs, although three-dimensional, are extended in only one direction. It would therefore seem to make sense to use regions which are only extended in one direction to represent them. This would lead to the system: 2_{10} region denotes 3_{100} volume; that is, a long region standing for a long volume. In this drawing, however, *lines* are used to stand for the arms and legs. Presumably this is because the child is not yet able to make a difference in his drawings between long regions and rounded regions, either because motor control has not yet developed to a point where this kind of differentiation is possible, as Olivier suggests, or because the ability to handle the symbolism involved in using two different kinds of two-dimensional primitives has not yet developed. Again, as with children's drawings of rectangular objects, we see the possibility of two different yet complementary types of explanation for each developmental stage: one in terms of motor control, picture-plane geometry and the drawing process, and one in terms of symbolic meaning. Again, the precise influence of each factor can only be teased out by careful experiment. Whichever is the explanation here, the use of lines to stand for long volumes is a 'default' solution. If the child cannot handle long regions, then using lines is the only way left to bring out the difference between rounded and long volumes.

Assuming that the child regards eyes as rounded surfaces, the eyes can be represented by a very simple system in which rounded regions are used to denote rounded surfaces. The potential problem is that a rounded region has already been used to denote the head; obviously, if just one kind of picture primitive is used to denote all sorts of scene primitives there is a danger of the drawing becoming too ambiguous. In this case, however, the regions used are of different sizes, lessening the danger of ambiguity; a further factor is the disposition of the parts of the drawing one to another, based very roughly on a system approximating to orthographic projection. If the primitives were scattered more or less at random across the page, as in so-called 'list' drawings, the ambiguity would be very much greater, *so right from the start there must be some kind of interaction between projection systems and denotation systems.*

Turning now to a more advanced drawing, Figure 4.6 shows a girl's drawing of a man, taken from Harris (1963). Harris' criterion for a more advanced drawing is that it depicts more features of the real world: whereas the previous drawing shows only the head/trunk, legs, arms and eyes, this drawing shows in addition the mouth, ears and feet. But another way of

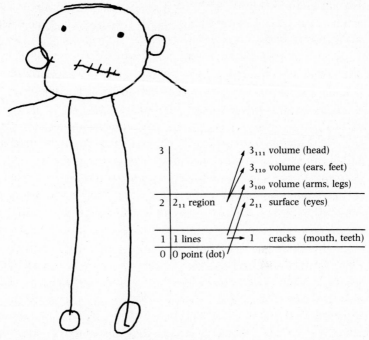

Figure 4.6 Analysis of a child's drawing of a man. (Drawing by a girl aged 6 years 6 months taken from Harris, 1963, Fig. 59.)

looking at the drawing is to say that a new element has been added to the repertoire of picture primitives. Whereas the previous drawing contained only two-dimensional primitives (regions) and one-dimensional primitives (lines), this drawing also contains zero-dimensional primitives (dots), in this case standing for eyes. The effect of this is to make it *possible* to represent more features: because the eyes have been represented by dots, the rounded regions are released to stand for other things: the ears and the feet, both of which may be regarded as rounded but flattish volumes. Notice, however, that the other conspicuous flattish features of the human figure, the hands, which might also have been represented by rounded regions, have been left out. This accords with the analysis of human-figure-drawing production in terms of the end-anchoring aspect of serial-position problems set out in Freeman (1980, Ch. 10); and therefore presumably one can take this particular drawing as a fairly representative specimen.

The drawing shown in Figure 4.6 does look rather more like a man than the drawing shown in Figure 4.5, but this is mainly because it depicts more features. For a drawing to look realistic or 'faithful', to use Gibson's term

(1971), the shapes in the drawing must either match the real shapes of the objects represented, or they must match the occluding contours of those shapes as they are delivered to the eye. This is possible only where the denotation relationships are intra-dimensional.

In the drawing shown in Figure 4.5 only one of the denotation relationships is intra-dimensional: 2_{11} region denotes 2_{11} surface (eyes). Here the extent to which the drawing can look realistic is limited only by the child's skill in matching the shapes of eyes in the real world. The other two relationships (2_{11} region denotes 3_{111} volume (head) and 1 lines denote 3_{100} volumes (arms and legs)) are both cross-dimensional, so the match between the shapes in the drawing and the shapes of real heads, arms and legs can only be more or less tenuous and accidental. In Figure 4.6, again, only one denotational relationship is intra-dimensional: 1 lines denote 1 cracks (mouth, teeth). Again, only this part of the drawing is potentially realistic.

In these circumstances there is obviously a limit to the number of features which can be depicted using only a limited number of kinds of picture primitives. One obvious way to depict more features, then, is to use more kinds of picture primitives. Figure 4.7 shows the analysis of a well-known drawing of a man with a saw, taken from Arnheim (1954). The number of picture primitives has been increased to four: dots, lines and two kinds of regions, rounded and long. The addition of a new kind of region, or rather the differentiation of a single kind of region into two kinds of regions, immediately allows the depiction of many more features in the real world, so the drawing is more advanced by Harris' (1963) criteria. This is, of course, made possible only by the child's ability to differentiate between two kinds of regions, so the drawing is more advanced by Olivier's (1974) criteria. There is, however, a more profound sense in which the drawing is more advanced: out of about the nine or more kinds of denotation relationship in the drawing, at least five are intra-dimensional. The actual realism is limited by the child's ability to match shapes: for example, to draw the teeth of the saw as triangles rather than as circles. Nevertheless, the potential for realism is much greater than in the previous two examples. But there is an even more important potential for development in the drawing. Using a long region (rather than a line) to depict a leg brings closer the possibility of matching the shape of the region to the shape of the real leg *as it is projected into the visual field*, and thus matching the shape of the line bounding the region to the shape of the occluding contour of the real object. A child who reaches this stage is beginning to use an adult denotation system: 1 lines denote 1 occluding contours.

The account of children's figure drawings given above must be regarded

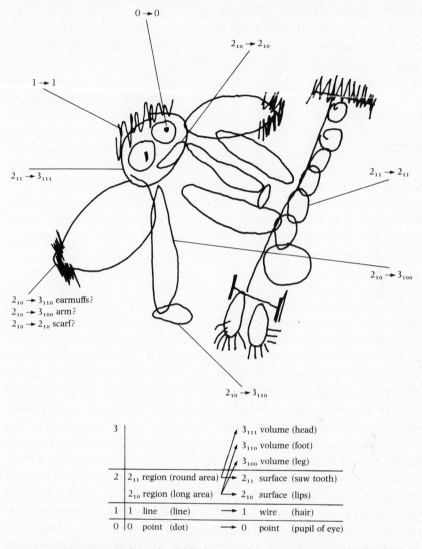

$0 \rightarrow 0$

$2_{10} \rightarrow 2_{10}$

$1 \rightarrow 1$

$2_{11} \rightarrow 3_{111}$

$2_{11} \rightarrow 2_{11}$

$2_{10} \rightarrow 3_{100}$

$2_{10} \rightarrow 3_{110}$ earmuffs?
$2_{10} \rightarrow 3_{100}$ arm?
$2_{10} \rightarrow 2_{10}$ scarf?

$2_{10} \rightarrow 3_{110}$

3			
		3_{111}	volume (head)
		3_{110}	volume (foot)
		3_{100}	volume (leg)
2	2_{11} region (round area)	2_{11}	surface (saw tooth)
	2_{10} region (long area)	2_{10}	surface (lips)
1	1 line (line)	1	wire (hair)
0	0 point (dot)	0	point (pupil of eye)

Figure 4.7 Analysis of a child's drawing of a man with a saw. (Drawing from Arnheim, 1954, p. 141.)

as very tentative; nevertheless, it does suggest some possible lines of research. Perhaps the first priority might be to decide, by experiment, the age at which children begin to use lines to denote occluding contours. My own guess would be that this would be at around the same time as they begin to take account of the orientation of the edges of rectangular objects in the visual field, that is, at about the age of between 10 and 12 years (Willats and Freeman, 1984);

but this is no more than a guess. Another obvious line of research would be to explore the distinction between the difficulties which children have in perceiving smooth forms, the difficulties with manipulating the picture-plane geometry and the difficulties with the symbolism of the denotation systems. Here, there is an obvious parallel with current lines of research in relation to the projection systems and children's use of oblique lines (Freeman, 1983). Studies of drawings of a cylinder, as reported in Duthie's chapter below, might give a point of contact. Another possible line of research might be to try to give an account of local or individual styles, in terms of the different marks which children use, and the selection rules which underlie their choice. Probably there is more scope for defining style in terms of the denotation systems than in terms of projection systems; the limitation on the number of projection systems available, as a result of the geometry of optics, makes the choice of systems very restricted, especially in the early years, and so gives only a narrow scope for stylistic variation.

9. Conclusions

Earlier work described the role of projection systems in describing children's drawings of rectangular objects. It now seems to be fairly well established that as children get older they use more complex and general projection systems, which allow them to produce better representations of three-dimensional shapes. One limitation of the projection-systems approach is that it cannot account for some kinds of drawings of rectangular shapes. An even more fundamental limitation is that it has little to say about children's drawings of smooth objects, the most important example of a smooth object being the human figure. The projection-systems approach is thus an essential component in the analysis of children's drawings and the description of the development of drawing ability. But it needs to be supplemented by an account in terms of other pictorial systems, and in the case of figure drawing an analysis in terms of denotation systems is especially important. Such an account, allied to analyses of children's executive expertise in getting the marks where they want them to go, is an essential step towards the specification of a psychologically real process-model of the development of depiction.

REFERENCES

Arnheim, R. (1954) *Art and visual perception*. Berkeley: University of California Press.
Clark, A. B. (1897) The child's attitude towards perspective problems. In E. Barnes (ed.), *Studies in education*, Vol. 1. Stanford: University Press.

Clowes, M. B. (1971) On seeing things. *Artificial Intelligence*, 2(1), 79–116.

Deręgowski, J. B. (1977) Pictures, symbols and frames of reference. In G. Butterworth (ed.), *The child's representation of the world*. London and New York: Plenum.

Dubery, F. & Willats, J. (1972) *Drawing systems*. London: Studio Vista.

(1983) *Perspective and other drawing systems*. London: Herbert Press.

Freeman, N. H. (1975). Do children draw men with arms coming out of the head? *Nature, London*, 254, 416–17.

(1980) *Strategies of representation in young children*. London: Academic Press.

(1983) Picture-plane bias in children's representational drawing. *Australian Journal of Psychology*, 35(2), 121–34.

Gardner, H. (1980) *Artful scribbles*. New York: Basic Books.

Gibson, J. J. (1971) The information available in pictures. *Leonardo*, 4, 27–35.

Goodnow, J. J. & Friedman, S. (1972) Orientation in children's human figure drawings. *Developmental Psychology*, 7(1), 10–16.

Guzman, A. (1968). Decomposition of a visual scene into three-dimensional bodies. In *Proceedings of the Fall Joint Computer Conference*. Washington, D.C.: Thomson Book Co., pp. 291–306.

Harris, D. B. (1963) *Children's drawings as measures of intellectual maturity*. New York: Harcourt, Brace and World.

Hartley, J. L., Somerville, S. C., Jensen, D. von C. & Eliefja, C. (1982) Abstraction of individual styles from the drawings of five-year-old children. *Child Development*, 53, 1193–214.

Hayes, J. (1978) Children's visual descriptions. *Cognitive Science*, 2, 1–15.

Huffman, D. A. (1971) Impossible objects as nonsense sentences. In B. Meltzer & D. Mitchie (eds.), *Machine intelligence*, Vol. 6. Edinburgh: University Press.

Ibbotson, A. & Bryant, P. E. (1976) The perpendicular error and the vertical effect. *Perception*, 5, 319–26.

Jahoda, G. (1981) Drawing styles of schooled and unschooled adults: A study in Ghana. *Quarterly Journal of Experimental Psychology*, 33A, 133–43.

Kennedy, J. M. (1974) *A psychology of picture perception*. San Francisco: Jossey-Bass.

(1978) Pictures and the blind. Paper presented at the American Psychological Association Meeting, Toronto, in the symposium 'First Encounters of a Pictorial Kind'.

Klein, F. (1939) *Elementary mathematics from an advanced standpoint (geometry)*. London: Macmillan.

Kosslyn, S. M., Heldmeyer, K. H. & Locklear, E. P. (1977) Children's drawings as data about internal representations. *Journal of Experimental Child Psychology*, 23, 191–211.

Lewis, H. P. (1963) Spatial representation in drawings as a correlate of development and a basis for picture preference. *Journal of Genetic Psychology*, 102, 95–105.

Marr, D. (1977) Analysis of occluding contour. *Proceedings of the Royal Society, London*, ser. B, 197, 411–75.

(1982) *Vision*. San Francisco: W. H. Freeman.

Marr, D. & Nishihara, H. K. (1978) Representation and recognition of the spatial organization of three-dimensional shapes. *Proceedings of the Royal Society, London*, ser. B, 200, 269–94.

Millar, S. (1975). Visual experience or translation rules? Drawing the human figure by blind and sighted children. *Perception*, 4, 363–71.

Minsky, M. & Papert, S. (1972) *Artificial intelligence progress report, memo 252.* Cambridge, Mass.: M.I.T. Artificial Intelligence Laboratory.

Olivier, F. (1974) Le dessin enfantin, est-il une écriture? *Enface*, 3(5), 183–216.

Pariser, D. (1981) Nadia's drawings: Theorizing about an autistic child's phenomenal ability. *Journal of Studies in Art Education*, 22(2), 20–9.

Phillips, W. A., Hobbs, S. B. & Pratt, F. R. (1978) Intellectual realism in children's drawings of cubes. *Cognition*, 6, 15–33.

Piaget, J. & Inhelder, B. (1956) *The child's conception of space.* London: Routledge and Kegan Paul.

Saenger, E. A. (1981) Drawing systems: A developmental study of representation. Unpublished Ph.D. thesis, Department of Social Psychology, Harvard University.

Selfe, L. (1977) *Nadia: A case study of extraordinary drawing ability in an autistic child.* New York: Academic Press.

Willats, J. (1977a) How children learn to draw realistic pictures. *Quarterly Journal of Experimental Psychology*, 29, 367–82.

(1977b) How children learn to represent three-dimensional space in drawings. In G. Butterworth (ed.), *The child's representation of the world.* London and New York: Plenum.

(1981a) Formal structures in drawing and painting. Unpublished Ph.D. thesis, Faculty of Art and Design, North-East London Polytechnic.

(1981b) What do the marks in the picture stand for? The child's acquisition of systems of transformation and denotation. *Review of Research in Visual Arts Education*, 13, 18–33.

(1984) Getting the drawing to look right as well as to be right: The interaction between production and perception as a mechanism of development. In W. R. Crozier & A. J. Chapman (eds.), *Cognitive processes in the perception of art.* Amsterdam: North-Holland.

Willats, J. & Freeman, N. H. (1984) Three modes of representation as a basis for children's depictions. Manuscript in preparation.

Wilson, M. & Wilson, B. (1982) The case of the disappearing two-eyed profile; or how little children influence the drawings of little children. *Review of Research in Visual Arts Education*, 15, 19–32.

(1983) Children's drawings in Egypt: Cultural style acquisition as graphic development. Paper given at the British Psychological Society International Conference on Psychology and the Arts, Cardiff, 1983.

5

The adolescent's point of view: studies of forms in conflict

R. K. DUTHIE

Editorial note by Norman Freeman. This chapter is a memorial to Mr Duthie, who tragically died before he could present to the public the results of two decades of original research involving nearly 100 experiments. By November 1980, he and I were criticising each other's work and starting to plan joint research. This endeavour died with him; but through the kind offices of Mrs Heide Duthie, I have had deeper access to the Duthie investigations. The chapter presented here is taken from his 1981 draft of 'Form' (86 pages) with transposition of sections 2 and 3; and his report of Experiment 28, conditions 1–4 (15 pages), in the light of formulations of the messages he was intending to convey which were contained in his letters to me: 20 October 1980, 26 November 1980, 23 February 1981 and 22 April 1981. Any virtues are due to his subtlety as investigator, and defects to my limitations as his editor.

A word of explanation is called for. It was Bob Duthie's habit to write his drafts without including references to other authors. He had a very critical mind, and would not simply draft in references without reservations. I have resisted the obvious temptation to insert the references *tout court*, merely cross-referencing to other chapters in this book. He also would try alternative formulations of some of the most important insights. In such cases, I have selected the more vigorous rather than the more cautious expressions, the more colloquial rather than the more formal and the more basic rather than the more theoretically complex. I aimed to capture the impression of him speaking through the printed word. Let this be a tribute to an active and committed art educator.

1. Introduction

The conventional approach to the topic of representing three-dimensionality on a flat surface is to regard it as a problem in representing depth: depth, that is, from the viewer outwards towards the horizon. Accounts are usually based on concepts such as those involved in the principles of linear perspective and depth-scaling. Such an approach misses the mark. It is not that perspective is irrelevant, but it is more important to query the premise upon which the conventional account is based. Why do we think that children even try to draw in depth? I shall argue that they probably don't. The evidence from several studies on adolescents' efforts to combine forms seems to sustain the case.

One study deals with the problem of combining two rectilinear forms, each of which is not only relatively easy to draw on its own, but when put together make up a configuration which is common in Scotland. Yet the effort of combining them leads to a wide variety of types of drawing solution. Another set of studies deals with the combination of curvilinear and rectilinear forms. Again, these are commonly observable, but apparently their mode of joining is not commonly observed. The argument is that what children have in their minds does not solve for them the problem of combining shapes on the page to represent forms in the world. Accordingly, let us begin with the nature of the distinction between drawn shape and object form, as seen in the plausibility of letting a shape on the page stand for a form in the real world.

Shape and form

A form is a configuration with a volume of space. Even when transformed as an image on a flat plane, the configuration on the page is constructed to retain, as far as possible, the visual property of space: that is, to depart from the picture surface and give an impression of space. The shape on the page appears to the viewer as lying within a range of credibility as a representation of a form within its own volumetric space. The concept of a range of representational credibility is crucial. Let us take the form 'pyramid' and draw out a range of shapes which we shall inspect for credibility. The shape given as Figure 5.1C is that preferred by the vast majority of adolescents whom I have worked with.

The shape A4 in Figure 5.1 can be seen as flat: as a rectangle made up of two triangles. But exactly the same two triangles can be seen as form by doing no more than changing the orientation of the rectangle (B4). It is now easy to imagine the top of the diagonal as the apex of a five-sided pyramidal form (four triangular faces and rectangular base). Although the orientation of the diagonal remains the same over series B, the longer the rectangle the more difficult it becomes to sustain the pyramidal form. Somewhere between B3 and B1, the *credibility* of four sides and a base cannot be sustained (and the pyramidal form becomes a four-sided compound wedge). This is not an optical illusion, nor is it a case of a multi-stable image such as the Necker cube. Indeed, some viewers may not be able to see *any* of the rectangles as pyramidal. Others will be able to see A4 as a pyramid stuck on a wall with

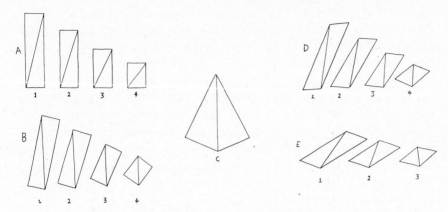

Figure 5.1 Ranges of shapes which possess different degrees of credibility as standing for the pyramidal form. Exploration in text.

the top corner of the diagonal as apex. But, once again, such credibility vanishes somewhere along the series back to A1.

Since there is such scope for variation from person to person, it is apparent that we are talking about degrees of credibility. It is important to note that credibility does not apply only to the visible shape, but applies to the sides of the form which cannot be seen: it is unlikely that anyone envisages the hidden base of the pyramid as having a curved surface, more likely that it is envisaged as a flat rectangle.

There are other variations which can be made to the basic shape on the page which affect its credibility. Figure 5.1D, E contains a set of parallelograms with the same ratio of sides as the previous rectangles. Again, the reader is invited to judge these for credibility. Orientation, size of angles and ratio of sides are the dimensions critical to the perception of pyramidal forms. But these dimensions carry different weights. Orientation may be thought of as a 'conditional form-factor': the credibility of the shape depends on how it maps onto the form's behaviour – real pyramids 'sit on' bases. In this factor, it is knowledge about possibly real objects – how they respond to gravity and balance or how they fit together with other objects – which determines what is acceptable to an individual viewer as a shape's resemblance to a particular form. Angle size and side ratio affect credibility rather differently, via a rule that an apex must be perceptually projecting from a base, irrespective of whether the apex is pointing up, down or sideways. Thus, this factor operates in free volumetric space, unlike the conditional form factor which operates in the constrained space of real relations.

The two factors together determine what may or may not fit together perceptually, and they determine where a given form will be placed on a scale of credibility when viewing a given shape. Any quadrilateral with *one* obtuse angle formed by the shortest sides and a straight line drawn from the obtuse angle to the opposite angle will appear as pyramidal in some orientation. In addition, the greater the ratio between the length of the short sides and long sides, the higher the apex will appear. The rule above is conditional on both baselines sloping *up* from the horizontal and certain limits on the angle of slope. Since this *is* conditional form, the optimum slope for the baselines depends on what each observer takes as an acceptable viewpoint. In general an angle somewhere around 20° to 25° from the horizontal for both baselines presents reasonable orientation.

If the conditions are fulfilled then it can be predicted that the two triangular parts can be perceived as a whole form.

The reason for spending so much time analysing the somewhat rarefied and meagre form of a pyramid is to drive home the point that perception of form is influenced by a predisposition toward certain tolerances of credibility. If one insists that pyramids must have bases resting on the ground then none of the upright rectangles will present credible pyramids. On the other hand, if one is willing to suspend any judgement about orientation of base but insists that pyramids must have a certain height apex then perhaps no rectangle or parallelogram will fulfil the conditions. It will then be necessary to consider other quadrilaterals. It is now easy to see what major problem faces adolescents when a pyramidal form is part of the array that they are attempting to represent. It is that they must work out how to put together the form factors which have, to them as individuals, credibility in that particular situation. This work occurs far beyond the retina; any image they form is truly trans-retinal.

I go some way toward the notion of canonicality (although I dislike the word!) as indicating that some shapes normally have greater credibility than others, but that notion cannot help us understand what problems face the adolescent in representing separate object volumes. Thus we may hold a canonical image of a church spire and one of a square tower, but what would be a canonical image of a church with square tower and spire? In a later section I show that adolescents find it difficult to combine credible forms. The credibility of a configuration is not a sum of the credibility of the separate forms which make it up. The next section explains why this should be so by drawing a distinction between picture space and picture depth.

⌁ 2. Space and depth

The child's view of the three-dimensional world – or at least as far as this world is depicted by the child in images – is a world where three-dimensional objects have space around them. The average child does not, perhaps even does not wish to, attempt to depict a homologous slice of the three-dimensional world seen from one viewpoint; depicted, that is, with every object in its correct relative position in depth, corresponding to a finite and particular volume of the real world. The three-dimensional world depicted by the child is a world of an undefined volume of space occupied by, and surrounding, every object.

Depth, in picture construction, always entails a coherent, internally consistent array of (implicit) parallel planes, whether straight or curved, lying from the front of the picture surface back to the furthest plane to be depicted. It should be noted that to depict depth it is not necessary to use orthodox linear perspective. Extraordinary depth realism can be achieved entirely by manipulation of overlap, transparency, texture gradients and colour contrast. However, if more than 20–30 cm of depth is to be depicted then it is necessary to construct a projection of the parallel planes in such a way that they remain consistent with a fixed viewpoint. The idea of fixed viewpoints is crucial to an understanding of linear perspective.

Space, unlike depth, does not necessarily entail a coherent or internally consistent array of parallel planes. Space can be thought of as the volume occupied by three-dimensional objects. And each object can be thought of as occupying a given volume of space that need not be, and in real life rarely is, seen as part of a uniform array of depth from one fixed viewpoint. Whatever is seen in depth is always more specific or less general than what is seen in space, because depth refers to the relation between parts of objects or between objects from a fixed viewpoint whereas space refers to the real volume of space that objects or parts of objects occupy irrespective of the viewpoint from which they are seen.

Estimating volume of occupied territory is more useful to the organism than seeing depth. For example, in a strange building I may be told that to get to the room I want, I have to go out of one door, down three steps, along a short corridor to a T-junction, turn right and enter the first door on my left. I cannot see my ultimate destination in depth, nor is it necessary for me to do so. I will be able to formulate an impression of where I will end up in space through clues about orientation: down, along, right, left and so on. All these words describe position in space. What is more essential for success in my immediate purpose of reaching the room is not just to *visualise space* but to perceive *in space*; that is, to see the available space I have to move in between the space occupied by other objects.

And as I move, my eyes move with me. Although this may be a commonplace observation it has serious implications. If I were to move, with my moving eyes, in depth rather than space then I would require to sift through an almost infinite range of changing viewpoints to find out where I am and where I am going. It is doubtful if anyone could depict even one of the immense number of changing views in depth when traversing the average room. Yet a great many people would be able to depict relative space, and the track taken, as a plan view. *And a plan view is the one viewpoint that certainly has not been seen by the walking traveller.* What evidence there is suggests that we do not continuously revise our viewpoint in depth but rather orientate our position and the position of objects in space.

While it is not yet known exactly how the visual input is processed to enable us to judge precisely where we and other things are, enough is known to indicate that we do not scan in the mind's eye millions of still frames of cine film each with its own unique viewpoint. Seeing in space rather than depth implies encoding many alternative orientations of one scene rather than a unique viewpoint of a succession of scenes. The encoding of alternative orientations introduces one more aspect of the perception of form that is hardly ever discussed in relation to how a child depicts form, and that is eye movement.

Even when the head is stationary the eyes are in almost continuous movement. The relevance of this observation to children's artwork becomes clear when eye movement is added to the body movement of the normal healthy child. The idea of a child drawing from a fixed viewpoint is a somewhat abstract notion to say the least. Yet millions of words written about linear perspective depend on a fixed viewpoint for their credibility. And of course the credibility of linear perspective has been elevated to virtually unassailable heights by the almost universal use of the fixed-lens camera: an optical system commonly taken to be similar in operation to the human eye but one that records precisely from a fixed viewpoint. Indeed, even the slightest camera movement from a fixed viewpoint results in a blurred image. Not so with the eye.

There can be little doubt that the movement of the person and of the eye plays a very important part in the way that children perceive form. For the moment it is enough to say that insufficient recognition of how eyes are actually used has led to serious misconceptions about depicting depth and space, about how children draw and about precisely what is to be taken as a retinal image. In the next section we take stock of the three key points made in this introduction: ranges of credible form, existence of objects in space rather than depth and a world seen from a multiplicity of orientations rather than from fixed viewpoints.

3. The task of combining form with space

By careful choice of configuration one can produce a pair of conjoined triangles that will be perceived by an individual only as a pyramidal form, and another pair that will be perceived only as a compound wedge. Between these two extreme configurations there are numerous stages of credibility. It was demonstrated that a change in the configuration of shapes may cause a change in perceived form. The crucial point is that what any observer will see at a particular stage does not depend on the figure *per se*, but on the observer's interpretation of the most credible alternative. This means that not all observers will see the same form at any given stage, but, at the same time, all observers will see one or other of the alternatives afforded by the given shapes. That credibility is essential to perceiving form is demonstrated beyond any doubt by the way we assume that the hidden parts of the form relate to each other in the same way as the exposed parts fit together. The implications of credible ranges will not be novel to artists whose stock-in-trade is maximum enhancement of one of a set of credible alternatives, even with such insubstantial entities as sunsets and hobgoblins. The whole form does depend on its shaped parts, but the whole form also depends on the credibility assigned to the relations between the parts, visible and hidden.

The proposition that perception of form should be considered from the position of credible alternatives does not mean that the conventional techniques of linear perspective, depth scaling and texture gradients do not produce credible images. Of course they do. Conventional techniques are techniques for maximising credible alternatives, especially when depicting depth. What is being maintained is that vision in depth is not the only way to look at form. And for the majority of school pupils it is not the most appropriate way.

The emphasis given in this introduction to space perception rather than depth perception leads almost inevitably to a concept of a real world of objects existing in relative space. More correctly, to a situation where space perception takes precedence over depth perception; for it is obvious that both forms of perception operate.

In practice the production problems of representing space are immense, because one cannot apply a simple set of systematic rules such as those of linear perspective. Each group of objects to be depicted in space requires separate solutions to arrive at what can only be the best of a set of possible compromises. And the best compromise will be the one which most closely offers both *credible form of objects* and at the same time *credible space between objects*. Not an easy task. A task certainly more exacting than linear perspective and certainly beyond the skill of most primary or secondary pupils. Why then do children choose naturally to attempt what appears to be the more difficult task of depicting objects in space? And moreover continue to do so even when offered a systematic solution of depth projection such as linear perspective? It cannot be that linear perspective is too difficult to understand. The rules of linear perspective are simple and few in number. Linear perspective is child's play compared with the problems of representing space; and yet children refuse to play with linear perspective and persist with dabbling in space.

It seems perverse, if not paradoxical, for children to start representing the world by choosing to tackle the difficult problem of representing the form of objects and their relative positions in space. But children do no such thing. Children depict form *and* space, not form and *related* space. Therein lies the difference. Children draw the form of objects as they perceive them and they represent them in space as individual objects. That is, children do not even attempt the really difficult problem of combining form with space in a coherent system. Now, as was demonstrated by the pyramid exercise, it is not difficult to depict form. In fact if one forgoes the requirement to depict form as it might exist in space, under the influence of gravity and so on, then it is extraordinarily easy to depict form. We are perceptually predisposed to interpret shapes as form whenever there is the slenderest possibility. We see form equally easily in random mottled wallpaper, in flickering flames and in doodles. Furthermore we have the knack of transposing one form onto another: the face in the tree trunk, the dragon in the clouds and scribbles on the page as cats or motor cars.

If no attempt is made to reproduce consistent space then the child's way of drawing turns out to be by far the easiest way to proceed. The blunt assertion that children do not depict the form of objects in *consistent related space* is made because the evidence is, without question, apparent in drawings made by all children. However, it does not follow from this assertion that children do not *want to* depict objects related in space. Perhaps they do; perhaps they don't: that is a matter for empirical investigation. The point has already been made that linear perspective provides a solution to depth representation but that children may be loth to use it. Linear perspective works as a system of depth projection for constructing pictures, but only provided two conditions are fulfilled: one, that the projection is from a fixed viewpoint; two, that the plane of the picture is at right angles to the line of sight. That these two essential conditions for linear perspective are also prerequisites for normal vision constitutes a major fallacy. We do not see the world from a fixed viewpoint (not, that is, unless we have our heads clamped and are squinting through an eyepiece) and normally we do not carry around in front of us a piece of glass at right angles to our line of sight upon which a picture of slices of the real world appear (for adults' use of such devices, see Pratt's chapter above).

A lot of people suppose that the system of linear perspective allows for a complete and accurate replica of the real world. This supposition is false. Linear perspective is a formal drawing system that affords a means to depict objects in depth and in so doing requires a subordination of the formal structure of the objects. That is, a perspective drawing of a collection of rectangular boxes will show in a consistent way how the boxes relate in depth at the expense of both the right angles and the parallel sides of all the boxes. At the expense, that is, of some form credibility. *No drawing system can simultaneously depict a collection of objects in correct relative depth and project the correct formal structure of the objects.* Even holography fails to fulfil both requirements.

A resistance to linear perspective can easily be demonstrated. Three hundred and eleven adolescents (12- to 13-year-olds) were shown the pictures in Figure 5.2 and were asked to choose the drawing that looked most like a group of real rectangular objects. Most of them rejected the drawing that was in 'correct' linear perspective. Only 14 per cent of the 12- to 13-year-old pupils tested chose A, the 'correct' perspective, whereas 43 per cent chose B, adjusted perspective (where all real parallel lines of small objects are represented as parallel), and 35 per cent chose oblique projection, C (where not only are all real parallel lines drawn as parallel but also a set of parallels are adjusted to the horizontal and retain right angles). The remaining 8 per cent chose isometric projection, D. A total of 86 per cent of the pupils chose one of the three drawings where all sides of rectangular objects were drawn as parallel lines.

When adolescents are asked to choose between (a) the information content of correct relative depth, (b) the information content of the structural form of objects and (c) the information content of the normal orientation of rectangular and circular objects, the great majority give priority to information content of structural form, then form plus normal orientation and *last of all* correct relative depth. It has to be emphasised that in this experiment pupils were not asked to draw the real objects and therefore there is no question of a failure due to inadequate drawing skill.

Images in which priority is given to structural form are idealised: drawings

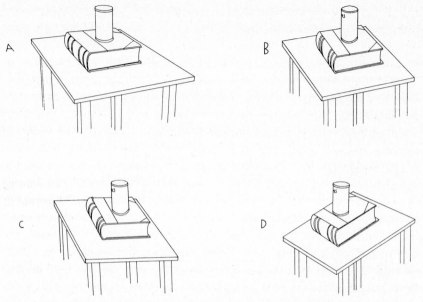

Figure 5.2 One array represented in various drawing systems for picture-choice experiment.

of objects freed from contexts. In so far as real objects usually exist in relation to other objects, the drawings are artificial. This kind of presentation, where a single object is depicted in normal orientation but in undefined space, necessarily emphasises the structure of the object.

The usual Necker cube is the kind of drawing of a cube that adolescents consider to be 'most like' a real cube. The cuboid structure represented by oblique projection is, without question, the only possible compromise that can depict at least some right angles as right angles and, all parallel lines as parallel and show three sides in correct relative size. No other way of drawing a cube can give this degree of compromise. The oblique projection cube is undoubtedly an 'ideal' compromise. In the case of cubes and other rectangular solids, the oblique-projection 'ideal' image matches closely the kind of image that adolescents make when they draw books, boxes and similar objects; and the 'ideal' rectangular solid represents a credible image of rectangular solids in normal orientation and in a normal context of lying on a table. The 'ideal' image of a table is also an oblique projection. When adolescents draw tables the overwhelming majority draw them in oblique projection. This is true whether the pupils are making their 'best drawing of a table' from imagination or are drawing an actual table, whatever its orientation to the line of sight of the pupils. There is one exception. When the table edge is horizontal to the line of sight then the majority of pupils draw the table top in conjoined orthography (side view combined with plan view), and the legs in single-point perspective.

Experiments with pyramidal forms revealed that pyramids also have an 'ideal' form. The pupils were asked to choose the 'most like a real pyramid' from pairs of drawings of pyramids displaying various proportions of sides and angles of baselines. The drawing 'most like a real pyramid' turned out to be in isometric projection with the apex directly above the centre of baselines of equal length and equal angle (Figure 5.1C).

The significant fact that emerges from the form experiments on the criterion 'most like' is that different 'ideal' forms require different *drawing systems*. The importance of this fact cannot be overstated. It is important in two ways. First, since the isometric projection necessary to produce a drawing of the 'ideal' pyramid is both different from, and incompatible with, the oblique-projection system necessary for producing a drawing of the 'ideal' rectangular solid, a uniform systems approach cannot produce ideal images. Thus, the question as to whether children do or do not want to depict objects in relative space is in part answered. For if they do wish to depict relative space then they cannot do so and at the same time preserve their 'ideal' image (see Hagen's chapter above for constraints on the depiction of relative space).

The second reason why it is an important fact that different drawing systems are required for different kinds of 'ideal' form is that combining these ideal forms must result in conflicting interpretations of spatial relations. For example, as will be seen in the next section, if the 'ideal' pyramid and cube are to be preserved then a square-section church tower capped by a four-sided spire must produce irreconcilable differences of structural form where spire meets tower. Confronted with this dilemma, typical of many problems of reconciliation, what will adolescents do? There are four main lines of approach. One, preserve the 'ideal' oblique projection of the tower and sacrifice the 'ideal' pyramid. Two, preserve the 'ideal' isometric projection of the pyramid and sacrifice the 'ideal' tower. Three, adopt a compromise between the angles used for isometric and oblique projection. Four, avoid the problem by using a completely different drawing system for objects that combine pyramids and cubes. In the next section, the results of empirical studies are discussed.

4. Combining rectilinear forms

The study involved 104 children aged 12 to 13 years, who were asked to draw a tower with a spire and also to choose a picture from a set. The style that

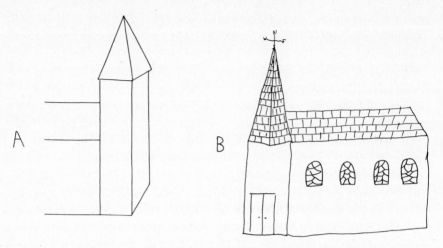

Figure 5.3 (A) Tower and spire in mixed-angle oblique projection, thought to be most like the real object; (B) drawing by 13-year-old who selected A as 'most like' but drew her own spire in isometric projection.

the vast majority regarded as 'most like' a real kirk, as reflected in their picture choice, is shown on the left of Figure 5.3. It has a steep oblique angle of around 60° for the *base of the tower* and a 10°–30° oblique angle for the *join between tower and spire*. This mixture of oblique angles could also go under the heading of 'adjusted perspective', and it is very probable that some children (and some adults too, for that matter) would suppose this to be perspective; but mixed-angle oblique projection is a more accurate description in terms of drawing systems. However, when they drew, the majority did not use the solution of mixed oblique. Only 19 per cent used small-angle oblique (30° or less) for the tower/spire join; of the remainder, 16 per cent chose to sacrifice the 'ideal' pyramid and retain the steep oblique angle of the 'ideal' tower, 21 per cent chose a straight-line-join compromise, 30 per cent chose isometric projection for the spire and sacrificed the 'ideal' tower (Figure 5.3B), 8 per cent avoided the problem by drawing the whole church as a flat orthographic view (these pupils were fully aware of systems for depicting three dimensions), 2 per cent used 'adjusted perspective' and 4 per cent could not be classified. It could be said that the 'ideal' solution for the tower and spire of mixed oblique angles gives a reasonably credible image, but only if one assumes a high-level viewpoint. However, a high-level view is not the most usual way to view a building. A crucial point is that with repeated testing, there was considerable fluctuation in drawing styles. Children's indecision about which way to depict this or that object can result in changes from drawing to drawing which often seem to be random. A pupil who opts to sacrifice the oblique church tower and preserve the 'ideal' spire on one day may readily reverse the process on another day. If the child cannot decide which alternative is best then the solution that is chosen is, to that extent, random. And since the possible extent of variation increases as the number and complexity of the picture contents increase so too will random choice increase. This sustains the present argument: it is fully in accord with the idea that even in late childhood the children's priority is not to select a drawing system which parcels out depth, but to select a method of bringing into contact the individual spaces of forms chosen from a range of credible forms.

The theory has served to identify an empirical problem. But it might be argued with hindsight that adolescents are simply not very adept at relating two strikingly disparate forms. However, the crucial prediction is that the same phenomenon will appear with more integral stimuli. All image-making demands a work of synthesis, and adolescents always operate by synthesising ideal forms: the effects of this ought to be salient even when one form is literally inscribed on a basic form. In such a case, all the visual information can be apprehended at a glance, yet the contention is that the adolescents

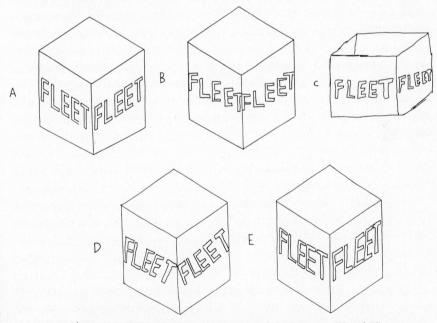

Figure 5.4 (A) Outline drawing which pupils had to copy. (B) and (C) are attempts by two individuals to reconcile cube and word projection. (D) is a typical rendering by 13-year-olds at average level in art, and (E) is a rendering by a pupil from the same class who had been rated top in general art ability by the teacher.

will draw as though they were confronted by the ideal forms, the spaces of each of which need to be reconciled. They will not use an integrated depth representation of the two.

The evidence comes from five tasks which were asked of some 600 children aged 12 to 14 years. The children were all taken from two classes in one school, and the sample was built up gradually over the years, with an equal number of boys and girls. One task was to copy an isometric projection of a cube with the word FLEET across the middle of both sides (see Figure 5.4A). The hypothesis is that the word, as a form to be drawn, would be perceived detached from the flat surface, so the letters would retain their right-angled property. In a second task, just the isometric cube was given, and the word had to be written on both sides. In a third condition, a real cube with the words was shown, for drawing in edge-on position. In a fourth, a real cube had three parallel lines drawn across the middle of the sides, corresponding to the top, middle and foot of the letters. In another task, there was just an oblique baseline with a vertical at either end, and the pupils had to draw three verticals between them at places indicated on the baseline. This is a control condition for the ability to construct acute angles/verticals on a diagonal, a task which is known to be difficult (see chapters below by Mitchelmore and Bayraktar). The results here were reassuring: 94 per cent of the pupils kept their lines to within 10 per cent of the vertical. In the light of this, the results from asking them to copy Figure 5.4A were most striking: 70 per cent of them consistently tilted the vertical of the two end letters, T, more than 10 per cent from the vertical, tending towards preserving the right angle in the letter. As might be expected, the majority of pupils did even worse at drawing from a real cube (see Chen's chapter below). The problem was not confined to verticals, nor to letters, for there was a correlation between poor performance at copying the words and at drawing the three lines in the place of the words: these were tilted towards the horizontal.

Some children were certainly aware that they were having a problem in reconciling the form of the cube and the form of the letters, and some 4 per cent rather dramatically drew the letters in a series of steps, as in Figure 5.4B, a configuration which certainly corresponds to no retinal image. Other examples of drawing styles are shown in the figure.

Although the experiments were originally designed to find out if words on a flat surface would retain the priority of the rectilinear right-angled structure of letters, it became clear very early on in the series that pupils considered by their teachers to be good at art were outstandingly better at drawing the word FLEET. The correlation was so compelling that the experiment which required pupils to copy the drawing of the cube with the word FLEET was used with older pupils: 80 Ordinary-grade art specialists (15-year-olds), 107 Ordinary-grade art specialists (16-year-olds), 50 Higher-grade who had gained 'O'-grade art the previous year (17-year-olds), 25 Higher-grade art specialists (17-year-olds) and corresponding numbers of non-art-specialist pupils from each of the year groups. The results were decisive. Art-specialist pupils in each category were significantly and consistently better performers than their non-art peers. Even more striking was the exceptionally high correlation ($r = 0.89$) between the ranking of the art specialists on class and examination results and the ranking of the drawings of the cube and the word. This was the first occasion on which any of the experiments mentioned so far produced results that unequivocally matched the performance of pupils' classwork and class teachers' assessments. Why the mechanical copying of a visually uninteresting drawing should correlate with artistic ability is an interesting question which cannot be dealt with here.

All in all, the errors made by so many adolescents when drawing the cube and word can be explained only by the image at the retina being reassembled in the nervous system according to a set of priorities. The set of priorities for cubes and words must be quite different from those in operation when drawing sets of single vertical lines. Perhaps priorities in the case of the experiments above entail no more than a child thinking, 'Here are vertical lines on an angled base line. I shall draw them vertical', and 'Here are letters that make up a word. I shall draw them as letters.' Thereafter, the actual drawing process is an on-the-spot stitching together, as best as can, the conflicts in spatial ordering.

At this point in the argument it is worth returning to the distinction between shape and form made at the outset. It could be argued that the problem for the adolescents arises because the cube is seen as form and the letters only as shape, whereupon the habits of writing bear heavily upon the process of representation. After all, the side of a cube is flat, as is a page, so the children may not be alerted to the problem of overcoming one represen-tational habit, letter formation, in favour of another, surface decoration. What would be expected if one alerted them by transforming the surface on which the letters are written? This can be done easily enough by providing a curvilinear surface: presenting the letters written on the side of a cylinder. Their tops and bottoms now form an ellipse, a most unusual contour for a word to take in normal writing. Yet every art educator knows that children find it extremely difficult to keep an ellipse steady over different drawing contexts.

The final set of studies, devoted to this very practical problem which plagues art teachers, is discussed in the next section, in the light of the theory so far.

Figure 5.5 Table scene by young child to show various representations of ellipse projections.

5. Curvilinear space

The point has been made repeatedly that the vast majority of adolescents depict objects *with space* rather than *in space* or *in depth*. To depict objects with space necessarily gives object volume priority over consistent spatial relations between objects. But that in itself does not guarantee that all the parts of the object will be given a consistent role in depicting that object volume. This will apply particularly where conditional form factors are involved, where part of an object may normally be contact points for other objects. In the case of the tower plus spire, this problem was salient, but it is even more salient in the case of a cylinder. The oval at the foot is often represented as a straight horizontal, presumably suitable as a representation of a base designed to rest stably on a flat surface (but see Willats' chapter above). This tendency can be readily seen in the drawings of 5-year-olds, and, as will shortly be shown, persists as a bias through adolescence.

What then would we expect for the top oval of the cylinder? If this too were represented in the same way, a rectangle would result. It seems counter-intuitive to expect a child to use a rectangle to represent a cylinder with its curves, but in fact it is extremely common. Figure 5.5 shows a child using rectangles to represent beakers, and straight-line closures at the top and bottom of the vase, despite manifest control over the oval shape for plates and heads.

The point of crucial importance for this account is that development does not occur gradually. The straight-line representation for the top of the vase may be retained when the base has flowers in it, because the relationship 'inside cavity' is credible enough without extra modification. When the vase is empty, the representation of 'cavity' demands that the cylinder top be represented as open, and here children swing to the opposite extreme, often using a complete circle. This is particularly marked after age 7 or so. The following experiment shows that the tendency to widen the cylinder's top ellipse and narrow the bottom remains strong many years later, in adolescence. For the majority of children, the only advance is to bring the ellipses somewhat nearer to each other in shape, with the top staying wider than the bottom. This is strange for the case of cylinder seen below eye-level, such as a can in the middle of a table seen by someone standing at the side, for there the top ellipse is visibly narrower than the bottom ellipse.

There were several tests, given in varied order to each individual separately out of 250 children aged 12 to 14 years. In one condition, the form was a white paper tube, viewed against a black background, with black lines, 2 mm wide, drawn around the top and foot of the tube. This was set for each child below eye-level in such a way that the foot ellipse appeared as roughly twice the width of the top ellipse. A tube is shown in Figure 5.6A (the word on it was deleted for this particular condition). As in all other conditions, the child was handed a sheet of paper with the two uprights drawn on it, and asked to complete the drawing.

When the drawings were measured, no account was taken of any irregularities in the contour of the ellipses. The only measurement was the vertical width of the ellipse to within 0.5 mm (approximately the thickness of a pencil line). The results were that 40 per cent managed to make the foot wider than the top, 6 per cent equalised them and 54 per cent made the foot narrower. The 40 per cent success rate is hopeful, but not a very impressive level of success. It may best be judged by comparison with the same condition in which the tube was made transparent, of clear acetate. Here the success rate rose to 64 per cent, with 8 per cent equalising the ellipses, and 28 per cent erring. But when the tube was suspended 20 cm off the ground, so that the foot did not act as a support, the majority (65 per cent) drew the two ellipses as equal. Presumably the two ellipses had equal status as attributes of the form cylinder since the bottom ellipse was not now a conditional form factor, despite the different retinal projection of the two ellipses. In another condition, the ellipses were presented quite out of context, drawn side by side

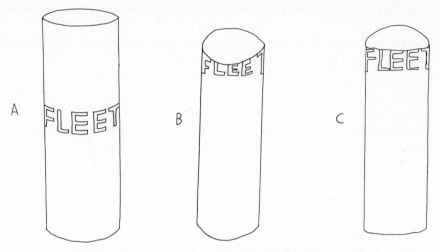

Figure 5.6 (A) Drawing to be copied in main experiment. (B) and (C) Two different solutions to the drawing problem when the word lies along the top edge of the cylinder.

on a sheet of paper. Now 99 per cent represented the difference in widths appropriately. So they can perceive the difference, but the more the ellipses form part of a real object, the greater the tendency to reverse the visual relationship. The fact that we are dealing with a reversal is crucial: it is not just a harmonious rescaling.

The next condition compares the top ellipse with the shape of the word FLEET (as measured by the displacement of the E's from two straight lines connecting the tops and bottoms of the F and T). The number of children erring was now 100 per cent. The letters had decisively flattened the ellipse. No child was now drawing what registers on the retina. How strong is the effect? An easy way to assess that is to adopt the logic of the tower-and-spire experiment: to join the word to the top ellipse. The critical difference is that the join is perfectly natural, with no drawing-system puzzle. Accordingly, in the next condition FLEET was inscribed shifted up to lie along the top of the tube. One can imagine various strategies of attempting to reconcile the curvature of the word and top. In the event, no fewer than 87 per cent of the pupils showed clear evidence of the drawing problem. This was made up of 53 per cent who made the top of the letters conform to the top ellipse and the bottom of the letters to a straight line (Figure 5.6B) and 34 per cent who opted for deforming the top ellipse by giving wide curvature to its further curve and straightening the curve, which contracted the letters to less than three-quarters of the further curve (Figure 5.6C).

Not one child managed to hold the tops and bottoms of the letters to a constant ellipse. A few, 7 per cent, did manage to come up to three-quarters of that aim, whilst 4 per cent did not even attempt to, and simply drew the letters in a straight line. One per cent attempted to solve the problem by 'stepping' the letters: pulling them out of alignment (each one being written as upright but on a different implicit baseline). Finally, one utterly unpredicted and inventive solution was shown by two children: it was to place the letters on a straight line with a U-curve to every horizontal component. These are indeed curved letters, but they do not form the larger structure, the curved word, nor do they relate in space to the even larger structure of the curved surface of the tube.

A final set of studies was devoted to probing small aspects of the studies. For example, it could be the case that complete ellipses, such as that at the top of the tube, oddly provoke wider swings than half-ellipses, such as the contour of the word. No such tendency appeared in tasks in which whole or half-ellipses had to be copied. Again, it could be that the whole demonstration is peculiar to writing habits being triggered. This turned out not to be the case. Children were asked to draw a strip of white paper wrapped around a grey tube. Here, 85 per cent of the pupils drew the two half-ellipses as equal, and, just as important, they narrowed them considerably, straightening them as had been done with FLEET. In the way that a row of letters 'reads' as a straight line, so too does a band: it becomes straightened even on a curved surface. The child has a problem in reconciling the cylinder and the band. *Reconcile* is the key term upon which this discussion will end.

6. Reconciliation

When the child is actually drawing, the nature of reconciliation is such that priority is given to retaining the internal structure that signifies the 'information content' of each part. It is obvious that as the number of individual parts in a scene increases, and the hierarchy of information becomes more diffuse, reconciliation becomes more difficult. Even with a moderately complex scene there can be no systematic approach by the child to spatial relations when she reassembles disparate entities. It is the difficulty of reconciliation, and the curious results in drawing that stem from recon-ciliations, that are the nub of 'production problems'. The particular aspect of drawings where production problems are most noticeable is inconsistency of spatial relations. It is at this level that I endorse recent attempts to analyse children's drawing as a problem-solving exercise for them.

Children do not so much depict space as require space. They require space for three major reasons. First, to show the independent existence and completeness of objects. Second, to show the order of importance of objects. Third, to allow enough room to include all the objects they think should be in the picture. As far as depicting space goes, the problem facing children is to evolve a way to satisfy the thematic needs of the picture, to evolve a way to retain the priorities of the items depicted and to evolve credible and consistent spatial relations between items. To construct a consistent system of spatial relations that at the same time can also take account of the features that children are concerned about is a task that would stretch to the limit the skill of an adult artist. There is no unified system that children can use to provide solutions to these kinds of spatial relations, and therefore the space to be depicted in each picture becomes, to a large extent, a unique problem of massive complexity.

The discussion may have given the impression that drawing is a serious matter, taxing to the limit the intellectual powers of adolescents. This is not the case. Drawing is not a serious matter for the majority of adolescents. Nor should it be inferred that all drawings children and adolescents make can be neatly compartmentalised. There is considerable variation in the artwork of adolescents: variations between individuals, and variations between drawings of the same object by the same child. Adolescents have a fairly wide tolerance of 'near enough' and therefore even when they may realise that their drawings may not be the very best they can do on any particular day, or of a particular object, they are often disinclined to do very much to alter their drawings. It should surprise no one that the drawings of the majority of children do not change to any marked degree after puberty. Nor should one be surprised that the majority of adolescents give up any serious study of art: the road they have taken toward realism is an immensely difficult path through a maze of problems. By the time most children become aware of the difficulty, they are too frustrated to backtrack and start on a *systematic* approach to problems of visual representation that would enable them to draw, and paint, sufficiently realistically to satisfy their own high demand for realism.

Commentary

N. H. FREEMAN and M. V. COX

The main theme so far, how to analyse the criteria for a successful depiction in the light of what is known about the perceiver's relationship to the scene, is one which many theories address. We have seen Gibson opposed to Marr, space contrasted with depth and projective geometry matched against denotation rules. Clearly this is a rich area for research. At the same time, the lack of common agreement is less important than the common focus of attention of all five authors. This common focus makes it easy to continue with an analysis of the many issues which were raised in the preceding chapters. Here are a few of them.

The importance of analysing the looking behaviour of the depictor is continued in Chapter 6, and a prediction is put forward in Chapter 10. Problems of choice of denotation are raised in Chapters 8, 15 and 20. The perpendicular bias, which dogged adolescents in using a flat page when depicting a word upon a cube's surface in the scene, is analysed with great rigour in Chapters 16, 17 and 18. The distinction between planned and on-the-spot decisions proves to be of vital importance in Chapters 15 and 19. The breaking down of the crude distinction between what we see and what we know is carried much further in so many of the succeeding chapters that it would be uninformative to list them here. The peculiar problem of squashing a three-dimensional scene onto a two-dimensional picture plane is laid out in terms of the geometrical primitives of the picture plane in a beautiful manner in Chapter 16; and the particular impact of this upon young children can be traced through Chapters 8 to 13.

For the present, the next chapters take up the problem of the mentality of the depictor. What is it about the structure of the mind which permits the actions of depiction, and what are the traps into which that may lead the depictor?

6

On the discovery, storage and use of graphic descriptions

W. A. PHILLIPS, M. INALL and E. LAUDER

1. Introduction: drawing as description-finding

Graphic creation is one of the most complex of human achievements. Its analysis encompasses a wide range of approaches. In this chapter we shall concentrate on just one aspect – the acquisition of the ability to produce line-drawings of realistic and representative views of simple solid objects. The primary problem in drawing seems to us to be that of finding appropriate descriptions of whatever is to be drawn. Remembering and using these descriptions are then the main secondary problems. We therefore tend to agree with those who treat drawings as a valuable source of information about internal mental representations, rather than with those who treat drawings as being largely a reflection of motor output ability. One of the experiments that we report does emphasise a problem that arises at the output stage, but this turns out to be a problem of perception and not a problem of motor control!

We shall present support for five simple propositions.

1. *Representational drawing is primarily a problem in description-finding.* Objects can in principle be described in indefinitely many ways. The descriptions normally made available by perception and imagination are not well suited to the production of realistic drawings. That is, they do not describe properties of the object's projection on a viewing plane. Learning to draw therefore requires the finding, remembering and use of these new graphic descriptions.

2. *Learning to draw includes learning specific graphic descriptions of specific objects.* One of the main differences between adults and children is simply that adults know how to draw more things.

3. *Acquisition of graphic descriptions of objects is not easy because the descriptions that are prominent are designed to facilitate interactions with objects, not with their projections.* Graphic descriptions are made easier to find by reducing the extent to which stimuli prompt these more habitual descriptions.

4. *Children are more dependent on their long-term-memory (LTM) schema of whole objects than adults because they are less able to create and maintain novel descriptions in visual short-term memory (STM).* The presence of a model to draw from is therefore less helpful to children. Adults are more able to compute rapidly novel descriptions of parts of the model and maintain them in visual STM for just as long as the immediate task requires.

5. *Because production is sequential and perception is context-sensitive, the appearance of the marks made may change as the drawing proceeds.* The interim stages will therefore sometimes not look at all 'right', and overcoming this difficulty may be an important part of learning to drawn.

We shall begin with a general discussion of the discovery, storage and use of graphic descriptions. The results of two investigations of the effects of training on children's drawings will then be reported, and they will be interpreted as providing some support for these propositions.

First, there is the problem of 'seeing' or otherwise computing what to draw, i.e. the problem of discovering graphic descriptions. There are indefinitely many descriptions that could be computed, even of simple objects. Representational drawing requires the discovery of descriptions that can be appropriately translated into lines or other marks on the picture plane. For example, the left-hand edge of the top of a cube in oblique projection (Figure 6.2, to be discussed later, shows such a cube – in cell 9) could be described as an oblique line joining a horizontal line beneath it at an acute angle. This description applies only to the projection, however: seen as a solid object, all edges are either horizontal or vertical, and all its angles are right angles. Objects can be described in many ways, and some of these descriptions will be much easier to use as a basis for drawing than others. Finding good descriptions may be difficult, however, both because there are in principle so many possibilities and because habitual descriptions dominate representation. The latter is a problem because habitual ways of 'seeing' are normally adapted to interactions with *objects*, not with their *projections*. A much more thorough analysis of this claim and of the procedures artists employ to reduce the difficulty is given in the chapter by Francis Pratt (this volume).

One of the messages to emerge most consistently from the work in Artificial Intelligence is that finding good descriptions is the major task in most problem-solving situations. Difficulties of description-finding in drawing may therefore reflect an important facet of cognition in general. Although the best description for realistic drawing is close to that directly produced by the visual optics, children, to a great extent, and adults, to a lesser extent, have difficulty in using this projective information to guide drawing. Furthermore, emphasising such descriptions by providing a simple projective line-drawing to copy does not remove the children's difficulty (Phillips, Hobbs and Pratt, 1978). For a thorough discussion of the projective descriptions that children do use, and of their gradual evolution towards the oblique projections which provide more representative and less ambiguous forms of depiction, see Willats, 1977, and Willats, this volume.

Second, once computed, the descriptions must be remembered for at least long enough to enable them to specify the motor-control parameters directly or indirectly. Even when drawing from life, information computed from the model must be maintained for at least long enough to enable it to guide production. If the information is stored in visual STM, then only very little information can be stored at any one time (Phillips, 1983). If, on the other hand, the information is stored in visual LTM, then habitual schema will be even more dominant, and the learning time needed to acquire new schema will be long, compared with the rate of input to visual STM (Avons and Phillips, 1980).

Furthermore, even though the amount of information that can be stored in LTM is effectively unlimited, the amount that can be used for computation at any one time is severely limited. Hinton (1979) demonstrates that even the structural descriptions of objects as familiar and as simple as cubes are beyond our ability to operate upon as a single integrated data structure. This limitation is not noticed, however, unless we are asked to compute something new that requires operation upon the data structure as a whole. An easy way to demonstrate the relevance of this limitation to drawing is to ask adults to draw pictures that make clear the essential structure of some of the simplest knots with which they are familiar. Unless they have already had experience of this particular task they are likely to find it very difficult. Their difficulties indicate that they cannot visualise the knot as a whole, but have to build it up sequentially, correcting errors as they go. Effective descriptions, therefore, will have to meet the constraints imposed by these very general memory limitations.

Third, sequential production is, of course, also an essential characteristic of the final output stage, and the motor-control difficulties that arise at this stage are commonly assumed to be the major ones in drawing. That this is not so can easily be demonstrated by comparing tracing with drawings made either from life or from memory. However, as a consequence of production being sequential, descriptions computed within the context of the whole object must be used to specify production within a context that changes as the drawing proceeds. Perception is, for good reasons, context-sensitive. The descriptions computed of parts of the drawing may not be static, therefore, but change as the drawing proceeds. Training procedures that may help children overcome this difficulty are investigated in the experiments reported below.

Within the conception of representational drawing as primarily a problem of finding and using appropriate descriptions, we designed two investigations of the effects of specific kinds of training. They show that some kinds of training can have large and lasting effects, and that others may have little or no effect. We will first describe these two investigations, and then ask whether the conception of drawing as an exercise in description-finding provides a useful framework within which to understand them.

2. Experiment 1: the effects of 'visual' and drawing training

If the discovery of projective descriptions is an important component of graphic skill then training procedures that emphasise such descriptions may be particularly effective. This possibility is investigated in this experiment in the context of both visual and drawing training. These two kinds of training were examined because there is evidence that both can be effective, and some disagreement as to which is the more effective. Our general approach suggests that the modality of training will matter less than the nature of the descriptions that it makes apparent.

In addition, this experiment was designed to investigate whether any effects of the training are specific to the particular objects drawn, or generalise to other objects. If what has been learned are specific descriptions of specific objects then they will not generalise. If what has been learned are general strategies for solving some of the problems involved in drawing then the training will generalise.

Children were asked to draw pictures of a cube and of a pyramid, which they viewed through a large reduction tube revealing an oblique view of the object. There were 25 boys and 35 girls with ages ranging from 6 years 7 months to 7 years 7 months. The children drew the objects before training, immediately after training and then again two weeks later. The 60 children were randomly assigned to five groups. Group 1 received drawing training on the cube. Group 2 received drawing training on the pyramid. Group 3 received visual training on the cube. Group 4 received visual training on the

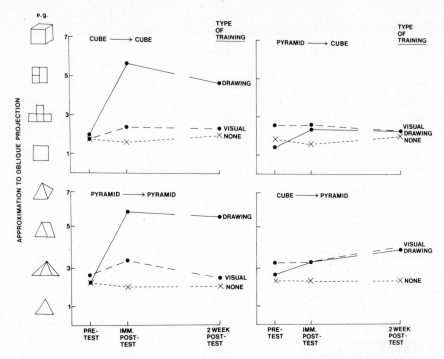

Figure 6.1 Experiment 1. The effects of training on children's drawings of cubes and pyramids. The objects were placed so that they could see only the oblique view illustrated, and they were asked to 'Draw what you see'. The two graphs on the left show the direct effects on the objects used in training (cube → cube, pyramid → pyramid). The two graphs on the right show the transfer of training to the other object (pyramid → cube, cube → pyramid). Drawings were given a score between 1 and 7 depending on their degree of approximation to the oblique projection. Each point plotted shows the mean score for 12 children.

pyramid. Group 5 received no training but drew whatever they liked for 10 minutes. All training also lasted for 10 minutes. Drawing training involved the experimenter drawing the edges of the object in the oblique projection viewed, while describing which edges and faces the lines represented. The slopes of the obliques and the number of faces shown were explicitly pointed out. After one demonstration the child drew together with the experimenter line by line. During this training the object was removed from view. Visual training was very similar except that the description of the visible edges and faces was addressed to the object viewed through the reduction tube rather than to the drawing of that view. The child was then questioned about the relevant properties of the visible edges and faces. The properties emphasised, and the order in which the edges were described, were kept the same as in the drawing training.

The results were clear, and are shown in Figure 6.1. Drawing training had a large and lasting effect. After training, the children's drawings were very much closer to the oblique projection viewed. This effect showed no significant reduction over a two-week interval. This large effect of drawing training was specific to the particular object used in training, however. It did not transfer to the other object. Visual training had no significant effect: the drawings produced were essentially as far from the oblique view as they were on the first attempt. For example, the drawings of the cubes still tended to be just drawings of a single square, or to have more than three faces, and with all lines being either vertical or horizontal. This lack of any effect is surprising, because during the visual training all children managed to describe correctly the number of visible faces and the slopes of the edges.

The drawing training, therefore, enabled the children to learn a procedure for drawing a specific object, but the visual training did not. There are many possible explanations for this difference. One hypothesis is that drawing was effective because it involved a sequence of motor acts. Another hypothesis, suggested by proposition 5 of the Introduction, is that drawing was effective because it shows those relationships between the parts that are more obvious in the intermediate stages than in the final product. To investigate these possibilities a second investigation compared the effects of two kinds of visual training and two kinds of drawing training.

3. Experiment 2: the effects of four kinds of training

Fifty-five new children were asked to draw a cube from memory, and were trained using a line-drawing of a cube seen from the same oblique projection used in the first experiment. Their ages ranged from 6 years 10 months to 7 years 9 months, and 27 were boys and 28 were girls. These were randomly divided into five groups of 11 children. Group 1 received drawing training much as in Experiment 1. Group 2 received drawing training as Group 1 except that only the experimenter drew, and the child just watched. Group 3 received visual training much as in Experiment 1 except that it was addressed to a cumulative sequence of line-drawings (Figure 6.2). This group therefore saw exactly the same intermediate stages as the drawing groups, but saw no drawing activity. Group 4 received visual training as in Group 3 except addressed to the whole line-drawing of the cube. Group 5 received no training and were just asked to draw whatever they liked for 10 minutes. Each kind of training also lasted for 10 minutes. The verbal descriptions accompanying training followed a prepared script which was very nearly the same for all four kinds of training, referring to the same properties of the model in the same order in all four cases.

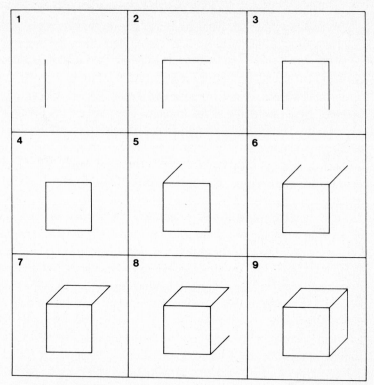

Figure 6.2 The sequence of line-drawings used in the cumulative visual-training condition of Experiment 2.

The children first drew a cube from memory. After training they were asked to copy the line-drawing of the cube. This was then removed and they drew a cube from memory. This testing was carried out individually. Two months later, in a group test of the children in their classroom, they were again asked for a drawing of a cube from memory.

The results of this experiment were also clear. Figure 6.3 shows the structures drawn from memory on the pre-test and on the immediate post-test. This time all kinds of training had significant effects, but both kinds of drawing training and cumulative visual training had significantly larger effects than wholistic visual training. There were no significant differences between drawing and cumulative visual training. There were no significant differences between the copies made at the end of training and the immediate post-test drawings from memory. The drawings produced from memory after two months were also similar to the immediate post-test drawings. The differences between the trained and untrained groups were still significant.

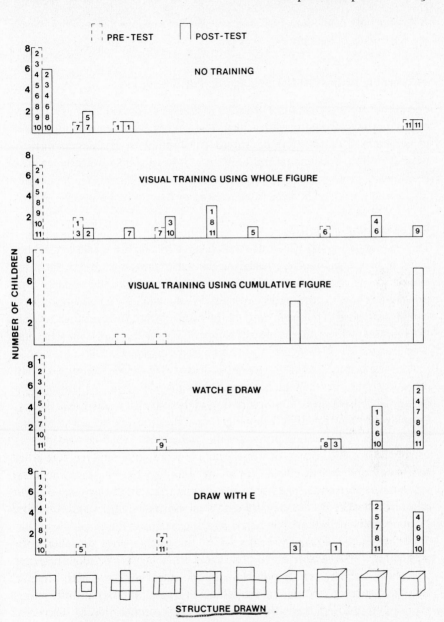

Figure 6.3 The frequency of structures produced from memory as drawings of cubes before and after five kinds of training. The small numbers within the histograms refer to individual children within each of the five groups of 11 children. (These data were not available for cumulative visual training.) A few drawings were not close to any of the 10 structures shown and these have been omitted.

After this long delay, however, there were no significant differences between the four kinds of training.

4. Learning to draw as learning appropriate descriptions

The effects of just 10 minutes' training of certain kinds had large and lasting effects on the way objects were drawn. The kind of learning involved in these experiments could therefore contribute substantially to the development of graphic skill that occurs naturally. What was learned does not seem to have been *general* strategies for looking at objects or for translating three dimensions into two, but to have involved learning graphic descriptions of specific objects.

The specificity of learning

The learning observed was thus very effective but highly specific. It did not transfer to a similar object tested at the same time and under the same conditions. It seems reasonable to conclude that what the children had learned was how to draw a specific object. We do not know whether the effects would generalise to different views of the same object. However that may be, the specificity of learning is clearly compatible with the view that what has been learned are descriptions of certain aspects of objects.

This result may be but one example of a very general feature of human cognition. One way in which complex acts may be produced is simply by looking up something we can already do and then doing it again. Alternatively, complex acts may somehow be put together at the time. Consider, for example, the problem of converting print into its spoken form. Such conversion can usually be achieved either by a *specific* whole-word (look–say) method, or by a *general* grapheme–phoneme conversion procedure (phonics) that puts the sequence of phonemes together at the time of translation (for readable and authoritative reviews of this work see Patterson, 1981, and Shallice, 1981). Computing the depiction of an object by the use of procedures specific to that object seems to be closely analogous to the whole-word procedures for translating a printed word into its associated phonology. These procedures are thought to address directly the whole phonological structure of the specific word, in contrast to the general procedures that work out the phonology from a representation of the word decomposed into pronounceable segments. Although described here as a dichotomy, it is possible that these two procedures are just examples from a spectrum defined by the complexity and specificity of the level at which translation takes place. The relative contributions of specific and general procedures to the computation of phonology from print is currently a central unresolved issue, but there is good evidence that even in highly literate adults the specific procedures still play a major role. Thus, whether we are dealing with drawing or reading, children or adults, highly specific procedures for computing one representation from another seem to play an important part in human cognition.

The suggestion that we are considering, therefore, is that all our training procedures have done is to create a new entry in the child's repertoire for producing specific graphic outputs given specific prompting inputs. If this is so, then two questions arise. First, why do so many kinds of experience fail to create these entries? Second, are there also more general procedures for finding or generating graphic descriptions, and if so how do they develop? These two questions will be discussed in relation to the problems involved in finding, remembering and using graphic descriptions.

5. Finding graphic descriptions

Looking at an object and verbally describing its appearance did not affect the way it was drawn. The same procedure applied to a line-drawing did affect drawing to some extent. It mainly led to children drawing three faces rather than one, but did not lead to correct depiction of the obliques. Drawing training and cumulative visual training were equally effective, and enabled the children to draw close approximations to a realistic view. Seeing the intermediate products seems to be more important than practising the motor acts that produce them.

How can these results be explained within the general conception we are exploring? When looking at a real object the many three-dimensional cues available lead to descriptions emphasising the three-dimensional structure. The training conversation is then taken to refer to aspects of that structural description. For example, in Experiment 1 the oblique edges were described as 'sloping away in this direction', together with the appropriate gestures. This attempt at an ostensive definition will be misunderstood, however, if the child represents the edges referred to as horizontal edges in the third dimension. Showing a whole line-drawing greatly reduces the cues to three-dimensional structure, and this seems to increase the chance that some of the projective properties will be noticed. Whole-object perception did still exert a strong influence, however, because most children still drew the oblique lines at right angles to the others. When these configurational cues to whole-object structure were absent or reduced, as in the intermediate drawings, the orientation of the oblique lines was correctly reproduced. Reducing the cues to other possible descriptions therefore increased the probability that projective descriptions would be reflected in the drawings. This clearly supports the conception of drawing as an exercise in finding appropriate graphic descriptions.

This discussion implies that children can learn projective descriptions but do not usually find them for themselves just by looking at the real object. If this is so, a question that arises is whether adults differ in this regard. Francis Pratt (this volume) presents a detailed analysis of professional artists' aids, and suggests that they can be interpreted as ways of reducing the dominance of habitual object-centred descriptions. This is therefore evidence that the general problem remains relevant at all ages and levels of skill. The phenomena of object 'shape constancy' and 'regression to the real object' seen in adults are further evidence for this view.

Nevertheless, by their early teens, children, in Western culture at least, can produce drawings of novel objects from life models that are much closer to realistic views than they could do earlier. This indicates that an ability to compute and use projective descriptions on the basis of natural views does develop. One suggestion about the nature of that development arises from the discussion of the next section.

6. Remembering graphic descriptions

In the Introduction we suggested that memory for graphic descriptions involves visual STM, visual LTM or some combination of them (Phillips, 1983; Pratt, 1983). The hypothesis that we wish to explore at this point is that children of 7 years or less are much more dependent on the use of visual LTM than adults, because their ability to create and maintain novel information in visual STM is very limited. In their research on the development of working memory, Hitch and Halliday (1983) have found strong evidence that the ability to maintain novel verbal information by sub-vocal rehearsal is not developed before about 7 years of age. Recent work at the University of Manchester by Catherine Pettipher and Graham Hitch (as yet unpublished) has extended this strategy to visual STM, and the results suggest that this ability is not well developed in 7-year-old children. At the University of Stirling, Lindsay Wilson has devised a novel pattern-span technique, and has found that a dramatic increase in visual pattern span occurs between the ages of 5 and 11 years. Further relevant evidence for this view is that in Experiment 2 copies of the line-drawing made at the end of training with the model still in view were no better than the drawings later done from memory (i.e. from LTM). It is also the case that young children look back and forth from model to copy very much less than adults (Pratt, 1984), and this also indicates that they rely more on visual LTM than on visual STM. Adults may therefore be better at drawing specific views from life because they are more able to transmit novel information about details of that view from perception to drawing without having to learn it. If children are less able to do this then they will be more dependent on LTM, and their drawings will consequently reflect more stereotyped conceptions.

7. The use of graphic descriptions

The finding that cumulative visual training was as efficient as drawing training is further evidence that motor skill is not a critical component of the development we are discussing. It does indicate, however, that the sequential nature of output is important. We discussed this result earlier in the context of the difficulty of finding appropriate descriptions of the model. In the context of production a slightly different perspective on this result arises. Consider, for example, the fifth drawing of the sequence in Figure 6.2. The oblique line at the top may at this stage be more likely to be perceptually described as being in the same plane as the square beneath than as receding in the third dimension. If this is so then learning a path to picture production may be analogous to solving a detour problem. One way in which this difficulty could be reduced in the course of development is by learning that perceptual descriptions are subtly influenced by context. Another possibility is that adults are more able to control the context that influences perceptual descriptions, perhaps by imagining the parts to be in contexts different from those in which they actually are. This would fit well with the earlier suggestion that developments in visual STM contribute to the acquisition of graphic skill.

8. Conclusion

We have shown that some kinds of training can have large and lasting effects. This is evidence against the view that children draw the way they do because of some very general and slowly evolving conception of space. It seems to us that the course of development is more that of finding and remembering appropriate graphic descriptions.

The descriptions that we have called appropriate are those appropriate to realistic views. It is reasonable to question the value of a course of development that seems to lead away from general abstract concepts and towards a concern for the particular and transitory aspects of experience. Our reply to this is that we believe the development to be toward a greater ability to *choose* between alternative representations. The basic problem facing intelligent life could be described as being that of relating enduring regularities to the realities of the moment. Sensitivity to alternative descriptions of immediate experience might enable a wider range of regularities to emerge, and thus contribute to the highly individualistic and creative lifestyle that is so characteristic of human evolution.

ACKNOWLEDGEMENT

The work reported in this paper was largely inspired by Francis Pratt.

REFERENCES

Avons, S. E. & Phillips, W. A. (1980) Visualization and memorization as a function of display time and poststimulus processing time. *Journal of Experimental Psychology*, 6, 407–20.

Hinton, G. E. (1979) Some demonstrations of the effects of structural descriptions in mental imagery. *Cognitive Science*, 3, 231–50.

Hitch, G. J. & Halliday, M. S. (1983) Working memory in children. *Philosophical Transactions of the Royal Society of London*, ser. B, 302, 325–40.

Patterson, K. E. (1981) Neuropsychological approaches to the study of reading. *British Journal of Psychology*, 72, 151–74.

Phillips, W. A. (1983) Short-term visual memory. *Philosophical Transactions of the Royal Society of London*, ser. B, 306, 295–309.

Phillips, W. A., Hobbs, S. B. & Pratt, F. R. (1978) Intellectual realism in children's drawings of cubes. *Cognition*, 6, 15–33.

Pratt, F. R. (1983) Intellectual realism in children's and adults' copies of cubes and straight lines. In D. Rogers & J. Sloboda (eds.), *The acquisition of symbolic skills*. New York: Plenum.

(1984) A theoretical framework for thinking about drawing. In W. R. Crozier & A. J. Chapman (eds.), *Cognitive processes in the perception of art*. Amsterdam: North-Holland.

Shallice, T. (1981) Neurological impairment of cognitive processes. *British Medical Bulletin*, 37, 187–92.

Willats, J. (1977) How children learn to draw realistic pictures. *Quarterly Journal of Experimental Psychology*, 29, 367–82.

7

Anomalous drawing development: some clinical studies

LORNA SELFE

1. Introduction

Many of the standardised tests of intelligence contain an item where the child is required to draw either a human figure or a geometrical design, and competence in such drawing tasks has been shown to correlate positively with abilities in a range of other intellectual skills. Harris (1963) summarises more than 10 studies which reported positive correlations between 0.05 and 0.92 between Goodenough scores on the Draw-a-man test and scores on individual items in other psychological tests. The assumption that children's drawings relate to their general cognitive or intellectual development is universally accepted and well established, although the nature of the association is ill defined. Children whose drawing skills are advanced for their age are assumed to be of above-average intelligence. Lark-Horovitz, Lewis and Luca (1967) state, 'Children who draw well are invariably bright...the mean I.Q. of artistically talented children is higher than that of average children of the same age and these children, rather than being one sided, i.e. gifted drawers only, are in fact mentally versatile. It seems quite clear that the ability to draw is a significant one and can help to forecast the young child's potential'. They conclude that very bright and artistically talented children go through the same stages in the development of drawing skills as do other children but at an accelerated rate. This raises the important empirical question of whether it is possible to achieve what are considered to be late accomplishments, such as linear perspective, without having passed through preliminary stages first.

2. Mentally retarded children

It is assumed that drawing ability will inevitably be associated with the general mental age of the child when the child is known to be mentally retarded. Harris

(1963), in his thorough review of the relationship between drawing development and intellectual maturity, says, 'it is instructive to compare the drawings of mentally retarded children with those of normal children...on almost every point on the scale, mentally retarded children are slower than normal to achieve success...Mentally retarded children are relatively more deficient on items of proportion and dimension and are relatively less handicapped on the inclusion of specific body parts.' (It is interesting to note here that Harris is assuming that 'advance' in drawing development is towards a photographically realistic representation.) Harris also quotes Goodenough's remarks (1926), 'They [retarded children] analyse a figure to some extent and by this means are able to set down some elements in a graphic fashion, but the ability to combine elements into an organised whole is likely to be defective and, in some instances, seems to be almost entirely lacking. It is this inability to analyse, to form abstract ideas, to relate facts that is largely responsible for the bizarre effects so frequently found among the drawings of backward children.'

Harris reviewed a number of studies which confirmed his thesis that retarded children draw at their mental age level. Two of the most notable were, first, one undertaken by Townsend in 1951, who found that graphic copying skills in children correlated highly with mental age. Using geometrical designs he found that copying skills correlated more highly with mental age than with chronological age. Second, Stotijn-Egge (1952) found that scores on drawing tests correlated highly with mental age in her sample of 2,000 severely mentally retarded subjects. Subjects who had no spoken language and who were severely retarded did not draw spontaneously, nor were they able to copy simple geometric shapes. Another general assumption is that, along with cognitive development, there is a hierarchy of skill acquisition in the development of representational drawing in children. It is assumed that the child slowly acquires more elaborate schemas (Phillips, Hobbs and Pratt, 1978); he gradually solves problems in planning and ordering his graphic production (Freeman, 1980); and pencil control is slowly mastered with increasing motor skill and manual dexterity (Elliott and Connolly, 1974).

The existence of phenomenal drawing ability in association with severe mental retardation was therefore an affront to reasonably held notions about child development and the acquisition of the hierarchy of skill. When I discovered a small number of children with severe learning difficulties who showed exceptional drawing competence from an early age, it was decided that it was very important that such an occurrence be investigated. In this chapter it is proposed to give details of these children and their abilities and to offer a possible explanation for the phenomenon. The discovery of the group derived from an earlier study which I conducted of a single child with exceptional and anomalous drawing ability (Selfe, 1977).

3. Nadia

This child, Nadia, was 6 years old when her mother referred her to the Child Development Research Unit in the University of Nottingham. Nadia had failed to develop any spoken language and it subsequently became apparent that her developmental patterns closely followed the autistic syndrome. Nadia was born in Nottingham to Ukrainian émigré parents in 1967. She was a second-born child in a family of three children. The other two children were developing quite normally and they were bilingual. Nadia had failed to develop language normally – the few words she had gained by 12 months of age slowly disappeared – so that when I worked with her from March to September 1974, she had an extremely limited vocabulary of some 10 single-word utterances. She used these only rarely and she was generally mute. At this time she attended a local school for severely subnormal children. She spent a good deal of time staring impassively into space. Nadia was very clumsy, poorly coordinated and excessively slow. She was unresponsive to question or to command, but it was extremely difficult to know whether she did not comprehend or whether she was refusing to cooperate.

At $3\frac{1}{2}$ years of age and after a period of separation from her mother, when her mother was in hospital, Nadia suddenly displayed an extraordinary drawing ability. These drawings were executed in fine lines, showing an outstanding manual dexterity which was notably absent in all other areas of her functioning. Her drawings were remarkable for their quality of photographic realism. The drawings were in perspective, proportions between and within elements were accurate and she used occlusion or hidden-line elimination. The final production was not only highly photographically realistic but also gave the adult viewer the impression of movement and vitality. The drawings were totally different from those normally produced by children of this age, and such competence is therefore described as anomalous to distinguish it from either accelerated or talented drawing ability.

I watched Nadia drawing on many occasions. She would draw with intense preoccupation for up to a quarter of an hour. On one or two occasions Nadia was seen to draw from life. This was during a phase when she was drawing legs and shoes. Most of her drawings, however, were done entirely from memory and she was never seen to copy directly from pictures. Generally the inspiration for the drawing came from a child's picture book in which the

Figure 7.1 Nadia, aged 5 years 6 months. Biro. Drawn from memory.

quality of the drawings was often rather crude. She studied such pictures with
great attention and several weeks later she would execute a similar drawing.
However, her drawings showed many changes and embellishments from the
original and she frequently experimented with the orientation of the subject.

Nadia was tested on a number of standardised assessment procedures. As
she lacked language and her behaviour was autistic, testing presented many
difficulties. The test results were therefore only an indication of her ability.
Testing and behavioural observation revealed profound deficits in language,

Figure 7.2 Nadia, aged 6 years 4 months. Biro. Drawn from memory.

Figure 7.3 Nadia, aged (5) years. Biro. Drawn from memory.

both with comprehension and with expression. She also appeared to lack many of the prerequisites for language development: she did not imitate, she could repeat monosyllables but not two syllables, and she was never seen to engage in symbolic play. Nadia's motor-development profile was very uneven. She could not hop nor walk upstairs one step at a time and her fine motor control was surprisingly deficient in view of her drawing ability. For example, she could not do up buckles or use a knife and fork together. However, on some visual matching tasks she passed items at her own age level. Using non-standardised tests it was discovered that although Nadia could match difficult items with the same perceptual quality, she failed to match items in the same conceptual class. For example, she could match a picture of an object to a picture of its silhouette, but she failed to match pictures of an armchair and a deck chair from an array of objects that could be classified on their conceptual basis. It would therefore appear that she was attending to the visual/perceptual characteristics of objects but not to objects as representatives of classes, i.e. their functional properties.

Since 1974, the diagnosis of retardation and autism has been confirmed. Nadia is now in a residential school for autistic adolescents. She has gained some expressive language, but this is rudimentary and she cannot hold a normal or even child-like conversation. She is unlikely ever to be self-sufficient.

4. Drawing development

As a result of the publication of this case a number of parents contacted me and the directors of the Child Development Research Unit in Nottingham claiming that their mentally retarded child had exceptional graphic competence. Through detailed correspondence two such cases were isolated as really exceptional or anomalous. Although the phenomenon of exceptional graphic competence and severe retardation is extremely rare, it seemed that it was not confined to the case of Nadia. It was therefore decided that if a sample of such children could be identified, then stable features and characteristics of the phenomenon could be elucidated and described. Paivio (1971) says, for example, 'calculating prodigies, mnemonists and other varieties of persons possessing unusual abilities for particular mental tasks, often while remaining otherwise average or below average intellectually...[is] of extraordinary interest here because the manifestation of modes of thought are thrown into relief, providing an unusual opportunity for the examination of both their natures and functions'. A systematic and representational search for such cases was therefore undertaken. The drawings of many hundreds of children were examined. A number of the drawings showed accelerated development of representational ability, associated with a high level of intelligence (as described by Lark-Horovitz, Lewis and Luca, 1967), that is, representational drawing at a level two or three years above the child's chronological age. One or two of these gifted children showed remarkable talent, although their ability was not anomalous in terms of the portrayal of photographic realism at an early age, but showed accelerated development of the depiction of symbolic schemas where the drawing was elaborated in terms of detail but where photographic or spatial aspects were frequently neglected. Also many of the outstanding drawings of these bright children were copied from pictures. I was able to identify a very small number of children whose drawings were truly anomalous and showed major departures from the norms of the development of representational drawing. These children exhibited a high degree of photographic realism in their drawings before the age of 8 years. These drawings were not necessarily detailed but they were drawn as if viewed from one fixed viewpoint, and almost all of their drawings were from memory. Drawing in linear perspective has been assumed to be a late accomplishment requiring the mastery of other simpler projection systems and devices (Willats, 1977; Freeman, 1980). Photographic realism is therefore defined as the reasonably accurate depiction of linear perspective and evidence of the use of sophisticated drawing devices. These drawing devices were categorised as follows:

1. The photographically accurate portrayal of proportion within objects and between objects, in depth.
2. The portrayal of other dimensions to objects, other than flat, frontal elevations.
3. The photographically accurate portrayal of diminishing size with distance.
4. The photographically accurate depiction of one object partially occluded by another nearer one.

In all, 11 children with anomalous development of graphic representational ability were identified. Most of these children were receiving special education, some in schools for severely subnormal children but most in schools for autistic children. Goodenough (1926) noted that even amongst normal children the gifted child artist is a rare event. A detailed examination of the psychological and physical development of all 11 children was undertaken and analysed and showed that they resembled one another in certain important respects. All of the subjects had severe learning problems and had some degree of mental retardation. All had many of the features of autism (Rutter, 1978; Newson, 1979). In particular, all of the children had suffered from delayed and deviant language development, and the majority still had very restricted or bizarre language. All the subjects had severe problems with social behaviour, and had had or still had obsessions, rituals and bizarre mannerisms. An analysis of their drawing habits showed that all the subjects had started to draw representational drawings at an early age and this had not been preceded by the usual stages of scribbling and experimentation. All the subjects' drawings, from a very early age, had been fixed-viewpoint drawings of scenes or objects, frequently those objects that were of obsessional interest to the child. The drawings are therefore described an anomalous. A brief history and the drawings of two of these children are included here.

Figure 7.4 Stephen, aged 5 years. Pencil. Drawn from memory.

5. Stephen

Stephen was adopted at 15 weeks, but his adopted mother was given his full birth history, which was perfectly normal. However, she reported that 'There was something wrong with Stephen from the start.' During his early years he had a number of short stays in hospital and his mother became concerned about his progress when his language failed to develop normally. At 3½ years he was referred by his local GP to a London teaching hospital and autism was diagnosed. He attended a playgroup at 2 years and was placed in a small unit for children with learning difficulties attached to an ordinary school at 5 years. By 7 years of age his educational problems were so severe that residential boarding education in a school for autistic children was recommended. Stephen started drawing at the age of 4 years.

6. Simon

Simon was born full-term after a normal pregnancy. His development appeared to be quite normal up to 1 year of age. However, he failed to pass screening tests for developmental milestones and before 2 years of age he was referred to a teaching hospital, but no specific diagnosis was made. At 4½ years he was placed in a small local private school, but by 7 years of age it was

Figure 7.5 Stephen, aged 5 years. Pencil. Drawn from memory.

evident that he could not cope with normal provision and he was removed. At about this age autism was finally diagnosed. As there was no specialised facility available to him in his home town he attended a physically handicapped school until he was 16 years of age. He has attended an occupational unit for the physically handicapped since then. Simon started to draw at around 5 years of age.

It is useful to compare the drawings of normal children with the drawings of the subjects using the drawing devices previously detailed.

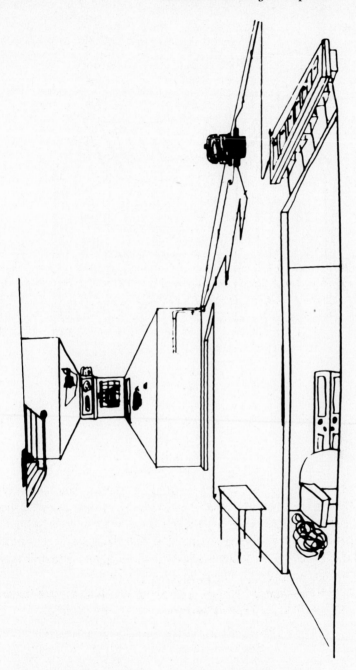

Figure 7.6 Stephen, aged 7 to 9 years. Pencil. Drawn from memory.

Figure 7.7 Simon, aged 6 years. Felt pen. Drawn from memory.

Figure 7.8 Simon, aged 7 to 9 years. Pencil. Drawn from memory.

Figure 7.9 Simon, aged 9 years. Pencil.

7. Normal and anomalous drawing compared

(1) *The depiction of proportion*

Commentators on the subject of children's drawings have noticed that young children have difficulty in portraying photographically realistic proportion (McCarty, 1924; Freeman, 1977; see also Allik and Laak's chapter below). It is well known, for example, that young children exaggerate the size of the human head in human-figure drawing. I investigated normal children's depiction of proportion in human-figure drawing (Selfe, 1983). I found support in the general observation that children produce more photographically realistic proportions in their free human-figure drawings with age. Even by the age of 10 years, head/trunk ratios were not photographically accurate and the tendency to overestimate the size of the head remained. It was also found that when a headless pre-drawn human figure was presented to young children so that all the major planning and production problems were solved in advance for them, and they were required merely to draw the head in, there was a marked tendency to underestimate the size of the head. Proportions between parts within the single object therefore are inaccurately portrayed by children under the age of 10 years. Moreover, proportions between objects, especially in depth, are notoriously difficult to portray accurately (Barnhart, 1942; Piaget and Inhelder, 1956; Freeman, 1980). Normal young children generally learn to solve this problem by using horizontal planes where the top and the bottom of the paper correspond to the near/far depth relationship. It is usually only haltingly and gradually that these planes become gradations of depth. It is clear from an examination of the drawings of the three autistic subjects that proportions between and within objects are far more accurately portrayed than in the drawings of normal children of the same age (see, for example, Figures 7.1, 7.6 and 7.8).

(2) Dimensions

Many authors report that in the early stages of drawing, children typically represent objects flat in two dimensions (Barnhart, 1942; Harris, 1963; Lark-Horovitz, Lewis and Luca, 1967). At the pre-schematic stage of drawing (approximately $2\frac{1}{2}$ to 5 years), a canonical representation of an object is confined to a single, one-sided representation where the characteristic and salient features are added. Either a front or a side elevation is depicted, whatever is the more characteristic of the object or will fulfil the child's aims. During the later, schematic stage the representation is elaborated and detail added. The child will attempt to incorporate more of the salient features and these may include side or even rear elevations of the object. These are usually, however, tacked onto the original canonical representation. Later still, and usually not until adolescence, children will be prepared to 'deform' their canonical representation in favour of a single, fixed view of the object. A single-fixed-viewpoint representation may frequently go against what the child knows of the object. For example, a single viewpoint of a car could incorporate only one wheel and yet the object be recognised as a car. The child gradually acquires an understanding of the use of a projection system to represent graphically what he sees in his visual world. These three autistic subjects from a very early age drew as if from a fixed single viewpoint so that all visible dimensions of an object are depicted. This ability to draw the photographic aspects of a scene or to use a projection system resembling linear perspective is considered to be very late accomplishment attained only in late adolescence, if at all (Willats, 1977).

— **(3) *Diminishing size with distance***
There has been rather little research into the development of the use of diminishing size with distance as a graphic device in children's drawing. Freeman (1977) discusses size-scaling but only for the drawings of single objects in relation to the size of paper offered to the child. I studied the phenomenon in a situation where the possibility of a photographic representation was optimised, where children were required to draw a missing lamp-post as a vertical line to complete the picture of a street in linear perspective. I found that in this optimum situation normal children up to 6 years tended to underestimate the true photographic size of the lamp-post, and even up to 10 years few of the children managed an accurate scaling. Again, it can be seen, especially in Stephen's drawings (Figure 7.6), that the autistic subjects had a well-developed understanding of size-scaling in depicting a scene in linear perspective.

(4) *Occlusion*
The development of the ability to draw a representation of two objects, one partly occluded of the other, in children's drawings has been discussed by several authors (Piaget and Inhelder, 1956; Lewis, 1963; Barnhart, 1942; Freeman, Eiser and Sayers, 1977; Cox, 1981; Light and Humphreys, 1981). Young children tend to depict the two objects as separate and complete or to draw the two objects as a 'transparency'. Only with increasing age is there a growing tendency to delete the invisible part of the occluded object. Freeman (1980) called this ability 'hidden-line elimination' (H.L.E.) and reported that it was only used by children after 7 years of age. It is clear from an examination of the drawings of the three autistic subjects that hidden-line elimination is accomplished from the age of 5 (see particularly Figure 7.5). In fact, the use of partial occlusion is a particular feature of all their drawings and again indicates that a static fixed single viewpoint is being used in their depictions.

Gibson (1979) produced an ecological theory of visual perception which is having a considerable influence on theories of representation and is discussed in detail elsewhere in this volume. Gibson described children's drawings in terms of the child representing what he has learned to attend to in 'the optic array'. Features that occur regularly and are attended to he calls 'invariants'. The child attempts to depict these invariants in his graphic work. Gibson suggests that in perception we are concurrently aware of persistence and change and that picture-making (drawing) is 'an arrangement of invariants of structure'. The different features of the optic array will have significance at different ages and stages in the child's life. An architect will attend to different features of a building than a stonemason or a carpenter or a demolition expert. But presumably in the process of socialisation and in communication the child is brought to see the world in a manner similar to other members in the society. This is an essential process before communication can commence. The drawings of normal children are a record of the conventional visual experiential features that are often important to all children in the shared culture. In Western cultures at least, and from 3 to 9 years of age, the essential features of the optic array which children choose to depict in their drawings appear to be objects and their defining characteristics. According to Arnheim (1974), the simplicity of children's schematic representation does not reflect graphic incapacity so much as it reflects the basic analytical categories through which the child organises his world. The drawing of the object is not limited to one fixed view and, in this respect coincides much more with the dynamic visual experiences of the child. He selects the symbolic form with defining features to represent this experience. According to Gibson, in perception the child apprehends the optic array, isolating those structural features which remain invariant across situations. For example, the expectation is that people will have two legs even if the legs aren't always visible. Children depict a table as having four legs of equal length in their drawings, since this is an invariant quality of tables.

The features that the autistic child draws, however, when he does attempt to draw, appear to be the lines, edges, contours and angles of the frozen fixed-viewpoint optic array. These are very different features from those attended to by normal young children of the same age. A number of developmental psychologists (Bruner, 1966; Vygotsky, 1962) point out that cognitive development in infants involves symbolising, codifying and cate-gorising experience. Bruner and his colleagues regard language as the most specialised system of symbolic activity and define three modes of representation, enactive, iconic and symbolic, where the symbolic system emerges last in development and seems to be more abstract and complex. It can be maintained that much the same symbolising activity characterises the drawings of the very young child. He represents those objects that have functional significance for him. The production of a characterising and meaningful symbolic representation appears to be more important than attention to idiosyncratic details or to a single view of an object. The autistic subjects, however, appear to be attending to non-symbolic aspects of visual experience. Objects are truncated or partially occluded and represented without their defining characteristics, as seen from one fixed viewpoint. This type of drawing is necessarily autistic and asocial in so far as one single viewpoint is possible only to one single viewer at one fixed spot. It is therefore hypothesised that the autistic child, in drawing, records objects in his optic array more as patterns – edges, contours and shapes – rather than as representatives of classes or symbols. It is perhaps coincidental that adult laymen generally value photographic realism in drawing and that this feature is the hall-mark in the drawings of the autistic group. Pariser (1979) concludes that 'Nadia's work demonstrates the fallacy inherent in assuming that realistic rendering is the end state towards which all art aspires.' It also demonstrates the fact that similar results do not always spring from similar processes.

8. Autism and realism

It is interesting to speculate what cognitive processes could account for the occurrence of photographically realistic drawing in association with autism. A possible explanation can be derived from current theories of visual imagery and from some experimental studies of autism. Paivio (1971) suggested that there are two distinct modes of internal representation in thinking processes; these he termed the imaginal and the verbal mode of thinking, and his theory is termed the dual-coding hypothesis. According to this theory, imagery is regarded primarily as a parallel processing system where images present themselves simultaneously and are characterised by their spatial arrangement. Although heavily criticised, the quasi-pictorial notion of imagery has an initial experiential plausibility to recommend it, and imagery has now been shown to have its measurable, behavioural correlates affecting reaction time, for example (Richardson, 1980). Paivio also suggests that the verbal system is specialised for sequential processing, for processing over time. Although the final product in representational drawing is an image, the act of drawing is sequential and temporal in so far as lines are drawn one after another and the normal young child possibly integrates both codes in the drawing process.

The notion of different modes of thinking was explored separately by O'Connor and Hermelin in 1978. They suggested that incoming stimuli or information could be coded in different ways according to whether the information was received by one sensory modality or another. They relate these modalities to temporal and spatial dimensions of information reception. Experimental work undertaken by Hermelin and O'Connor (1970) and by Hermelin (1978) has shown that autistic children have difficulty in transposing information received by one sensory modality to another mode. If autistic children are presented with visual information such as a visual sequence of letters, for example, they were found to be less likely to recode them internally into nonsense words as normal children do. Normal children were found to process information in that sensory system which had the greatest capacity for handling those particular data.

Hermelin and O'Connor concluded that autistic children have difficulty involving a transposition between verbal/temporal thinking into spatial/imaginal thinking and vice versa. Hermelin (1978) says, 'Autistic children, though able to receive the complete range of sensory information, nevertheless seem to use only such data as are at the moment presented to them. This lack of mental mobility in handling information, and their tendency to remain stimulus bound, can make them operationally blind or deaf or even both.'

Using this model it can be seen that restricted transposition and the inflexible use of representational cognitive codes may help to account for the fact that the autistic subjects draw more photographically realistically and that spatial information is more accurately portrayed. Presumably it could be claimed that the autistic child is using the visual/spatial modality without the interaction and integration of the temporal/verbal mode, which may occur normally. It is far too soon to push such an explanation too far, since there are many critics of the dual-coding hypothesis and there are many conflicting theories as to the nature of cognitive deficits in autism. It is also important to reiterate that these cases of autistic children with drawing ability are extremely rare. Most autistic children have no special drawing ability and in fact show a retarded development in graphic representation, if they can be persuaded to draw.

Whilst it is important to attempt some sort of explanation for this phenomenon, I have to conclude that I remain baffled, but not without clues. Hopefully an explanation will emerge as we understand more about autism and about representational drawing in normal children (see Selfe, 1983, for a full discussion of these points).

To sum up, it would appear that, in drawing, normal young children are dominated by the need to set down their conceptual understanding of an object; the child represents the characteristics of an object rather than the idiosyncratic, fixed viewpoint. The transition from earlier symbolic forms to the depiction of photographic realism is a gradual development which usually appears to require the elaboration of skills and techniques. Linear-perspective drawing, for example, is not usually attempted until early adolescence and has frequently to be taught to normal subjects. These rare autistic subjects are able to record a single fixed view of static spatial configurations almost invariably from memory and from a young age, but it is argued that this may well be due to the nature of autism where symbolic and verbal abilities are severely retarded and where there appear to be problems with the integration of sensory information.

One very important conclusion must be that what may at first blush appears to be phenomenal and accelerated graphic competence could in fact be as much a symptom of autism in these three subjects as is echolalia or bizarre mannerisms, but if this is a pessimistic conclusion it is also evident that such children can show an elaborate and detailed memory of their visual experience through their drawings.

REFERENCES

Arnheim, R. (1974) *Art and visual perception*. Berkeley: University of California Press.

Barnhart, E. (1942) Developmental stages in compositional construction in children's drawings. *Journal of Experimental Education, 11*, 156–84.

Bruner, J., Olver, R. & Greenfield, P. (1966) *Studies in cognitive growth*. New York: Wiley.

Cox, M. V. (1981) One thing behind another: Problems of representation in children's drawings. *Educational Psychology, 1*, 275–87.

Elliott, J. & Connolly, K. (1974) Hierarchical structure in skill development. In K. Connolly & J. Bruner (eds.), *The growth of competence*. London: Academic Press.

Freeman, N. H. (1977) How young children try to plan drawings. In G. E. Butterworth (ed.), *The child's representation of the world*. New York: Plenum.

(1980) *Strategies of representation in young children*. London: Academic Press.

Freeman, N. H., Eiser, C. & Sayers, J. (1977) Children's strategies in drawing 3D relations on a 2D surface. *Journal of Experimental Child Psychology, 23*, 305–14.

Gibson, J. J. (1979) *The ecological approach to visual perception*. Boston: Houghton Mifflin.

Goodenough, F. (1926) *Measurement of intelligence in drawings*. New York: World.

Harris, D. B. (1963) *Children's drawings as measures of intellectual maturity*. New York: Harcourt, Brace and World.

Hermelin, B. (1978) Images and language. In M. Rutter & E. Schopler (eds.), *Autism – A reappraisal of concepts and treatment*. New York: Plenum.

Hermelin, B. & O'Connor, N. (1970) *Psychological experiments with autistic children*. London: Pergamon.

Lark-Horovitz, B., Lewis, H. & Luca, M. (1967) *Understanding children's art for better teaching*. Columbus, Ohio: Charles Merrill.

Lewis, H. (1963) Spatial representation in drawing as a correlate of development and a basis for picture preference. *Journal of Genetic Psychology, 102*, 95–107.

Light, P. & Humphreys, J. (1981) Internal spatial relationships in young children's drawings. *Journal of Experimental Child Psychology, 31*, 521–30.

McCarty, S. (1924) *Children's drawings*. Baltimore: Williams and Wilkins.

Newson, E. (1979) *Making sense of autism: an overview*. University of Nottingham: Child Development Research Unit.

O'Connor, N. & Hermelin, B. (1978) *Seeing and hearing and space and time*. London: Academic Press.

Paivio, A. (1971) *Imagery and verbal processes*. New York: Holt, Rinehart and Winston.

Pariser, D. (1979) *A discussion of Nadia*. Technical Report No. 9. Cambridge, Mass.: Harvard University Project Zero.

Phillips, W. A., Hobbs, S. B. & Pratt, F. R. (1978) Intellectual realism in children's drawings of cubes. *Cognition*, 6, 15–34.

Piaget, J. & Inhelder, B. (1956) *The child's conception of space*. London: Routledge and Kegan Paul.

Richardson, J. T. (1980) *Mental imagery and human memory*. London: Macmillan.

Rutter, M. (1978) Diagnosis and definitions. In M. Rutter & E. Schopler (eds.), *Autism – A reappraisal of concepts and treatment*. New York: Plenum.

Selfe, L. (1977) *Nadia – A case of extraordinary drawing ability in an autistic child*. London: Academic Press.

  (1983) *Normal and anomalous representational drawing ability in children*. London: Academic Press.

Stotijn-Egge, S. (1952) *Investigation of the drawing ability of low grade subnormals*. Leiden: Luctor et Emergo, 158, 172.

Townsend, E. (1951) A study of copying ability in children. *Genetic Psychological Monographs*, 43, 3–51.

Vygotsky, L. (1962) *Thought and language*. Cambridge, Mass.: M.I.T. Press and Wiley.

Willats, J. (1977) How children learn to draw realistic pictures. *Quarterly Journal of Experimental Psychology*, 29, 367–82.

Commentary

N. H. FREEMAN and M. V. COX

The line of argument probed in Chapters 2, 6 and 7 is that depictors work from a mental model of the scene. This is also the centre of gravity of one of the arguments in Chapter 14, which uses the strengths of the mental-model idea to contest the notion that children's drawings can best be explained in terms of the way in which an urge to inform gets hold of the children. Amongst the many other issues which previously cropped up is the question of depiction training, and this can be traced further in Chapters 16 and 19. Just as important, the issue of how best to test children's expertise, which was dealt with in Chapters 5 and 7, is a most important consideration in Chapters 9, 10, 12, 16, 17, 18 and 19.

In the next few chapters, two strands of evidence from the previous chapters are maintained. One concerns the particular drawing devices which are at children's disposal. How do they select from amongst them when they are needed? One device is that of *segregation* of parts of a scene: if a scene contains separate bits, they may be drawn visibly separated on the picture plane. Another device is that of *hidden-line elimination*, whereby two figures are related through sacrificing a part of the contour of one or both of them. Of course, these two particular devices may be in competition one with the other. The analysis of the selection of drawing devices is expounded in Chapters 9, 10, 14, 15 and 20. The other strand of evidence concerns the peculiar problem of representing the third dimension (the azimuth) on a two-dimensional picture surface, at a level of generality much higher than just that of selecting a particular drawing device. Both these strands of evidence are used in order to examine the status of the child as a depictor. *What information about objects and dimensions do children typically try to capture, and what developmental account is the most appropriate?* This section of the book runs from Chapters 8 to 14, with a basic description of the area in Chapter

8, and with Chapter 12 acting as a place for taking stock. In fact, the particular questions in italics formulated above can be found in Chapter 12.

In the next few chapters, these issues are examined in a wide variety of ways. A brief guide to the sequence of chapters may be found in the 'plan of the book' section of the Introduction.

8

Young children's representational drawings of solid objects: a comparison of drawing and copying

MAY JANE CHEN

1. Introduction

Young children's attempts to represent depth relationships in their drawings have been the subject of many studies in recent years. Three types of observation can be identified: those concerned with depth relationships between two objects (e.g. Cox, 1978; Freeman, Eiser and Sayers, 1977; Light and MacIntosh, 1980; Light and Humphreys, 1981), those concerned with one object having discrete defining features such as a cup (e.g. Davis, 1983; Freeman and Janikoun, 1972), and those concerned with the three-dimensionality of a single solid object (e.g. Chen and Cook, 1984; Phillips, Hobbs and Pratt, 1978). Most of these studies have used a single scene, and the main questions include 'How do children depict the three-dimensional scene on a two-dimensional picture plane?' and 'What are the distinctive characteristics of their drawings at each age level?'

To draw one object behind another, an adult drawer would normally use partial occlusion to depict the 'behind' relationship. The absence of an attempt to represent the occlusion of a farther object by a nearer one in young children's drawings has been noted by many authors. For example, Freeman, Eiser and Sayers (1977) asked children to draw one apple behind another without showing the apples to the children. They found that few children before the age of 8 used partial occlusion in their drawings. Instead, they drew the apples either side by side or one above the other. These findings were confirmed by other studies where real objects were shown as models (Cox, 1978; Light and MacIntosh, 1980; Light and Humphreys, 1981).

Use of occlusion has also been investigated in drawing a single object. For example, Freeman and Janikoun (1972) studied children's tendency to include a defining feature of a cup (the handle) even when this feature was not in view. Most children between the ages of 5 and 7 included the handle in their drawings. However, Davis (1983) found that when children between the ages of 4 and 7 years were asked first to draw a single cup with its handle not in view, then to draw two cups together, one cup with its handle visible to the child and the other with its handle not in view, many children under the age of 6 years, who initially drew the handle in the single-cup task, went on to omit the occluded handle in the two-cup task. Davis' findings suggest that young children are sensitive to the context in which a drawing task is performed and that they are more capable of expressing what they see in their drawings than is generally realised. Evidence from other studies also suggests a powerful effect of context, instruction or other task variables on children's drawing performance (e.g. Cox, 1978; Taylor and Bacharach, 1982). Unfortunately, most of these studies are concerned with children's ability to use occlusion in drawings and very few have examined children's graphic representation of other depth relationships.

2. Effect of models on drawing performance

One task variable which has been found to affect children's representational drawings of a three-dimensional scene or a solid object is the model used. Although research has looked at children's ability to draw from a real three-dimensional model, at their ability to copy a picture of a three-dimensional scene and at their ability to draw a nominated scene or object from memory (Deręgowski, 1976 and 1977; Phillips, Hobbs and Pratt, 1978; Willats, 1977), few attempts have been made to compare children's drawings made from a three-dimensional scene with their own copied drawings from a picture of the scene. One such study was reported by Freeman (1980, p. 257) in which Hayton and Freeman compared children's spontaneous drawing with their own copied drawing of the same object. They asked children between 10 and 11 years of age to draw a table and then to copy a drawing of a table which was within their own drawing system. A majority of the children did it with ease. However, when given a more advanced drawing to copy, only one out of 20 managed the copying task. Phillips, Hobbs and Pratt (1978) compared children's drawings made from copying a perspective line-drawing of a cube with their own drawings of a cube from memory. They found that the copied drawings were to some extent affected by what the children were copying and that few children copied the cube pattern by drawing exactly the same structure that they drew from memory. The copied drawings were more similar to the line-drawing model than were the drawings made from memory. Phillips *et al.* attributed this difference to the opportunity children had in copying a line-drawing model of a cube in which a solution to the problem of translating the depth information onto a picture surface was shown. These results suggest that children's drawing performance can be influenced by the models provided. One difficulty with both of these studies, however, is that each was a comparison of a copied drawing (using a line-drawing model) with a spontaneous drawing of an object from memory or general knowledge. This latter condition, being relatively uncontrolled, potentially allows a variety of factors to influence the drawing, e.g. children's general experience or creativity or imagination.

The present paper reports the use of more complex techniques to examine the effect of a model on children's representational drawings of solid geometric forms, with an attempt to control the comparability of different drawing conditions. Specifically, it reports a series of experiments on children's ability to draw pictures of solid objects under three drawing conditions.

In each experiment, children were asked to draw what they see from a real-life solid object and also to copy from a photograph as well as a line-drawing of the same object. By comparing their performance in these three drawing conditions, it was hoped to isolate some of the difficulties manifested by young children in drawing solid objects. The advantage of comparing drawings produced by the same children in different tasks is that it provides a control over task demand. The picture which is to be copied can be matched precisely to the model which is to be drawn from life, so that quantitative comparisons between the child's performance on the different tasks can be made.

3. Structural-directed *versus* content-directed strategies in drawing

The main issue in drawing a three-dimensional scene on a picture plane is the conveying of depth information. The drawer must decide the level of abstraction appropriate for the task, what aspects of the subject are to be included in the drawing and, most important, must solve the problem of translating the three-dimensional information onto a two-dimensional plane. In a three-dimensional scene, the depth information comes from various sources arising from the light reflected from the scene (Haber, 1980), e.g. surface perspective transformation, local depth cues and retinal disparity. The surface perspective transformation describes a set of rules that relate the arrangement of light-reflecting surfaces to the pattern of reflected light projected on the retinal surface. Texture gradient is one such rule. Occlusion is a local depth cue that specifies the retinal-image relations when one surface occludes another; however, it only specifies adjacent discontinuities. Finally, retinal disparity (motion or binocular) is produced between two retinal images whenever the light-reflecting surfaces are at different distances. Of these, only the retinal disparity is unique to the three-dimensional scene and cannot be represented on a picture plane.

Chen and Cook (1984) suggest that the capacity to draw projectively is mainly dependent on two factors. The first is the possession of a learned repertoire of drawing devices. These devices are standardised ways of representing (projectively) specific classes of objects within a culture, and are ways of depicting surface perspective transformation and local depth cues. The second is the capacity to attend to the appearance of the object, as opposed to its perceived spatial structure, and to represent this appearance on paper.

— In a drawing task, i.e. to draw a picture from a three-dimensional model, children must rely on their learned drawing devices to represent depth relations in the three-dimensional scene. In a copying task, i.e. to draw a picture by copying a two-dimensional model, children who can literally copy the line structures of the depicted object on paper, even if they do not have the specific drawing device in their repertoire, would be able to produce adequate drawings. This is described as a structure-directed strategy. While it might be expected that a structure-directed strategy would generally yield more 'accurate' or visually realistic drawings, the mere fact that a copy is well drawn does not necessarily indicate the use of this strategy. Children with advanced drawing devices which are as complex as that depicted in the two-dimensional model should be able to draw from a life model as well as to copy the object's picture accurately. If children's acquired drawing devices are far less advanced than that depicted by the two-dimensional model, then they may be expected to have difficulties in both tasks, and to rely more on their own knowledge about the object. This is described as a content-directed strategy. A mixed pattern of results showing that children can copy the two-dimensional model more accurately than they can a three-dimensional model may suggest that these children are adopting a structure-directed strategy in copying. Such children may be in a transitional stage of development of graphic skills and are therefore more susceptible to task variations than children at the more extreme stages. These hypotheses are derived from the theoretical premise that, with development, children become less dependent on object knowledge in drawing and rely more on the appearance of the object and the more advanced drawing devices they gradually master.

Furthermore, when the model is a real solid object, the scene comprises homogeneously coloured surfaces whose boundaries are marked only by spatial cues and discontinuities in luminance. In producing a drawing from a three-dimensional model, children would attempt to translate not only the depth information onto the picture plane but also the boundaries to lines. A photograph of a three-dimensional scene which is taken from the child's viewing position is retinally matched with the real model, and a line-drawing model is a line reduction of the photograph. If there is no difference between performances in copying the photograph and copying the line-drawing of the same object, this would suggest that boundary-to-line translation which is required by the copy-from-photograph task would not be a problem. Thus, if copied drawings are superior to drawings made from three-dimensional models, this difference would be attributed to the difficulty in translating the depth information in a three-dimensional scene onto the two-dimensional plane.

4. A developmental scale of depth-drawing devices

Studies on children's representational drawings of solid objects have focused on the three-dimensionality of the objects. For example, to draw a cube, an adult would normally (at least in Western cultures) draw a perspective representation with certain features and conventions such as using lines for boundaries, acute angles for receding surfaces, or T-junctions for intersecting boundaries. A developmental sequence of children's drawing characteristics of depth relationships has been suggested in various forms. Willats (1977), for example, has proposed six drawing systems to account for children's performance in drawing a table top while others (e.g. Deręgowski, 1977) suggest a developmental sequence in which a cube is drawn. It is conceivable that for every three-dimensional scene there exists a developmental scale with progressive stages of drawings made by different age children. Unfortunately, these developmental scales are often not comparable to each other, because drawings of different objects require different skills or drawing devices.

The establishment of a developmental scale on which different objects could be placed, or a rule-based scale representing the development of drawing devices for depicting the depth relationships of solid objects or any three-dimensional scene, would probably be more useful. This kind of scale has the advantage of cutting across different objects and tasks. The following six-point scale, which is generalisable to many objects and is defined in terms of approximation to correct linear perspective, was proposed. Earlier research which helped provide a sound basis for this scale includes: Willats' work (1977) on classifying drawings of a table top, Mitchelmore's (1978) developmental stages of drawing regular solid figures and Deręgowski's (1977) classification of cube drawings. The six classes of drawings on the scale are:

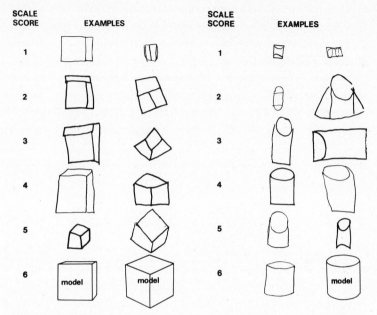

Figure 8.1 Examples of cube and cylinder drawings assigned to each class on the six-point scale.

Class 1. Drawings which reveal only basic defining features, e.g. a square or squares for a cube and a circle or circles for a cylinder.

Class 2. Drawings which show no attempts to represent near–far relationships and tend to represent both visible and occluded surfaces of the depicted object.

Class 3. Drawings which manifest primitive attempts to depict near–far relationships by use of oblique lines or modification to angles or curvature, and show only visible surfaces of the depicted object.

Class 4. Drawings which show more advanced attempts to depict near–far relationships than those in Class 3 and are therefore more similar to the perspective representation of the depicted object. In drawings assigned to Class 4, the top–bottom and the side–side relationships were correctly represented.

Class 5. Drawings which were correct in perspective representations in all respects except the foreshortening of the tilted surfaces.

Class 6. Correct perspective representations.

Figure 8.1 shows examples of drawings of two geometric forms (cube and cylinder) assigned to each class on the scale. This scale suggests a developmental sequence of children's ability to draw a solid object in perspective, and it is

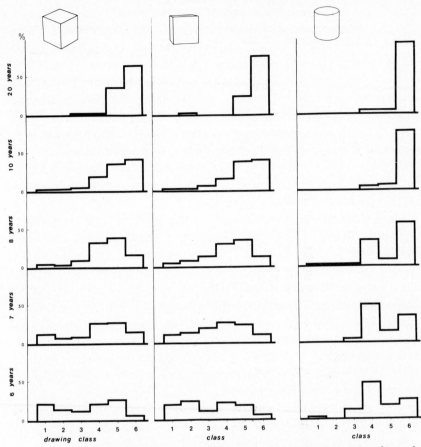

Figure 8.2 Histograms showing percentages of copied drawings assigned to each class for a point-on cube, a face-on cube and a cylinder, by five age groups.

expected that different objects will yield different rates of progress along this scale. A study was conducted by Chen and Suen to test the adequacy of this scale in assessing children's ability to depict a solid object. Subjects were 1,150 students, ranging from 6 to 20 years of age (five age groups with 230 students in each) drawn from five schools and from National Taiwan University in Taipei. Students were asked to copy line-drawing pictures of a point-on cube, a face-on cube and a cylinder. A random sample of 100 drawings of each shape was drawn from the pool of drawings made by all students and these sampled drawings were rated by two independent judges. The interrater correlation coefficients ranged from 0.84 for the point-on cube and 0.85 for the face-on cube to 0.88 for the cylinder.

The results are shown in Figure 8.2. They are summarised as follows: (a) there was, with age, a trend towards using a more advanced class of drawing (in terms of linear-perspective representation); (b) skills for copying cylinders were mastered earlier than those required for copying cubes; (c) performance on copying the two cubes did not differ; and finally (d) there was a significant age-by-shape interaction. That is, the discrepancies between copying cubes and copying cylinders decreased with age. Apparently, therefore, the six-point scale is useful in discriminating drawings at different levels of approximation to the perspective representation of the depicted objects. This expanded scale supports the findings of Mitchelmore (1978) using a four-stage scale. Both studies claim that there is a steady improvement with age in children's representational drawings of solid objects and that the rate of development varies with different objects.

Three experiments are summarised in this paper. The first experiment examined the effect of three-dimensional and two-dimensional models on drawing four solid objects (cube, cylinder, tetrahedron and cone) with two age groups, 6 and 8 years (Chen and Cook, 1984). The second experiment was a two-year longitudinal study with two new groups of children of the same age range tested at 12-month intervals (Chen, Therkelsen and Griffiths, 1984). This study specifically examined the development of cube and cylinder drawings of the 6- and 8-year-olds over a two-year period and observed changes in their sensitivity to the pictorial cues of depth relations in the two-dimensional models. The third experiment compared children's ability to copy a picture of a solid object and their ability to draw one from memory after a brief viewing of the picture. This study was designed to test the durability of the effect of the two-dimensional models on children's drawing performance. Children between the ages of 5 and $9\frac{1}{2}$ were chosen because it has been shown that children under the age of 10 have difficulties in depicting depth relationships (Freeman, 1980).

5. Experiment 1: comparison of drawing and copying performance

The first study focused on comparing children's ability to draw pictures of four solid objects under three conditions: drawing from a life model, copying a photograph, and copying a line-drawing of the same object. Two groups of 20 children were tested. The kindergarten group ranged from 5 years to 7 years with mean age 6 years 4 months. The first-grade group ranged from 7 years 6 months to 9 years 6 months with mean age 8 years 6 months. The results show that older children were more advanced in their drawings (in terms of the six-point scale) and that the two-dimensional models were effective in improving children's drawings at each age level. More advanced drawings were found in the copied drawings than in the drawings of real objects by the same children. Similarly, the copied drawings from line-drawing models were more advanced than the copied drawings from photographs for cylinder and tetrahedron but not for cube and cone.

A detailed account of the comparison between drawing and copying performance is provided by examining the cube and cylinder drawings only. On cube drawings, about one-quarter of the first-grade children and none of the kindergarten children produced reasonable perspective drawings, i.e. drawings attaining scale scores five or six on the six-point scale, in both drawing and copying tasks. This suggests that these children must have acquired the necessary drawing devices and could draw a cube with these devices under either condition. About one-quarter of the children in each group showed copying performance superior to drawing performance, which suggests that elements of a structure-directed strategy are operating in their copying performance. However, there was still a substantial proportion of the first-grade children whose drawings were not visually realistic in any of the two tasks. That is, these children (about 30 per cent when copying a photograph and 25 per cent when copying a line-drawing model) did not benefit from the suggested solution to the three-dimensional $\rightarrow$ two-dimensional translation problem in the two-dimensional models. They were very much 'content-directed' in their drawing. The majority (75 per cent) of the kindergarten children also fell into this category.

On cylinder drawings, more than 60 per cent of the first-graders were able to produce reasonable perspective drawings under both real-life and copied drawing conditions, and fewer than 20 per cent of the kindergarten children did also. Twenty-two per cent of the first-grade children and 20 per cent of the kindergarten children who did a good perspective cylinder drawing when copying a two-dimensional model could not draw an equally advanced picture of a cylinder when they were given a real-life model to draw. Furthermore, about 40 per cent of the kindergarten children's drawings did not differ between the two tasks, both showing errors in depicting depth relationships of the cylinder, whereas only 3 per cent of the first-grade children fell into this category.

Finally, in order to show the extent to which children's representational drawings of different objects manifest similar levels of proficiency or consistency of performance across different object shapes, a comparison between cube and cylinder drawings by the same children was made. Only the drawings produced from real-life models were included in the analysis. About 30 per cent of the kindergarten children and 5 per cent of the first-graders drew both cube and cylinder with no depth features (scores of 1 or 2); none of the kindergarteners but 35 per cent of the first-graders drew both objects in perspective (scores 5 or 6). Furthermore, apart from one child in each group whose cylinder drawings showed fewer depth features than their cube drawings, the majority of children (65 per cent of kindergarten and 50 per cent of first-grade) produced more advanced cylinder drawings than their cube drawings.

In summary, this study examined the effect of three-dimensional and two-dimensional models on children's representational drawings of four solid objects. The results suggest that models have a significant effect on young children's drawing performance. Many children under the age of $9\frac{1}{2}$ who usually draw a picture of a solid object with little or no depth features when drawing from a real three-dimensional model tend to draw a visually realistic picture of the same object when copying a photograph or a line-drawing model of the object. This is explained in terms of the difficulties children experience in translating the three-dimensional scene onto a two-dimensional plane and the strategies they adopt to cope with this problem. Furthermore, for cylinder and tetrahedron drawings, it is more difficult for these children to copy a photograph than to copy a line-drawing model of the object. This suggests that, in addition to the three-dimensional → two-dimensional translation problem, they also experience difficulty in translating boundaries to lines when drawing the cylinder or the tetrahedron. This shows that children's response to the two-dimensional models is also affected by the shape of the object.

6. Experiment 2: development of drawing and copying skills

The development of children's skills in producing a perspective drawing of a solid object was investigated using a longitudinal design. For a clear assessment of developmental changes, it is preferable to obtain repeated measurements on the same children over a period of time, because differences between age groups in a cross-sectional design do not always reflect the nature of individual growth.

Forty children, 20 6-year-olds (Cohort A) and 20 8-year-olds (Cohort B) at the first session, were sampled. Each child was tested three times at 12-month intervals over two years. In each session, the child was asked to draw a cube and a cylinder under three conditions: to draw from a three-dimensional model, to copy a photograph and to copy a line-drawing of the same object. An additional group of 40 children was sampled as two control groups with 20 children in each. They were comparable to the two longitudinal samples in age (Cohort C being 8 years of age and Cohort D being 10 years of age

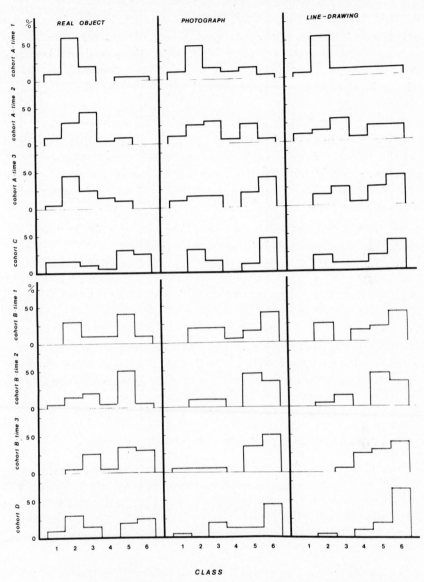

Figure 8.3 Cube drawings over three test sessions at 12-month intervals by Cohorts A and B on drawing from real object, copying a photograph and copying a line-drawing model. Results of the control groups (Cohorts C and D) are also shown.

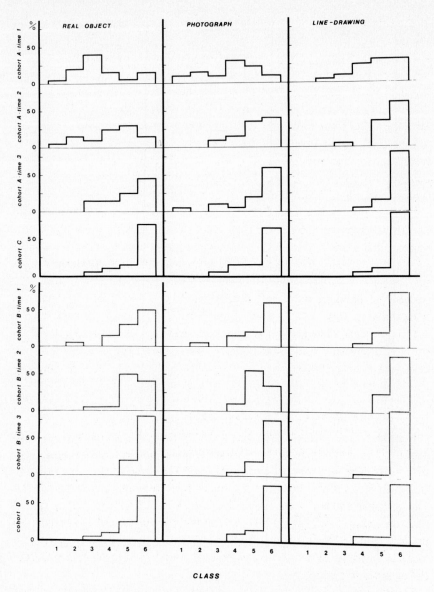

CLASS

Figure 8.4 Cylinder drawings over three test sessions at 12-month intervals by Cohorts A and B on drawing from real object, copying a photograph and copying a line-drawing model. Results of the control groups (Cohorts C and D) are also shown.

at the third testing session), but each child was tested once only at the third session.

The results are shown in Figures 8.3 and 8.4. They were generally in accordance with those found in the first study: the 8-year-olds did better than the 6-year-olds; the copied drawings were more advanced than the real-life drawings; and cube drawings attained lower scale scores than did cylinder drawings. The results also showed that there was no difference between the longitudinal groups and their corresponding control groups in drawing performance. This suggests that familiarity with the drawing tasks is not a contributing factor to performance, and reinforces the notion that it is age which most significantly affects children's drawing performance.

Furthermore, children in both age groups progressed towards more advanced perspective representation over time when drawing cubes from real three-dimensional models. Over half of the children in Cohort B drew the cube in perspective at every test session over the two-year period, whereas only 10 per cent of the younger children (Cohort A) did. The difference between the number of children in Cohort A who drew cube pictures in reasonable perspective at Time 3 (10 per cent) and those who did in Cohort B at Time 1 (50 per cent), both groups being 8 years of age at the time, is difficult to explain. It is probably attributable to a random sampling error of the children in Cohort A, because children of comparable age in the control group (Cohort C) did as well as those in Cohort B. In contrast, on cylinder drawings, the majority of the children in Cohort B had succeeded in drawing the cylinder in perspective at Time 1, and had remained at the asymptote level of performance over the two-year period. This suggests that they must have acquired the drawing devices necessary for drawing the cylinder by the age of 8 years. The fact that they continued to struggle with the cube-drawing task must mean that cube drawings require different kinds of drawing devices. The younger children (Cohort A) also improved in their cylinder drawings with age. Only two (10 per cent) of the children in Cohort A managed to produce cylinder drawings in perspective at Time 1; the percentage increased to 45 per cent at Time 2; and by Time 3, 70 per cent of them could draw the cylinder in perspective.

Thirdly, when real-life drawings and copied drawings were compared over time, the following pattern of results emerged. (Orientation was included in the analysis because correct orientation reflects children's awareness and their attempt to represent the appearance of the object.) At Time 1, 14 of the 20 6-year-olds in Cohort A drew the cube from a three-dimensional model as square(s) (attaining scores 1 or 2); 8 drawings did not show the correct orientation. Eleven of these children continued to produce the same drawings when copying from a photograph with 6 of them making errors in depicting the orientation of the object. Twelve of the initial 14 drew square(s) again when copying a line-drawing of the cube, but only two made errors in depicting the orientation. These children apparently had not acquired the necessary drawing devices for drawing the cube in perspective, and had not learned to employ the structure-directed strategy in copying, thus allowing their object knowledge to take control in what they drew, i.e. adopting a content-directed strategy.\ They had, however, been able to depict the orientation in their drawings when copying a line-drawing model. In successive testing sessions, although the children had not shown noticeable improvement in their drawings of a cube from a three-dimensional model, their copied drawings were more advanced than their earlier attempts under the same conditions. There were practically no errors in depicting the orientation of the model, which was a good indication of their attempts to represent the appearance of the depicted object and of their tendency to employ a structure-directed strategy. For the children in Cohort B, only 6 out of 20 at Time 1 drew the cube from a three-dimensional model as square(s), and 4 of them showed errors in depicting orientation. Four of these 6 children drew square(s) again when copying from a photograph, but only 1 continued to draw square(s) at copying a line-drawing model. No orientation error was made in any of the two copying tasks.

On cylinder drawings, the effect of the three drawing models differed for each group. As most children did not make mistakes in depicting the orientation of the cylinder models and as there was little room for improvement by the children in Cohort B, the analysis focused on the performance of the children in Cohort A over the two-year period. Their cylinder drawings were more visually realistic when copying a line-drawing model than when copying a photograph, and copied drawings from the photograph were in turn more advanced than drawings made from a real-life model. This relationship was consistent over the three testing sessions and suggests that the translation of boundaries → lines is difficult for the younger but not for the older children.

In summary, the results in the longitudinal study suggest that the development of representational drawing skills is a gradual process, and age, not familiarity with the task, is the prime determinant of drawing performance of solid objects. The findings which have demonstrated children's amazing ability to depict correct orientation of the models could mean that they are attempting to depict the appearance of the object at an age much earlier than 8 years. Most children at 10 years of age would probably not have acquired a command of drawing a cube in perspective, although they have, by this age, successfully acquired the skills to draw a cylinder in perspective.

7. Experiment 3: comparison of copied drawing and memory drawing

In the first two studies, all drawings were produced in front of a model. It has been demonstrated that children can produce more advanced drawings by copying a two-dimensional model (either a photograph or a line-drawing) of a solid object than they could in a drawing made from a three-dimensional model. This difference is attributed to the requirements of translating the depth information in the three-dimensional scene onto a picture plane in a real-life drawing task, and to the presence of the suggested solutions to this three-dimensional → two-dimensional problem in the two-dimensional models. If children produce drawings of a solid object in perspective, whether they are drawn from a three-dimensional model or copied from a two-dimensional model, then they are said to have acquired the necessary drawing devices for this task. On the other hand, if children's drawings do not contain any depth features, irrespective of the model used, then they are described as being content-directed. Finally, if children's copied drawings are more advanced than their real-life drawings, this could suggest that they are in a transitional stage of acquiring a specific drawing device and are, therefore, more susceptible to the suggested solution in the two-dimensional model. They may adopt a structure-directed strategy by literally copying the line configuration in the two-dimensional model. If the model is taken away from them, then their drawings may regress to a less advanced representation, because they are forced to rely on their object knowledge in drawing a picture of the object.

The following experiment was designed to test the durability of the effect of the two-dimensional model on children's representational drawings. It involved asking a child to draw a picture of a solid object by copying a two-dimensional model and by drawing a picture of the same object from memory after a brief inspection. All children who took part in this study were chosen on the criterion that their copied drawings were superior to their real-life drawings in both cube and cylinder drawing tasks. Two groups with 25 children in each were included in the sample. The younger group ranged from 5 years 10 months to 8 years 3 months (mean age 7 years 6 months, and s.d. 7 months) and the older group ranged from 8 years 5 months to 11 years 2 months (mean age 9 years 9 months; s.d. 11 months). There were 22 girls and 28 boys, equally divided between the two groups. Each child was asked to perform three tasks: copying a picture (photograph or line-drawing) of a cube and a cylinder, drawing from memory immediately after a picture of the solid object was presented for five seconds, and drawing from memory 20 seconds after a picture was presented for five seconds. The photograph and line-drawing models were used alternately between children for the no-delay and the delayed conditions.

A comparison of children's copied drawings with their drawings produced from memory in either the immediate or delayed conditions revealed the following results. Overall, the no-delay and delayed conditions did not yield different results in children's drawing performance. On cube drawings, almost half of the older children produced perspective drawings of a cube under both copied and memory conditions, whereas only a small proportion of the younger children did (12 per cent for the no-delay and 20 per cent for the delayed conditions respectively). The rest of the older children drew more advanced cube drawings when copying than they did when drawing from memory. The remaining younger children either produced no-depth drawings of a cube under both conditions or did a more advanced cube drawing under the copying condition. On cylinder drawings, over half of the older group and over one-third of the younger group drew the cylinder in perspective under both copying and drawing-from-memory conditions. Most of the remaining children in both groups produced a more advanced cylinder drawing when it was copied from a two-dimensional model than they did when it was drawn from memory.

In summary, children's copied drawings were markedly more advanced than their memory drawings produced under either immediate or delayed conditions. Performances in the two drawing-from-memory conditions did not differ, but were similar to their drawings produced from life models. The present results are in accord with that of Phillips, Hobbs and Pratt (1978), despite the different paradigms used. In the present study, children were shown a real solid object (cube or cylinder) briefly prior to the drawing-from-memory task whereas Phillips et al. asked similar aged children simply to draw a cube with no reference to the object to be depicted. Both studies found that there were more deviations from the perspective view among the drawings produced from memory than among the copied drawings. Furthermore, the present study shows that the difference between copied drawings and memory drawings was independent of age (7 and 9 years), type of two-dimensional model (photograph and line-drawing) and shape of solid object (cube and cylinder). The results seem to suggest that the effect of the two-dimensional model is limited. As children have not acquired the specific drawing devices needed to draw a picture of a solid object (as determined by their better ability to produce a perspective drawing when copying than when drawing from life models), the removal of the two-dimensional model would have prevented them from adopting a structure-directed strategy and therefore abolished the advantageous effect of the two-dimensional model on copied drawings. The fact that there was no difference between the immediate and the delayed-memory drawing conditions lends further support to this view.

8. Discussion and conclusion

The present paper focused on children's graphic representation of solid objects with specific interest in their ability to depict depth relationships of the objects on a picture plane. Previous research (e.g. Freeman, 1980) has shown that young children have difficulties in drawing depth relationships and their problems seem to derive from an inability to perform a translation of the three-dimensional scene onto a two-dimensional surface. The issue addressed here is whether children can benefit from a model which suggests a solution to the three-dimensional → two-dimensional translation problem in their representational drawings. By comparing children's drawings made from a real-life three-dimensional model with their copied drawings from a two-dimensional model of the same object, the effect of the two-dimensional model can be investigated.

The present study showed that if children were asked to copy a picture of a solid object, their copied drawings were usually more advanced than their drawings made from a real-life model. This is attributed to the line configuration of the picture, which suggests to the children a solution of mapping the depth relationships of a solid object onto a picture plane. Phillips, Hobbs and Pratt (1978) found that children between 6 and 10 years of age manifested intellectual realism in their drawings when copying a two-dimensional model of a cube. That is, their drawings tend to show general properties of the object (squares). Phillips *et al.* explained the results in terms of computational complexity and subsequent selection of appropriate or available graphic motor schema for execution. They suggested that when copying a drawing, the internal description created by seeing the drawing as a solid object will presumably describe the form of that object in three-dimensional space. Thus, children will have the same problem of generating graphic instructions in a two-dimensional medium from a description which is not two-dimensional. This seems unlikely, however. The present results suggest that children do not always produce the same pattern when drawing from a real-life model as that which they produce by copying a two-dimensional model. Additionally, with increasing age there is a tendency to produce a more advanced drawing (towards perspective representation) in copying a two-dimensional model than the drawing they produce from a three-dimensional model.

Older children who have already acquired the specific drawing devices for drawing the depicted object produce drawings in reasonable perspective in both copying and drawing-from-life tasks. Younger children who have not learned these drawing devices would also produce the same types of drawings in the two tasks. With this group, however, both drawings would manifest errors in depicting depth relations in perspective or no depth features at all, thus showing the control of their object knowledge in drawing. These children are described as adopting a content-directed strategy. Those children whose copied drawings are more advanced than their real-life drawings but who could not maintain this level of superiority when the two-dimensional model is removed have probably adopted a structure-directed strategy in copying. The content-directed and structure-directed strategies are distinguished on the basis of children's copied drawings and their drawings made from a real-life model. These strategies concern drawing processes rather than products and provide a heuristic framework for discussing children's representational drawings.

REFERENCES

Chen, M. J. & Cook, M. L. (1984) Representational drawings of solid objects by young children. *Perception*, 13, 377–85.
Chen, M. J., Therkelsen, M. & Griffiths, K. (1984) Representational drawings of solid objects: A longitudinal study. *Visual Arts Research*, 10, 27–31.
Cox, M. V. (1978) Spatial depth relationships in young children's drawings. *Journal of Experimental Child Psychology*, 26, 551–4.
Davis, A. M. (1983) Contextual sensitivity in young children's drawings. *Journal of Experimental Child Psychology*, 35, 478–86.
Deręgowski, J. B. (1976) Coding and drawing of simple geometric stimuli by Bukusu schoolchildren. *Journal of Cross-Cultural Psychology*, 7, 195–208.
    (1977) Pictures, symbols and frames of reference. In G. E. Butterworth (ed.), *The child's representation of the world*. New York: Plenum.
Freeman, N. H. (1980) *Strategies of representation in young children*. London: Academic Press.
Freeman, N. H., Eiser, C. & Sayers, J. (1977) Children's strategies in producing three-dimensional relationships on a two-dimensional surface. *Journal of Experimental Child Psychology*, 23, 305–14.
Freeman, N. H. & Janikoun, R. (1972) Intellectual realism in children's drawings of a familiar object with distinctive features. *Child Development*, 43, 1116–21.
Haber, R. N. (1980) How we perceive depth from flat pictures. *American Psychologist*, 68, 370–80.
Light, P. H. & Humphreys, J. (1981) Internal spatial relationships in young children's drawings. *Journal of Experimental Child Psychology*, 31, 521–30.
Light, P. H. & MacIntosh, E. (1980) Depth relationships in young children's drawings. *Journal of Experimental Child Psychology*, 30, 79–87.
Mitchelmore, M.C. (1978) Developmental stages in children's representation of regular solid figures. *Journal of Genetic Psychology*, 133, 229–39.

Phillips, W. A., Hobbs, S. B. & Pratt, F. R. (1978) Intellectual realism in children's drawings of cubes. *Cognition*, 6, 15–33.

Taylor, M. & Bacharach, V. R. (1982) Constraints on the visual accuracy of drawings produced by young children. *Journal of Experimental Child Psychology*, 34, 311–29.

Willats, J. (1977) How children learn to draw realistic pictures. *Quarterly Journal of Experimental Psychology*, 29, 367–82.

9

Some children do sometimes do what they
have been told to do: task demands and
verbal instructions in children's drawing

M. D. BARRETT, A. V. BEAUMONT and M. S. JENNETT

1. Introduction

Imagine the following situation. You are seated at a table, with one other person sitting by your side. This person places a model of a house in the centre of the table in such a position that you can see the front and one side of the model house from where you are sitting. While the model is being positioned, you notice that the only door on this model is situated at the rear, and hence cannot be seen from where you are sitting. This person then gives you a pencil and a blank sheet of paper, and says, '*Look very carefully at this house. I would like you to make the best drawing of this house that you can do.*' He then falls silent and awaits your execution of the drawing. Throughout the time in which you are working on your drawing, he gives you no further indications as to whether he either approves or disapproves of your drawing.

What are the decisions which you will have to make in the course of producing this drawing? First, it will be necessary for you to decide how you are going to cope with the three-dimensional nature of this model house which has to be drawn on a two-dimensional surface. Should you try to use linear perspective in order to depict both the front and the side of the house which are visible to you, or should you instead try to use a simpler linear projection system (for example, an orthographic projection which would simply depict the front of the house alone) which will perhaps enable you to produce a less sophisticated but clearer representation of the house? Having made this decision, it will then be necessary to decide upon the position, the orientation and the scale of the drawing upon the sheet of paper. Should the drawing be placed centrally, to one side, or towards the top or the bottom of the sheet of paper? Should the drawing be orientated squarely on the paper, or should it be orientated at an angle to the paper's edges? Should the drawing be scaled in such a way that it completely fills the sheet of paper, or should it be scaled somewhat smaller? Another decision which will have to be made concerns the sequence in which the drawing is to be executed. Should the roof or the front wall of the house be drawn first? Whichever element happens to be chosen, should you then draw the remainder of the outline of the house, or should some of the details (for example, the chimney or the windows) first be added to the element which has already been drawn? Finally, there is the problem of the door. Is it necessary to include a door in the drawing in order to make it quite clearly recognisable as a drawing of a house, or is it better to simply omit the door altogether even though the resultant drawing might then look a little peculiar and rather different from all the other drawings of houses which you have ever produced?

It can be seen from this example that the process of producing a drawing is not a simple affair. As Freeman (1977, 1980) has previously remarked, when a person is given a pencil and a blank sheet of paper and is asked to draw an object, that person is being placed in a situation in which there is an immense amount of freedom in which to operate, and the drawing that will eventually be produced will be the result of many decisions which that person has had to make throughout the planning and execution processes. Furthermore, the hypothetical drawing situation which has been described above is not a caricature which has been designed merely to illustrate this point, but is, on the contrary, an extremely close approximation to the standard procedure used in research on children's drawings (see, for example, Freeman and Janikoun, 1972; Barrett and Light, 1976; Light and Humphreys, 1981; Davis, 1983). Consequently, it is useful to examine this drawing situation in a little more detail, in order to explore its implications for our understanding of the processes which might be involved in the production of drawings by children.

2. Making decisions

It has been seen that the production of a drawing entails making many decisions. To some extent, the problem of making these various decisions may be partially alleviated for the drawer, in so far as the outcome of some decisions may constrain the manner in which some of the other decisions are made. Thus, to continue with our example, if the decision to use linear perspective is made, and if it is also decided to begin the production of the drawing with a line representing the base of the front wall of the house, then these decisions will serve to constrain several of the subsequent decisions. For this baseline will then need to be positioned, orientated and scaled in such a way that it enables the remainder of the drawing to fit onto the sheet of paper and, once this line has been drawn, the position, orientation and scale of the subsequent elements of the drawing will then have to be produced in relationship to this baseline in accordance with the rules of perspective.

But although some of the subsequent decisions may be constrained by the outcome of the initial decisions, the drawer will still face the problem of having to make these initial leading decisions. And in order to make these decisions, it seems reasonable to suppose that the drawer will take into account any information which he has received about the purpose of the drawing. For example, if he has been told that his drawing is to be used as a test of his ability to depict a three-dimensional object in depth, then it seems likely that he will decide to employ linear perspective. If, on the other hand, he has been told that the drawing is to be used as an illustration of the architectural details and decorations which adorn the front of the house, then he may decide to employ an orthographic projection instead. Thus, it seems likely that the drawer will use any information which he has been given about the purpose of the drawing in order to interpret what is required and hence to constrain his leading decisions.

Alternatively, however, the drawer may not be given any explicit information about the purpose of the drawing. In these cases, he may have to infer what is required on the basis of limited information which is contained in the verbal instructions. Consequently, these instructions may be more or less helpful to him, depending upon the amount of information which they contain. For example, if he is given the instructions '*Here is a model of a house. Can you please draw it for me*', then he would probably find these instructions to be fairly unhelpful, as they contain little information about the task demands and hence do not place many constraints upon the decisions which he will have to make in the course of producing the drawing. If, on the other hand, he is given the instructions '*Here is a model of a house. Can you please draw it for me exactly as you can see it from where you are sitting*', then he would probably find these instructions to be much more helpful, as they would enable him to form a much more precise interpretation of the task demands and they would therefore place considerable constraints upon his leading decisions. Thus, in response to these instructions, he would probably produce a drawing in which linear perspective is used, the front of the house is orientated at an angle and the door is omitted from the drawing. In other words, it seems likely that the drawer will attempt to interpret the task demands of the drawing situation by taking the verbal instructions into account, and that he will then use this interpretation in order to select a response strategy which he thinks is appropriate to this particular task.

It should be noted, however, that the preceding account is based upon two assumptions. First, it assumes that the person producing the drawing has available at command a multiplicity of different drawing strategies for tackling the task, and that he uses his interpretations of the task demands to select that particular strategy which he judges to be the most appropriate to the given situation. This is an important point because, if we try to extrapolate these considerations to children, it could be the case that they have not yet acquired multiple graphic response strategies, and that they instead have at their command only a single strategy for responding in any particular drawing task. And if this is the case, then it would be predicted that those children would produce the same drawings irrespective of the precise nature of the verbal instructions which they are given.

Second, the discussion above also assumes that the person producing the drawing is sensitive to verbal instructions and is able to use the information which these instructions contain in order to select an appropriate response strategy. Once again, this point is important when we try to extrapolate these considerations to children. For it could be the case that children do indeed have multiple graphic response strategies, but are insensitive to verbal instructions. And if this is the case, then it would be predicted that the manipulation of the instructions alone would not be sufficient to affect those children's drawings.

3. Recent evidence

Against this background, we should now like to report the results of three experiments which we have recently conducted in an attempt to explore some of these issues in greater detail. Cox (1978 and 1981) has reported evidence which tends to suggest that the drawings of 5-year-old children may indeed be affected by the nature of the verbal instructions which are given to the children in the drawing situation. However, this previous evidence is complicated by the fact that the different verbal instructions that were used were given in tasks which employed different models. Consequently, in the first of our experiments, we decided to examine the effects of varying the instructions while holding the model constant, in order to see whether or not children are able to modify their drawings solely in response to a change in the verbal instructions. The full procedure which was used has been reported in Barrett and Bridson (1983); the essentials of it were as follows. A total number of 71 children, aged between $4\frac{1}{2}$ and $7\frac{1}{2}$ years, were asked to draw a model of a house which was positioned in such a manner that the front and one side of the house were visible to the child (see Figure 9.1). Each child was asked to draw the house using just one of the following instructions:

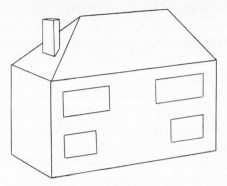

Figure 9.1 The model of the house used in the first experiment, as it was viewed by the children.

Instructions 1: '*Please can you draw this for me. Do not touch it or leave your seat.*'

Instructions 2: '*Please can you draw this for me exactly as you can see it from where you are sitting. Do not touch it or leave your seat.*'

Instructions 3: '*Please can you draw this for me exactly as you can see it from where you are sitting. Look very carefully at it while you are drawing it so that you can draw it just as you see it. Do not touch it or leave your seat.*'

These three sets of instructions were devised in the expectation that, if children are sensitive to verbal instructions, Instructions 1 through to 3 would increasingly channel the children towards producing accurate representations of their own view of the model house.

The 71 drawings which were obtained were scored according to the accuracy with which the children had represented their own view of the house. There were seven important aspects here: the shape of the front of the house, the shape of the roof, the vertical chimney on the left side of the roof, the difference in size between the lower and upper windows, the absence of a door, the absence of any other details such as drainpipes or curtains, and the three-dimensional nature of the model house. A score of 7 for a drawing reflected a faithful rendering of all these details of the child's own view of the model house, while a score of 0 reflected a totally inaccurate rendering of that view.

The scores that were obtained by using this procedure were found to average out at 3.4 for the group of children who received Instructions 1, 3.8 for the group who received Instructions 2, and 4.9 for the group who received Instructions 3. This was found to be a statistically reliable trend. These results therefore show that the instructions which were given to the children did have an effect upon the drawings that were produced, with Instructions 3 resulting in the most accurate representations of the children's own view of the model house.

But although this experiment serves to establish that children's drawings may vary depending upon the verbal instructions which are given in the drawing situation, there is a problem concerning the conclusions which can be drawn from the findings. The house was a complex model with a variety of different features and, in scoring the drawings of this model, the accuracy with which all of these different features were depicted was taken into account. However, it could be the case that the accurate depiction of each of these different features requires the deployment of different skills by the child. Consequently, the obtained results can only be interpreted as reflecting, in a rather global manner, the effects of the instructions, without enabling any very specific conclusions to be drawn concerning the effect of verbal instructions upon any particular graphic skill.

It was clearly necessary to design and conduct a second experiment in which a much simpler model was employed. In view of the large amount of research which has been conducted using a model that contains a single depth relationship between two objects (Freeman, Eiser and Sayers, 1977; Cox, 1978 and 1981; Light and MacIntosh, 1980; Light and Humphreys, 1981; Light and Simmons, 1983), it was decided to use this type of model in this second experiment. It was also decided to limit the age range of the children who were tested to the upper portion of the age range tested in the previous experiment, these being the children whom one would expect to be maximally sensitive to the manipulation of the verbal instructions (see Light and Simmons, 1983).

Consequently, in this experiment, 144 children aged 7 years were asked to draw a model which consisted of two identical balls. One of these balls was placed on a table at a distance of about two feet from the child, with the second ball being placed directly behind the first ball so that it was partially occluded from the child's point of view. The children were asked to draw this model, using either one of the following instructions:

Instructions 1: '*Please can you draw this for me. Please do not touch it or move from your chair.*'
Instructions 2: '*Please can you draw this for me exactly as you can see it from where you are sitting. Look very carefully at it so that you can draw it just as you see it. Please do not touch it or move from your chair.*'

These instructions were chosen in the light of the results obtained in the first experiment, in the expectation that they would elicit maximally differing types of drawing.

All the drawings which were obtained contained an attempt at representing

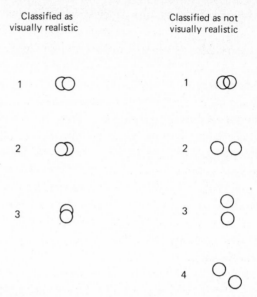

Classified as visually realistic	Classified as not visually realistic

Figure 9.2 The classification of the drawings of the balls obtained in the second experiment.

both balls. Consequently, the 144 drawings were classified into just two types. In order for a drawing to be classified as *visually realistic*, that drawing had to depict one ball as being partially occluded by the other ball by the successful implementation of hidden-line elimination. All other drawings were classified as being not visually realistic (see Figure 9.2). It was found that only 6 per cent of the drawings elicited by Instructions 1 were visually realistic, while 35 per cent of the drawings elicited by Instructions 2 were visually realistic. This was, statistically, a highly significant difference. These results thus demonstrate that some 7-year-old children are indeed able to take the verbal instructions into account when they are presented with a task which involves the depiction of partial occlusion. And this experiment therefore implies that the findings of the previous studies which have employed this type of model need to be interpreted with caution, in so far as the results obtained might apply only when the particular verbal instructions which were given to the children in those studies are used.

This experiment alone, however, does not reveal whether the same sensitivity to verbal instructions also exists in younger children, or whether such sensitivity only emerges at a relatively late stage in development. Consequently, a third experiment was designed and conducted, in which a group of younger children was also tested, in addition to a group of 7-year-olds.

We also included a second drawing task (which required the use of a linear-projection system for the depiction of depth) in this third experiment, in order to examine the possible generality of the findings across different tasks.

Sixty children aged between 5 and 6 years, and 67 children aged between $6\frac{1}{2}$ and $7\frac{1}{2}$ years, were tested in this third experiment, in which two different models were employed. One of these models was the one which had been used in the second experiment. The other model was a plain white cube which was positioned on the table at an angle so that the child could see two of the vertical faces of the cube from where he was sitting (see Mitchelmore, 1978 and Phillips, Hobbs and Pratt, 1978 for previous research into children's abilities to draw cubes). The child was asked to draw the model using either Instructions 1 or Instructions 2 (as used in the second experiment). Each child produced just one drawing (of either the balls or the cube), in order to avoid the possibility of inter-task interference.

The drawings which were collected in this way were then classified into two types. In the case of the drawings of the balls, the same criteria for classification were used as had been used in the second experiment. In the case of the drawings of the cube, if any drawing included a depiction of the two vertical faces of the cube that were visible to the child in the drawing situation (either with or without including a depiction of the top horizontal face of the cube), then that drawing was classified as *visually realistic*. All other drawings of the cube were classified as being not visually realistic (see Figure 9.3).

The total percentage of visually realistic drawings that were obtained in each condition is shown in Table 9.1. A statistical analysis of the results revealed that the nature of the model (drawing a cube as opposed to the balls) had not affected the proportions of visually realistic drawings which had been obtained from the children (i.e. there were no significant differences within each pair of results shown in Table 9.1, row 4). Consequently, the results were pooled across the two models to facilitate further analysis (see Table 9.1, row 5). This revealed that changing the instructions had not affected the drawings of the younger children, but had affected the drawings of the older children. In addition, it was found that the drawings of the older children were not significantly different from the drawings of the younger children when Instructions 1 had been used, but were different from the younger children's drawings when Instructions 2 had been used.

This experiment therefore shows that, with $6\frac{1}{2}$- to $7\frac{1}{2}$-year-old children, the effects of providing explicit instructions to pay attention to the visual appearance of the model are not specific to drawing tasks which involve the

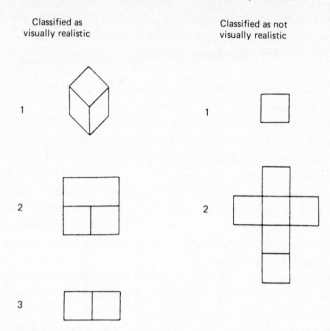

Figure 9.3 The classification of the drawings of the cube obtained in the third experiment.

Table 9.1. *The results obtained in the third experiment*

Children	Younger				Older			
Instructions	1		2		1		2	
Model	Balls	Cube	Balls	Cube	Balls	Cube	Balls	Cube
% of visually realistic drawings produced	0	0	0	0	11	19	65	44
% of visually realistic drawings produced irrespective of model	0		0		15		55	

depiction of partial occlusion: these effects are also present to the same extent in tasks which involve the use of a linear-projection system for depicting depth. This finding, which pertains specifically to the older children, is therefore consistent with the idea, advanced earlier in this chapter, that more explicit instructions can serve to constrain the leading decisions of the drawer, by cueing him into a particular interpretation of the task demands. That is to say, the more explicit instructions used in this experiment did appear to cue these older children into the interpretation that they were required to depict their own *view* of the model (as opposed to, say, the internal structure of the model). And, once this leading decision had been made, the children's choice of a particular drawing device (for example, the choice of hidden-line elimination for depicting partial occlusion, or the choice of perspective for depicting the depth of the cube) was then affected and constrained by the outcome of this initial leading decision.

However, this third experiment also shows that children's ability to select a particular graphic strategy in response to the task demands implied by the verbal instructions may not arise until the age of about $6\frac{1}{2}$ to $7\frac{1}{2}$ years. Before this age, children appear to produce the same drawings irrespective of the instructions which they are given, and they cannot be cued into producing visually realistic representations depicting depth simply by instructing them to pay attention to the visual appearance of the model. This finding is perhaps not surprising in the light of the classic descriptions that have been given of the drawings of 5- to 6-year-old children, which draw attention to the fact that children at this age adopt highly inflexible drawing strategies and frequently employ stereotyped designs for representing objects irrespective of the actual features of any present objects which they are asked to draw (see Freeman, 1972). More recent studies have also shown that the drawing strategies of 5- to 6-year-old children cannot be easily modified, either by manipulating the information which they are given about a particular model before drawing it (Barrett and Light, 1976) or by manipulating the communicative purpose which the resultant drawing is intended to serve (Light and Simmons, 1983). The results of this third experiment therefore contribute a further line of evidence concerning the relative inflexibility of the drawing strategies employed by 5- to 6-year-olds.

4. How flexible are children?

As noted earlier, however, this inflexibility of the younger children could have been due to either one of two different factors. It could have been the case that these children had not yet acquired multiple graphic strategies, and were therefore unable to modify their drawings in response to the task demands implied by the verbal instructions. Alternatively, however, it could have been the case that these younger children had acquired multiple strategies, but were instead insensitive to the changes in the verbal instructions. Thus, the manipulation of the verbal instructions alone might not have been sufficient to cue these children into overriding their habitual, routine strategies. The studies by Cox (1978 and 1981) indicate that 5-year-old children have indeed acquired multiple strategies for depicting the depth relationship between two objects in partial-occlusion drawing tasks; this would therefore imply that the latter explanation is the correct one, and that the inflexibility displayed by the 5- to 6-year-olds in the present experiment should be attributed to their insensitivity to the task demands that were implied by the verbal instructions, rather than to their lack of multiple strategies (at least on the partial-occlusion task). And this in turn implies that the acquisition of the flexibility which characterises the drawing behaviour of older children should be attributed, at least in part, to the acquisition of a greater sensitivity to the variable task demands which can be implied by different verbal instructions, and not solely to the acquisition of additional drawing devices for depicting objects in depth.

It is apparent that these three experiments, when considered together, contain important implications for the manner in which experiments into children's drawings should be conducted. For if it is the case that the verbal instructions can affect the nature of the drawings which children produce, then it is clearly necessary to control carefully the exact format of the instructions which are used in this type of experiment, so that any observed changes in those drawings can be unambiguously attributed to the experimental manipulation, and not merely to changes in the instructions which have been used.

In addition, these three experiments also imply that when we attempt to interpret the results of any given study into children's drawings, it is necessary to bear in mind the fact that those results might only be specific to that particular task and might not extrapolate to other tasks in which different verbal instructions are used. This is an important point, because it means that we cannot simply assume that the drawings which are obtained from children in any particular study are necessarily documenting the full range of those children's drawing abilities, or that these drawings necessarily represent the children's very best attempts at producing, say, visually realistic drawings: it could be the case that if either more or less explicit instructions were to be used, then those same children might prove themselves capable of producing a radically different style of drawing. Consequently, it would seem necessary for us to exercise considerable caution when we are attempting to interpret the results of experiments into children's drawings, and to take due notice of the precise format of the instructions which have been used before we try to draw any conclusions about the extent and the limitations of children's drawing abilities.

REFERENCES

Barrett, M. D. & Bridson, A. (1983) The effect of instructions upon children's drawings. *British Journal of Developmental Psychology, 1,* 175–8.

Barrett, M. D. & Light, P. H. (1976) Symbolism and intellectual realism in children's drawings. *British Journal of Educational Psychology, 46,* 198–202.

Cox, M. V. (1978) Spatial depth relationships in young children's drawings. *Journal of Experimental Child Psychology, 26,* 551–4.

(1981) One thing behind another: problems of representation in children's drawings. *Educational Psychology, 1,* 275–87.

Davis, A. M. (1983) Contextual sensitivity in young children's drawings. *Journal of Experimental Child Psychology, 35,* 478–86.

Freeman, N. H. (1972) Process and product in children's drawing. *Perception, 1,* 123–40.

(1977) How young children try to plan drawings. In G. Butterworth (ed.), *The child's representation of the world.* New York: Plenum.

(1980) *Strategies of representation in young children.* London: Academic Press.

Freeman, N. H., Eiser, C. & Sayers, J. (1977) Children's strategies in producing three-dimensional relationships on a two-dimensional surface. *Journal of Experimental Child Psychology, 23,* 305–14.

Freeman, N. H. & Janikoun, R. (1972) Intellectual realism in children's drawings of a familiar object with distinctive features. *Child Development, 43,* 1116–21.

Light, P. H. & Humphreys, J. (1981) Internal spatial relationships in young children's drawings. *Journal of Experimental Child Psychology, 31,* 521–30.

Light, P. H. & MacIntosh, E. (1980) Depth relationships in young children's drawings. *Journal of Experimental Child Psychology, 30,* 79–87.

Light, P. H. & Simmons, B. (1983) The effects of a communication task upon the representation of depth relationships in young children's drawings. *Journal of Experimental Child Psychology, 35,* 81–92.

Mitchelmore, M. C. (1978) Developmental stages in children's representation of regular solid figures. *Journal of Genetic Psychology, 133,* 229–39.

Phillips, W. A., Hobbs, S. B. & Pratt, F. R. (1978) Intellectual realism in children's drawings of cubes. *Cognition, 6,* 15–33.

10

One object behind another: young children's use of array-specific or view-specific representations

M. V. COX

1. Introduction

When adults draw a picture of a scene they usually draw it as they see it from a particular point of view. Any part of the scene which is not actually visible from that particular perspective is omitted from the drawing. If an object is *partially* hidden by another, the depiction of *partial occlusion* by the device of *hidden-line elimination* (cf. Freeman, 1980, pp. 214–17) on the page is used to indicate that, from the observer's viewpoint, part of an object is obscured by one that is nearer. In a complex scene, adults may decide to temper this convention, but then sophisticated rules are needed to accomplish that successfully.

A general finding with young children, below about 8 years of age, is that they do not readily use this technique of partial occlusion. Instead they draw the complete contour of the partially hidden object. Various studies have traced the developmental progression from a period characterised by the depiction of the complete object to a later period in which the hidden part of the object is omitted. One of the earliest studies was that of Clark (1897), who asked children to draw a model of an apple with a hatpin through it. He found that younger children drew the line of the hatpin right across the apple even though, in the model, the middle part of the pin could not be seen. At about 8 or 9 years of age, children began to omit the middle part of the hatpin and drew two parts, one joined to each side of the apple.

In Clark's model the objects were physically joined together: regardless of one's point of view the hatpin was *through* the apple. Not only were the objects *structurally* integrated, they also *looked* to be united too. The children preserved this relationship by uniting them on the picture plane. Freeman (1980, pp. 236–46) replicated Clark's task and confirmed the findings. He then altered the task so that the two objects still *looked* united, but because one was placed behind the other they were no longer *structurally* united. Of the children who drew both objects in their complete form, most segregated them on the picture plane, thus attempting to capture the structural difference in the array.

Young children seem to concentrate on the structure of the scene at the expense of the way it looks. Thus, they will depict a complete object when they can in fact see only part of it; they will separate objects on the picture plane if they are separate in the scene, and they will unite them on the picture plane if they are united in the scene. Luquet thought that these younger subjects are dominated by an *intellectual realism*. Their way of responding has been referred to, in the literature, as *array-specific* or *object-centred*. It appears, in contrast, that older children and adults draw a scene 'as it looks' even though there may be some ambiguity about its structure (e.g. whether a pin goes through or behind an apple). Luquet (1927) and, later, Piaget and Inhelder (1956 and 1969) regarded these older subjects to be in a stage of *visual* realism; they attempt to draw a scene from a particular viewpoint. This way of responding is often called *view-specific* or *viewer-centred*.

This chapter is concerned with children's drawing of objects which are structurally separate but which present a united visual configuration. One object is placed directly behind another on a table, so that the observer sees the farther object partially occluded by the nearer.

2. The problem of classification

When researchers talk about a view-specific representation of, for instance, one object behind another, they are referring to a partial occlusion. And by 'partial occlusion' they mean that only the visible part of the partially occluded object is outlined in the drawing *and* is united with the outline of the nearer object. The spatial arrangement of the two objects should correspond with the scene: for example, if the partially occluded object is seen over a nearer object in the scene, then a vertical arrangement should be produced on the page. Some researchers (e.g. Willats, 1977; Ingram, 1983) also specify that the contours of the occluded object should meet the occluding object at 'junctions'. There seems to be a consensus in the literature that this partial-occlusion configuration is the 'best' example of a view-specific response, and indeed often the only response regarded as view-specific. It is illustrated in Figure 10.1a; the drawings represent a ball placed behind a block.

The definition of this response as outlined above involves a number of criteria. Perhaps the most important one is that only the visible part of the partially occluded object should be shown. If this criterion is met, however,

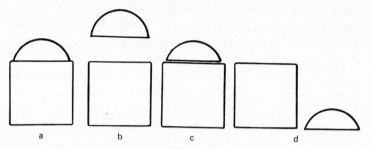

Figure 10.1 Drawings of a ball partially masked by a block.

it does not follow that the others will be too. In other words, the subject may draw the visible part of the object only, but may not place it above the other object on the page (Figure 10.1d), may place it above but *separate* it from the other object (Figure 10.1b), or may unite it vertically with the object but in very close proximity rather than by using junctions (Figure 10.1c). These examples are all taken from my own data. The number of cases of any one type (b, c, d) is actually quite small. But if researchers are to use classification schemes reliably and unambiguously then we need to be more specific about what we mean by a 'partial occlusion' or a 'view-specific response'.

I want to suggest that Figures 10.1a and c should have equal status as partial occlusions. They both show only the visible part of the ball, this is placed vertically above the block, and it combines with the block in a unified configuration. The difference between them is that in (a) the outer contour only of the visible part of the ball is drawn and the 'ends' join into the block, but in (c) the whole visible part of the ball has been outlined, forming a closed shape which rests on the line of the block. In my own research to be discussed in this chapter I have included pictures such as those in Figure 10.1a and c as partial occlusions, but not those in (b) and (d).

It might be objected that Figure 10.1a is more in accord with the way the subject is supposed to generate the view-specific response, viz. by *hidden-line elimination*. The subject is assumed to generate a mental image of the complete object (a circle in this case) and then to delete that part which is not seen. We do not know, however, that this is the way that these responses are made. If they *are*, then one would expect that a large proportion of errors would be interposition (or overlapping) errors; yet children produce very few of these. It might be that a subject may directly generate the shape of the visible part of the object, in which case she would produce a closed semicircle. Indeed, subjects may be able to do either, or there may be individual preferences.

Even if researchers agree with me regarding Figure 10.1c, I think there will be disagreement about (b) and (d). I would feel uneasy about according these the same status, but I would also hesitate to label them as 'separate' arrangements since these usually imply two *complete* but separated objects. Rather than trying to classify each picture exclusively in one category or another, it would be more useful to apply the criteria independently. This would mean that we could talk about the elements in a picture being unified, for instance, quite apart from the way in which this is achieved or the spatial arrangement produced. The questions we might ask are:

1. Is the partially occluded object shown in its complete form or visible part only?
2. Does the spatial arrangement in the picture accord with that in the array (e.g. vertical, horizontal)?
3. Do the objects form a unified configuration (i.e. joined by junctions, or proximity)?
4. How is the visible part represented (i.e. by open or closed shape)?

It is quite easy to decide that in Figure 10.1b, for instance, only *part* of the ball is represented. The closed semicircle is distinctly different from a complete circle. It may be more difficult with some arrays, for instance two blocks, to decide if a whole block or only part is present, since the shapes are both rectangular. I suspect that many drawings of two blocks have been classified as 'vertical-separate' when in fact the child has actually drawn only the visible part of the occluded block. This problem of classification is particularly relevant to younger children. Researchers may need to find out from the child precisely what she thinks she has drawn.

3. Freeman's model of the development of hidden-line elimination

Freeman, Eiser and Sayers (1977) attempted to draw up a model which would account for the main developmental changes in children's drawings of one object behind another. They asked children and adults to draw one apple behind another. From their review of the existing literature on children's drawing they predicted that there would emerge a series of approximations to the adult style of partial occlusion based on the accretion of discrete rules. Specifically, they expected that: (1) very young children would arrange the objects side by side on the page; this arrangement would be the least informative of a 'depth' relationship; (2) the addition of the rule 'up the page means behind' would lead to a separate-vertical arrangement; (3) a superimposition rule would result in overlapping circles; (4) by inserting a 'delete' instruction into this 'program' partial occlusion would be produced.

With age, then, there should be a shift from a horizontal to a vertical arrangement and from a tendency to separate the two objects to a tendency to unite them.

In general, the predictions were supported: 5- to 6-year-olds drew the apples separately, side by side; 7-year-olds drew them with the further object vertically above the nearer; children of 9 to 10 years old and adults drew partial occlusions. One notable difference between the predicted and the actual responses was with regard to the 'superimposition' rule. Very few children overlapped two complete circles; the rate never rose above 7 per cent for any age group. Clearly, as mentioned above, when the objects in the scene are structurally separate, children who draw both objects in their complete form tend to separate them on the picture surface. It is difficult to say whether this segregation is a device used deliberately to get around the drawing problem or whether it is simply a way of relating two separate objects. I favour the latter explanation because, as I shall argue later, in these kinds of drawing tasks children may not *intend* to draw only what they can see, so view-specificity may not be a 'problem' for them.

A main problem with the Freeman *et al.* study was that no model of the apples was actually present. This criticism has been detailed elsewhere (Cox, 1978 and 1981, study 1). Cox (1981, study 2) found that when a model is present throughout the task *and* the child's attention is drawn to the spatial relationship between the two objects the crossover from a horizontal to a vertical arrangement is between 4 and 5 years whereas Freeman *et al.* found it to be between 6 and 7 years. In general, though, Freeman *et al.*'s developmental pattern was supported: horizontal-separate gave way to vertical-separate, which gave way to partial occlusion at age 8 years.

4. Explanations for the young child's response

There are a number of possible reasons why the younger children do not use the technique of partial occlusion. One is that they simply may not be aware of it, i.e. they may not notice it in other people's drawings or, if they do, they may not understand its use. We have evidence, though, which shows this is not the case. Hagen (1976) asked 3- to 7-year-olds to select a three-dimensional scene to match each of a number of pictures. She found that almost all the children matched a picture involving partial occlusion with a scene which had one complete object behind another. I have also observed that children as young as 2 years will interpret 'disembodied' heads in their story books in terms of 'she's hiding behind that tree' or 'she's peeping out'; they seem to accept that a whole person is there but is masked by another object.

Table 10.1. *Copying task: percentage of children giving each kind of response*

Age	a	b	c	d	e	f	N
5	81	5	5	4	1	4	78
6	91	0	4	2	1.5	1.5	82
7	92	1.5	4	2.5	0	0	91

If children do understand the use of partial occlusion in other people's drawings, do they perhaps lack the graphic skill to produce the configuration for themselves? This may well be so. In free human-figure drawing (see Allik and Laak's chapter below) children seem unwilling to use a common boundary between head and body, preferring each part to have its own complete contour. This issue certainly requires investigation.

First of all we can check whether children actually possess the skill to draw the partial-occlusion configuration. I simply asked them to copy a line-drawing, but I did not tell them what it represented. Most children as young as 5 years drew their figure in exactly the same way as older children, that is, a complete circle with an arc joined to it (see Table 10.1). If an actual scene of, say, a ball behind a ball had been presented these responses (1a) and perhaps those in 1b and 1c would have been acceptable as view-specific representations.

Next we can take away the drawing component of the task and instead give the child a selection task. Freeman (1980, pp. 241–6) compared a drawing task with a picture-selection task using a pencil-behind-apple model. He found that children below 8 years selected partial occlusions more often than they drew them. Cox (unpublished data) also gave a drawing and a selection task using a ball-behind-ball model. The results were very similar to Freeman's: there was no difference between the two tasks in the use of partial occlusion at age 8, but among 6-year-olds 56 per cent of the selection group chose partial occlusions, whereas only 25 per cent of the drawing group actually produced them. The results of these two studies, then, show that the young child's problem may be a graphic one rather than a more general representational one. MADONNA.

Freeman (p. 245) pointed out, though, a weakness in the experimental design, namely that the two sets of data come from different subjects. An experiment by Cox (1981, study 3) in fact gave the two tasks to the same subjects (with the order of presentation varied) and found no difference in the types of response given: below age 8 years the children drew the balls separately and also selected a picture showing them complete and separate. In contrast to the studies outlined above, this study found that young children's failure to produce partial occlusions was *not* confined to the drawing mode of representation, but occurred also in a selection task.

So young children understand the use of partial occlusion and they have the skill to produce the configuration themselves in a copying task. It is clear that a problem arises when the child is presented with a three-dimensional scene which she has to 'translate' onto the page.

5. The 'cops and robbers' task

Since most of the existing research showed that young children do not use partial occlusion to represent one object partially masked by a nearer one, even when asked to draw 'exactly what you can see' (although see the chapter above by Barrett, Beaumont and Jennett), I began to look for ways in which the notion of view-specificity (i.e. how the scene *looks*) could be made salient to them. It seemed to me (Cox, 1981, study 5) that one of the main points about partial occlusion is that it indicates that part of an object is hidden from view. I argued that if a task were designed in which the idea of *hiding* was given prominence, then young children might see the need to represent it in their drawings. Flavell (1968) pointed out that even if a child is capable of adopting a particular point of view, she may not see the need to do so. (For further studies of children's perspective-taking skills, see Flavell, 1974 and 1978, and Flavell, Flavell and Green, 1983.) This problem may arise in our study of children's drawing. A ball behind another one or a pencil behind an apple do not seem to be the kinds of arrays which immediately suggest the idea of hiding. So I devised a 'cops and robbers' task, rather similar to that used by Hughes and Donaldson (1979) and that proved to be important in their work on perspective-taking: a policeman chased a robber who hid rather unsuccessfully behind a wall, his head being visible over the top. The child was asked to represent the policeman's view (which was the same as the child's own view). The objects used – a man and a wall – did not pose difficult projection problems; a head-shape and a rectangle were all that was required. Thus, the semantic content of the situation was enriched without the need to rely on verbal instructions (see Barrett's chapter) and, importantly, without

solving the depiction problem for the children. This task was given to children
from 4 to 10 years and to a group of adults. As in previous research, most
of the older children and adults used partial occlusion, but so did most of the
6-year-olds and 44 per cent of the 4-year-olds. Obviously the hiding game
facilitated the use of a *particular* drawing device. We need to investigate how
it did so. There are many differences between the cops-and-robbers task and
those such as a ball behind a ball, used in previous research. The objects used,
the actual instructions given and the procedures followed differ considerably,
so we do not know which variable (or combination of variables) is important
in eliciting partial occlusion.

The next step was to try to tease out the important variables. First a direct
comparison was made between the two sets of objects using the same
procedure and instructions. Some children were asked to draw one ball behind
another and another group was asked to draw a man behind a wall. In each
case, the model remained visible throughout the task. Within each task it was
made verbally explicit to half the subjects that one object was *hidden* behind
the other one, whereas half the subjects were simply asked to draw one object
behind another. The notion of hiding, then, was manipulated in the verbal
instructions with both sets of materials. Subjects within each age level (4, 6,
8, 10 years and adults) were randomly allocated to one of the four
experimental conditions. The results are shown in Table 10.2.

The results of the condition in which subjects were simply asked to draw
one ball behind another (condition 1) can be compared with other studies (e.g.
Cox, 1981, study 2). They are very similar: below 8 years of age, the majority
of subjects did not use partial occlusion. When the hiding instruction was
added (condition 3) the pattern was essentially the same, except that more
of the 8-year-olds used partial occlusion. The man–wall materials produced
partial occlusions from the majority of 6-year-olds (condition 2) and the
addition of the hiding instruction (condition 4) elicited partial occlusions from

Table 10.2. *A comparison of ball–ball and man–wall materials and two types of
instruction* (*percentage of subjects using partial occlusion*)

Age	One object behind another		One object hiding behind another	
	1. Ball–ball	2. Man–wall	3. Ball–ball	4. Man–wall
4	13	36	13	57
6	21	64	31	64
8	67	87	100	93
10	93	100	100	100
Adults	100	100	100	93

57 per cent of 4-year-olds. Overall, significantly more partial occlusions were produced using the man–wall materials than with the two balls, but the two types of instruction did not have a significant effect.

The important factor which produces reliably different effects in this experiment is the task materials. It seems that it is not necessary to present the task as a game nor even to mention the word 'hiding' to the child: a man placed behind a wall will elicit more partial occlusions at a younger age than a ball behind a ball. At this stage, then, it seemed inappropriate to be thinking in a rather general way about the 'human sense' of the task (see Cox, 1981, study 5); instead, I set about looking at the task materials themselves to discover what the important variables are.

6. Manipulating the task materials

To begin with, I asked, 'Can any object be placed behind a wall and achieve the same high rates of partial occlusion, or is there something special about a human figure?' I presented different objects (a man, a bottle, a ball, a disc, a cube and a rectangle) behind a red rectangular block to different groups of 4-, 6- and 8-year-olds. In all cases the partially occluded object was directly behind the block but not touching it; the experimenter made quite sure that the children could actually see the upper part of the occluded object. The children were then asked to draw exactly what they could see from where they were sitting; no reference was made to 'hiding'. The percentage of children drawing a partial occlusion in each condition is given in Table 10.3.

Clearly it is not only a man behind a wall which will elicit partial occlusions; although these materials do elicit the highest rates, among 6-year-olds at least, a bottle and a ball behind a block also elicit high rates. When a disc is used, the rate dramatically falls and when a cube or another rectangular block is used the rate is extremely low indeed.

The pattern which emerges from Table 10.3 is that the task materials to the right elicit partial occlusions whereas those to the left lead children to separate the objects on the page. What seems to be happening is that the *similarity* of two objects in the scene in terms of shape leads children to separate the objects. When there is a *difference* in shape, more children use partial occlusions. As more differences are added the partial occlusion rate becomes higher. Developmentally, the object materials with the largest difference between them elicit partial occlusions at age 4 years, and with increasing age the partial occlusion technique is applied more to similar objects; no doubt if we extended the study to older age groups, high rates of partial occlusion would extend to pairs of identical objects.

Table 10.3. *Percentage of children drawing a partial occlusion when presented with various objects partially occluded by a rectangular block* (N = *approximately 25 in each condition at each age level*)

Occluded object Occluding object	Block Block	Cube Block	Disc Block	Ball Block	Bottle Block	Man Block
Age 4	0	0	0	0	13	21
Age 6	8	6	38	68	70	75
Age 8	52	19	63	80	100	94

Table 10.4. *Percentage of 6-year-olds drawing a partial occlusion in each condition*

(a)	(b)	(c)	(d)	(e)	(f)
Block–block 8	Cube–block 6	Disc–block 38	Ball–block 68	Bottle–block 70	Man–block 75
Cube–cube 11	Block–cube 20	Ball–cube 31	Disc–cube 62		Man–cube 62
Ball–ball 7		Cube–ball 27	Block–ball 52		Man–ball 62
Disc–disc 14	Ball–disc 30	Block–disc 26	Cube–disc 52		Man–disc 62

Is this pattern confined to pairs of objects in which a rectangular block is the occluder or does it apply to other pairs of objects as well? The data for 6-year-olds in Table 10.4 suggest that the answer may be 'yes' to the second part of the question. Identical pairs of objects (column a) produce very low occlusion rates, and indeed there are plenty of examples of this in the literature (Freeman *et al.* 1977; Cox, 1978 and 1981; Ingram, 1983; Light and Humphreys, 1981). When one dimension is changed, either depth, as in column b, or shape, as in column c, more children use partial occlusions. (I suspect that the cube-behind-block condition is a rather odd one.) When more than one dimension differs between the two objects (columns d, e and f) the partial occlusion rate is higher still. The effect is strongest when the occluder is a block, perhaps because it is a particularly effective screen-like object.

If it turns out, as these data suggest, that asymmetry between the objects leads to more use of partial occlusion whereas similarity leads children to separate the objects in their drawings, we want to know why. Could it be that the more similar the objects the more ambiguous becomes the drawing? Anyone looking at my own drawings of a cube behind a cube might think that only one object is being represented, whereas a partially occluded ball in my drawing is less likely to be confused with an occluding rectangle. This explanation does not convince me, since it rests mainly on the similarity of shape between the two objects. Yet if the shape remains the same but depth is changed (a ball behind a disc) this also leads to an increase in partial occlusion.

Perhaps the results can be explained in terms of the way in which children set about the drawing task itself. To begin with, the child scans the scene. If the objects are identical she accesses a mental representation for the first object and then simply repeats it on the page without referring back to the scene itself, thereby producing a drawing in which the two objects are quite separate. If the two objects are different in some way this may prompt the child to look again after she has drawn the first object, since she realises that a simple repetition may not be adequate. At this point she may notice that only part of the 'behind' object can be seen *and* may also make a decision about separating the objects or putting them together, depending on the ambiguity which may result in the drawing. We can investigate this possibility in at least two ways.

First of all we can simply observe the child's looking patterns: we should find fewer visual checks by the child with identical objects than with different objects. Another method of investigation would be to try to manipulate the child's looking pattern experimentally. So, for instance, we could take an identical-objects scene and ask the child to look at the occluded object after the first one had been drawn. We already have a hint that this might be effective. In Ingram's third experiment (1983) he presented one cube behind another and asked the children to draw the array; after they had drawn one cube, he asked them to point to the corresponding cube in the array, and then to continue with their drawing. He found that there were more partial occlusions with this procedure than without. Unfortunately, however, the results were confounded because whereas he had previously used same-sized blocks, he now changed to different-sized blocks. Thus, it was not clear whether the asymmetry in size within the array or the procedure affected the partial occlusion rate. Amanda Stapeley and I have recently sorted this out and found that asymmetry in size within the array had no significant effect on the children's responses, but the procedure was important; children produced significantly more partial occlusions with the 'interrupted' procedure.

So far, I have concentrated on the responses of the 6- and 8-year-olds. Whereas these children did not need the man–wall task presented as a hiding game in order to produce partial occlusions, the data suggest that the younger children may do. In Table 10.3 it is the man–block condition which elicits the highest rate among 4-year-olds and in my previous studies these materials have elicited even higher levels. Most other materials have produced no partial occlusions at all. With very young children it does seem to be important that the task materials and the way they are presented should provide very strong cues to suggest that one object is masked from the viewer by an occluder. Indeed, this revives my idea about 'hiding' as an inherent part of the materials. Nigel Simm and I have recently presented the *same* materials to 4-year-olds, but one group was told a man was behind a *wall* whereas another group was told a man was behind a *block*; further groups were presented with a ball behind a wall and a ball behind a block. The ball–wall and ball–block conditions produced very low rates of partial occlusion (7 per cent and 6 per cent respectively). The man–block condition produced 33 per cent partial occlusions, and the rate in the man–wall condition rose to 66 per cent. Very young children will produce partial occlusions when particular objects are presented in such a way that they suggest to the child the point of the task, i.e. the drawing must show what can be seen and omit what is hidden. A description of two objects such as 'a man behind a wall' may make it easier for young children to impose a relationship on two otherwise separate objects, that is, it enables them to see the objects as a unified scene rather than as two separate and unrelated objects. In turn, this may facilitate a decision to represent how the *scene* looks. In contrast, it may be more difficult for a young child to 'see' how a ball and a block are related; they may be seen as two separate and unrelated objects, and may then be represented as such.

7. Conclusions

At the beginning of this chapter I stated the widely held assumption regarding children's drawings of two objects which lie one behind the other along their line of sight, that is, whereas older children and adults show the nearer object complete and the farther object partially or wholly occluded by it, younger children draw two complete objects quite separately. Initially, I took this statement about children's representations to reflect young children's normal way of responding to such arrays. I then became interested in trying to find ways in which I could *curb* their tendency to show the hidden object in complete form. At first I expected that one would need to use highly salient materials presented in the form of a well-known hide-and-seek activity in order to convey the message to the child that our interest was in *how things look* and which parts are *hidden*. It transpired that much of this effort was not necessary. Six-year-olds responded to cues within the array itself and these are sufficient to elicit a view-specific response. As yet we do not know precisely which cues in the array are important. However, the results so far indicate that dissimilarity between the objects is important and we are beginning to be able to grade this. It may also turn out, though, that some occluders are more effective than others. I suspect that using a wall-like occluder will be more effective than using, say, a ball or a cube. With very young children, say age 4 years, it may well be the case that highly salient materials are necessary; from my own studies it is certainly 'contextually powerful' scenes which have been the most successful in eliciting partial occlusions.

The results presented suggest that the young child first applies the technique of partial occlusion, drawing only what she can see and omitting what she cannot see, to familiar materials and situations. From her picture books she already understands that the technique can be used to indicate that people, animals, etc. are hidden by other, occluding objects. It is these kinds of figures and ideas in the scene which cue her to use partial occlusion in her own drawings. The technique is applied later, and, it turns out, in a rather systematic fashion, to other 'decontextualised' sets of objects, and eventually the strategy is adopted for all scenes in which one object is behind another. The general conclusion of previous research including some of my own, that young children do not use partial occlusion, has been based on tasks which have been selected unwittingly from the 'difficult' end of a continuum; young children are a good deal more 'view-specific' than we have given them credit for.

REFERENCES

Clark, A. B. (1897) The child's attitude towards perspective problems. In E. Barnes (ed.), Studies in education, Vol. 1. Stanford: University Press.
Cox, M. V. (1978) Spatial depth relationships in young children's drawings. Journal of Experimental Child Psychology, 26, 551-4.
 (1981) One thing behind another: Problems of representation in children's drawings. Educational Psychology, 1, 275-87.
Flavell, J. H. (1968) in collaboration with Botkin, P., Fry, C., Wright, J. & Jarvis, P. The development of role-taking and communication skills in children. New York: Wiley.
 (1974) The development of inferences about others. In T. Mischel (ed.), Understanding other persons. Oxford: Blackwell.
 (1978) The development of knowledge about visual perception. In C. B. Keasey (ed.), Nebraska symposium on motivation. (Vol. 25.) Lincoln: University of Nebraska Press.
Flavell, J. H., Flavell, E. R. & Green, F. L. (1983) Development of the appearance–reality distinction. Cognitive Psychology, 15, 95-120.
Freeman, N. H. (1980) Strategies of representation in young children. London: Academic Press.

Freeman, N. H., Eiser, C. & Sayers, J. (1977) Children's strategies in producing three-dimensional relationships on a two-dimensional surface. *Journal of Experimental Child Psychology, 23,* 305–14.

Hagen, M. A. (1976) Development of ability to perceive and produce pictorial depth cue of overlapping. *Perceptual and Motor Skills, 42,* 1007–14.

Hughes, M. & Donaldson, M. (1979) The use of hiding games for studying the coordination of viewpoints. *Educational Review, 31,* 133–40.

Ingram, N. A. (1983) The representation of three-dimensional spatial relations on a two-dimensional picture surface. Unpublished Ph.D. thesis, University of Southampton.

Light, P. & Humphreys, J. (1981) Internal spatial relationships in young children's drawings. *Journal of Experimental Child Psychology, 31,* 521–30.

Luquet, G. H. (1927) *Le dessin enfantin.* Paris: Alcan.

Piaget, J. & Inhelder, B. (1956) *The child's conception of space.* London: Routledge and Kegan Paul.

  (1969) *The psychology of the child.* London: Routledge and Kegan Paul.

Willats, J. (1977) How children learn to draw realistic pictures. *Quarterly Journal of Experimental Psychology, 29,* 367–82.

11

The canonical bias: young children's drawings of familiar objects

ALYSON M. DAVIS

1. Introduction

Even young children can often undertake to produce a recognisable drawing with no model in front of them as a guide. Figure 11.1 shows a drawing made by a 5-year-old child who was asked to draw a cup from memory. The positioning of the ellipse suggests a cup's usual upright orientation, and the handle makes the drawing easily recognisable as a cup rather than, say, a bowl. The drawing is a canonical representation, in that it depicts the object in an orientation which contains the important structural features necessary for recognition (Freeman, 1980, p. 346). The same child who produced the drawing in Figure 11.1 made an almost identical drawing when presented with a model cup positioned with its handle *hidden* at the back. Therefore, while the second drawing was again easily recognisable, it does not convey the true orientation of the cup as seen by the child. In other words, the child has drawn what he knows (that the cups have handles) rather than what he sees (that the handle is hidden). This tendency by young children not to encode viewpoint in their drawings has been widely reported (e.g. Piaget and Inhelder, 1956; Freeman and Janikoun, 1972; Light and Humphreys, 1981). Piaget, following on from Luquet (1927), made the distinction between intellectual realism (children drawing what they know) and visual realism (drawing what they see).

The concern of this chapter is with the way young children draw familiar objects when copy-drawing from a model. This paradigm of asking children to draw from a model taps the children's use of two major potential sources of information. The first source hinges on the *familiarity* of the model; that is, children may bring with them to the situation relevant object knowledge about the structure and function of the object to be drawn. The second source of information is that derived from the fact that by using a model the

Figure 11.1 Drawing of a cup from memory made by a 5-year-old child.

child's *viewpoint* can be specified so that the model is seen in a particular orientation.

The canonical bias in cup-drawing referred to earlier was first noted by Freeman and Janikoun (1972). The Freeman and Janikoun study showed that most children of 5 to 7 years of age drew the handle on the side of a cup despite the fact that the handle was *not* visible from the child's viewpoint. The underlying problem posed by this type of canonical bias is that it seems that presenting a familiar object in a non-canonical orientation essentially acts to elicit an object-centred representation of the object. Young children appear to be concerned with representing their knowledge about the object rather than their view of the object when these two sources of information conflict. The question is whether children will endlessly hang onto this object-centred mode of representation or whether there are situations where they will avoid a canonical bias in favour of representing viewpoint. In short, we need to know if object-centred representations are the only means by which young children draw familiar objects.

This issue regarding the extent of the canonical bias in children's drawings will be examined here by considering some recent experimental evidence. Part one of this chapter focuses in particular on the way children represent a familiar object when it is presented across a variety of contexts, contexts in which the number, type and orientation of the objects presented in the array are manipulated. Although other chapters in this volume also look at the influence of changes in the array, the emphasis here is quite different. This chapter focuses on object-centred representations by using *single*, integral objects. In some of the new studies that I shall report, the relationship between objects will be manipulated only as a possible means of influencing the drawing of each separate object. In contrast, the chapters by Cox and Light, for example, are concerned primarily with how children deal with representing *between-object* spatial relationships. These two issues are quite separable yet complementary. The evidence considered in the second part of this chapter again rests on children's responses to a three-dimensional array but where the array itself remains constant while the task instructions are manipulated.

Figure 11.2 The paired-cup task used in Davis (1983a).

There is a point of contact here with Barrett, Beaumont and Jennett's chapter (above), whose approach is to stress literally to the children, via the task instructions, that a viewer-centred drawing is called for. However, the changing of the task instructions in the present chapter is not aimed at emphasising the task demands, but instead it attempts to change the social context in which the drawings are produced.

In sum then, this chapter starts by looking at children's drawings in situations in which the arrays themselves are manipulated while the task instructions remain constant (Davis, 1983a and 1984) and shifts to situations where the reverse is true; that is, where the arrays are constant but with changing instructions (Davis, 1983b).

2. Canonicality: object knowledge *versus* the encoding of viewpoint

An experiment by Davis (1983a) presented 4- to 7-year-old children with a cup positioned with its handle hidden, as in Freeman and Janikoun's (1972) study. The children's performance in this task provided a baseline for the canonical bias. Not surprisingly, in keeping with the results of Freeman and Janikoun, the majority of children made a canonical error by drawing the hidden handle on the side. The next step was to leave the cup in the same position (still with its handle hidden) but to add a second cup to the array with its handle clearly visible at the side (see Figure 11.2). Will the extra cup help the children with the target cup?

Across these two tasks there is a comparison of each child's drawing of the target cup (handle hidden) in two different contexts: one where the target cup is presented in isolation, and another where it is paired with another cup in its canonical orientation. The comparison between contexts proved striking. Many of the children who had made an object-centred representation of the target cup by drawing the handle on the side when it was presented on its own managed to omit drawing the handle on that same target cup when it was paired with a canonically orientated cup. There is then a strong context effect whereby the presence of a canonically orientated cup strongly influences the way in which children draw a cup out of its canonical orientation. This effect was most powerful for the 5- to 6-year-old children; the 4-year-olds tended towards a canonical bias by producing object-centred representations in both tasks, whereas the older children tended to produce viewer-centred representations. The importance of the context effect is that it shows clearly that children can avoid the canonical bias in order to represent viewpoint. The question, of course, is why these children should shift their mode of representation across these two tasks.

Davis (1983a) argues that children are concerned to represent the strong visual contrast which results from the two differently orientated cups in the paired-cup situation. Children are concerned to mark this contrast and thus differentiate one cup from the other. At the same time the contrasting orientations of the two objects may act to draw the children's attention to the deliberate orientation of the target cup when it is presented in isolation. This hypothesis was upheld by the finding of a strong order-of-presentation effect. The paired-cup task resulted in a high proportion of children encoding viewpoint irrespective of order of presentation. However, performance on the single cup was significantly enhanced if the paired-cup task was presented first. So it seems that children show a sensitivity to orientational contrast which may in turn facilitate their overall appreciation of the task demands.

Given this sensitivity to the visual information in the array, the investigation can be taken one step further by manipulating *only* the visual appearance of the object while maintaining the object's orientation and function. Transparent glass cups (plain-sided beer tankards) were used instead of opaque cups (Davis, 1984). Thus, all other factors were kept constant: scene structure, task instructions, between-object relations and the child's position relative to the array. The target glass was positioned with its handle turned away at the back. Of course, with the glass, the handle is not occluded but remains visible at the back, appearing as a straight rod. Hence the visual appearance is quite different from that of the opaque cup. The results showed that even more children made a canonical error on the glass than had done on the cup (Davis,

1984; Freeman, 1980). Relatively few children represented the handle 'correctly' at the back by drawing it within the main body of the glass. This is a somewhat surprising finding, since the use of a glass allowed the children both to draw a handle and at the same time represent their own view (see Freeman, 1980 and Davis, 1984). Therefore this canonical bias goes beyond a graphic concern of the children to include a handle in their drawing – it suggests the children's primary concern is that their representations should be object-centred rather than viewer-centred.

— There is, however, another possibility as to why children produced object-centred representations of the glass. Some recent evidence demonstrates that children might 'reserve' the area within the main body of a container (such as a cup or glass) to depict the spatial relationship 'inside'. For example, an experiment by Light and MacIntosh (1980) showed that when a toy model house was placed literally inside a transparent (handleless) beaker about half the 5- to 6-year-old children drew the house within the main body of the glass. In contrast, when the model house was presented *behind* the beaker (the visual experience being similar to the 'inside' condition), the predominant tendency was to segregate both objects and draw the house and beaker either side by side or one above the other. So it could well be that in the glass experiment children avoided drawing the handle at the back in case this might be misinterpreted as representing 'inside'. This intriguing possibility was suggested by Freeman and Janikoun (1972) and tested by Taylor and Bacharach (1982). Here opaque cups were used as models. In one condition a flower motif was attached either to the front of the cup or literally on the inside of the cup. In both conditions the model was carefully presented to the child so that the flower was clearly visible. The main finding was that the children were prepared to draw the flower within the main body of the cup when it was inside, but tended to avoid drawing it when it was on the front. Taylor and Bacharach took this as evidence supporting their hypothesis that the area within the outline of the main body of the cup is used by children to depict the spatial relationship 'inside'.

Hence, there may be two main reasons why children fail to encode viewpoint when presented with a glass positioned with its handle at the back. The first is a general tendency towards a canonical bias. The second is that children may employ a drawing device which maintains that within boundary space depicts the spatial relationship 'inside' rather than behind. The next step is to try to test between these ideas in an experiment.

The paired-cup task demonstrated that the tendency towards a canonical bias can be overcome by providing visual contrast. Would the same hold for glasses? To this end the target glass (handle at the back) was paired in exactly the same way as the cups were; that is, a second glass was placed next to the target glass with its handle clearly visible at the side. The results were strikingly similar to those obtained from the cup study. A large group of children who had made an object-centred representation of the target glass when it was single produced a viewer-centred drawing (i.e. one which encodes viewpoint) of the target glass when it was paired (Davis, 1984). Here is further evidence that the canonical bias is indeed influenced by the context within which the object is presented. But the truly interesting point is the way in which children represented the orientational contrast of the paired glasses; i.e. the handle of the target glass was drawn within the main body of the glass. The option was open to the children simply to omit the handle of the target glass altogether to contrast it with the canonically orientated object. In fact, only one child omitted the handle, while the remaining children encoded the exact contrast. The results are not congruent with the conflicting-drawing-device hypotheses. The fact that children were prepared to draw the handle within the outline of the glass shows that, in this situation at least, children are not concerned with this being misinterpreted as being literally 'inside'.

Taken together my studies indicate a strong contextual sensitivity by young children when drawing an array in which two objects differ only in terms of their orientation. This sensitivity was towards the visual contrast. It was also suggested that there is an adaptation to the task demands (i.e. to encode viewpoint) which results from contrasting two objects. If this is the case, then would children continue to encode viewpoint even if the information available to them was conflicting? That is, what might happen if children are presented with another object which they could examine before drawing and which differs from the cup in terms of structure but not appearance? In the next experiment, the target cup (handle hidden) was paired with an otherwise identical sugar bowl. Here there is no visual contrast but there is a conflict in terms of object knowledge. The cup and bowl are known to be different (in terms of handleness), but they appear the same in the way they are positioned. Would children concern themselves with representing this difference in object knowledge? The short answer is that they did – most children reintroduced the handle on the cup (at the side) in their drawings despite the fact that they had avoided drawing it in the paired-cup task. In a further study a black spot was added to the bowl. This simple alteration to the array led children to avoid the canonical representation of the cup and content themselves with marking the visual contrast of 'spottedness'. The results of the cup studies can be summarised as follows: children are concerned to show a difference between two objects which they know to differ – either in terms of object knowledge or visual appearance. The way in which they mark this difference is determined by the context. In the paired-cup array the objects differ only in orientation, so the children mark this by omitting the occluded handle. If the two objects differ in 'handleness', as in the cup-and-bowl task, the children include the handle to show the difference. However, if they differ in 'spottedness' and 'handleness' the visible spot is used in preference to the hidden handle to mark the difference, since this information both is available from the child's viewpoint and serves to mark a contrast between the two objects.

All the experiments discussed so far involved verbal task instructions that the array should be drawn exactly how it looks from the child's viewpoint. Hence, any shift in terms of the children's mode of representation away from canonicality reflects an active decision on the children's part to convey information other than the object knowledge which determines a canonical representation. As has been stated earlier, a canonical representation is a highly effective means of stating what the object is; the drawing of a cup with a handle at the side is clearly *recognisable* as a cup. However, a drawing consisting of two canonically drawn cups simply does not communicate the fact that the two cups are in contrasting orientations and therefore look different. Clearly, even young children are aware of this fact when they shift to encoding viewpoint in the two-cup situation. Underlying this is the assumption that children appreciate that drawings can convey different types of information in different situations. In short they appear to understand the communicative value of their representations. The question, of course, is what are their drawings communications of and for *whom*? In other words, do the children's drawings simply reflect that they themselves know about 'cupness' and contrast, or do they also appreciate that their drawings could be used by another individual to derive information about the scene? This is a truly complex question which lies at the heart of representational drawing. The data from the studies discussed above serve as an important baseline of children's contextual sensitivity, a baseline which allows us to take on board some broader issues about the communicative function of drawings.

3. Drawing for a reason

The preceding section established an essential prerequisite for the evidence to be considered here. That is, it showed that individual children can selectively shift their mode of representation. The question is the extent to which children can convey particular types of information appropriate to a given situation. In order to do this the child will not only have to decide what information is available (over and above object knowledge), but also correctly infer that this is the *relevant* information to depict in the drawing. One attempt which has been made to allow children to appreciate the 'relevant information' is the setting up of drawing tasks as communication games. The basic experimental paradigm is to tell children that their drawing of an array of objects will be used by another person to establish the *viewpoint* from which the drawing was made. The idea is then that the child will realise that viewpoint-encoding is called for and that any other representation would be unsuitable for the particular task at hand.

This approach was used by Light and Simmons (1983), who were investigating children's depiction of depth relationships. Typically 5- to 6-year-old children, when asked to draw one object behind another, depict both the visible and the occluded object (Cox, 1981; Light and Humphreys, 1981). A communication-game setting was used to see if children would utilise occlusion in the interests of specifying the viewpoint from which the drawing was made. In fact the results showed that the 5- to 6-year-old children did *not* produce significantly more occlusion drawings in the communication condition than in a control condition. So it seems that the communication setting does not have much impact on the children's representation of the spatial relationship 'behind'.

However, there are a few studies which have looked at communication games and the canonical bias. The first is an experiment by Vanessa Moore (cited in Freeman, 1980). Infant-school children were presented with a row of cups in differing orientations. A sweet was dropped into a target cup which had its handle hidden at the back. Each child was told to draw the target cup so that another child could use the drawing to establish which particular cup had the sweet in it. Thus the onus here is on the child to differentiate one cup from the others on the basis of how it appears from the child's viewpoint. The results showed that there were *more* canonical errors, drawing the handle on the side, in the communication condition ('draw for another') than in the neutral condition ('draw what you can see'). So, whereas the Light and Simmons experiment showed no real effect on the children's drawings, here children's performance is towards a greater canonical bias. Light and Simmons (1983) have suggested that the effect of the communication game in Moore's experiment may well have been to direct the child's attention to the target object and in doing so to the fact that the handle is there even though it is hidden. Davis (1983b) has some evidence to support this idea. It comes from a replication of Vanessa Moore's experiment using a series of instructions varying in the degree to which the communication aspect is stressed. The overall findings supported the original one: that the canonical bias is increased in a communication-game setting. However, examination of the children's patterns of response provided a clue as to what may be going on. The target cup which the children were asked to draw had a flower painted on the front and its handle hidden at the back. In the neutral condition (i.e. using the instructions 'draw exactly what you can see'), the majority of children's responses were divided into those who drew a cup with a handle at the side but who omitted the flower and those who appropriately omitted the handle and included the flower. The former was the most frequent response. But in the communication condition, a 'new' pattern of response emerges: here most of the children draw both the visible flower *and* the non-visible handle. Thus, there is an effect of introducing the communication game, but it does not seem to be towards making the children represent their own view. Rather it seems that children respond to the task demands by marking the presence of the flower while at the same time increasing the tendency towards canonicality.

— This counter-productive effect of the communication game is striking. How might it be accounted for? In the Davis experiment and Moore's experiment, children had to differentiate one target cup from a set of others rather than one viewing position from a set of alternatives. It was suggested earlier that children seem quite good at differentiating one object from another on the basis of orientation. Therefore, it is surprising that children tend not to do this in the communication games involving a row of cups. It could be, of course, that it is one thing to differentiate one object from another object, and quite another problem to differentiate one object from a set of four others. Alternatively, it could be our poor grasp of what is happening in communication games. *Clearly, communication games do not serve to make the younger children represent their own view despite the fact that they do influence the children's responses.* In other words, while we might see communication games as being an obvious way of encouraging viewer-centred representations, it looks as if this is not the way young children interpret them. Indeed Light's and Cox's chapters (this volume) emphasise the need to take heed of this warning. They contain evidence to suggest that what had originally appeared to be a communication-game effect could well have resulted instead from children responding to a contrast within a two-object array rather than as a direct response to the communication game itself.

One of the assumed 'benefits' of the communication-game paradigm is that it directs the children's attention to the target model and consequently to the orientation of the model. But, as Light and Simmons (1983) point out, encouraging children to focus on the model may even increase their reliance on object knowledge and thus paradoxically result in more object-centred rather than viewer-centred representations. Perhaps then a very different kind of manoeuvre is called for; if emphasising the orientation of the target model is counter-productive, then would directing children's attention *away* from the model's orientation prove more successful? This was the aim of a study by Davis (1983b). Again glass cups were used, so the object knowledge was available to children, but it was given an irrelevant role in the task as a whole. The task was as follows: children (4 to 7 years old) were presented with a row of four glasses, all with their handles turned away. One of the glasses was full of milk so that the handle was completely occluded; one was half full, exposing part of the handle; and another contained only a small amount of milk, which left the handle completely visible. The fourth glass was empty, so the handle was, of course, visible. From previous evidence (Davis, 1983b and 1984) it is known how children respond to each of these glasses *separately*, with the instructions 'Draw the glass exactly how it looks' (neutral instructions). The aim of the present experiment was to investigate the effect on the canonical bias of requiring children to draw the glass to show how much *milk* was in each. Two hypotheses were made: first, that children would be more likely to include the milk level in this task than when the neutral instructions were used; second, that the number of object-centred representations would be lower than when the neutral instructions were used. In sum, it was predicted that by focusing the children's attention on the milk they would be led to draw the milk rather than convey object knowledge about cups and their handles.

Each subject drew each glass starting either with the empty glass or the full glass. The results were clear. The first hypothesis was substantiated – *all* the children drew a line to represent (with impressive accuracy) the levels of the milk. This compares with between 30 and 50 per cent of children who included the milk in their drawings under neutral instructions. So clearly the children are adapting to the task demands with respect to the milk. But what was the effect on the canonical bias? The number of canonical representations of the first glass to be drawn (either empty or full) was the same in this experiment as in previous experiments using neutral instructions: roughly 75 per cent on the empty glass, and 25 per cent on the glass full of milk. The truly interesting finding was that the individual children maintained their response across each drawing. That is, if the first glass to be drawn was empty, most children drew the handle at the side and continued to do so on the subsequent trials, in which each glass with its respective milk level was drawn in turn. Similarly, if the full glass was drawn first, most children appropriately omitted the handle and omitted it on all the other glasses. It is not, however, simply the case that children produce the *same* drawing for each glass – they do not. Nearly all the children accurately depicted the differing levels of milk, making it possible to distinguish each glass from the others on the basis of how much milk was in each. Obviously the children were able to convey the relevant information in their drawings.

Again we have run up against a paradox similar to the one which emerged from the communication-game studies: the effect on the children's drawings following the change in the task instructions is by no means clear-cut. What is needed are data from an experiment in which the initial glass to be drawn contains some milk *and* the handle is at least partially visible. This would allow two possible explanations to be teased out. The first is whether the canonical bias is so great on the empty glass when it is drawn first, not just because the handle is visible (at the back) but also because there is no milk level to be drawn. Clearly, being able to see the handle at the back is not in itself sufficient for a strong canonical bias, since the canonical bias is avoided on *all* the glasses if the initial glass is full of milk. The second possibility leads on directly from this. It is possible to argue that to avoid the canonical bias on all the glasses, the first glass to be drawn has to have its handle totally occluded by the milk. One would suspect that the critical factor is whether or not the glass contains *any* milk, rather than whether the handle is visible or occluded. In short, this particular study raises a host of new questions. Nevertheless, it does have clear implications for future empirical work which should provide answers.

4. Summary

The starting point of my own research was with one end of a previously established developmental trend (children's increasing tendency with age to encode viewpoint in their drawings). Those children who took part in the studies reported here were in the 4- to 7-year age range, and I have argued how, as a group, contextually sensitive these children are. However, this in itself raises theoretical issues which are, primarily, *developmental* ones. And although the discussion here has not focused on relatively minor age differences (for example, apparent differences between 4- to 5- and 5-to 6-year-olds) these should not be overlooked. Our ability to map rather gross developmental changes, however valid, cannot provide the theoretical benefits of being able to pinpoint more micro-developmental changes within a narrower age range or indeed within a given task.

To sum up, the relative success or failure of finding situations in which young children will encode viewpoint in their drawings has rested on the extent to which the task demands have been more clearly defined in the way we set them, and our sensitivity to the way in which the children interpret those demands. Children rely on various sources of information in making representational decisions; their own view is only one of these sources. Young children are highly contextually sensitive; they are sensitive both to the immediate context of the array and to the context of the task itself, as demonstrated by manipulation of the task instructions or the use of communication games. The problem, then, is to establish how this information is organised. That is, when will children rely on one source rather than another? One way of dealing with this is to pit one extreme against another; and this has proved a reasonable method in the work for showing when children will avoid the canonical bias. The evidence from the communication-game studies points to a wide gap in the research. How do children evaluate their own and other children's drawings? A satisfactory model of children's drawings will have to incorporate the social cognition involved in graphic representation.

REFERENCES

Cox, M. V. (1981) One thing behind another: Problems of representation in children's drawings. *Educational Psychology*, 1, 275–87.
Davis, A. M. (1983a) Contextual sensitivity in young children's drawings. *Journal of Experimental Child Psychology*, 35, 478–86.
   (1983b) Contextual sensitivity in young children's drawings of familiar objects. Unpublished Ph.D. thesis, University of Birmingham.
   (1984) Noncanonical orientation without occlusion: Children's drawings of transparent objects. *Journal of Experimental Child Psychology*, 37, 451–62.
Freeman, N. H. (1980) *Stategies of representation in young children*. New York/London: Academic Press.
Freeman, N. H. & Janikoun, R. (1972) Intellectual realism in children's drawings of a familiar object with distinctive features. *Child Development*, 43, 1116–21.
Light, P. H. & Humphreys, J. (1981) Internal spatial relationships in young children's drawings. *Journal of Experimental Child Psychology*, 31, 521–30.
Light, P. H. & MacIntosh, E. (1980) Depth relationships in young children's drawings. *Journal of Experimental Child Psychology*, 30, 79–87.
Light, P. H. & Simmons, B. (1983) The effects of a communication task upon the representation of depth relationships in young children's drawings. *Journal of Experimental Child Psychology*, 35, 81–92.
Luquet, G. H. (1927) *Le dessin enfantin*. Paris: Alcan.
Piaget, J. & Inhelder, B. (1956) *The child's conception of space*. London: Routledge and Kegan Paul.
Taylor, M. & Bacharach, V. R. (1982) Constraints on the visual accuracy of drawings produced by young children. *Journal of Experimental Child Psychology*, 34, 311–29.

12

The development of view-specific representation considered from a socio-cognitive standpoint

PAUL LIGHT

1. Introduction

In this chapter I shall review a series of experiments bearing on the handling of the third dimension in young children's drawings of simple 'in depth' arrays. My concern throughout these experiments has not been with *how well* children draw at particular ages, but rather with what information they appear to be trying to 'catch' in their drawings. The specific content of the chapter, then, concerns how young children typically organise their drawings when asked to draw one object placed behind another *vis-à-vis* themselves. At a broader level, though, the chapter is concerned with the kinds of explanation that may be appropriate for age-related changes in children's drawings. Some introduction is needed in respect of this broader issue, and I shall attempt to couch such an introduction in terms of the venerable concept of intellectual realism.

The notion that young children draw what they know rather than what they see is amenable to a number of interpretations. Take the case where a child is presented with an object and asked to draw it. The child may produce a picture which clearly represents the object presented (i.e. that *particular* object) but which incorporates features of the model not visible from the child's viewpoint. Features that the child knows the object to possess are drawn in, even though they cannot be seen. Thus the object may be drawn as if from another point of view or as if from several points of view simultaneously, or even (as in the case of transparencies) in a way inconsistent with any possible point of view.

The potential for this particularistic or object-centred kind of intellectual realism exists whenever the child has more knowledge of the object he is drawing than is available in his view of it at the time, a condition which may be met with a relatively novel and unfamiliar object. With highly familiar objects, though, we may see a rather different kind of intellectual realism, which might be termed generic, or class-centred. Here the child's attention to the presented object apparently extends only far enough to classify it, and the resulting drawing depicts the *type* of the object rather than its particular properties. Barrett and Light (1976) explored this by presenting children with atypical exemplars of familiar types of objects – a doorless house, for example. They found that most 5- and 6-year-olds included a door in their drawings of such a house, even after being told a story which emphasised that this particular house lacked one.

In both its particular and its generic sense, the term intellectual realism is more descriptive than explanatory. However, in practice the term has tended to acquire certain 'explanatory overtones' which seem rarely to have been rendered fully explicit. In drawing research, as elsewhere, work typically proceeds on a very local and piecemeal basis, and there is little incentive for us as researchers to examine our broader assumptions about appropriate explanatory approaches. In the present case such explanatory approaches may be classified as negative or positive. The predominant view, which I shall term negative, appears to treat intellectual realism as a fault, reflecting some kind of limitation on the part of the child. But it is possible to take a more positive view of intellectual realism, seeing it as a product of a deliberate strategy on the child's part.

Negative explanations are often couched in terms of the failure of inhibitory processes. Thus, for example, Crook (this volume) suggests that intellectually realistic drawings of particular, novel objects may arise as a result of the child constructing a mental list of the properties of the object. The child is envisaged as having difficulty inhibiting the tendency, while drawing, simply to run through this list of properties. The generic sense of intellectual realism is closely allied with the concept of canonicality (Hochberg, 1978). Familiar types of objects are held to be mentally represented in particular 'canonical projections'. Drawings may tend to echo the form of this canonical projection simply because the child fails to inhibit the output of this standard form for long enough to modify it in line with the model (Freeman, 1980, esp. pp. 251–2).

A positive explanation, in the sense intended here, would be one which treats intellectual realism more as a product of a conscious strategy than as an aberration of the cognitive processes involved in picture production. Thus the child may be envisaged as recasting his or her view of an object in order to show those features held to be of significance, in much the same way that an adult might do in producing a diagram or an engineering drawing. Any such explanation is likely to imply a motive to inform, and to treat the drawing very much as an intentional product which *conveys* rather than simply *contains* information (Costall, this volume). From such a perspective the generic form of intellectual realism might be seen as arising from the word-like function of the drawing. Just as the word 'house' is generic or classificatory in function, so may a young child's drawing of a house be envisaged as designating the type of the object rather than representing its particular properties. This of course also raises the interesting possibility that the 'canonical projection' might itself be more a matter of social convention than is at first apparent.

It is this 'positive' approach to explanation that I wish to explore in the present chapter, writing as I do from the standpoint of a general interest in social cognition and a more particular interest in the social construction children put upon cognitive tasks presented to them. The experiments described in the following pages were conceived as contributions to the integration of the study of drawings into the wider field of social cognition research. The earlier, published, studies will be described briefly to provide a context for a rather more detailed consideration of some more recent work. The concluding discussion will return to the issues raised here and will also bring out some of the more immediate points of contact between the studies described here and other contemporary work on children's drawings.

2. One thing behind another

The problem of representing the third dimension on a two-dimensional picture surface is an obvious starting point for a study of children's drawings. Three into two, after all, won't go. In the late 1970s a number of papers appeared which described experimental studies of children's responses to requests to draw one object behind another. It did not appear to make much difference whether actual models were present (as in Cox, 1978) or not (as in Freeman, Eiser and Sayers, 1977). Children from about the age of 9 or so onwards responded by showing the nearer object complete and the farther object partially or wholly occluded by it. Younger children responded quite differently, drawing the two objects separately, either side by side or one above the other.

In considering alternative explanations of this developmental shift, an obvious possibility is that the younger children simply lack certain graphic skills necessary to the production of occlusion. In this spirit, Freeman (1980) proposed that 'hidden-line elimination' might pose particular problems in graphic production. However, it occurred to Elizabeth MacIntosh and me that such production problems would not presumably arise if the nearer of the two objects was *transparent* (cf. Davis, this volume; Freeman, 1980), since in this case the farther object can still be quite clearly seen and no hidden-line elimination is necessary.

To check on this we examined the responses of 6- and 7-year-olds to a model in which a small object, a toy house, was placed behind a transparent glass beaker (Light and MacIntosh, 1980). The tendency to segregate the two objects on the page persisted – in fact the children responded just as they would have done had the nearer object been opaque. Any 'negative' explanation in terms of graphic skill limitations is thus in some difficulties. The results might be taken to indicate that children at this age are in fact simply unconcerned with the depiction of spatial relationships, being concerned only to show all of the objects present in their drawings. However, in the same study we found that when the toy house was placed *inside* the beaker (an array which looked almost identical from the child's station point) *none* of the children segregated the objects in their drawing – the house was always drawn within the beaker.

It was evidently not the case, therefore, that the children were unconcerned with showing spatial relationships in their drawing. Rather it seemed that they might be encoding only relationships intrinsic to the array itself, i.e. those which are independent of the observer's point of view, like 'insideness'. By contrast, the children may be making little or no attempt to encode relationships like 'behindness', which are entirely dependent upon the observer's station point.

Of course, 'behindness' *can* be integral to the array and independent of the viewpoint of the observer. Imagine, for example, one pig following in file behind another. If they are processing towards the observer, the farther pig can be said to be behind the nearer in two distinct senses, the first relative to the observer and the second relative to the leading pig. The interpretation offered above would lead one to expect that the young child would be more concerned to encode 'behindness' in the second sense than in the first.

John Humphreys and I conducted a study to investigate this (Light and Humphreys, 1981) using, amongst other things, a pair of ceramic 'piggybank' pigs, one red and one green. These were placed in file, the red pig following the green pig. Thus when they were oriented towards the child, the child could see the head of the green pig with the red one largely hidden behind it. When they were oriented away from the child, the backside of the red pig was nearest to the child, with the green pig largely hidden behind it. When asked to draw these arrays, 5- and 6-year-olds tended, predictably, to draw the pigs separately on the page, either side by side or one above the other. However, what was most striking was that although such drawings departed quite radically from what the children could see from their viewing position, nonetheless they very faithfully preserved the real relationships obtaining between the objects in the array. That is, in this instance, over 80 per cent of the 5- and 6-year-olds' drawings clearly showed the red pig *following* the green pig, as it was in the model.

It is tempting to suppose that the use of such 'meaningful' materials had something to do with how the results turned out, but in fact similar results were obtained with multicoloured blocks: the younger children disregarded their own viewpoint in favour of a notional viewpoint giving maximal information not only about the objects but also about their relationships to one another. The older children (8 and upwards) most commonly drew only the nearer end of the nearer object, for example the face of the green pig, or the nearer surface of the nearer block. Certainly in the case of the blocks, these drawings were graphically simpler rather than more complex. They specified the drawer's viewpoint, but at the cost of much information about the objects present and their relationships to one another.

These two studies, taken together, suggest that the pronounced developmental shifts in children's responses to such tasks are not in any simple sense a matter of graphic skill. They seem rather to reflect a change in the importance children at different ages attach to the encoding of various kinds of information, or perhaps a change in their interpretation of the kinds of information the experimenter wants them to encode.

3. Communication games: a first attempt

One of the reasons why it is often difficult to decide whether age changes really reflect graphic or cognitive incapacities on the part of the younger child, or simply a different conception of the drawing task, is that the task demands of the situations we use are often rather ambiguous and unclear. Brian Simmons and I have tried to tackle this by using a 'communication game' to clarify and to manipulate the effective task demands (Light and Simmons, 1983).

When we analyse drawings in terms of the information they successfully encode we are in effect treating drawings as more or less successful acts of communication. But we rarely consider who is communicating what to whom and why. The idea behind our experiment (an idea which incidentally owes much to Vannessa Moore's study cited in Freeman, 1980) was to use an *explicitly* communicative framework to try to establish whether young children, who typically do not encode viewpoint-specific information in their drawings, would prove capable of doing so in a situation which clearly demanded such a response. We compared drawings produced under two conditions. In one ('standard'), the task demands were the usual somewhat ambiguous ones implicit in tasks of the 'draw that' variety. In the other ('game'), a communication game was used as a means of creating a highly explicit task demand for view-specificity.

Two balls, one red and one blue, were placed on a platform on a square table around which were four chairs. In the standard condition children were tested singly. Each child was brought in to the testing room and shown the set-up, and the tester and child walked round the table discussing which chair the child should sit in. Finally they settled on a chair from which the red ball was directly behind the blue. The child was then given paper and felt-tipped pens and asked to 'Make the best drawing of the balls that you can.' Approximately 20 5- and 6-year-olds, 20 7-and 8-year-olds and 20 9- and 10-year-olds were tested in this condition.

In the game condition children were brought in in pairs and it was explained to them that one of them was going to wait outside the room while the other made a drawing from one of the chairs. The waiting child would then come in again and would have to use the drawing to discover which chair the child who produced the drawing had been sitting in. It was emphasised that they should help each other as much as they could. When one child (selected at random) had been sent outside, the other was treated just as in the standard condition, being seated in a chair from which the red ball was largely obscured behind the blue. He was asked to 'Make the best drawing of the balls that you can, so that it will be a clue to (child's name) to find out which chair you sat in.' Approximately 20 pairs of children were tested in each of the three age groups in this condition.

Some 90 per cent of all the drawings produced in this experiment fell into one of two categories: horizontal (two balls drawn separately, side by side) and occlusion (farther ball partially or totally hidden by the nearer). Horizontals accounted for over 80 per cent of the youngest children's drawings, dropping to some 30 per cent in the oldest group, while occlusions rose commensurately. So the general age trends were consistent with those found in previous studies.

The key question was whether the 'game' condition would elicit a higher proportion of occlusions (which accurately specified the drawer's view) than would the 'standard' condition. Figure 12.1 shows the frequency of occlusions as a percentage of all drawings at each of the three age levels. Amongst the older and the younger groups the difference between the two conditions was minimal. Amongst the 7- and 8-year-olds, though, the difference was very marked, and highly significant statistically.

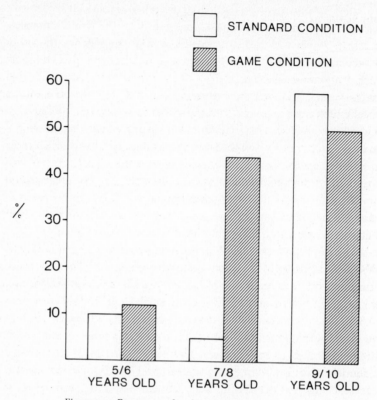

Figure 12.1 Frequency of occlusions (as a percentage of all drawings) at each of the three age levels in the Light and Simmons (1983) study.

The 5- and 6-year-olds, then, disregarded their own viewing position not only in the standard condition but also in the game. A subsidiary study with just this age group, in which children had an opportunity to play the game through more than one round, also failed to show a significant conditions difference (Light and Simmons, 1983). By contrast, the 9- and 10-year-olds tended to produce drawings which specified their own view not only in the game condition but also in the standard condition, even though nothing in the verbal instructions demanded this. At 7 and 8 the children's responses in the standard condition resembled those of the younger group, while in the game condition their responses resembled those of the oldest children. They showed an adaptive flexibility of response which the older children were in effect not called upon to show and the younger children failed to show.

4. Communication games: a second attempt

Negative results are never entirely convincing, and we were reluctant to accept, simply on the basis of this one study, that the younger children could not be brought to modify their drawings in the light of different communication requirements. In the Light and Simmons study, a 'game' condition demanding view-specificity had been compared with a relatively neutral, or ambiguous, standard condition. A more powerful test of flexibility would be possible if a game condition calling for view-specificity was compared with *another* game condition calling equally explicitly for depiction of the objects themselves, irrespective of view. We therefore designed a further study (Humphreys and Light, unpublished) comparing a 'view-centred' task with an 'object-centred' task. Both departed from the pattern of the preceding studies in that they involved drawing only a single object, namely a multicoloured block.

The subjects for this experiment were 40 5- and 6-year-olds and 40 9-year-olds, divided equally between the two conditions. Children were brought singly into a testing room and seated at a table. They were shown two large elongated blocks, each painted in two colours. The child was asked to name the colours and then the blocks were arranged on the table. Figure 12.2 shows the colours and arrangement of blocks in the view-centred task and in the object-centred task. For the view-centred task the blocks were actually identical, differing only in orientation to the child. For the object-centred task the two blocks were actually different, but were oriented so as to present the child with a similar view.

The procedure was exactly the same for the two conditions. After placing the blocks the experimenter produced a very small flat key and, drawing the child's attention to what he was doing, hid it under one of the two blocks (designated as the 'target' in Figure 12.2). The child was told, 'We are going to play a game. I'm going to ask the next child who comes in to sit just where you are and tell me which block the key is under. You can help by making a drawing. He should be able to guess from your drawing which block the key is under. The only rule is that you're not allowed to draw the key or make marks on the drawing to show it.' The child was given a pack of coloured pencils to use for his drawing.

Our intention was that the children should respond by drawing just the target block, and almost all of them did so. The real question at issue was whether the children would represent the target block differently in two conditions. In both cases what they had to do was to differentiate the target block from its neighbour. In the object-centred task this called for a clear picture of the target block, with viewpoint information being irrelevant and

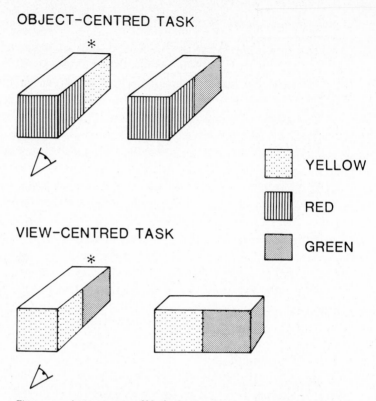

Figure 12.2 Arrangements of blocks for the object-centred and view-centred tasks (Humphreys and Light, unpublished). The asterisks indicate the block under which the key was hidden.

potentially confusing. In the view-centred condition, on the other hand, viewpoint information was critical to distinguishing between the blocks.

Drawings were categorised as side (or top) view with the long axis of the block drawn either horizontally ('Horizontals') or vertically ('Verticals') on the page, or as end views. The end views were divided into those which showed only the nearer end of the block ('End Only') and those which involved some attempt to show the side as well, and included both colours ('End + Side'). The most obviously interesting categories are the Horizontals, which are entirely appropriate for the object-centred condition but disastrous for the view-centred task, and End Only drawings, which specify the view very effectively but contain insufficient 'object information' to be useful in the object-centred condition. Thus effective adaptation to the differing demands of the two conditions should be reflected in there being more Horizontals in the object-centred condition, more End Onlies in the view-centred condition.

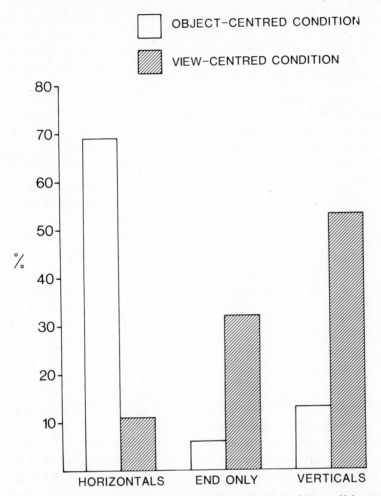

Figure 12.3 Frequency of 'Horizontal', 'End Only' and 'Vertical' drawings in the object-centred and view-centred conditions (5- and 6-year-olds only) (Humphreys and Light, unpublished).

Amongst the 9- and 10-year-olds, Horizontals were indeed more frequent in the object-centred (30 per cent) than in the view-centred (0 per cent) condition, while End Only drawings were more frequent in the view-centred (45 per cent) than in the object-centred (5 per cent) condition. More interestingly for us, as Figure 12.3 illustrates, a similar pattern of adaptation was shown by the 5- and 6-year-olds as well.

The trade-off between Horizontals and End Only drawings is clear here too, but, as Figure 12.3 shows, Vertical drawings were also much more frequent in the view-centred than in the object-centred condition. These drawings always showed the nearer end of the block lower down the page. The children were not 'drawing what they saw' in these cases, but nonetheless such drawings are specific to the child's own view and represent an interesting adaptation to the task demand for view-specificity.

The shifts in response between the two conditions were highly statistically significant at both age levels. They show that the children's ways of depicting the objects are not fixed; on the contrary, they appear to be adapting sensibly to the informational demands of the differing contexts. In this study, then, unlike its predecessor, we had managed to induce even 5-year-olds to 'bring themselves into' their drawings by specifying their own viewpoint. The evidence of flexibility of response, which had eluded us in the previous study, was abundantly present in this one. Less clear, however, was what the flexibility was in response *to*. Since the context of a communication game was used in both conditions in this experiment, we had no way of knowing whether this aspect of the task was an important one or not. Indeed, some evidence from contemporary experiments by Davis (this volume) suggested that it might not be.

Davis has shown that young children will tend to mark in their drawings any *contrast* between two objects presented simultaneously, even if this contrast is only of orientation. The two 'communication game' studies described here differ in terms of the contrasts they presented to the subjects. In the Light and Simmons task, described earlier, the child in the 'game' condition was required to differentiate his or her *own* perspective on the two balls from the three alternative perspectives represented by the other chairs. Thus to succeed the child had to differentiate in the drawing between a visually present 'target viewpoint' and a set of non-present (imagined or remembered) alternative viewpoints. No simultaneous contrast was involved. However, in the subsequent Humphreys and Light study the target block and that from which it was to be differentiated were simultaneously present in the child's visual field. The greater flexibility evidenced by the 5- and 6-year-olds in this latter task might therefore very well owe as much to the simultaneous contrasts involved as to any communication requirements embodied in the instructions.

And so it proved. Christine Allibone and I have just completed a study in which we have shown that one can strip away all the paraphernalia of the communication game from the Humphreys and Light design and still get the same results. We used 80 5- and 6-year-old children. The Humphreys and Light design was replicated exactly, except that the target blocks used for the two conditions were identical in colours as well as orientation. The results were highly similar to those obtained previously. Different materials were also tried out – model trains in place of coloured blocks – and the result was an even sharper differential response to the object-centred and view-centred conditions. But for both blocks and trains the tasks were also used (on a 'between subjects' basis) without the key being hidden under one of the blocks and without anything being said about another child having to use the drawing to identify one of the objects. The tester simply pointed to the target block, or train, and asked the child to draw it. The results were virtually identical to those for the corresponding 'communication' conditions.

Where does this leave us? The 5- and 6-year-olds who were producing such inflexible object- or array-centred responses in the earlier experiments are here demonstrating an ability to switch to view-centred responses. But if, in the spirit of the kind of 'positive' explanation characterised in the Introduction, we interpret this in terms of strategic adaptation to task demands, we are faced with a grave difficulty. If that *were* the case, surely the level of adaptation would be increased by framing the drawing task as a communication game. The fact that this modification makes *no* difference (and we are not dealing here with ceiling effects) clearly seems to militate in favour of an alternative 'negative' form of explanation, perhaps couched in terms of attentional mechanisms. Thus it may be that for the 5- and 6-year-olds a contrast in object properties within the array cues attention to these properties, irrespective of orientation, while a contrast of orientation between two otherwise similar objects cues attention to orientation. Such attentional selectivity might be envisaged as operating prereflectively, and thus independently of any *intention* on the child's part to differentiate between the two objects in his drawing. If, as in the last two studies described, the child's sensitivity to such contrasts renders his or her drawings more 'successful' as messages, it may be more by luck than judgement.

So we come back to the beginning again. Before pursuing this issue of the child's reflective awareness of his or her objectives and intentions in making a drawing, though, it may be useful to provide a brief overview of the studies described and to pick out a few points of contact with other contemporary work.

5. Overview and concluding comments

At the beginning of this chapter I characterised the predominant form of explanation of intellectual realism in children's drawings as negative. The term may be applied more generally to all those explanations of developmental change in drawings which implicitly assume that all subjects interpret a given task in the same way and that the younger child's drawing is best seen as a more or less incompetent attempt at what the older child successfully brings off.

I suggested that against this must be set the possibility that the younger child might differ from the older more in what he or she is *trying* to do than in what he or she *can* do. We do not have to make a blanket choice in favour of one type of explanation or the other: both may be appropriate to particular aspects of the drawing process. However, the studies described in this chapter have been motivated by a concern with the latter type of explanation, and have therefore focused on the information which children do and do not include in their drawings at different ages, and on the extent to which their 'selections' may be sensitive to manipulations of the social context of the drawing task.

The first experiment described (Light and MacIntosh, 1980) investigated the tendency amongst young children to segregate in their drawings objects which in fact were presented one behind the other. This tendency was shown to persist even when the nearer object was transparent and thus did not occlude the farther one. This suggests that such segregation does not reflect an inability to manage the depiction of occlusion. The ensuing study (Light and Humphreys, 1981) used pairs of more complex objects, again one behind the other with respect to the child. The results showed that the young children's 'segregations' were quite systematic, so that while view-specific information was lost their drawings faithfully depicted the spatial relationships between the objects themselves.

It was argued on the basis of these studies that, for children in the 5- to 8-year range, information about the *array* took precedence in their drawings over information about their *view* of that array. These kinds of information are not necessarily incompatible, and many of even the 5-year-olds' drawings will be faithful to their view as well as to the array (as when objects are presented side by side *vis-à-vis* the child – see Light and Humphreys, 1981). But when it is difficult to show the array and the view at the same time, as when one object is behind the other, then the young children, unlike their elders, will systematically sacrifice the view information.

There seems, in turn, little room for doubt that if children at this age were presented with an array so arranged that it was difficult or impossible adequately to depict the objects themselves and at the same time their relationships to one another, the latter information would be sacrificed to the former. A clear demonstration that this was the case would be a useful addition to the literature at this point, but even without it we can see that we seem to be dealing with a hierarchical system in which certain requirements take precedence over others in the organisation of the drawing. The child could not sensibly be said to be at this or that (object-centred; array-centred) *stage* of development, since all these possibilities exist in his or her repertoire. Within such a scheme it seems natural to conceptualise any age changes (towards 'visual realism', for example) as a reflection of shifting priorities within the hierarchy, rather than in terms of newly emerging capabilities. If new graphic skills are involved at all it may be nearer the mark to see them as driven by, rather than driving, the changes in the child's drawing practices.

There are in fact a number of recent indications that the use of partial occlusion with 'hidden-line elimination' is not in any case confined to children over 7 or 8. In a study by Smith and Brown (1982) two balls were placed one *partly* behind the other, and children were given highly explicit instructions of the type 'You can't see all of this ball, can you? Draw exactly what you see.' This elicited quite high frequencies of view-specific partial occlusion from children as young as 4 and 5. Cox (1981) reported a study in which she explored the effects of imbuing the spatial relationship between objects with 'human sense', using a cops-and-robbers format. Many children even as young as 4 responded by producing partial-occlusion drawings. However, it is not clear what aspects of the task were important. As in the Smith and Brown study, objects were deliberately *partly* overlapping, and in this case they were also of very different shapes. An unpublished study by Teresa Foot and myself suggests that the element of 'human sense' provided by the cops-and-robbers format is actually relatively unimportant. Cox, in her chapter in this volume, reports new evidence on the apparently complex factors influencing the prevalence of partial-occlusion drawings. One might suggest that if 'human sense' is involved here, it is at the level of the 'sense' in which the child takes the task.

However this may be, all of these studies suggest that the very low levels of partial occlusion observed in some of the studies reported here and in earlier studies such as Cox (1978) and Freeman, Eiser and Sayers (1977) may be the exception rather than the rule. In all these cases two similar objects were placed one directly behind the other *vis-à-vis* the child. It may be that this particular configuration generates a high degree of uncertainty on the child's part as to what is expected of him. If so, the child's performance could be expected to show a high degree of contextual sensitivity. It should thus be possible to clarify the basis of this performance not only by varying the *content* of the drawing task, as in the studies mentioned in the preceding paragraph, but also by varying its *context*. Indeed, from this standpoint our 'communication game' studies might best be seen as attempts to disambiguate the task by manipulating the context, rather than the content, of the drawing task.

In the Light and Simmons (1983) study the 7- and 8-year-olds behaved just as we had expected, showing little concern for view information in the standard task, but accommodating to the need to convey this information in the communication game. Five- and 6-year-olds, however, failed to accommodate in this way.

Barrett, Beaumont and Jennett (1983) have obtained similar results simply by varying the instructions children were given. Children aged $6\frac{1}{2}$ to $7\frac{1}{2}$ tended not to encode their own view in their drawings given relatively neutral instructions but shifted their response towards view-specificity when given highly explicit instructions to do so. The younger children (5 to 6), however, failed to encode their own view and were quite unaffected by instructions. In both of these studies, therefore, the difference between the 5-year-olds and the 7-year-olds is not so much in their preferred mode of drawings as in their flexibility of response to varying task demands.

Our attempts to improve on the communication-game design (Humphreys and Light) provided unexpectedly clear evidence of flexibility in the 5- and 6-year-olds. However, as our subsequent replication and extension of this study have made clear, this flexibility was in response to the contrasts provided by the objects within the arrays rather than in response to any explicit demand to differentiate the objects for the purposes of communication. As was pointed out earlier, this finding is at least consistent with the notion that the visual contrasts in the array might directly affect the child's perceptual encoding of the array (cf. Crook, this volume). No reflective awareness of alternatives need necessarily be imputed to the child.

The insensitivity of 5- and 6-year-olds to manipulations of the instructions and social context of the drawing task is doubtless relative rather than absolute, but it is striking nonetheless. These children, though clearly possessing a good deal of tacit know-how about drawing and showing responsiveness to the characteristics and contrasts of the presented array, may perhaps have little explicit knowledge about their drawings. The findings are reminiscent of those of the Robinsons (e.g. Robinson and Robinson, 1981; Robinson, 1983) on verbal communication abilities in the same age range. Five- and 6-year-olds have well-developed verbal communication skills in naturalistic situations, but what the Robinsons term their 'metacommunicative knowledge' seems very limited. For example, in structured testing situations, where communication fails the children regularly blame the recipient of the message rather than the message itself, even when the message is ambiguous or misleading. They seem to have little explicit awareness of what is involved in formulating an effective message.

This issue of 'metacognitive awareness' (Lefebvre-Pinard, 1983; Robinson,

1983) is of course closely bound up with the concept of egocentrism. Piaget (at least in his better moments), along with Vygotsky and Mead, characterises the young 'egocentric' child as being fundamentally unconcerned with points of view, lacking in awareness as much of his own point of view as of any other, and engaged in the world in an essentially pre-reflective fashion. Piaget has blotted his copybook by using the concept of egocentrism in quite other and indefensible ways, but Mead and especially Vygotsky have provided the theoretical backcloth for much of the recent work in social cognition. The process of development is increasingly being construed as a matter of growing reflective self-awareness, growing awareness both of alternative courses of action and of the relativity of points of view. This interpretative stance finds at least an echo in the work reported here on children's drawings.

This is not an ending, of course, merely a holding position. In offering the inevitable conclusion that more work is needed it is a pleasing (if uncomfortable) thought that, given the vigour with which research in this area is being pursued at present, the 'more work' may already have been done before the present work comes to press.

REFERENCES

Barrett, M. D., Beaumont, A. & Jennett, M. (1983) The effect of instructions upon the representation of depth in children's drawings. Paper presented at the Conference on Graphic Representation, University of York, April.
Barrett, M. D. & Light, P. H. (1976) Symbolism and intellectual realism in children's drawings. *British Journal of Educational Psychology*, 46, 198–202.
Cox, M. (1978) Spatial depth relationships in young children's drawings. *Journal of Experimental Child Psychology*, 26, 551–4.
   (1981) One thing behind another: Problems of representation in children's drawings. *Educational Psychology*, 1, 275–87.
Freeman, N. H. (1980) *Strategies of representation in young children*. London: Academic Press.
Freeman, N. H., Eiser, D. & Sayers, T. (1977) Children's strategies in producing three-dimensional relationships on a two-dimensional surface. *Journal of Experimental Child Psychology*, 23, 305–14.
Hochberg, J. (1978) *Perception*. 2nd ed. Englewood Cliffs, N.J.: Prentice-Hall.
Lefebvre-Pinard, M. (1983) Understanding and autocontrol of cognitive functions. *International Journal of Behavioural Development*, 6, 15–35.
Light, P. H. & Humphreys, J. (1981) Internal spatial relationships in young children's drawings. *Journal of Experimental Child Psychology*, 31, 521–30.
Light, P. H. & MacIntosh, E. (1980) Depth relationships in young children's drawings. *Journal of Experimental Child Psychology*, 30, 79–87.
Light, P. H. & Simmons, B. (1983) The effect of a communication task upon the representation of depth relationships in young children's drawings. *Journal of Experimental Child Psychology*, 35, 81–92.

Robinson, E. (1983) Metacognitive development. In S. Meadows (ed.), *Developing thinking*. London: Methuen.

Robinson, E. & Robinson, W. (1981) Ways of reacting to communication failure in relation to the development of the child's understanding about verbal communication. *European Journal of Social Psychology*, 11, 189–208.

Smith, P. & Brown, J. (1982) Eliciting drawings of partial occlusion from young children. Paper presented at the Conference on Graphic Representation, University of York, April.

13

Three into two won't go: symbolic and spatial coding processes in young children's drawings

NIGEL INGRAM

1. Introduction

In this chapter I shall report the results of comparisons made between two experiments, both of which were part of an interlinking series of six studies designed to establish how children between 3 and 8 years represent three-dimensional spatial relationships on a two-dimensional picture surface (Ingram, 1983). The results of the comparisons suggest two coding processes for representation: a *symbolic code* which is consistent with Luquet's theory of intellectual realism, and a series of *view-specific* spatial codes not predicted by Luquet's theory. Both these codes may be available to young children, but only become integrated between 5 and 7 years. This suggests that Luquet's (1913 and 1927) theory concerning the developmental transition from intellectual to visual realism may have to be modified, since even very young children can draw what they see, from where they see it.

The results from a number of experiments reported in the literature suggest that attempts to represent the partial occlusion of a further object by a nearer one are infrequent in the drawings of young children and that they typically draw the objects separate, side by side, or vertically one above the other (Freeman, Eiser and Sayers, 1977; Light and MacIntosh, 1980; Ingram, 1980 and 1983).

Several explanations of this phenomenon have been put forward. A first hypothesis is that these drawings may be explained by reference to Luquet's (1913 and 1927) theory concerning the developmental transition from intellectual to visual realism. Luquet asserted that there is a general tendency for conceptual knowledge, which involves some kind of stereotypic mental description of the objects being depicted (intellectual realism) to dominate young children's drawings. The drawings produced by children in the experiments reported by Freeman *et al.* and by Cox (1978) may be said to belong to the stage of intellectual realism, in that the children draw what they 'know' of the objects rather than what they see. They draw what they know in the sense that the objects being represented evoke some kind of mental description of an already acquired concept. A child may not occlude the farther object in his/her drawing, since to do so would involve breaking into an already occupied space on the paper. The child 'knows' that this does not occur in the real world, where one object can occupy only one place at one time. Such an explanation of the vertical or horizontal depiction of an 'in-depth' array emphasises the conceptual status of the child.

The development of children's drawings may also be related to the work of Piaget and Inhelder (1969), who adopted Luquet's stages of development and incorporated them into their own theory. They linked intellectual realism with the topological phase, and visual realism with the projective and Euclidean phases of the development of spatial intelligence. Drawings produced by younger children are said to be topological representations: topological in the sense that objects are represented on a page as separate, but in proximity to each other. Furthermore, Piaget and Inhelder maintained that the drawings may be considered to be topological, since they reflect an inability to draw from one fixed viewpoint. Such an approach treats children's drawings as spatial representations in their own right, albeit at different developmental stages.

A view similar to that of Piaget and Inhelder is held by Willats (1977 and 1981), who describes children's drawings in terms of 'drawing systems'. Willats' theory is a more sophisticated account of Piaget's, and similar in that he also linked children's drawings with the development of an 'object-centred' topological phase, i.e. objects are drawn largely irrespective of the child's viewing position, through to axonometric perspective projections, where the child uses Euclidean rules to depict 'view-centred' information vis-à-vis the child's line of sight. Like Piaget, Willats also claims that children's drawings are rule-governed, and that the child has to learn these geometric rules before he/she can successfully represent three-dimensional spatial relations on a two-dimensional picture surface. An interesting feature of Willats' (1981) work is his assertion that depicting objects in depth from a particular viewing position involves hidden-line elimination (H.L.E.) in the drawings (a term first used in computer graphics by Marr (1977) to refer to points where lines meet or cross in the objects being represented). The ability to omit lines and form junction points is, Willats maintains, an essential skill for the realistic portrayal of spatial depth relations. Willats' work is important, since his drawing taxonomy provides a useful classificatory system for the analysis of children's drawings.

A further theory not unrelated to Willats' account is suggested by Light and MacIntosh (1980), Light and Humphreys (1981) and Light and Simmons (1983). They tend to stress the social and communicative aspects of children's drawing and suggest that the vertically or horizontally orientated drawings of objects presented in depth reflect the children's concern to show array-specific information, largely irrespective of their viewing position. In their experiments the authors showed that there was an age-related change from depicting array-specific information to showing view-specific information when the apparent relationship between the objects is seen from a particular viewpoint. Light and Humphreys (1981) also claim that younger children, when depicting array-specific information, i.e. when depicting objects presented in depth as vertical or horizontal separate, are, in fact, unconcerned with, or insensitive to, perspective differences in the model.

Another theory is that children are unable to portray a spatial depth relation by partial occlusion of the further object by the nearer one, because they lack technical competence and have organisational difficulties (Berman, 1976; Freeman, 1980). According to this view, children draw objects separately, in either a vertical or horizontal orientation, because they lack the graphic or organisational skills needed to integrate the objects. Finally, it has been suggested that the possible symbolic content of the objects being drawn, the media used and the instructions given all trigger off the use of different coding processes by children in the representation of the spatial orientation of objects (Gesell and Ames, 1946; Bassett, 1976; Cox, 1978; Freeman, 1980; Light and Humphreys, 1981). For example, it is well established, particularly by Freeman, that young children generally draw the human figure in a vertical orientation and in a frontal position on the paper, and draw cars and animals in side view. Does this mean that children rotate objects irrespective of the orientation and relative positions in which the objects are presented in order to preserve the canonical form of the objects being drawn? Furthermore, to what extent does the symbolic content of the presented objects affect their representation?

2. Canonical orientation and stereotypic representations

The experiments to be reported here present evidence for the *simultaneous availability of two types of coding processes* among children as young as 3 years. This claim is based on the results of comparisons made between two experiments, one of which was specifically designed to study the effects of canonicality on the representation of spatial orientation in drawing. According to Freeman (1980, p. 345) the word 'canonical' refers to 'an optimal method of conveying basic structural information'. Thus, in this description of a process, a canonical representation of an object is one in which an object is drawn in a specific orientation, containing the salient 'core' features of that object or array. For example, the human figure is typically drawn in a vertical and fronted position, a car is drawn in side view and a beer glass or cup will include a handle, although the handle may, at the time of drawing, be hidden from the child's line of sight. A number of studies have addressed the issue of canonical representations in children's drawings (e.g. Freeman and Janikoun, 1972; Bassett, 1976; Freeman, 1980; Davis, 1983). The results from several of these studies indicate that, first, children may not necessarily produce canonical representations of objects. Indeed, canonicality may be avoided in order to differentiate between two similar objects which often differ only in terms of their orientation (see Davis' chapter above). Second, the studies cited raise the question of context: what sources of information are available to children in drawing tasks and the situations under which they will rely on one source rather than another? For example, to what extent does the *symbolic* content of the presented arrays affect their representation?

One explanation which may account for the phenomenon of canonicality is that of intellectual realism. For example, are the drawings of figures, cups and cars stereotypic representations triggered off by having an obvious connection with a previously acquired concept? Historically the concept of stereotypes in drawing is often discussed within the context of Luquet's theory concerning the developmental transition from intellectual to visual realism. A good example of the transition from intellectual to visual realism involving some kind of stereotypic mental image is cited by Freeman and Janikoun (1972). Children were asked to draw a cup with a flower on the front, which was presented in such a way that the handle of the cup was hidden from view. They found that children below 8 years made drawings which included the handle (the hidden feature) but omitted the flower, whilst the older children included the flower but omitted the handle. Freeman and Janikoun explained that the cup was a functional, familiar object with a distinctive feature (the handle), for which the children might have a stereotypic mental equivalent. They therefore suggested that one reason why the younger children included the non-visible handle might be that they were responding to the cup by producing a stereotype (intellectual realism). The older children included the flower because they were drawing what they could see from one viewpoint (visual realism). Another related reason might be that the younger children included the non-visible handle, because otherwise the drawing might not be recognised as representing a cup. In this sense, the drawing of the cup was a stereotype brought about by having an obvious connection with an already acquired concept.

3. The experimental evidence

It was noted in the Introduction that each of the experiments to be reported here forms part of an interlinking series of six studies designed to establish how young children represent three-dimensional spatial relationships on a two-dimensional picture surface (Ingram, 1983).

In each successive experiment an additional cue was added to the model to be drawn by the children, and all the experiments were interlinked through a constant control condition, usually a vertical (pile) or in-depth (file) condition. This permitted crucial comparisons to be made within and between the drawings of the array relative to the control.

In Experiment 1 two plain-faced but different-sized blocks, joined by a bridging pin, were presented to the children in four sets of spatial relations. In Experiment 2, doll-like features were added to the smaller of the two blocks and presented in the same spatial configurations. Comparisons were made between the experiments to establish the effects of this controlled change to the model on the children's drawings (see Figure 13.1). One of the main purposes of Experiment 2 was to discover whether adding doll-like features to the previously plain-faced blocks would induce the children to preserve the canonical form of the doll, and, if so, how would they achieve this?

Plain-faced, neutral blocks were used in Experiment 1 since they lacked any socially recognisable and familiar features, familiar for example in the sense that the cup was functionally familiar to the children in Freeman and Janikoun's study. Although it may be argued that neutral blocks have symbolic uses (they may be used to represent houses) and that children perhaps 'know' them in a topological sense, plain-faced blocks have no particular connections with already acquired concepts. For example, although the vertical drawings (see Table 13.1) may be classed as stereotypes of blocks, i.e. they are typical ways of representing blocks, the blocks are not seen as representative of something *else* – they represent blocks, whereas doll-like features have direct symbolic connotations, the presence of which may (and did) radically change the children's depictions of the model.

A total of 60 children in five age groups served as subjects for each separate experiment. There were 12 subjects in each age grouping: 3–4, 4–5, 5–6, 6–7 and 7–8 years (six male and six female in each).

In Experiment 1, the children were shown two plain wooden blocks, one

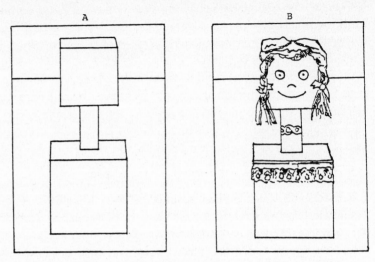

Figure 13.1 Arrays presented in various orientations for children to draw.

Table 13.1. *Categorisation of children's drawings by age of the non-featured and featured arrays presented in file: Small Front.*

(EXPERIMENT 1)   N = 60   AGE : YEARS

ARRAY	CATEGORY	3	4	5	6	7	TOTAL
File	VERTICAL: Large Top*	7	5	0	0	0	12
	Large Top	2	2	7	3	0	14
	OCCLUSION: Small Front	3	5	5	9	12	34

(Non-featured)

VISUAL SUMMARY

Bridge Pin Omitted

Vertical:
Bottom Small First
Top Large Second
Bridge Pin Third

Partial Occlusion:
Small Front First
Bridge Pin Second
Large Back Third

(EXPERIMENT 2)   N = 60

File	TADPOLE: Small Only	7	1	0	0	0	8
	VERTICAL: Small Top	4	8	4	1	0	17
	Large Top	1	3	6	5	1	16
	OCCLUSION: Small Front	0	0	2	6	11	19

(Featured)

VISUAL SUMMARY

Tadpole Stereo-type

Small Top First, Features 2nd, Large Bottom 3rd

Small Bottom First
Large Top Second
Features Last

Partial Occlusion:
Small Front First
Large Back Second
Features Last

*Bridge-pin omitted

6.5 cm in size and the other 5 cm, joined by a 4×2 cm bridge-pin. In Experiment 2, features were added to the model to give a doll-like appearance to the blocks. The children were seated approximately 50 cm from the model, which was placed on the surface of a table.

In each separate experiment, each child completed four drawings, one for each task, with order counterbalanced. The tasks were as follows:

 (i)   The small block (or head) in front of the large block (or body): file;
 (ii) The large block in front of the small block: file;
 (iii) The small block on top of the large block: pile;
 (iv) The large block on top of the small block: pile.

In Experiment 1 each child was asked to 'Draw the objects on the table as you see them from where you are sitting.' Questions were countered by asking the child to do the best drawing he/she could. No child was allowed to touch the model or to rotate the paper when drawing. In Experiment 2 the instructions were the same except that the word 'doll' was substituted for 'objects' and 'it' was substituted for 'them'. This may seem a pedantic point, but Berman (1976) and Cox (1978) found that instructions given markedly affect drawing performance (see also Barrett, Beaumont and Jennett's chapter above). After each child had completed drawing the small or large block (the head or body) each child was asked to point to the model and match the drawing to the appropriate block in the model. This procedure allowed the experimenter to check the referent of the different-sized blocks in the drawings and also to monitor the temporal order sequence.

The main purpose of making comparisons between the two experiments was to establish how the addition of features to the model changed the children's drawings with respect to:

 (i)   age;
 (ii) orientation and relative positions of the different-sized blocks;
 (iii) temporal order of drawing.

These comparisons will provide evidence for two types of coding processes. The tables have been paired with a 'visual summary' so that the reader may easily compare the results of each experiment and note the changes in the children's drawings which occurred as a result of the changes made to the model.

File Arrays: Small Front

Table 13.1 categorises the children's drawings of the non-featured and featured array, presented in file with the small block (or head) in front of the larger block.

If we first consider the drawings of the *non-featured array*, Table 13.1 shows that at age 3 there was a preference to omit the bridge-pin and depict the array as vertical, which gave way to occlusion with line eliminations at age 6. One of the most interesting results concerns the vertical drawings. All the children systematically rotated the further, larger block in the model to the top of the picture plane. There were no inversions of the blocks. Furthermore, the *bottom* small (or front block in the occluded drawings) was always drawn first. We also see, excluding the 3-year-olds, that there was a change with age in the *sequence* in which the different-sized blocks and bridge-pin were drawn. It was only when the blocks were occluded in the drawings that the relative proximity of the blocks in the model was drawn with respect to the children's viewing position, i.e. small block drawn first, bridge-pin second and large back block last. Thus, in general, the spatial relations between the blocks in the array are carefully preserved in the drawings.

If we now turn to the drawings of the *featured array* and compare them with the drawings of the non-featured array (Table 13.1) we see that the addition of doll-like features to the model changed the children's depictions of the spatial orientation and relative positions of the blocks. The 3-year-olds who depicted the doll in Tadpole form all drew the small single front block first and added features second, attaching arms and legs last. From age 4, as there was a change in the block placements in the drawings from vertical small to large top, there was a corresponding change from drawing the small block first, with features second, to drawing the small block first, large block second and the features *last*. From age 6, as the vertical drawings gave way to occlusion, the small *front* block was drawn first and the features last. The change with age in the order in which the features were drawn was highly statistically significant (Jonckheere test; $Z = 12.58$, $p < 0.001$).

These results are important, since they provide the key to understanding why the vertical-small-top rotation errors occurred in this experiment. They show that, when the younger children started their drawings with the small block and added features second, they always rotated the features to preserve the canonical form of the doll. Once the features were normalised with respect to the child's position, a vertical depiction inevitably followed. The children became 'locked' into the intrinsic features of the doll and always drew the large block underneath the small block in the vertical plane. For the older children, however, the reverse held. They concentrated upon the internal spatial relations of the blocks and were less likely to be influenced by the canonical form of the doll. Although they also drew the small block first, they always drew the features *last*. They were thus able to avoid the vertical-small-top rotation errors.

File Arrays: Large Front

Table 13.2 categorises the children's drawings of the non-featured and featured array, presented in file with the large block in front of the smaller block.

When the drawings of the *non-featured array* were considered, Table 13.2 shows that most of the 3-year-olds omitted the bridge-pin, and were equally likely to occlude the blocks as depict them vertically. Of the vertical drawings, all systematically rotated the small rear block in the model to the top of the picture plane in their drawings, these gradually giving way to occlusion with line eliminations at age 7. The bottom large (or front block in the occluded drawings) was always drawn first. We also see that there was a change with age in the *sequence* in which the blocks were drawn. As with the drawings of the non-featured array (Table 13.1), it was only from age 5 that the relative

Table 13.2. *Categorisation of children's drawings by age of the non-featured and featured arrays presented in file: Large Front.*

(EXPERIMENT 1) N = 60		3	4	5	6	7	TOTAL
ARRAY	CATEGORY	3	4	5	6	7	TOTAL
File	VERTICAL: Small Top*	5	3	0	0	0	8
	Small Top	1	2	5	3	0	11
	OCCLUSION: Large Front*	5	1	0	0	0	6
	Large Front	1	6	7	9	12	35

(Non-Featured)

VISUAL SUMMARY

Bridge pin Omitted	Vertical Joined or Partial Occlusion: Bottom/Front Large 1st, Small 2nd, Bridge pin 3rd	Partial Occlusion: Large Front 1st, Bridge Pin 2nd, Small Block 3rd.

(EXPERIMENT 2) N = 60							
File	TADPOLE: Large Only	7	0	0	0	0	7
	VERTICAL: Small Top	4	12	10	6	1	33
	OCCLUSION: Large Front	1	0	2	6	11	20

(Featured)

VISUAL SUMMARY

Tadpole Stereo-type	Small Top First, Features 2nd, Large Bottom Last	Large Bottom 1st Small Top Second Features Last	Partial Occlusion: Large Front First Small Back Second Features Last

*Bridge pin omitted

proximity of the blocks in the model were drawn with regard to the children's viewing position. An interesting feature of these results concerns the omission of the bridge-pin by the younger children. This omission also occurred in the 3-year-olds' drawings of the plain file when the small block was in front of the large block (Table 13.1). Yet here it occurs even with an increase in occlusion drawings. This seems to suggest, perhaps, that in the depiction of the files the bridge-pin was not visible to the children from their viewing positions. However, since a repeated-measures design was used, the children were surely aware that the pin was indeed there.

Overall, these results show that the children differentiated the file arrays by the relative positions of the blocks and the order in which they drew them. They also show that, in general, the children drew the different-sized blocks in a definite sequence with (for the older children) the temporal order of production corresponding with the block-and-bridge-placements in the model.

Turning to the drawings of the *featured array* we again see that the addition of doll-like features to the model changed the children's depiction of the spatial orientation and relative positions of the blocks. Apart from the seven Tadpole drawings at age 3 (which occurred as a consequence of the features or 'frontedness' of the model) all of the drawings which depicted the blocks vertically, rotated the small rear block in the model to the top of the picture plane. Across age, the Tadpole preference (large only) gave way sharply to vertical small top at 4 years. The vertical preference decreased smoothly with age, and gave way to occlusion at 7. When the temporal order of drawing was considered, there was a change with age in the order in which the features were drawn. The 3-year-olds who depicted the model in Tadpole form drew the nearer large block only first, added features second and attached arms and legs last. Of the vertical drawings the younger children drew the small block first and features second, yet at age 5 drew the large bottom block first (perhaps as an 'anchorage'?) and features last. When the blocks were occluded, the large front block was drawn first and the features were always added last. The change with age in the order in which the features were drawn (irrespective of the relative *positions* of the blocks) was statistically significant (Jonckheere test, $Z = 4.56$, $p < 0.001$).

So, in the drawings of this model, when the large block was in front, although there was a change in the temporal order of drawing, the change did not correspond to a change in the block placements when the doll was depicted vertically. Perhaps this was due to the small featured block being hidden from the child's viewing position?

When comparing the results with those from the non-featured array, when the large block was always drawn first, we see that the additional features to the model did affect the temporal and spatial order in which the blocks were drawn, particularly when the file was depicted vertically. This suggests that, although the children were concentrating upon preserving the canonical form of the doll, they were *also* influenced by the large front block in the model from their viewing position.

It is also interesting to note that *distance* in visual space is represented as *lateness* in time. The further the block is from the child in visual space, the higher up the vertical plane and the later it is drawn. This is seen in the drawings of the file arrays when the bottom and nearer blocks were drawn first. Hence, spatial order is preserved in the temporal order of production.

Pile Arrays: Small Top

Table 13.3 categorises the children's drawings of the non-featured and featured array, presented vertically with the small block on top of the larger block.

When the drawings of the *non-featured array* were considered, Table 13.3 shows that the blocks were invariably depicted in the correct orientation and in their correct relative positions on the paper. The bridge-pin was included in all the drawings and only three children drew the blocks separately. With

Table 13.3. *Categorisation of children's drawings by age of the non-featured and featured arrays presented in pile: Small Top.*

(EXPERIMENT 1) N = 60		3	4	5	6	7	AGE:YEARS
ARRAY	CATEGORY	3	4	5	6	7	TOTAL
Pile	VERTICAL: Small Top	12	12	12	12	12	60

(Non-Featured)

VISUAL SUMMARY				
	Vertical Separate: Bottom Large First Small Top Second Bridge Pin Third		Vertical Joined: Bottom Large First Bridge Pin Second Small Top Third	

(EXPERIMENT 2) N = 60		3	4	5	6	7	
Pile	TADPOLE: Small Only	7	0	0	0	0	7
	VERTICAL: Small Top	5	12	12	12	12	53

(Featured)

VISUAL SUMMARY			
Tadpole Stereotype	Small Top First Features Second Large Bottom Last	Large Bottom First Small Top Second Features Last (Anchorage?)	

regard to the temporal order of production all of the younger children drew the large bottom block first. Across age, there was a gradual shift from drawing the small block second to drawing the bridge-pin second and the small top block third at age 7 (Jonckheere test, $Z = 4.33$, $p < 0.001$). Overall these results show that the children preferred to start with the large block, using it as an 'anchorage point' and then working up the page in a systematic order.

As the reader will see from Table 13.3, when the *small featured block* was presented on top of the large block, almost all the drawings, with the exception of seven Tadpole drawings, depicted the blocks in the correct orientation and in their correct relative positions. Across age, there was again a significant change in the order in which the blocks were drawn. The younger children drew the small block first and features second, whilst the older children drew the bottom large block first and features last (Jonckheere test, $Z = 8.42$, $p < 0.001$).

Although from age 4 all the block placements in the drawings represented the model correctly, the change in the order of drawing showed that the younger children concentrated upon the canonical form of the doll and worked down the paper. The older children, however, used the large bottom block as an anchorage point, and concentrated upon the internal spatial relations intrinsic to the model. They always drew the large bottom block first, and worked up the page in a definite order.

A comparison of these results with those from Experiment 1 (non-featured array) showed that the features added to the model again changed the children's representations of the array, especially with regard to the temporal order of drawing, since when the blocks were non-featured all the children drew the large rather than the small block first.

Pile Arrays: Large Top

Table 13.4 categorises the children's drawings of the non-featured and featured array presented vertically with the large block on top of the smaller block.

Table 13.4 shows that for the *non-featured array* the blocks were again depicted in the correct orientation and in their correct relative positions on the paper. There was, however, a change in the temporal order of drawing when compared with Table 13.3. The majority of the younger children drew the large top block first. This preference gave way with age to drawing the small bottom block first at 7. In general these data show that, across all conditions, there was a shift with age from concentrating upon the different sizes of the blocks to concentrating upon the spatial relations between the

Table 13.4. *Categorisation of children's drawings by age of the non-featured and featured arrays presented in pile: Large Top.*

		AGE : YEARS					
(EXPERIMENT 1) N = 60							
ARRAY	CATEGORY	3	4	5	6	7	TOTAL
Pile	VERTICAL: Large Top	12	12	12	12	12	60

(Non-Featured)

VISUAL SUMMARY

Vertical Separate:
Large Top First
Small Bottom Second
Bridge Pin Third

Vertical Joined:
Bottom Small First
Bridge Pin Second
Large Top Third

		AGE : YEARS					
(EXPERIMENT 2) N = 60							
ARRAY	CATEGORY	3	4	5	6	7	TOTAL
Pile	TADPOLE: Small Only	8	1	0	0	0	9
	VERTICAL: Small Top	3	7	7	1	0	18
	Large Top	1	4	5	11	12	33

(Featured)

VISUAL SUMMARY

Tadpole Stereotype

Small Top First
Features Second
Large Bottom Last

Large Top 1st,
Small Bottom,
Second,
Features Last

Small Bottom
First, Large
Top Second,
Features Last

blocks, with the drawing sequence corresponding to the models by 7 years, as seen from the child's point of view.

Table 13.4 shows that when the large block was presented on top of the *small featured block*, a pattern of results occurs similar to that shown in Table 13.1. Surprisingly, in 30 per cent of the drawings, the blocks were completely rotated, showing the small block on top of the larger block. Across age, the Tadpole preference gives way to vertical small top at 4, which decreases at age 5, giving way to large top, which increases to a ceiling at 7.

The overriding feature of all the results reported concerns the changes in the children's drawings brought about by the inclusion of the doll-like features to the model. These are now discussed within the context of Luquet's taxonomy and other theories of pictorial representation.

4. Two codes

The most interesting results of comparisons made between these two experiments concerns the evidence for the simultaneous availability of two types of coding processes: a symbolic code which is consistent with Luquet's theory of intellectual realism and a series of view-specific spatial codes, both of which may be available even to very young children and become integrated between 5 and 7 years.

— First, consider the evidence for the spatial codes, particularly with regard to the children's depiction of the non-featured array. It was noted in the Introduction that Light *et al.* (1980 and 1981) suggest that the vertically (or horizontally) orientated drawings of objects presented in file reflect the child's concern to show array-specific information, largely irrespective of their viewing position. Since the vertical (or horizontal) drawings preserve the internal spatial relations of the array, i.e. were array-specific, they take this as evidence that the young child is, in fact, unconcerned with, or insensitive to, perspective differences.

However, there are difficulties with this explanation, since the results presented in Tables 13.1 and 13.2 provide evidence that the younger children's vertical drawings of the file in Experiment 1 may be regarded as containing view-specific information, and that the children are *not* insensitive to perspective differences in the model. The fact that the younger children, in their depiction of the file arrays, systematically rotated the farther small or large block in the model to the top of the picture plane and drew the blocks in a definite sequence suggests that the children were aware of relative size differences and that the vertical drawings were an elementary form of view-specificity. In a personal communication, Paul Light agrees with this interpretation, but stresses that the verticals may be both array- and view-specific. Across age there was also a systematic change from depicting the file arrays as vertically separate to partial occlusion at age 7, involving either partial or complete line eliminations, these drawings also being view-centred. Interestingly, partial line deletions from age 5, where the child interrupted the drawing line by lifting the pencil and continuing the line the other side of the block, occurred only when the small block was in front of the larger block in the model. This suggests that the increased use of partial occlusion (in relation to the number of partial occlusions in Experiment 2) may reflect the fact that this spatial configuration taps a view-centred code – optimally, since *both* objects are visible to the child from his viewing position.

Further evidence in support of a view-centred mode (and against intellectual realism) is provided by considering the children's omission of the bridge-pin in their depiction of the plain file arrays. As was noted earlier, the pin was omitted largely by the 3-year-olds, yet it was always included in the drawings of the vertical, pile arrays. A crucial point for the acceptance of these drawings as being view-centred concerns whether the children could see the bridge-pin *before* they started drawing. Since a repeated-measures design was used and

Freeman, N. H. (1980) *Strategies of representation in young children.* London: Academic Press.

Freeman, N. H., Eiser, C. & Sayers, J. (1977) Children's strategies in producing three-dimensional relationships on a two-dimensional surface. *Journal of Experimental Child Psychology, 23,* 305–14.

Freeman, N. H. & Janikoun, R. (1972) Intellectual realism in children's drawings of a familiar object with distinctive features. *Child Development, 43,* 1116–21.

Gesell, A. & Ames, L. B. (1946) The development of directionality in drawing. *Journal of Genetic Psychology, 68,* 45–61.

Ingram, N. A. (1980) Use of vertical and horizontal axes in drawing. In Freeman, 1980, pp. 228–30.

(1983) Representation of three-dimensional spatial relationships on a two-dimensional picture surface. Unpublished Ph.D. thesis, University of Southampton.

Light, P. H. & Humphreys, J. (1981) Internal spatial relationships in young children's drawings. *Journal of Experimental Child Psychology, 31,* 521–30.

Light, P. H. & MacIntosh, E. (1980) Depth relationships in young children's drawings. *Journal of Experimental Child Psychology, 30,* 79–87.

Light, P. H. & Simmons, B. (1983) The effect of a communication task upon the representation of depth relationships in young children's drawings. *Journal of Experimental Child Psychology, 35,* 81–92.

Luquet, G. H. (1913) *Les dessins d'un enfant.* Paris: Alcan.

(1927) *Le dessin enfantin.* Paris: Alcan.

Marr, D. (1977) Analysis of occluding contour. *Proceedings of the Royal Society of London,* ser. B, 197, 441–75.

Piaget, J. & Inhelder, B. (1969) *The psychology of the child.* London: Routledge and Kegan Paul.

Willats, J. (1977) How children learn to represent three-dimensional space in drawing. In G. E. Butterworth (ed.), *The child's representation of the world.* New York: Plenum, pp. 189–202.

(1981) Formal structures in drawing and painting. Unpublished Ph.D. thesis, Council for National Academic Awards.

14

Knowledge and appearance

CHARLES CROOK

1. Introduction

Children's drawings are, at one level, very economical in their style: lines are sparsely deployed to capture likeness in a schematic manner. Yet, in a different sense, they are not economical at all, for they often include many features of a scene – whether it be imagined or real – that may indeed be present in that scene but which would not be visible to anyone taking up the artist's viewing point. It is this quality of being over-inclusive which comes closest to summarising the general feature of early drawing to be discussed here. I shall argue that it is an intrusive by-product of young children's considerable conceptualising ability and not necessarily an indication of how children prefer their drawings to be.

The theme of this paper is the idea that our ability to capture the appearance of a scene is in some important way affected by the things that we know about it. In fact, knowledge of a scene's structure may serve to make drawing it a difficult task. This is certainly no new idea; it is at least as old as John Ruskin's account of the 'innocent eye'. Moreover, Gombrich (1960) was led to make broad reference to the relationship of knowledge and appearance as he traced the development of technique in representational painting. Neither is this idea new to the domain of concern here: children's drawing. In one of the earliest child psychology texts it was proposed that the child's 'sense perceptions have, for artistic purposes, become corrupted by too large an admixture of intelligence' (Sully, 1896, p. 396). More modern accounts of children's drawing still reflect this view but take Luquet's (1927) concept of intellectual realism as their focal point: the child draws 'what he knows, not what he sees'. For a long time this particular formula survived rather well, partly because Piaget chose to adopt it in an enthusiastic, if somewhat cavalier, manner but also because it really does seem to express something very striking

248

about childhood drawing. Unfortunately, it cannot take us very far. Just what is meant by 'knowing' a scene is always left unclear. One aim of the present chapter is to explore this question and to pursue Luquet's goal of forming a cognitive basis to drawing development. As it happens, the recent research literature presents some resistance to such an enterprise. Emphasis is currently placed on the child's intent to be 'informative' in drawing, so that intellectual realism becomes merely a descriptive term for strategies that realise such a motivation. In pursuit of a cognitive account of early drawing it will therefore be necessary to question this contemporary view. That will be an important aim of this chapter.

It is necessary to begin with a clear idea of the features of early drawing that commonly inspire this appeal to some influence of 'knowing'. They seem to be of two kinds. The first is associated with children's attempts to represent certain objects. These are frequently shown in stereotyped aspects, some of which could never be realised. This may lead to pictures having what Piaget called 'a medley of viewpoints'. Thus, features of an object not visible in the given view are, in some manner, added on – after all, the child knows they are there. Secondly, there is an intellectual realism at work in depictions of the spatial relationships that exist between discrete objects in a scene. In particular, attempts may be made to specify fully such relationships in a drawing, even though this may involve including objects, that are partially or totally occluded at the viewer's position. It is these familiar characteristics of early drawing that the present chapter is particularly concerned to understand. These are senses in which knowledge may be said to intrude into the child's drawing. What is at stake is the extent to which that intrusion is an incidental by-product of cognitive activity rather than an intentional strategy. The cognitive view will be argued for here, but first we must see how the alternative, more motivational, account has emerged.

The dichotomy of intellectually realist symptoms established in the preceding paragraph may be an imperfect one, but it is convenient, for it maps onto two theoretical advances which have come to displace reference to intellectual realism in accounts of early drawing. Consider the first of the tendencies above. A concrete example would be Freeman and Janikoun's (1972) illustration that if shown a cup with its handle pointing away, the young child may well include that handle in her drawing even though it is not visible. Freeman (1980) and others chose to account for these cases by reference to the concept of 'canonical forms'. This expresses the notion that there are preferred or ideal projections for certain objects. Like intellectual realism, this is an idea with a history (cf. the 'orthoscopic forms' of Buhler, 1918) and, again, it has a strong intuitive appeal: children's drawings are indeed marked by common stereotypes. It is also proving to be a powerful notion for its promise of links with other areas of cognitive development (cf. Freeman, 1980). But it has real limitations. One is the difficulty of defining canonical forms independently of the drawings which they are intended to explain. Another must be that it cannot always apply to the second class of intellectually realist phenomena identified above, namely those idiosyncrasies arising in the expression of spatial relationships in a scene. Such relationships are not always canonical.

A concrete example of this second form of intellectual realism may be seen in an experiment which I have reinvestigated and will describe more fully later in this chapter. Children who witnessed a hatpin pushed through an apple (Clark, 1897) copied this rather bizarre scene with a line representing the pin drawn across a circle representing the apple. In other words, the children *seemed* to try to show the actual arrangement of objects by treating the apple as though it were transparent. Now, a further theoretical device that attempts to deal with such phenomena is the distinction between view-specific and array-specific representation (Light and MacIntosh, 1980). This is expounded in Light's chapter above. Another formulation, from Marr's work (1982), is to make a distinction between two types of mental representation which the viewer has access to, viewer-centred and object-centred; children become stuck at the object-centred level. This is expounded in Willats' chapter above. On these accounts, the young child is said to express in her drawings the object relationships of the array itself, rather than those relationships specified at the artist's particular view.

We now have two elaborations of the old intellectual realism concept, but, at first sight, neither the concept of canonical projection nor the distinction between array-specific and view-specific modes seems to provide any greater explanatory power. However, this may not be so. They do share common ground by each implying a role for *informativeness*: both canonical forms and array-specific organisations amount to 'good' or informative views. So, if it is claimed that children have this urge to inform motivating their drawing style, then we have a broad account that seems to generate some testable predictions. Children are communicative in their drawing: they furnish a message about the best view. However, this is not an account that rests easily with the ideas to be developed here, and this particular reformulation of intellectually realist phenomena will be the one to be questioned in what follows.

In the next section, I shall explore this claim that children's communicative attitude to drawing can account for their intellectually realist style. I shall argue that we are not bound to accept such a theory and I go on to propose an alternative, more cognitively specifiable, account of the same material, taking up a theme developed in the chapter by Phillips, Inall and Lauder above. Later, some experiments will be reported whose results do not at all favour the informative motive as an explanation of children's drawing.

2. Drawings as messages

It is widely recognised that the content of children's drawings may provide insight into their feelings and thoughts about their world. Thus, clinicians may quite rightly regard drawings as potential 'messages'. But in accepting this projective quality of drawing one must be careful not to generalise the insight too freely. It does not directly follow that those idiosyncrasies of drawing style which we call intellectually realist should also be interpreted as communicative in nature. Certainly it must be admitted that drawings in which hidden parts of objects are included, and spatial interrelationships become elaborated, are drawings that are reasonably termed 'informative'. Since they usually tend to involve the child in more graphic work than just omitting the hidden lines would, the claim that children must be intending their drawings to be informative in this way is an appealing one. The consequences of refusing to accept this claim seem clear. If such drawing does not reflect either the child's preference or his interpretation of what is expected, then we must suppose that capturing scenes as they appear from particular views is, in some way, a particularly difficult thing to do. As it happens, the argument for drawings as messages derives from denying there is such a difficulty rather than from any direct evidence of an intention to inform.

Such a denial emerges from experiments employing a particular kind of paradigm. A scene is taken which typically gets drawn with either canonical projections of some object or with array-specific representation of spatial relationships. The experimenter then manipulates the way the task is arranged for the child in order to provoke a more view-specific drawing. It is important in such experiments that the appearance of the original scene is always preserved unchanged. For instance, more elaborate instructions (Barrett and Bridson, 1983) or a different way of actually constructing the final appearance of the scene may be provided (Light and MacIntosh, 1980; Crook, 1984). A concrete example should clarify this, and the Light and MacIntosh study provides a particularly elegant one. A toy house is viewed through a glass behind which it has been placed; however, young children will often draw these two things beside each other, or the house above the glass. These are array-specific representations. This hardly seems a 'lazy' strategy; just as much drawing is involved as would be in the view-specific solution of putting the house within the lines of the glass. But the key point is a claim that the alternative possibility, of children finding such a solution in some way too difficult, is also ruled out: when the same final appearance is constructed by placing the house inside the glass, then all children now shift to the view-specific solution. So it is argued that, since a condition has been found such that the child is shown capable of representing the given scene in a view-specific manner, the conditions in which he fails to do so must represent a misinterpretation of what he is supposed to be doing. Executive incapacity has been ruled out by success with the 'inside glass' control.

Note that this control does not directly demonstrate the existence of an informative motive. In fact, my own view is that its value is less in what it 'rules out' (usually a rather improbable incapacity) than in what it reveals: namely, some of the extent to which the child's knowledge of scenes can serve to disrupt and distract from the ideal drawing strategy. Controls such as this 'inside' one should not be closing up the issue; they should be multiplied and extended in order that the relation between favoured drawing devices and particular scene structures can be properly mapped out. However, this is a view that must be properly argued in what follows.

It may be apparent why the debate concerning accounts of intellectually realist drawing is conducted in the context of copying tasks. They supply a paradigm in which models are objectively defined and in which subtle task manipulations may indeed allow executive problems (of a sort) to be ruled out. But the conclusions apply as much to free drawing as to copying. These conclusions are said to suggest that an urge to inform leads young children to exercise intellectually realist tendencies in their drawing, such as including objects that are hidden from their view. I wish to question this motivational interpretation and later will present material that is not easily explained in these terms, but first I shall sketch an alternative theoretical framework in which the various drawing phenomena described above may be better understood.

3. The cognitive basis of early drawing

The force of much contemporary research on intellectually realist drawing is to stress how its idiosyncrasies are not usually located in problems of perception or of execution. If that is the case, then we must turn to consider psychological processes which intervene. Thus, in the preceding section we encountered an interpretation based upon intervening processes of a social-motivational nature. Here I shall encourage consideration of intervening cognitive factors and, in particular, consideration of (a) the kind of *mental model* a child might construct for a scene and then (b) how such a representation might influence the management of drawing.

This is rather in the spirit of Luquet's original enterprise. There is insufficient space to formalise that earlier account here but it should be recognised that he proposed something more detailed than the slogan of intellectual realism. Luquet's full theory has been neglected because there is no English translation, but useful secondary sources do exist, e.g. Read (1943) and Freeman (1972). One feature of Luquet's account involved the specification of an internal model that mediated between the child's observation of a scene and her drawing. In pursuing that path here it is proposed to work from a conception familiar to students of Artificial Intelligence, namely, the structured description (e.g. Palmer, 1977).

This device has been developed partly in an attempt to integrate the various phenomena composing human representational activity, although the debates surrounding that particular effort need not detain us (see Kosslyn and Pomerantz, 1977). In its simplest expression, this form of representation involves a list of objects that occupy a scene, any one of which may itself be unpacked into a further list of features. In addition, there is propositional information: abstract structures functioning to express precise relations that exist between the entities listed. Such propositions carry truth values and, although they are not linguistic structures, they may frequently be approximated by simple declaratives, as in: 'The house is behind the glass.' Thus, in viewing a scene, the child transforms it into a representation that approximates a catalogue of constituents appropriately tagged with information concerning spatial relationships.

Prior to a drawing exercise, the child is considered to construct a mental representation of just the kind above. Of course, there may also be generated a mental image with more direct pictorial properties; it is not necessary to debate here the possibility or status of such images. The point is only to recognise the independent existence of a cognitive representation of the scene more articulated than any such pattern-matching image. This structured description of a scene is the consequence of intellectual activity carried out upon it – processes of interpretation and extrapolation. In a sense, then, the young artist may work from two sources: a pattern of surfaces available as her view and a structured description that is the outcome of mental work spontaneously carried out upon that view. It may be that the anomalous drawers described by Selfe (this volume) have more ready access to the former;

the crucial point for the present account is that most young children are dominated by the latter – a particular kind of mental representation of the scene they have to draw.

In short, it is proposed that the child's cognitive activity interferes with an ability to produce view-specific drawing. In this sense, knowledge is disruptive and we may wish to say that children fail to 'inhibit' this knowledge, so identifying the account as 'negative' as opposed to the 'positive' flavour of the more motivational interpretation (Light, this volume). It will certainly be difficult to distinguish between these two accounts, as they both seem to anticipate 'informative' drawings most of the time. Nevertheless it is important to try and make this discrimination, for, at the very least, there are likely to be different implications for practical strategies aimed at cultivating drawing skill.

A note of qualification to this theoretical dichotomy may be necessary. As emphasised earlier, the communicative motive is only under examination with respect to the intellectually realist *style* of drawing. The actual topics chosen for drawing, and even certain other aspects of style, may well have message-like characteristics. It must also be stressed that the accounts being contrasted here are not mutually exclusive. In particular, there may certainly be occasions when psychologists and others construct such peculiar arrangements for drawing that children may well become confused as to what it is that is expected of them.

Given these qualifications, what is now outstanding is clarification of just how the child's mental model of a scene does interfere to make drawing difficult. In all of what follows, emphasis will be on the problems that are created for representing simple spatial relationships. However, the general account applies as much to the intellectual realism earlier associated with the canonical form as it does to the intellectual realism of array-specific drawing. I shall now identify two ways in which the structure of the child's knowledge of a scene interferes with expressing spatial relations in a drawing.

The mental representation that the child is inclined to reference when making a drawing has a list-like structure. First, it is proposed that drawing decisions guided by such a structure lead to a tendency towards itemisation in drawings. Moreover, this itemisation of objects on the picture plane may be apparently accentuated so that each object is made to occupy its own space (Goodnow, 1977). Such *segregation* does seem to be a basic and early feature of drawing development. It may also be deployed for the representation of spatial relations. Thus, Luquet identifies a very early stage (perhaps only fleetingly seen) that he refers to as 'synthetic incapacity'. In this, segregated items are simply juxtaposed with a lack of respect for their spatial organisation in a scene. Arms and legs become separated from a body and so on. However, management of simple relationships is mastered fairly quickly from here, and the device of segregation comes to help code relational information – as when placing the toy house above the glass (for 'behind') in the example cited earlier.

Perhaps the more basic tendency behind segregation is that of maintaining the unitary nature of the particular things in a scene. It is proposed that this reflects reference to a mental representation comprising a list of discrete entities. So the first manner in which intrusion of our mental representation may cause difficulties is in respect of this commitment to itemisation: it will get in the way of executing certain graphic tricks that are necessary to express depth on the picture plane. In the extreme, the child fails to suppress inclusion of objects that are totally occluded at the artist's viewpoint. But also partial occlusions can hardly be compatible with maintaining the unitary quality of objects. To employ hidden-line elimination means not only diminishing the unitary nature of the object which has been partially 'rubbed out' but blending its boundary with that of another object.

Problems in the expression of spatial relationships do not only rest upon the management of occlusions. Light and MacIntosh's children failed to express the house behind the glass in a view-specific manner, even though the solution involves no occlusion – nothing gets hidden in the scene. The second manner in which mental representation may intrude concerns cases of that kind. Earlier it was proposed that structured descriptions involve propositional information whereby objects are tagged for their spatial inter-relationships. We suppose that in accessing the information 'behind', say, the child has a limited number of drawing rules or conventions that can be called upon to get that 'behind' information into the picture. Problems could then arise if the relative placement of objects dictated by the view called for the execution of a convention that normally means something else. To be specific: it is likely that drawing a house within the boundary of a glass would normally be a solution to coding 'inside', or possibly 'in front of' (and we may speculate that the nature of these early conventions derives from an isomorphism with the actual actions that would be involved in manipulating the objects themselves). So in adopting a segregation solution to the house *behind* the glass, Light and MacIntosh's children are not so much making a positive effort to convey array-specific information as they are avoiding a tension generated by employing an 'inside' rule in a situation they know to involve 'behind' relations. Thus, some scenes may offer views comfortably compatible with the drawing rules available to express what is known about them (house inside glass); others may present a conflict (house behind glass). Of course, these rules are not immutable and it is important to establish the boundary conditions of their application: Davis (this volume) has explored this issue with respect to the 'inside' rule.

So it is that the intrusion of knowledge is further disruptive: the view-specific solution may be judged to violate an established drawing convention. Such a formulation is by no means *ad hoc*; evidence already exists that the expression of certain canonical forms can be explained in just these terms (Taylor and Bacharach, 1982). Moreover, I shall present empirical evidence in a later section that strongly reinforces this line of reasoning.

Two points have been made above in clarifying the mechanisms whereby knowledge in the form of particular mental representations can disrupt the drawing of view-specific relations. First, a pressure towards itemisation undermines the expression of occlusions. Second, even when occlusions are not involved, drawing conventions may be insufficiently flexible or versatile to render comfortably the organisation of certain views. Our final step must be to provide empirical justification for these claims: the first requires clear interpretation of the ubiquitous segregation tendency and the second requires manipulating the information contained in a scene in order to play it off against the child's commitment to certain drawing conventions. The following two sections consider each of these in turn.

4. Interpreting segregation

The most casual study of early drawing will bear witness to the young artist's reluctance to make objects disappear or blend into each other. The child knows that in reality this does not happen. Unfortunately, the look of things can very often only be described in just this way: the world may be full of discrete objects, but it is a cluttered place and hence there occur spatial transformations that lead to the occlusions characterising our various views. Such transformations require that, in drawing, some things must be cancelled altogether or (with partial occlusions) their boundaries must become shared. It is an apparent reluctance to acknowledge this that is associated with array-specific representations.

The issue with respect to the theories contrasted in this paper is whether the tendency to segregate represents a particular approach to drawing tasks – the informative attitude – or whether it reflects the drawing dictates of a particular mental representation of scenes. One approach to evaluating these alternatives might be to study situations where two objects really do blend into each other through actual contact. To maintain their segregation in a drawing would not be properly informative of the spatial relations that exist,

Figure 14.1 Drawings of terraced houses taken from a class of 31 5-year-olds. One of the two models shown at top left was supplied: starred drawings match to starred model. Four groups of children are distinguished and their treatment of the shared boundary is discussed in the text.

but it could be said to reflect the robust influence of a mental model of the basic situation.

For example, houses are popular topics in early drawing and they are pleasingly discrete things in our thinking, but in reality they are also things that often come joined together in pairs or in terraces. Each child in the reception class of an infant school was shown one of the two models reproduced at the top left of Figure 14.1 and asked to make a drawing that looked just the same. They found three basic solutions to the shared boundary. Some children (Figure 14.1: 1–7) depicted it as given, others drew two segregated houses (Figure 14.1: 8–23), and a third group simply drew one house (Figure 14.1: 24–31). A clear sub-group of segregated drawers (Figure 14.1: 8–13) went to some length to stress the 'closeness' of the houses by making a minimal gap between them. (Note the synthetic incapacity of Figure 14.1: 28: both sets of windows have been placed in the one frame.)

It is clear that the segregation tendency has not been readily inhibited. However, it could be argued that these children have a cavalier attitude to the task: they are indifferent to our pleas to make their drawings 'just the same', or perhaps they are still set on providing a 'message' but one which communicates how things are in the real world, not in this particular model of the world. What makes these proposals unconvincing is the extreme care that characterises their copying of *other* features in the models (they were made to be subtly different). Thus, details of chimney and fenestration are faithfully captured. It is against this that we must interpret any apparent flouting of the spatial relationship between the two dwellings.

I propose that the task is made difficult by the child constructing a mental representation comprising either 'house' or 'one house and a second house'. In the latter case, there is an intrusion of this representation such that the integrity of these two things will not easily be undermined by any terracing transformations we may perform. These drawings certainly do not favour explanation of segregation in terms of a strong urge to be informative; but it must be said that neither do they conclusively rule it out. The experiments reported in the next section are more definitive and concern the second form of influence we are ascribing to these cognitive intrusions: the tension associated with knowing a spatial relationship in the scene and accessing a drawing convention that appears to violate that relation.

5. Interpreting a transparency

One of the earliest reports of intellectually realist drawings was Clark's (1897) study of the apple and the hatpin described earlier. Having seen the pin pierce

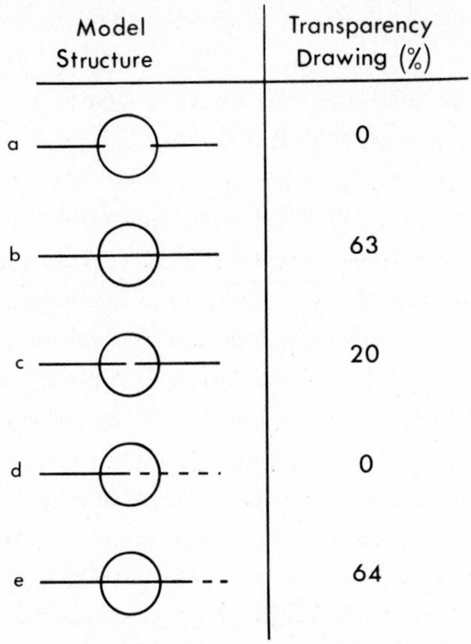

Model Structure	Transparency Drawing (%)
a	0
b	63
c	20
d	0
e	64

Figure 14.2 Five ways of arranging a model in which two sticks emerge from opposing points on the surface of an opaque ball. The percentage of 5-year-olds copying the ball as transparent is shown for each case. In (c) the two sticks do make contact; the dotted lines in (d) and (e) indicate a red/black colour contrast on a single stick.

the apple, his children often drew something that implied that the apple was transparent. Such transparency drawing is quite a common solution to partial occlusions (see Cox, this volume).

The appearance of this model – a round thing with two straight bits coming out at opposite points – can actually be created in at least three ways. Freeman (1980) reports one in which a stick is simply made to rest on a concealed support behind, and separate from, a ball. It is common for children to draw this construction as segregated, with the stick *above* the ball. I have reported other variants on this task with 5-year-olds, whose responses will be summarised with respect to Figure 14.2. Thus a second construction that leads to the same general appearance involves simply placing two separate sticks each in the opposing points on the ball (Figure 14.2a). The children always produced a view-specific drawing, never a transparency. On the other hand, Clark's original arrangement of pushing a single stick right through led to a transparency in the drawings of 63 per cent of the same children.

These three different ways of drawing a model of identical relation to the viewer evidently reflect the influence of different things the children know about its construction. A motivational account of how knowledge exerts this influence would claim that children were trying with their segregation to code 'behind', and with their transparencies they were trying to convey 'through'. This interpretation would have to regard the two-stick model of Figure 14.2a as the traditional control that rules out executive problems as a source of inability to interrupt the single straight line of the pin.

⌐ At first sight, these transparency solutions may not seem in tune with the more cognitive account being developed here. It might be supposed that drawing across the circle is more usually reserved for an 'in front of' relation and so the child should be concerned about violating a drawing convention. However, it is proposed that a tendency to keep the two objects intact, coupled with a relatively unfamiliar drawing relation 'through', leads the child into a solution whose final ambiguity is not anticipated. In fact, the experiment described here exploits this situation by highlighting the violation of a drawing convention while leaving the actual appearance of the scene unchanged. Consider the single-stick condition (Figure 14.2b): it is supposed that a structured description exists that comprises two things (ball and stick) related by 'through'. Of course, from the point of view of drawing, this structured description is a hindrance because the 'push through' transformation has, in appearance, made the stick into two bits where it was previously one. The singular nature of the children's original coding of the stick must either be abandoned or updated. The 'through' relation is probably rather unfamiliar to novice drawers, but the action of putting the pen down at a point outside the circle (the end of the stick) and then drawing right across its centre to an equivalent point is a drawing action that probably resonates with the real action on the real objects. In any case, it is a reasonable guess that the children do not anticipate the ambiguity inherent in the outcome (that the ball will appear to be transparent, or the stick will appear to be in front of the ball).

Fortunately, this analysis allows the two accounts outlined above to be pitted against each other. If the child's intention in drawing a transparency is to inform what is hidden by the ball, then increasing the information concealed in this manner should only serve to increase the tendency towards transparency drawing. However, an account that has these children running through their mental representation of the scene will predict *fewer* transparencies; for, by making drawing marks within the circle the children will be made to confront the ambiguity in their solutions more immediately. Accordingly, in a further experimental condition, information concealed was increased by having the two sticks pushed together until they were felt to meet (Figure 14.2c). No children represented the new information of this join in their drawings but some (20 per cent) produced the familiar transparency, suggesting they had conceptualised the situation as a new single stick.

Transparencies were thus reduced in this situation, 20 per cent compared with 63 per cent with the single stick of condition 2.

In a further study a single stick was employed, sometimes painted half red and half black, so that the break would be concealed within the ball when pushed through (Figure 14.2d) and sometimes painted three-quarters one colour and one-quarter the other such that the join could still be drawn but now occurred outside the ball (Figure 14.2e). Transparencies were at their normal frequency in the latter case (64 per cent) but did not occur at all with the symmetrically painted stick. Thus, in situations where the information to convey is increased (a physical or a painted join), children are actually less likely to produce a transparency.

Even with the most charitable interpretation, this result hardly suggests an urge to inform. My argument is that the requirement to make discrete drawing marks within the circle confronts the child with his violation of an acquired drawing convention. Putting the pen down in such a way must normally mean 'in front of' or (if it were transparent like a glass) 'inside'. Moreover, in the present situation, the salience of the join or colour break probably marks it as a starting point for drawing and so forces the child into contact with ambiguity right at the outset of his drawing. Perhaps such modest experiences might even be quite valuable if they precipitate active reflections on the bases of one's drawing decisions and thereby contribute to the development of a more view-specific attitude.

To summarise the argument so far: a young child's drawing is not always faithful to the scene as given at her viewpoint; it may include hidden or extra detail. These elaborations usually reflect the child's knowledge of the scene's structure. So in a sense, children's drawings may often be more informative than we expect. But this need not imply the child actually does possess a communicative attitude. There is no direct evidence to support such a notion and studies described above are hardly consistent with it. Rather it is suggested that intellectually realist drawings emerge from the structured descriptions that children spontaneously generate in response to viewing objects and arrays. It is reliance on these models and their particular characteristics that leads to the many familiar idiosyncrasies of early drawing.

6. A note on production problems

In fact, using the concept of intellectual realism only accounts for a modest range of graphic idiosyncrasies. In elaborating it, we have been able to say something about the selection of items for inclusion in a drawing and offer some insight into how those items are sometimes deployed within the available space. But understanding the composition of early drawings evidently has much further to go. Intellectual realism has been one theoretical device in traditional accounts of this topic; another has been the concept of a production problem (cf. Freeman, 1980). It would be normal to contrast these two ideas: intellectual realism reflects the impact of knowledge on drawing, while production problems are difficulties of execution that persist when all the meaning in a topic has been removed (and thus 'knowledge' of it cannot interfere). For example, there may be executive difficulty in forming certain angles or parallels or particular shapes.

The influence of production problems may, however, be overstated. The only example that has been clearly articulated is that of orientation biases. One striking feature of early drawing is a failure to get certain perpendicular relationships as they should be: water level stays perpendicular to the sides of a glass even when it is tilted, chimneys jut out of roofs at right angles to them, and so on. The case for regarding these as production problems rests initially on the demonstration by Ibbotson and Bryant (1976) that when a totally abstract angle-copying task is given to young children they tend to make copying errors towards the perpendicular: a so-called perpendicular bias. However, we must be alert for sleight-of-hand in this argument. Close examination of the errors made in such abstract tasks reveals that these biases are neither sweeping nor substantial (Crook, 1983). The magnitude of the error diminishes as the target angle itself approaches 90°, but in any case the error at 45° is still normally only of the order of 10°. This is hardly sufficient to account for the strong perpendicularisation characteristic of spontaneous drawing.

What happens in drawing trees on hillsides and chimneys on roofs is a more dramatic error and, again, must surely reflect an intrusion from what the child knows of such situations – implicit knowledge of gravity and so on. Freeman (1983) has opened up the study of these kinds of influences by managing to manipulate the symbolic content in an angle-drawing problem. As his models took on more meaning, so the angular relationships that were drawn changed in the size of error.

Thus it is not merely depth relationships that may be disrupted by what the child knows; orientation relationships are also vulnerable. In the final section below it remains to give brief consideration to how these general influences of knowledge might be mastered.

7. The promotion of view-specific drawing

It may be argued that organised attempts to direct children's early drawing development are improper. One interesting reason for contemplating such intervention is that drawing may be a neglected experience relevant to the cultivation of more broadly based cognitive skills. In particular, it may provide inroads into the family of childhood dispositions we label as 'egocentrism'. Light and Nix (1983) have confronted the apparent paradox of how children's emphasis on their own view in traditional perspective-taking tasks (Piaget and Inhelder, 1956) is coupled with a resistance to taking the view-specific attitude in drawing. They have proposed that spatial egocentrism may be wrongly formulated as a preference for 'own' view; it is really a preference for 'best' view, or array-specific view. Many previous studies have confounded these two. Thus, children may be dominated by their structural descriptions of scenes, not just in production tasks (drawing) but also in perspective-taking choice tasks (the three-mountains study). This analysis raises the possibility that experiences gained in the arena of drawing may have a more significant role in promoting cognitive development than is commonly claimed. Moreover, if this is so, it only serves to highlight the need for separating the two theoretical interpretations of early drawing discussed in this chapter.

The interpretation favoured here supposes there are two kinds of developments that could underlie advance towards view-specific drawing. Either the child comes actively to resist the intrusion of a mental model as drawing decisions are made or such models come to assimilate more view-specific information. Arguably, the former strategy is preferable if view-specificity in drawing is the main goal; on the other hand, the latter strategy may reflect a more generally important cognitive advance in so far as the child is acknowledging that descriptions of things may not remain invariant across changes in the location of someone viewing them. Consider the manipulations designed to undermine canonical drawings of cups that are described by Davis (this volume). A cup with its handle turned out of sight is likely to be drawn by young children with its handle included on the side. This canonical projection can be undermined if such a target cup is positioned adjacent to another one that does have its handle in view. Here, the contrast may be inducing the child to inhibit reference to any mental coding of the scene in favour of more direct examination of its structure, but, more likely perhaps, the mental coding of objects may itself come to incorporate view-dependent information. Thus, *a* cup becomes *the* cup (the cup-with-the-handle) and this view-dependent property is incorporated into the cognitive representation.

Such contextual variables may work their effects either through the cultivation of more richly differentiated mental representations which continue to serve as a basis for drawing, or by tempting the child to abandon those mental models and turn to the geometry of the scene. This volume documents a considerable range of circumstances that prompt more view-specific drawing in children. We may at last be in reach of theoretical integration having implications for the instruction of drawing and, perhaps, of identifying a more central role for drawing experiences in early cognitive development than has hitherto been recognised.

At the outset it was noted that the place of knowledge in drawing has a history of discussion by artists and their commentators. As has been observed in other areas, it may be inappropriate to imply that young children are somehow qualitatively different or peculiar in their understanding compared with the more mature thinker. So it may be in drawing. In fact, some instructional techniques for developing drawing in adults make much of the difficulties resulting from one's knowledge of a scene (Edwards, 1979) and the need to break normal viewing habits (Pratt, this volume). We may be unconscious of the nature of this knowledge and its shortcomings but its impact can be considerable and cumulative.

The fact that how we know a scene does affect drawing is clear, and its influence on our drawing may often be dissatisfying. The core of this discussion is well enough captured in Sully's reference to a child's remark: 'First I think, then I draw my think' (Sully, 1896). This is a rather ugly motto compared with Luquet's, but it is more potent for stimulating research. The pressing task is one of specifying the structure of that 'think' and, from there, the consideration of how it may be mastered, curbed and put to work.

REFERENCES

Barrett, M. D. & Bridson, A. (1983) The effect of instructions upon children's drawings. *British Journal of Developmental Psychology*, 1, 175–8.
Buhler, K. (1918) *Die geistige Entwicklung des kindes*. Jena.
Clark, A. B. (1897) The child's attitude towards perspective problems. In E. Barnes (ed.), *Studies in education*, Vol. 1. Stanford: University Press.
Crook, C. K. (1983) The perpendicular error and the vertical effect. Paper presented at the Conference on Graphic Representation, University of York, April.
    (1984) Factors influencing the use of transparency in children's drawing. *British Journal of Developmental Psychology*, 2, 213–21.
Edwards, B. (1979) *Drawing on the right side of the brain*. USA: J. Tarcher.
Freeman, N. H. (1972) Processes and product in children's drawings. *Perception*, 1, 123–40.
    (1980) *Strategies of representation in young children*. London: Academic Press.

(1983) Picture-plane bias in children's representational drawing. *Australian Journal of Psychology*, *35*, 121–33.

Freeman, N. H. & Janikoun, R. (1972) Intellectual realism in children's drawings of a familiar object with distinct features. *Child Development*, *43*, 1116–21.

Gombrich, E. H. (1960) *Art and illusion*. London: Phaidon.

Goodnow, J. J. (1977) *Children's drawing*. London: Fontana.

Ibbotson, A. & Bryant, P. E. (1976) The perpendicular error and the vertical effect. *Perception*, *5*, 319–26.

Kosslyn, S. M. & Pomerantz, J. R. (1977) Imagery, propositions, and the form of internal representations. *Cognitive Psychology*, *9*, 52–76.

Light, P. H. & MacIntosh, E. (1980) Depth relationships in young children's drawings. *Journal of Experimental Child Psychology*, *30*, 79–87.

Light, P. & Nix, C. (1983) 'Own view' versus 'good view' in a perspective-taking task. *Child Development*, *54*, 480–3.

Luquet, G. H. (1913) *Les dessins d'un enfant*. Paris: Alcan.

Marr, D. (1982) *Vision*. San Francisco: Freeman.

Palmer, S. E. (1977) Hierarchical structure in perceptual representation. *Cognitive Psychology*, *9*, 441–74.

Piaget, J. & Inhelder, B. (1956) *The child's conception of space*. London: Routledge and Kegan Paul.

Read, H. (1943) *Education through art*. London: Faber and Faber.

Sully, J. (1896) *Studies of childhood*. New York: Appleton.

Taylor, M. & Bacharach, V. R. (1982) Constraints on the visual accuracy of drawings produced by young children. *Journal of Experimental Child Psychology*, *34*, 311–29.

15

The head is smaller than the body:
but how does it join on?

JÜRI ALLIK and TIIA LAAK

1. Introduction

The way children draw their pictures may look queer to adults, but children are inclined to repeat their queerness from one picture to another. The underlying graphic vocabulary of children's drawing seems to be quite limited. Everyone who has studied children's pictures knows that many features of their drawings are extremely stereotyped in the individual child. The child borrows a limited number of graphic 'formulae' (Goodnow, 1977) from the age-specific graphic vocabulary, attempting to use them on many occasions. A particular graphic 'formula' which happened to be useful on one occasion is used in the hope of success when the child is locked in confrontation with another blank page. We can regard drawing as a problem-solving exercise for the child (Freeman, 1977 and 1980). In some sense the situation is similar to cats' movement-pattern stereotypy in a puzzle-box; there is a strong tendency for the animals to repeat the precise movements leading to escape from being boxed in.

The concept of stereotypy is a general one referring to those aspects of children's drawings which exhibit great consistency from one drawing to another. Stereotypy of drawings can manifest itself at different levels of abstraction. Provisionally, one can speak about three levels of abstraction at which drawing stereotypy can be described. The first level is the mental representation of the external world. Usually young children's drawings have been developed with the intention of representing real objects and the relations between them. The children's concept of objects and space is stereotyped and, as such, influences the final product of drawing. If we understand it correctly, Piaget's theory lays the main stress upon the relationship between the graphic image and the corresponding mental representation (Piaget and Inhelder, 1956). The end product of children's drawing is not *uniquely determined* by the underlying mental representation, but rather it imposes some general constraints on the drawing organisation. Without going into details one can cite canonicality as an example of a stereotyped aspect of mental representation. The most obvious manifestation of canonicality is seen in drawing a familiar object in canonical orientation (Freeman and Janikoun, 1972; Ives and Houseworth, 1980), for instance, a cup drawn with its handle visible at the side. This is studied in Davis' chapter in this volume. It is worth mentioning that canonical representation is a central requirement in Marr's three-dimensional-model representation (Marr and Nishihara, 1978; Marr, 1982). In order to provide a unique description of any object, Marr and Nishihara propose that the three-dimensional representation should be canonical in the sense that the same object seen from any point of view will always yield the same object-centred description.

The second level of stereotypy manifestation is that connected with planning and picture-production strategy. Any picture containing many items has to be produced in serial order. The strategy by which internal representation is translated into graphical image seems also to be subject to stereotypy: the sequence in which the parts of a human figure are produced is quite stable (Bassett, 1977; Goodnow, 1977; Freeman, 1980), at least for an individual child. There are some indications that children use not only surface picture properties but genuinely abstract entities to guide their drawing. For example, it can be demonstrated that some aspects of children's drawing depends on relative size (the body–proportion effect) and the centre of the figure (firebrush figures) (Kellogg, 1969; Freeman, 1975 and 1980; Freeman and Hargreaves, 1977; Goodnow, 1977).

Finally, the stereotypy of children's drawing can be analysed at the level of drawing performance. Children's pictures are made up of a variety of graphic units, the number of which is partly limited by their motor skills. In general, we mean by drawing performance a variety of *local decisions* which the child makes when he/she draws. Such local copying devices are termed by Freeman (1980) 'drawing devices': four of them (segregation, interposition, enclosure and hidden-line elimination) have been described in more detail. Just like the more abstract properties, the same drawing devices are used by children on many occasions: they are plurifunctional.

For the child, making a picture is the result of a considerable effort, solving many planning and performance problems. It is nothing but an illusion that a free-drawing task imposes no limitations at all on the children's drawing. For example, the spatial layout of the parts of the human body is produced in a relatively fixed serial order. Starting from the head, as is most commonly done, children may create a problem by failing to leave enough room on the page for the body. In this respect the first item drawn on the paper has an obvious advantage. Then in drawing each following item, children must take into account, in addition to the edges of the page, the spatial layout of what they have already completed. Because it is difficult to persuade children to draw the trunk before the head, the latter has a clear advantage over the rest of the body. Quite a few properties of the drawn human figure, especially the size of the body parts, can in principle be attributed to problems of serial production.

How might one reverse the children's natural drawing order? The completion of a partly pre-drawn figure is one possible method. One can make use of children's readiness to interpret every situation as a game, giving them a sheet of paper with a pre-drawn headless body and asking them to complete the figure which was 'left unfinished by another child'. In this situation the natural drawing sequence is reversed: the child has to draw the head after the trunk. By varying the size of the pre-drawn figure one can test the question of how the size of the head changes when it has been made in an unusual order, and how it depends upon the size of the components already laid down. In short, the method of completion solves, partly at least, some planning problems for the child.

There is always a discrepancy between children's intention and their ability to put this intention into effect (and there is no reason to think that this is untrue of adults, too!). The completion of an unfinished drawing, or the starting of a new one, causes, in addition to planning problems, many other problems intrinsic to the children's graphical performance itself. In order to get free from some of the limitations imposed by the children's drawing performance, instead of drawing one can ask the child to complete the unfinished figure by selecting one item from a set of cut-out pieces. In this case the translation from mental representation to the graphical image is less influenced by sheer motor skill.

Usually it is very difficult to use drawing as evidence about mental representation and planning. We are very far from believing that the comparison of free drawing, completion and cut-out assembly data allows us *directly* to separate planning problems from the properties of mental representations. We can say that some natural constraints inherent in the free drawing are diminished in the completion task and the latter, in its turn, is more restrictive compared with the assembly technique, in the sense of the demands imposed upon coordination skill. Unfortunately, there is nothing which could prove that completion is but a free-drawing task minus an additive constant eliminated in the completion task. On the contrary, it is more natural to suppose that an unfinished figure, usually carried out in a non-childish style, imposes some new problems the child has not encountered in the free-drawing task. This is the case when we wish to compare the completion task with the assembly game where graphic constraints are relaxed. Nevertheless, we believe that the comparison of these three principal methods – free drawing, completion and assembly – can tell us something about the origin of stereotypy in children's drawing. Let us suppose that we were to discover a stereotyped property which is encountered only in free drawing. In this case, there will be more temptation to attribute it to graphic vocabulary rather than to characteristics of mental representation. In turn, if we find a phenomenon manifested invariably in all drawings and assembly tasks, one has every reason to suggest that this very phenomenon is a characteristic of mental representation.

2. Size stereotypy

Many investigators are inclined to think that the scale of children's drawings is used as a symbolic tool by which the importance of the represented object is conveyed. The symbolic interpretation of children's drawings' scale can only be strengthened by the existence of many iconographical systems in which the scale of a portrayed figure *directly* reflects its social and religious importance. Byzantine iconography is certainly one of the best examples of this kind. Since the chosen scale of a portrayed figure depends on its rank in the celestial hierarchy, in Byzantine icons and frescoes the image of the Virgin or Jesus Christ has a greater size than the apostles (Lazarev, 1971, p. 104). It is interesting that, following the tradition of Byzantine symbolism, Sechrest and Wallace (1964) proposed that the scale of children's drawings reflects the social importance of the represented personage. In particular, they found that the size of Santa Claus in drawings is systematically larger than the scale used for drawing an ordinary man, the difference becoming more pronounced as Christmas approaches. Subsequent studies have questioned the relation between Christmas and the size of Santa Claus in children's pictures. Particularly, Wallach and Leggett (1972) demonstrated that children of 5 to 6 years of age do not draw Santa Claus larger on average just before Christmas than they drew earlier, or after Christmas is over. However, the size of drawings, showing the high degree of consistency from one occasion to another even across the five-week period, was significantly different for Santa Claus and ordinary man drawings. As may be expected on the mere basis of intuition, Santa Claus figures, whose prototype includes a necessary hat, are considerably larger overall than figures of a man (by some 20 per cent). So, at least in this particular case, the chosen scale of a drawing conveys some information about the importance of the portrayed person.

Nevertheless, the quoted examples say little, if anything at all, about the *universality* of the symbolic use of size in children's pictures. For example, children older than those tested in the studies cited above failed to show the expected change in the size of drawings of the U.S. presidential candidates Carter and Ford as the election approached (Truhon and McKinney, 1979). Moreover, many children had expressed their *dislike* for a candidate in pictures bigger than those of the preferred one. Together with empirical findings one can have more deep-rooted theoretical doubts about generality of size symbolism in children's pictures. It is quite possible that size, like many other pictorial attributes, comes into the canonical representation of an object. Usually canonicality primarily means the most salient orientation or form which is used for representation of a set of objects. There is no logical reason which would prevent including size in the list of canonical features. Objects occur in typical sizes as well as typical distances from self, etc. In this case the size of Santa Claus drawings would simply indicate that its canonical representation bears no relation to a Byzantine-like hierarchy of social roles.

It can be hypothesised that children attempt to draw every new element in a certain proportion to the parts of the human figure already drawn, and the first item drawn on the paper in a certain proportion to the space available on the page. Freeman (1980) presents many illustrative data showing children's sensitivity to ratios and proportions. However, the relative-size concept, at least in its strict sense, is neither a universal nor the only one which controls children's picture production. Gridley (1938) reported that children could, on request, draw another figure of a different size though they could not rescale all the parts of the body in proportion. Children's inability to maintain harmonious relations among parts of the body during rescaling can be interpreted as supporting a stereotyped concept of size in the children's minds. For once it may sound strange that children show a high degree of consistency of drawing scale from one drawing to another. In the above-cited paper, Wallach and Leggett (1972) collected drawings of Santa Claus and a man from kindergarten children at various points in time before and after Christmas and were able to demonstrate that drawings made on any given topic would have a size that is characteristic of each person, regardless of the occasion on which the drawings are produced. The size of the drawing which they call a 'stylistic' aspect of the behaviour shows a high degree of consistency from one occasion to another across a five-week period. Size consistency accounted for about 30 per cent of total variance. Summing up, the child has a relatively stable concept of the size in which any given topic has to be drawn and is able to carry it across a considerable time period.

In fact, there have been some earlier reports indicating children's tendency to adopt a characteristic size (or proportions) for their drawings (e.g. Harris, 1950 and 1963; Nash and Harris, 1970). These reports have shown a considerable stability in the size of drawing over a period of time. Agreement among drawers, as well as self-consistency over a number of drawing trials, is greater in head length than in leg length: Nash and Harris (1970) proposed that the greater consistency in the drawing of the head is due to the relative amount of attention paid to the head and legs respectively.

3. Stereotypy in connecting parts of the figure

The choice of an appropriate scale for a new drawing item is not the only problem met by the child. Starting with a new item, the children have to solve the problem of how to *connect* this new item with the items already drawn. Young children are notoriously poor at putting parts of a drawing together in their appropriate relative positions (Freeman, 1980, p. 278). But even if relative positioning has been successful, a problem still remains: how to show, by graphic means, that two parts of the drawing represent a physically connected single object. It is crucially important to note that children's drawing is not simply a *list* of parts but a *number of connections* fastening one part to another. One has reason to think that connection technique is also subject to stereotypy. To our knowledge this type of children's drawing stereotypy has been neglected to date (for an exception see Laak and Rüütel, 1983). It seems that the stereotyped connection technique is an ingenious way to overcome a fundamental discrepancy existing between young children's ability to draw only one discrete item after another and the integrity of the depicted object. As Goodnow (1977) has observed, in some sense the drawings of very young children are 'asyntactic', since each graphical element is assigned its own space so that it is clearly segregated from the remaining elements on the page. Later, children make attempts to join boundaries between neighbouring parts of the drawing.

The most natural object of study for the problem of connecting the parts of the figure is the boundary between head and trunk. First of all, there may be complete separation of the two (Goodnow, 1977, pp. 44ff). To this primitive option are opposed several other types where the boundaries of head and trunk are contiguous (Kellogg, 1969). In general, we have been able to classify all children's drawings by using seven different types of head–trunk connection styles, which are schematically shown in Figure 15.1.

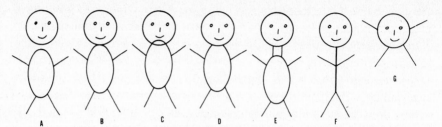

Figure 15.1 The classification of head–trunk connection types in children's drawings. A = unconnected-figure; B = tangent-point-figure; C = intersection-figure; D = tangent-line-figure; E = neck-figure; F = stick-figure; G = tadpole.

Unconnected-figure. This type is characterised by the head having no contact with the trunk.

Tangent-point-figure. In this type the contours of the head and trunk have only one point of contact.

Intersection-figure. The contours of the head and trunk intersect.

Tangent-line-figure. The figure is drawn so that there is a common line belonging simultaneously to the head and trunk. Usually, the tangent line is formed by eliminating one of two intersecting contours belonging either to the head or to the trunk. Formally, this figure type has two singular points with three arcs going out from each point specifying a particular type of joining topology.

Neck-figure. The head is connected to the trunk by two nearly parallel lines denoting the neck. This type, already having four singular points, is of late origin, rarely encountered before the age of 4 years.

Stick-figure. The contour of the trunk is collapsed onto a single line which is directly attached to the head.

Tadpole. Finally, in addition to the described types, we have to put tadpoles into a separate class: a human figure with the legs and arms apparently coming out directly from the head.

The types described can be relatively easily identified, and only in a few cases which we have seen was there some doubt as to how to classify a given picture.

Finally, it is an important aspect of drawing that the same graphical device can effectively be used for different purposes. That is why the present list of head–trunk connection types is in many aspects similar to the list of graphic devices by which children depict behindness in their drawings (Freeman, Eiser and Sayers, 1977). For example, hidden-line elimination can be used for conveying an idea that one object is behind another one (see Cox's chapter above), as well as another idea that two parts, head and trunk, belong to a single integral figure.

The general idea on which the experiments reported below were based is very simple. Various tasks, such as free drawing, completion and assembly, impose specific limitations on different aspects of children's representation. By recording inter-task and intra-task consistency, one can advance hypotheses about the origin of stereotypy in size and connection style of figure parts. To anticipate the results, our data support the idea that the child is guided by a simple relational-size concept which is *not specific to drawing per se*: the head must be smaller than the body. Contrary to this, the figure-parts connecting style appears to be a quite *local drawing device* depending, particularly, on the order in which the items were drawn. It is not surprising that we were not able to find any systematic dependences between figure-parts size and connecting-type stereotypy; that is another indication of their different origins.

4. Experimental studies

The first experiment was mainly focused on a comparison among free drawing, completion and assembly tasks. The second experiment, on the other hand, aimed to test for drawing consistency over successive occasions, and for the influence of different size-cues on the connecting style and relative size of figure parts in children's drawings.

Experiment One

The sample included 74 children, ranging from 2 years 8 months to 6 years 11 months of age (mean age 5 years 3 months). The experimenter had a private room where children were asked to perform six tests: (1) free drawing of a man; (2) completion of a pre-drawn headless body; (3) completion of a pre-drawn head; (4) selection of a head to add to the pre-drawn body from a set of cut-out heads; (5) selection of a body to complete the pre-drawn head; and (6) construction of the human figure from two pieces, head and headless body, from cut-out pieces of different size. The drawings and completion tests were performed on a standard sheet of white paper 21×15 cm.

The experimental session always started and ended with a free-drawing task. A sheet of clean paper was given to the child with the following instruction: 'Draw a person, please. You may draw yourself, or Mummy, or Daddy, or anybody else.' On the final occasion the experimenter usually added: 'I like your pictures and I'd like you to make me another man drawing.' The sequence of other tasks was chosen at random.

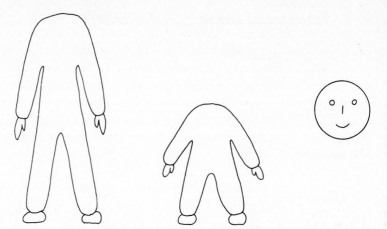

Figure 15.2 Examples of the pre-drawn head and headless bodies that have been used in the completion and assembly tasks. Note that the scale of figures was the only important variable.

Head drawing. Each child was given a sheet of paper with the pre-drawn human headless body, the height of which was 5 cm, as shown in Figure 15.2. The instruction was: 'Here is a headless man; only the body and legs are drawn. Please finish this figure so that the man will come out.'

Body drawing. A sheet of paper with the pre-drawn head (height 5 cm) of Figure 15.2 was given, with a request to complete this figure.

Head selection. Again the same pre-drawn human headless body was presented, and in addition six cut-out heads of different sizes. The instruction was: 'Please choose one head from these that you think is the best one for this body. Put the chosen head in its place so that a man will come out.' The diameters of the heads were: 2.0, 3.5, 5.0, 6.5, 8.0 and 9.5 cm. The arrangement of the heads on the table was random.

Body selection. A sheet of paper with the pre-drawn head was given with the request to complete this figure with a body from a collection of six headless bodies of varying height: 3.5, 5.0, 6.5, 8.0, 9.5 and 11 cm. As in previous, and all other, experiments, the arrangement of bodies was random.

Construction (assembly). Six cut-out heads and six cut-out headless bodies were placed in front of the child, with the instruction: 'I should like you to put together a man from these pieces. Please choose just one head and one body, and make the best man you can.'

For two repeated drawing tasks and two completion tasks (the head and the trunk drawing) the type of each drawing was determined according to the classification in Figure 15.2. In the drawing tasks the size of the drawn

Table 15.1. *Means and standard deviations in the height of drawn and selected body parts, in mm, in two free-drawing, pre-drawn figure-completion and figure-construction (assembly) tasks*

Task	Code	Mean	sd	Reliably different from
First free drawing				
Head	H1	29.6	(14.0)	H3, H4, H5
Body	B1	67.0	(28.3)	B3, B4
Final free drawing				
Head	H2	31.6	(16.4)	H3, H5
Body	B2	71.0	(31.3)	B4
Body completion				
Head drawing	H3	23.0	(10.0)	H1, H2, H4, H5
Head selection	H4	40.5	(25.1)	H1, H3
Head completion				
Body drawing	B3	81.0	(26.4)	B1
Body selection	B4	90.9	(22.5)	B1, B2
Figure construction				
Head	H5	49.4	(26.1)	H1, H2, H3
Body	B5	79.6	(29.1)	—

head and the trunk was measured, defined as the vertical height from the lowest point to the highest.

The data are shown in Table 15.1. Pairwise comparison of means shows no differences between free drawing done at the start and the end of the session, so there was some stability in performance (see the last column in Table 15.1). There was no difference in the mean size of the selected head and body in completion and construction tasks. However, in the completion of the pre-drawn headless body, the drawn head was reliably *smaller* than that in free drawing. In contrast, the size of the completed body was magnified in comparison to the free-drawing body. What can this contrast tell us? First of all, it turned out that the pre-drawn body was *smaller* than would be done spontaneously by the child, and, contrary to this, the pre-drawn head was somewhat *larger* than the head drawn spontaneously. Thus it seems that the children were governed by a simple relational-size concept: the larger the head, the larger has to be the body. As may be expected, the pairwise Pearson product-moment correlation between sizes of the drawn heads and bodies in the free-drawing tasks was highly positive. But the largest correlation was found between the size of the selected head and body in the construction task ($r = 0.666$), which accounts for about 44 per cent of the variance. The

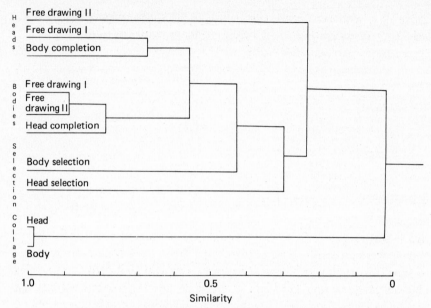

Figure 15.3 The solution of a hierarchical cluster analysis applied to the data of Experiment 1. For other details consult the text.

relational-size concept will be studied in more detail in Experiment 2 by varying the size of the pre-drawn figures and the format of the paper.

The covariance between the sizes of drawn and selected figure parts shows the high degree of similarity of those parts of the drawing. More formally, the coefficient of correlation can be transformed into a distance measure, characterising the degree of similarity between items, by the following equation: $d = 1 - (r+1)/2$ (note that if $r = 1$ then the corresponding inter-item distance will be 0). To the reformulated matrix of distances, a Johnson's hierarchical clustering analysis was applied. From a number of classificatory schemes realised in the program (cf. Lance and Williams, 1967), we selected the nearest neighbour distance 1, since it is shown to be invariant in respect of monotonic transformation of distance matrix (Johnson, 1967).

— The obtained solution is shown as a dendrogram in Figure 15.3. The degree of similarity between any two elements is represented by the horizontal distance from the root of the graph to the node where these two particular elements join into a cluster. From inspection of Figure 15.3 it is immediately obvious that the construction task is different from all other tasks. Another finding of the hierarchical cluster analysis is that all drawn bodies are very similar to each other. As concerns other elements from different tasks, they join the general graph quite randomly; perhaps only the second free-drawing

Table 15.2. *Response-frequency distribution of the different figure types (see Figure 15.1) in free-drawing and pre-drawn figure-completion tasks*

Figure type	Free drawing		Completion	
	I	II	Body	Head
1. Unconnected-figure	2	2	7	0
2. Tangent-point-figure	31	31	19	32
3. Intersection-figure	4	6	28	12
4. Tangent-line-figure	0	1	9	2
5. Neck-figure	23	22	11	19
6. Stick-figure	6	5	—	2
7. Tadpole	8	7	0	7

task is oddly separate from the others. It is rather interesting that the drawn body is the most sensitive element showing the highest degree of consistency in size. This result can be compared with developmental data showing that children prefer to hold head size relatively constant and increase trunk size with increase in age (Laak, 1981). Consequently, if it is at all reasonable to speak about disproportionality in young children's drawing it seems to be the trunk that is too small in relation to the head. In this respect it is worth remembering that 4-year-olds believe that the big trunk is much funnier than the big-headed figure (Freeman, 1980).

In two free-drawing tasks and two completion tasks, we were able to determine the type of the drawn figure. The results are shown in Table 15.2. Chi-square tests reveal no reliable differences between two free-drawing and pre-drawn head completion tasks. The body-completion task, in which children draw the head, was reliably different from all other tasks. As may be expected, when completing the headless body, children never draw tadpoles. Also it is worth mentioning that the number of intersection-figures was dramatically increased at the expense of tangent-point-figures. The number of neck-figures roughly halved. It is not surprising that the head–trunk connection type changes with the change of pre-drawn incomplete figure. Evidently, the tasks of drawing with different incomplete figures, bodiless head and headless trunk, have different 'demand characteristics' (as it was named by Golomb, 1974). First of all there seem to be different graphic conventions used by children to draw the head and body of a human figure. The form of the head, for example, is certainly more stereotyped in being more reliably circular. The form of the body is far more variable. One possible reason for the changes in method of joining between them, apart from what may be induced by the reversal of the natural drawing order, is that the child may feel difficulties with eliminating part of a contour in a more regular figure, that is, the circle. Presumably that is why the number of intersection-figures was significantly increased when the child drew a head in completing the headless trunk. The sensitivity of figure parts' connection types to the form of the pre-drawn figure can be regarded as supportive of the idea that connection type is a rather specific drawing device, being not integral to the child's mental representation as such. But as a specific drawing device, head–trunk connection type is quite stable. Although there is no information about inter-individual consistency in Table 15.2, in fact we found that an individual remains true to the connection type once chosen, using the same type in free-drawing tasks as well as in the pre-drawn head-completion task, in good agreement with our earlier data (Laak and Rüütel, 1983).

One can ask how the connection type and the size of body parts are related. We were not able to discover any systematic relations between the figure parts' connection types and the size of those parts. One can conclude that these two aspects of children's drawing stereotypy are relatively independent of each other, probably having different origins in the drawing process. Still it is obviously necessary to probe the stability of performance under different drawing conditions. To this we now turn.

Experiment 2

Eighty kindergarten children (mean age 5 years 3 months) were asked to draw a man or to complete pre-drawn headless bodies and heads. The experiment involved two sessions, with an interval of two weeks between them.

Free drawing. The child was asked to draw any man he/she liked, the instructions being the same as in the previous experiment.

Completion of 6.5-cm pre-drawn headless body. The task was to complete a pre-drawn headless body, 6.5 cm in diameter.

Completion of 11-cm pre-drawn headless body. Exactly the same body, but with a height of 11 cm, was given to the child for completion.

Completion of 2-cm pre-drawn head. The child had to draw the missing parts.

Completion of 5-cm pre-drawn head. The same as on the previous occasion.

The experimental session always started with the free-drawing task, the sequence of the other tasks being random. After two weeks the experiment was repeated. Each child went through the same tasks, performing finally one additional task: free drawing made on a larger sheet of paper, 30 × 21 cm. So in total there were 11 drawings per child.

For each drawing the size of the drawn head and/or body was determined in the way previously described, and was classified according to the type of head–trunk connection. The data are shown in Table 15.3.

Table 15.3. *Means and standard deviations in the height of drawn and selected body parts, in mm, in free-drawing and pre-drawn figure-completion tasks. Two values, upper and lower, in each row, correspond to two successive occasions respectively; since there were no reliable differences between these, the averages in the third data-column were used to compute the results of the final column*

Task	Code	Mean	sd	Overall Mean	sd	Reliably different from
Free drawing						
Head	H1	24.0	(13.9)	25.2	(13.0)	H4
		26.4	(12.0)			
Body	B1	68.1	(30.3)	70.9	(30.8)	B3, B4
		73.6	(31.2)			
Body completion						
6.5 cm	H2	24.1	(11.5)	23.4	(9.7)	H3, H4
		22.7	(8.0)			
11.0 cm	H3	28.4	(10.7)	29.8	(11.3)	H2, H4
		31.2	(11.9)			
Head completion						
2.0 cm	B2	79.8	(35.2)	81.1	(36.0)	B3, B4
		82.3	(36.9)			
5.0 cm	B3	94.5	(32.6)	95.7	(30.9)	B1, B2, B4
		96.9	(29.2)			
Free drawing (paper 30 × 21 cm)						
Head	H4	42.1	(19.5)	—	—	H1, H2, H3
Body	B4	123.6	(53.0)	—	—	B1, B2, B3

There was good agreement between two successive occasions (*t*-tests failed to find reliable differences between means). The completion of pre-drawn figures seemed to obey a simple rule: the larger the pre-drawn part of the figure, the larger will be the added head or body.

In Table 15.4 the frequency distribution of different figure types in free-drawing and figure-completion tasks is shown. Once again, the completion of the pre-drawn headless body seemed to be different from the other tasks. This was confirmed by chi-square: the distribution of figure types in free-drawing and head-completion tasks differed reliably from the figure-type distribution in all body-completion tasks. No reliable difference was discovered when free-drawing and head-completion tasks were compared among themselves; but there were differences amongst the body-completion tasks themselves. As in the previous experiment, intra-individual connection-style consistency was observed: a child using a given head–trunk connection type on the first occasion almost always used the same type on the second occasion.

Table 15.4. *Response-frequency distribution of the different figure types in free-drawing and pre-drawn figure-completion tasks. The upper number in each cell of the table corresponds to the first drawing occasion, the lower number to the second drawing occasion. All measurements are in cm*

	Free drawing		Completion			
Figure type	Page 21×15	Page 30×21	Small body (6.5)	Big body (11)	Small head (2)	Big head (5)
1. Unconnected-figure	1	0	2	3	1	1
	1	1	4	5	1	1
2. Tangent-point-figure	47	0	35	34	50	50
	52	52	30	32	54	55
3. Intersection-figure	3	0	25	23	3	1
	4	3	30	25	4	4
4. Tangent-line-figure	2	0	4	5	0	0
	1	2	5	7	0	0
5. Neck-figure	21	0	14	15	20	23
	17	18	11	11	17	16
6. Tadpole	6	0	0	0	6	5
	5	4	0	0	4	4

In order to find similarities among different drawing tasks, a matrix of Spearman product-moment correlations was computed, then transformed into a matrix of inter-item distances to which Johnson's hierarchical clustering scheme ('nearest neighbour') was applied. The solution in the form of a tree is shown in Figure 15.4. The solution turned out to be very intelligent. It is possible to distinguish three clearly separate levels: on the first level a single cluster joins all drawn headless bodies; on the second level a new cluster was formed which united all heads which were drawn to complete an unfinished body; and, finally, on the third level, the heads drawn in free-drawing tasks joined the tree. Bearing in mind that the horizontal distance from the root to the node where two elements are joined in one cluster represents similarity, it is obvious that the *body* was the most stable element in the children's drawings. The mean correlation among seven bodies that children drew in this experiment was $r = 0.506$, which accounts for about 26 per cent of the variance. If we compare the bodies drawn in the course of *one* session, then the consistency among body heights was even larger, accounting for more than a third of the variance.

In general, the results of this experiment are in good agreement with data that have been obtained in the first. In particular the children's relational-size concept was strong and relatively stable over time.

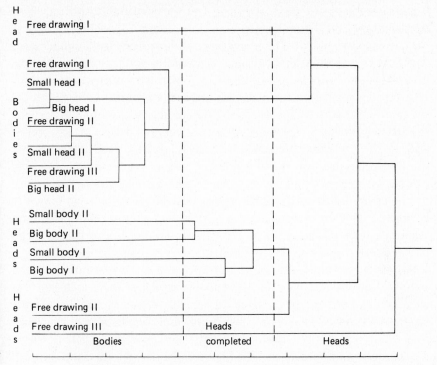

Figure 15.4 The solution of a hierarchical cluster analysis of data obtained in Experiment 2.

5. Re-evaluation of drawing performance

Size consistency. In this study we found support for children's tendency to adopt a characteristic size in their drawings. Size consistency, measured by product-moment correlation, was manifest to a different degree depending on the part of the drawn figure. On the basis of two experiments one can speak about *two* forms of consistency. First, the size of an item showed a high degree of consistency from one drawing task to its repetition across a two-week period. This result is in good agreement with the data reported by Wallach and Leggett (1972). We can assert on the basis of our second experiment that size consistency can account for about a quarter of total variance at least. Second, size consistency extended from one specific drawing task to another. The results of both experiments showed that, knowing the size of the head or the remaining figure, one can with some confidence predict the height of head or body which the children draw on request to finish an uncompleted human figure.

It is rather natural to propose that the first item laid on the paper may have an advantage over the remaining parts of the figure. Therefore, head length may be expected to have a relatively larger self-consistency than other parts of children's drawing. What we found is precisely *opposite* to this conjecture. The head size, overwhelmingly the first drawn item, turned out to be a relatively inconsistent element in the children's pictures. Contrary to the conclusion of Nash and Harris (1970), we can hypothesise that, in drawing the first item, children experience difficulties with the *choice* of an appropriate scale for their drawing. There may be many reasons for these difficulties, but the most plausible one seems to be the lack of an immediate frame of reference. Therefore a partially pre-drawn figure provides a frame of reference for the child. Following this line one can conclude that the head drawn to complete a headless body is more consistent in size than that drawn on a request to draw a man on an empty page. Inspecting Figure 15.4 one can find evidence supporting this proposal.

Surprisingly enough, we found the body size to be the most self- and intertask-consistent element in the children's drawing. This conclusion was supported by both our experiments (cf. Figures 15.3 and 15.4). Usually the product-moment correlation between trunk–limb heights was in the range from 0.4 to 0.7, which accounts for a large amount of the variation. It is of special importance to note that the high correlation does *not* mean the *exact* reproduction of the same characteristic size on two different occasions. Thus, in the second experiment, where our young subjects completed 2- and 5-cm heads, on the second occasion the trunk height was reliably larger for the 5-cm head than for the smaller one. This means that the children were able to rescale their drawing, but they did this in proportion to their previous pictures.

Although size consistently extended from the free-drawing task to the completion task, the *absolute* size of the assembly element selected for completion of a half-done figure was not too consistent with the absolute size of the same element children drew with a pencil. What we found is a responsiveness to *relative* size in the assembly task: the children believe that the smaller head must also have a smaller body, and, in turn, the larger head is united with the larger body.

Connection-type consistency. The head–body connecting type proved to be consistent. Although Tables 15.2 and 15.4 contain only average results, type consistency was a characteristic of individuals. Tadpole-drawers, for example, were the same children. Children stuck to their preferred type even after the two-week period. The head–body connecting stereotype is not only confined to the free-drawing task. If a child were asked to complete a half-done figure representing a head, s/he was most likely to use the same connecting type as in the free-drawing task (with the tangent-point-figure and neck-figure being the most popular ones). The dramatic changes occurred when the pre-drawn head was replaced with the headless body. As we mentioned above, in this case the distribution of types was reliably different from all other cases. In the body-completion task the natural drawing order is reversed: the head was drawn after the trunk and limbs. With the reversal of the natural drawing order the relative position of items on the paper was also reversed. In the normal case the next item joined to the previous one was below it. Adding the head to an unfinished human figure, the already finished items were below and new elements had to be drawn above them. The connecting type changed remarkably. The number of tangent-point- and neck-figures diminished, and the number of intersection-figures increased. In some sense this type change can be interpreted as a backwards step. Neck-figure-drawers were on average older than those who preferred other types, especially tadpoles. Completing the headless human figure, there were far fewer necks compared with the free-drawing and head-completion tasks. It should also be noted that tangent-figures require more coordination than does intersection. We believe that for a young child it is more difficult to draw two contours having contact only in one tangent point rather than freely intersecting each other. From these observations, one can conclude that the connecting type is specific to the drawing-production system. Children seem to have a formula on which their human-figure drawing is based, and alteration of the normal sequence may lead to omissions and changes in drawing items. This is what we observed when the children were asked to complete a headless body. However, it is not the completion task *per se* which alters the type of drawing but the reversal of the normal drawing order of human-figure elements. In short, the connecting type is likely to be a *local drawing device* helping to cope with the problems posed by drawing.

As noted in the introductory section, the different connection types bear a strong resemblance to the set of drawing devices (segregation, interposition and hidden-line elimination) which Freeman, Eiser and Sayers (1977) studied in a different spatial problem. In their study, the children were asked to draw one object behind another: the younger ones segregated the two items on the page, whereas older ones used hidden-line elimination, which is similar to the tangent-line method in this chapter. The chapters by Crook and by Cox in this volume also deal with the device of hidden-line elimination. We can thus see here that different spatial tasks can result in similar problems on the picture plane and children then adopt rather similar solutions. Drawing devices are indeed plurifunctional.

Size concept. From the results one can draw some conclusions about children's concept of what size a body part ought to be. In the first experiment the same pre-drawn figure was completed by drawing and by selection from a set of items. From Table 15.1 it is apparent that the selected element, head or body, was larger than the same element drawn for the completion. In the second experiment we observed that the increase of size in the pre-drawn item induced an increase of size in an item drawn in the completion. This means that the children had a tendency to draw the next item in proportion to the previous element already drawn on the page (Table 15.3). Inspection of Table 15.3 can readily confirm that there was no single feature, like area available on the page or the size of already drawn figure parts, which predicted the *exact* size of the rest of the figure parts. For example, if the pre-drawn head increased in size from 2 cm to 5 cm the size of the added body increased only 1.2 times instead of the expected 2.5. Of course, one could try to find more sophisticated relations between different measures, but we are doubtful about the existence of something like an interval scale here, on more general grounds. It is more natural to suppose that the child is guided in her/his drawing by a simple relational concept: the head must be smaller than the rest of the body together with the legs. This simple concept is valid not only for the free-drawing task but for the completion and assembly tasks as well. Since this regularity proved to be independent of particular tasks, the concept 'the head is smaller than the body' can be attributed to their mental representation, being a canonical aspect of the latter.

6. In conclusion

Previous studies have shown that children have a tendency to adopt a characteristic size for their drawings. But with the change of drawing task the scale of children's drawing is also changed. In spite of this, the correlation between sizes of figure parts remains; that is, the children who preferred a relatively larger scale for their figures in one task preferred a relatively larger scale in another task also. Relatively new in our study was a demonstration that the children's tendency to draw the next item in proportion to the previous element already on the page is specific to the element's content, not to the order in which they have been produced. The proportions were determined by a simple principle: the head must be smaller than the body. In addition, we discovered a new type of stereotypy in children's drawings, that governing head–trunk connection. We were able to show that expression of the concept of relative size was insensitive to change of task, whilst the connection-type stereotypy was sensitive to this change. Consequently, the children's concept of size is more likely to be integral to their mental representation and the connecting stereotype is most likely a specific drawing device, depending, particularly, on the spatial position and production order of drawn items. It is to be hoped that research such as this will lead to a reclassification of drawings, distinguishing between those aspects which are directly governed by the child's mental representation of the topic and those which are local, on-the-spot, solutions to the drawing problems which arise on the page during the course of production. Both are aspects of the problem-solving nature of representational drawing and they demand rather different theoretical formulations.

ACKNOWLEDGEMENT

We owe a special debt to Norman Freeman for his special efforts in bringing the manuscript into its present form.

REFERENCES

Bassett, E. M. (1977) Production strategies in the child's drawing of the human figure. In G. Butterworth (ed.), *The child's representation of the world*. New York: Plenum, pp. 49–59.

Freeman, N. H. (1975) Do children draw men with arms coming out of the head? *Nature, London*, 254, 416–17.

(1977) How young children try to plan drawings. In G. Butterworth (ed.), *The child's representation of the world*. New York: Plenum, pp. 3–29.

(1980) *Strategies of representation in young children: Analysis of spatial skills and drawing processes*. London: Academic Press.

Freeman, N. H., Eiser, C. & Sayers, J. (1977) Children's strategies in producing three-dimensional relationships on a two-dimensional surface. *Journal of Experimental Child Psychology*, 23, 305–14.

Freeman, N. H. & Hargreaves, S. (1977) Directed movements and the body-proportion effect in preschool children's human figure drawing. *Quarterly Journal of Experimental Psychology*, 29, 227–35.

Freeman, N. H. & Janikoun, R. (1972) Intellectual realism in children's drawings of a familiar object with distinctive features. *Child Development*, 43, 1116–21.

Golomb, C. (1974) *Young children's sculpture and drawing*. Cambridge, Mass.: Harvard University Press.

Goodnow, J. (1977) *Children's drawing*. London: Open Books.

Gridley, P. F. (1938) Graphic representation of a man by four-year-old children in nine prescribed drawing situations. *Genetic Psychology Monographs*, 20, 183–350.

Harris, D. B. (1950) Intra-individual vs. inter-individual consistency in children's drawings of a man. *American Psychologist*, 5, 293.

(1963) *Children's drawings as measures of intellectual maturity*. New York: Harcourt, Brace and World.

Ives, S. W. & Houseworth, M. (1980) The role of standard orientations in children's drawings of interpersonal relationships: Aspects of graphic feature marking. *Child Development*, 51, 591–3.

Johnson, S. C. (1967) Hierarchical clustering schemes. *Psychometrica*, 32, 241–54.

Kellogg, R. (1969) *Analyzing children's art*. Palo Alto: Mayfield.

Laak, T. (1981) Body proportions in children's human figure drawing: Developmental changes. *Acta et Commentationes Universitatis Tartuensis*, 568, 65–72.

Laak, T. & Rüütel, M. (1983) Head size stereotype in children's human figure drawing. *Acta et Commentationes Universitatis Tartuensis*, 638, 66–78.

Lance, G. N. & Williams, W. T. (1967) A general theory of classificatory sorting strategies. I. Hierarchical systems. *Computer Journal*, 9, 373–80.

Lazarev, V. N. (1971) *Byzantine painting*. Moscow: Nauka Publisher. (In Russian.)

Marr, D. (1982) *Vision*. San Francisco: Freeman.

Marr, D. & Nishihara, H. K. (1978) Representation and recognition of the spatial organization of three-dimensional shapes. *Proceedings of the Royal Society of London*, ser. B, 200, 269–94.

Nash, H. & Harris, D. B. (1970) Body proportions in children's drawing of a man. *Journal of Genetic Psychology*, 117, 85–90.

Piaget, J. & Inhelder, B. (1956) *The child's concept of space*. London: Routledge and Kegan Paul.

Sechrest, L. & Wallace, J. (1964) Figure drawings and naturally occurring events: Elimination of the expansive euphoria hypothesis. *Journal of Educational Psychology*, 53, 42–4.

Truhon, S. A. & McKinney, J. P. (1979) Children's drawings of the presidential candidates. *Journal of Genetic Psychology*, 134, 157–8.

Wallach, M. A. & Leggett, M. I. (1972) Testing the hypothesis that a person will be consistent: Stylistic consistency versus situational specificity in size of children's drawings. *Journal of Personality*, 40, 309–30.

Commentary

N. H. FREEMAN and M. V. COX

The classical account of children's development, that they are locked into 'intellectual realism' until saved by a realisation that they can depict what they see around the age of 7 or 8, now seems very thin indeed. Even 3-year-olds may have some access to a viewer-centred mode (Chapter 13) and 5-year-olds certainly do. It is not yet clear how to characterise the possession of more than one mode. The options canvassed include drawing a specific object/drawing a class-exemplar (Chapter 12), symbolic/view-specific codes (Chapter 13), object-centred/array-centred modes (Chapter 12), object-centred/viewer-centred coordinate systems (Chapters 4, 11), scene-structure/scene-appearance (Chapter 10), short-term-store/long-term-store descriptions (Chapters 6, 14), structure-directed/content-directed strategies (Chapter 8) and so on. This multiplicity is vexing, but it has a healthy side. The distinctions do not easily pack down into two neat piles: many of them capture different impressions of the mind of the depictor (this is particularly clear in a comparison of Chapters 4 and 12). Thus one is not called upon to make a legislative decision as to which term will be, henceforth, regarded as kosher. Rather the challenge is to identify the points at which any two terms appearing to lie on the same side of the divide actually fail to tessellate, and that will indicate the position of an interesting problem for the next round of research.

Whatever the fate of that new research, it seems that there is substantial agreement that the slogan 'children below the age of 7 or so draw what they know rather than what they see' has had its run. The newer one might run 'children below the age of 7 aren't flexible enough in the choice they make from the options available to them to do themselves justice'. Not very snappy as a slogan, but a bit closer to the mark.

We know much more about children's strategies now, but what we still do not know is how good they are with any one strategy. We were told in Chapter 5 that children may set themselves a very hard depiction puzzle even when an easier one is on the agenda, and in Chapter 4 we were shown some of the complexity of operating even a simple denotation system. In Chapter 15 we gained some insight into the plurifunctional nature of certain specific drawing devices. All this means that there is ample scope for error to occur, in the sense of a deviation in the product from that which is intended by the producer. One can envisage a loss of nerve as the emerging depiction fails to look as though it is coming right (Chapter 6), or a slippage in the planned sequence of drawing (Chapters 13 and 15), or even a hasty bungling of an on-the-spot implementation of a drawing device which had not been foreseen (Chapters 5, 13, 15, 19).

It is easy to catalogue possible sources of error. But interpretation of their effects is an enterprise of an altogether harder nature. That is because we do not yet know the noise level against which such error signals would be expected to occur. How accurate are young children when everything possible is done to assist them? In the final few chapters we begin with an analysis which draws upon many of the previous themes, examine some specific problems in great detail, and end with material which poses a direct challenge: how many of the previous insights can be focused to illuminate the happy, free-drawing child?

16

Geometrical foundations of children's drawing

MICHAEL C. MITCHELMORE

1. Introduction

Most of the chapters in this book are concerned with the geometry of children's drawings in relation to that of the stimulus figure. Duthie, Willats, Phillips and Chen, for example, analyse drawings of three-dimensional objects in terms of the overall structure of the drawing or the directions of individual lines, comparing these with some ideal representation derived by projection onto the picture plane. Davis, Cox, Ingram, Light and Barrett are more concerned with the representation of the spatial relations between objects, analysing them using concepts such as separateness, order and orientation. Pratt, Crook, Bayraktar and Bremner, on the other hand, consider direct copies of two-dimensional figures, where the notion of projection or representation does not enter, in terms of angles, distance and symmetry.

Despite all this interest in geometry, few researchers have examined two fundamental relations used in the analysis of Euclidean space, namely *parallels* and *perpendiculars*. As soon as we think of three-dimensional space, we think of three perpendicular directions (length, breadth and height, usually) and it is the representation of these three directions on paper which presents the first problem in drawing three-dimensional objects. All lines in any one of these directions are parallel to each other, and the preservation of this relation in the drawing enables one to depict all rectangular objects, the most basic of which are the cube and cuboid. Mathematically, parallels and perpendiculars form the basis of the rectangular coordinate system which is so widely used in both theoretical work and practical applications.

Parallels and perpendiculars are also fundamental in a logical sense. Since the time of Euclid, mathematicians have tried to build geometry on a foundation of axioms – supposedly self-evident properties for which no proof is required. Euclid's famous Fifth Postulate is the axiom which expresses the properties of parallels as we experience them in the real space around us. It has been shown that a perfectly consistent geometry can be constructed without any axiom relating to parallels, but this geometry cannot cope with metric ideas (i.e. ideas related to measurement: length, angles and so on). Addition of the Fifth Postulate produces a richer system in which angles can be defined in terms of parallels: one can define a direction as a set of lines which are all parallel to each other; an angle is then simply a pair of directions. A congruence axiom is required before angles can be compared; perpendiculars can then be defined as lines whose intersection creates four congruent angles. Further axioms are required before measurement concepts can be fully incorporated into the system.

Are ideas of parallels and perpendiculars present at an early age, before ideas of angle and direction? In fact, can they be regarded as 'primitives' in the perception and concept of space? Can, and do, children use them in their drawings? And do they operate in the same or in different ways depending on whether the child is copying a two-dimensional figure or a three-dimensional model?

This chapter is devoted to a discussion of these questions. The plan is as follows. As a necessary preliminary, the first section clarifies the essential differences between two-dimensional and three-dimensional drawing. The second section reviews the evidence on children's cognition of parallels and perpendiculars in isolation. This is followed by two sections which report research on the conflict between the representation of parallels and perpendiculars, first in two-dimensional and then in three-dimensional drawings, and the final section considers how far children's performance in these two spheres can be related.

2. Isographs and homographs

Both two-dimensional and three-dimensional drawings are two-dimensional, in the sense that they are necessarily restricted to a two-dimensional surface. In order to express more clearly the difference between them, I propose to call them *isographs* and *homographs* respectively. The reason for choosing these terms is given below.

Isographs

In what was previously called two-dimensional drawing, the intention is usually to produce a more or less exact copy of a given two-dimensional stimulus figure. Because the drawing is also two-dimensional, its accuracy can be tested by placing it on top of the stimulus (imagine that the drawing is made on tracing paper, if you will); the drawing should match the stimulus at every point, within some acceptable range of drawing error. Mathematically, the response should in theory be *congruent* to the stimulus. The tasks discussed in the chapter by Laszlo and Broderick fall squarely into this category.

There are other occasions where a drawing represents a two-dimensional object without being congruent to it. Many designs produced by commercial artists, for example, are actually scaled-down or scaled-up versions of a shape which is intended to be applied to a surface or cut from a flat sheet of some material. Especially when drawing very large or very small objects, we do not expect a drawing to be congruent to the original, but we do expect that it would be congruent (and could then be matched point by point) if it were enlarged or reduced. In this case, the response is geometrically *similar* to the stimulus. Each angle in the response is equal to the corresponding angle in the stimulus, and the ratio of any two lengths in the response is equal to the corresponding ratio in the stimulus.

In these two cases, we shall call the response an isograph of the stimulus. The term is modelled on the mathematical term 'isomorphic', which is applied to a one-to-one correspondence in which certain features are faithfully preserved. An isograph is (in intention, at least) in a one-to-one point-by-point correspondence with the stimulus figure, and angles and ratios of lengths are copied exactly. The vast majority of two-dimensional drawings, if you think about it, are isographs.

Homographs

In a so-called three-dimensional drawing, a view of an object is constructed by projecting onto a picture plane according to some standard system (Dubery and Willats, 1983). The projection from the object onto the picture plane is unique, but the object cannot be uniquely reconstructed from the picture: an infinite number of objects give the same projection (for a discussion of why we tend to interpret these inherently ambiguous drawings in a unique way, see Perkins and Cooper, 1980). A three-dimensional drawing is therefore different from an isograph in that it is not in one-to-one correspondence with the stimulus object. Even after enlarging or reducing the drawing, there is no hope of being able to lay it on top of the object to see if it fits exactly.

Nevertheless, a three-dimensional drawing does accurately represent many features of the object, for example (if one includes the hidden edges and excludes singular station points) it shows the number of vertices on the object, how they are linked by edges, and the number of edges of each face. Three points in line on the object will also be in line and in the same order in the drawing, and if two lines meet in the object they will meet in the drawing.

Angles and lengths are distorted, but the ratio of lengths measured in the same direction is often approximately equal in stimulus and response. We shall therefore call such three-dimensional drawings homographs, from the mathematical term 'homomorphic' which is applied to a many-to-one correspondence in which certain features are faithfully preserved. The vast majority of three-dimensional drawings that children and the average adult deal with are homographs.

A grey area: two-dimensional homographs

The distinction between an isograph and a homograph may seem obvious, but the literature suggests that they are often confused.

Consider, for example, Piaget's water-level task (Piaget and Inhelder, 1956). This seems to be a two-dimensional task, in that the drawing represents a section through the bottle and the water level is assumed not to slope in the depth dimension. Do we therefore call it a two-dimensional drawing? Can we validly model it by an isographic task, as Ibbotson and Bryant (1976) claimed to do? The answer is that you can call the drawing anything you like but you cannot make it into an isographic task: drawing the water level is essentially homographic, a two-dimensional representation of a three-dimensional phenomenon.

It is necessary to distinguish three-dimensional stimuli which effectively lie entirely in the frontal plane (such as Piaget's water-level and hillside tasks) from those which lie in a non-frontal plane (drawing a receding road) or use all three dimensions (drawing trees next to the road). The task children face in drawing homographs of frontal-plane stimuli *may* be equivalent to that of drawing an isograph, but in view of the vast theoretical distinction between a homograph and an isograph it need not be; no one has ever adduced any experimental evidence to support this assumption.

3. The psychological primitivity of parallels and perpendiculars

Parallels

Many studies have shown that quite young children are very sensitive to the alignment of two lines, that is, to their parallelism. For example, Bryant (1969) showed that the performance of 4- to 6-year-old children on a memory task, involving the discrimination of right- and left-sloping oblique lines, was considerably enhanced when an auxiliary line parallel to the target line was included in the stimulus and the response. This was not simply a matter of providing a cue to the left–right distinction, because the provision of an auxiliary line in the same quadrant but not parallel to the target line had no such effect. From this and similar results, Bryant (1974) argues that young children's judgements of orientation are largely made in terms of parallel alignment to salient features in the surroundings, such as the edges of a sheet of paper or of furniture and buildings. Freeman (1980) has extended this argument to explain the well-known finding that young children find tasks involving vertical or horizontal lines much easier than similar tasks involving oblique lines on the basis that there are many more naturally occurring verticals and horizontals to provide alignment cues; one might add that such naturally occurring obliques as do exist show a wide variety of inclinations.

Abravanel (1977) showed the primitivity of parallels in a different way, finding that 4-year-old American and Indian children tended to judge a pair of parallel lines to be more similar to a pair of parallel lines in a different direction than to a pair of non-parallel lines in approximately the same direction. Also, Leppig (1978) found that all the first-grade German children he tested could pick out lines which 'ran in the same direction' in a parallelogram; but the success rate fell to 30 per cent for a more complex figure in the form of a double trapezium. Most interestingly, two-thirds of the children stated that two converging lines in a homograph representing parallel edges on a cuboid ran in the same direction.

Studies by Naeli and Harris (1976) and Freeman, Chen and Hambly (1984) have confirmed that young children use parallel-alignment cues in constructive tasks. They showed that accuracy on the normally difficult task of placing a square card in the same orientation as an oblique square improved substantially when both squares were set in an oblique frame, and that, conversely, the accuracy of copying the orientation of a square in the standard orientation fell dramatically when both were set in an oblique frame.

Parallel alignment also enhances isographic drawing accuracy. Data on the simplest task, drawing a line parallel to another line, are rare – possibly because it is such an easy task for children brought up in a Western culture. The performance of Jamaican children has, however, been assessed by Mitchelmore (1983). In his tasks, the mean absolute errors among Grade 1 children (mean age 7 years 4 months), many of whom will have used a pencil only since entering school and even then rarely for drawing, were 2.6° for horizontal parallels, 5.8° for vertical parallels and 7.4° for oblique parallels (sloping at 30° to the horizontal); between Grade 3 and Grade 9, only 9.4 per cent of the drawings showed an absolute error of more than 5°. These results compared starkly with the accuracy in drawing simple angles; on 10 tasks requiring the copying of 30° and 60° angles, the mean absolute error in Grade 1 was 16.1°, and 61.2 per cent of the drawings in Grades 3–9 showed an absolute error of more than 5°. For more complex drawing tasks, the effect of parallel alignment is amply probed by Bayraktar's studies, reported in her chapter below.

Perpendiculars

There is also strong evidence that perpendiculars are primitive in children's spatial cognition. The major evidence comes from studies of isographic drawing. First, perpendiculars appear to be drawn accurately from an early age. Among 5-year-old English children, Bremner and Taylor (1982) report mean absolute errors of 2.3°, 2.1° and 7.2° respectively for copying horizontal, vertical and oblique lines perpendicular to another line. Mitchelmore (1983) obtained corresponding mean absolute errors of 4.5°, 6.0° and 9.6° among his Grade 1 Jamaican schoolchildren, and only 16.7 per cent of the drawings made by older children showed an absolute error of more than 5°. It will be noted that these errors were only slightly larger than the children's errors in copying parallels, and that, as for parallels, the oblique case, although drawn with greater error, was still drawn quite accurately.

Secondly, we note the so-called perpendicular bias in isographic drawing (discussed by Crook, Bayraktar and Bremner in this volume). This term refers to the common finding that young children copy acute angles with a systematic error towards the perpendicular (the only exception found to date occurring when an angle of 45° or more is drawn to a vertical baseline). The size of the bias decreases steadily with age (Mitchelmore, 1983) but is still discernible in undergraduates (Freeman and Mitchelmore, unpublished data). A similar effect which occurs in homographic drawing is discussed later in this chapter.

Experimental evidence on the use of perpendiculars in perceptual and placement tasks is rare. Ibbotson and Bryant (1976) mention an unpublished study by Bryant and Kaptynska which showed that 5-year-old children could distinguish perpendiculars from other angles better than they could distinguish between the other angles. Many of the parallel-alignment studies have overlooked the fact that children could also have been using perpendicularity. For example, the accurate placement of a square card of any orientation within a square frame of the same orientation requires each edge of the card to be perpendicular to two sides of the frame as well as parallel to the other two sides. Furthermore, it may be argued that the significance of the horizontal direction in our conception of the world derives largely from the fact that it is perpendicular to the vertical direction. For there are sound gravitational reasons why man-made uprights should be accurately vertical, and we carry a built-in vertical sensor in our inner ear; but the reason for

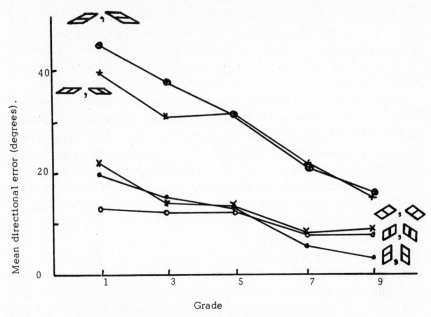

Figure 16.1 Mean directional error on parallelogram-median copying tasks, by figure and grade.

making floors horizontal is to facilitate both the building task and the sense of upright (as you will find if you try to build a house on, or walk along, a tilted surface).

4. Drawing parallels in isographs

Parallel alignment versus perpendicular bias

Young children can copy a line parallel to another line with considerable accuracy, but when the target line is inclined at an angle to the baseline they generally show a systematic error towards the perpendicular direction. What happens when the two effects – parallel alignment and perpendicular bias – are in conflict? I shall report three experiments which bear on this question.

Mitchelmore (1983) gave groups of Jamaican children aged 7 to 15 several parallelograms in which a median line (that is, a line joining the mid-points of two opposite sides and therefore parallel to the other two sides, as in the stimuli on the right of Figure 16.1) was drawn, and asked them to copy the median line in a congruent parallelogram alongside. The sides of the parallelogram were either horizontal, vertical or sloping at 30° to the horizontal, one side was approximately twice the length of the other (lengths varied from 18 mm to 46 mm), and the median was always parallel to the shorter sides. Figure 16.1 shows the mean directional error in each grade on each parallelogram. The two parallelograms with an internal angle of 30° and the three with an angle of 60° gave very similar trends. The mean error was remarkably high. In over 60 per cent of the drawings made by children in Grades 1 to 5 the target line was drawn nearer to the perpendicular than to the given direction, and even in Grade 9 the average drawing showed the line rotated a quarter of the way towards the perpendicular. The error was at each age greater, and in many cases several times greater, than the simple perpendicular bias shown in children's copies of single angles of the same size and orientation. The fact that the median was oblique to two sides of the parallelogram seemed to accentuate the perpendicular bias, and the fact that it was aligned to the other two sides of the parallelogram did not seem to have any great effect.

Mitchelmore (1983) proposed the following model of children's drawing errors in figures with both parallels and oblique 'baselines'. Suppose that, in the absence of any other lines, a child would copy a target line at a variable inclination which has a certain mean value. The effect of a parallel line would be to reduce the deviation of the drawn line from the target direction, and two parallels ought surely to reduce the deviation even further. The effect of an oblique baseline would be to reduce the deviation of the drawn line from the perpendicular to the oblique, and again one would expect two baselines to have a greater effect than one. In the presence of both parallels and baselines, the simplest assumption is that the two effects would be additive.

Mitchelmore and Freeman (1984a) attempted to test this model by giving 6-year-old English children drawing tasks based on the parallelogram-median tasks of Mitchelmore (1983) but in which the figure contained either no, one or two parallels and either no, one or two baselines. The tasks were administered individually; the target line was always 50 mm long and sloping at 45° to left or right, and the baseline was always horizontal and 68 mm long. The mean errors obtained are shown in Figure 16.2. The apparent interaction was significant, and can be summed up as showing that the one-baseline, one-parallel figure gave smaller errors (mean 4.3°) than all the other cases, which were not significantly different (mean 10.8°). These results certainly demonstrate the parallel-alignment effect clearly enough, but they show only a weak perpendicular bias; furthermore, they offer no evidence that two baselines have a stronger effect than one baseline and they actually suggest that two parallels have a weaker alignment effect than one parallel. There are so many differences between this experiment and that of Mitchelmore (1983) that it is difficult to say that the results are contradictory; they are

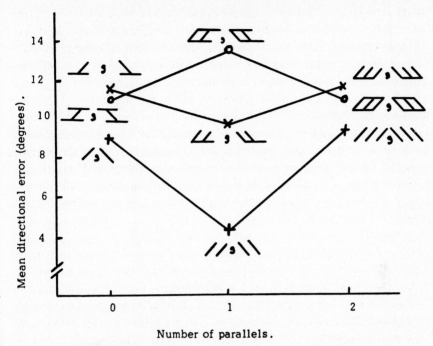

Number of parallels.

Figure 16.2 Mean directional error on parallel copying tasks, by numbers of baselines and parallels.

nevertheless surprising and all sorts of *ad hoc* explanations can be given. If the results of Mitchelmore and Freeman (1984a) are replicable, they would show that our analysis of children's isographs of geometrical figures should proceed on a very different basis from the additive model proposed by Mitchelmore (1983). It would seem as if the 6-year-old children in this study were either unable to extract the parallel-alignment information from any but the simplest figures, or they were unable to use it successfully in their drawings (perhaps it was too difficult to keep a line parallel to two lines at once), or both.

In a second study, Mitchelmore and Freeman (1984b) tried to find whether the source of children's errors lay in the stimulus-analysis or the response-production phase of 6-year-old children's drawings. The basic task was to copy a line parallel to a line inclined at 45°; in other tasks, either a second parallel or a horizontal baseline was added to either the stimulus or the response sheet or to both. It was argued that if difficulties in stimulus analysis were a source of children's errors then mean errors would be different for different stimuli, and if difficulties in producing a response were a source then mean errors would be different for different response formats. The results showed that both effects were present and acted independently. The addition of a line oblique to the target line had an approximately equal biasing effect whether it was added to the stimulus or the response; and the addition of a second parallel had no effect in either case. The failure of the second parallel to improve alignment was consistent with the results of the first experiment.

Attention to parallels

The weakness of parallel alignment in counteracting a perpendicular bias is unlikely to be due to children's inability to recognise the parallels in the stimulus figures. It might, however, be due to a failure to attend to the parallels in the presence of other orientation relations. If the child does not notice the parallels in the stimulus, there can be no alignment effect in the response.

To test this possibility, Mitchelmore and Freeman (1984a) taught a random half of their subjects to identify pairs of 'friendly' (parallel) lines. After only two examples and two counter-examples, there were fewer than 3 per cent errors in judging the friendliness of 16 pairs of lines inclined at either 0°, 15° or 30° to each other, thus confirming that 6-year-olds already possess the cognitive mechanisms to recognise parallels. However, the error rate rose substantially (to 22 per cent) in a more complex task in which children judged whether a line joining points on the two parallel sides of a trapezium was parallel to one or both of the other two sides. This result is in agreement with that of Leppig (1978) cited earlier, and supports the contention of Mitchelmore and Freeman (1984b) that the apparent weakness of the parallel-alignment cue at the stimulus-encoding stage is attributable to the complexity of the figure. It would appear that children do not notice the parallels in more complex figures because it is actually quite a different task for them to analyse the figure and pick out the parallels.

Mitchelmore and Freeman (1984a) then readministered their drawing tasks to all their subjects, but before each drawing asked children to point to the 'friends' of the target line; and errors were corrected before the copy was drawn. In the control group, lines were 'friendly' if they were drawn in the same colour; half of these pairs were also parallel. There was only a small and unreliable difference between the mean errors among the two groups of children, thus indicating that drawing children's attention to the parallel-alignment cues in the stimuli had no detectable effect on their drawing errors. So even if children do not normally notice parallel relations in geometrical stimuli, this cannot be the sole source of their errors; there is clearly also a production effect operative, as Mitchelmore and Freeman (1984b) claimed to have shown.

(a)   (b)

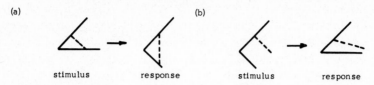

stimulus   response   stimulus   response

Figure 16.3 'Topological' responses to a copying task. The broken line is the target line.

A further possible explanation for the results observed is that children of the age tested, although they are sensitive to parallel alignment in a complex figure, do not accept it as a criterion of an 'exact copy'. It is unfortunate that Mitchelmore and Freeman (1984a) did not ask their experimental subjects how many 'friends' the lines they had drawn had; but it seems quite likely that children would have recognised that their lines had no 'friends' and yet have seen no contradiction with the fact that the line they copied had two 'friends'. There are, after all, many situations where it is not necessary to preserve such Euclidean features; for example, children of this age will just have learnt that M, M and *M* all represent the same sound and are therefore to a large extent interchangeable.

A similar disrespect for Euclidean relations occurred in some anomalous results in a second study reported by Mitchelmore and Freeman (1984b). The basic task there was to copy a line perpendicular to a line inclined at 45°, but in other tasks various lines were added to the stimulus or the response sheet or both. One-third of the children produced copies similar to those shown in Figure 16.3: they had made topologically exact copies of the whole figure instead of isolating and copying the Euclidean relation (perpendicularity) as had been intended. Further illustrations of 'errors' made by young children who clearly have not accepted the criterion of congruence are given by Mitchelmore (1984).

5. Drawing parallels in homographs

Perpendicular bias in homographs

It is well known that young children tend to draw the water level in a tilted bottle perpendicular to the side of the bottle rather than parallel to the table it is standing on, and trees perpendicular to a hillside instead of parallel to a vertical direction (Piaget and Inhelder, 1956). However, as noted above, it is not clear whether such tasks should be regarded as homographic or isographic. A clearly homographic task demonstrating perpendicular bias was used by Mitchelmore (1975). He asked Jamaican children to add telegraph

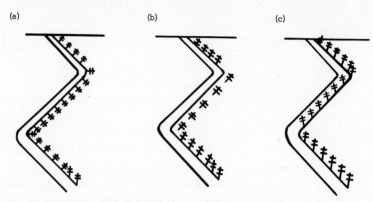

Figure 16.4 Typical drawings of telegraph poles alongside a road as drawn by Jamaican children aged (a) 7 years, (b) 11 years and (c) 15 years.

poles alongside a drawing of a winding road receding into the distance and found that 7-year-olds generally drew the poles perpendicular to the road in the plane of the paper; it was not until age 15 that most children drew the poles more or less parallel to the 'vertical' edge of the paper (Figure 16.4). Specially interesting was the finding that there was a gradual changeover from one extreme to the other, so that the intermediate-age children drew poles which were tilted towards the perpendicular and even the oldest showed a small but consistent bias in that direction.

It is very difficult to interpret such results in purely geometrical terms because of the intrusion of the physical concepts vertical and horizontal. An obvious explanation is that young children do not understand that telegraph poles are vertical and therefore parallel to each other, and so do not attempt to draw parallels in their homographs but rely on the only relation they are sure about: the poles are perpendicular to the road. But it could also be that they do understand about verticals but are unable to represent the resulting parallels. To investigate the conflict between parallels and perpendiculars in homographs, we must use a stimulus where the parallels are more obvious.

Homographs of rectangular solids

Drawings of a cube have been the subject of much recent research (Caron-Pargue, 1979; Dolle, Bataillard and Guyon, 1973; Gaillard, Assel and Brull, 1974; Koops, 1981; Phillips, Hobbs and Pratt, 1978). Figure 16.5 shows typical drawings of a cuboid at each stage of development. The sequence, first obtained in Jamaica (Mitchelmore, 1978), has since been confirmed in the U.S.A. (Mitchelmore, 1980a), England (Mitchelmore, 1980b) and West Germany (Mitchelmore, 1982). The conflict between parallels and perpendi-

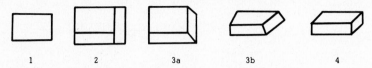

1   2   3a   3b   4

Figure 16.5 Typical drawings at each stage of development in the representation of a cuboid.

culars is quite clear. Both parallels and perpendiculars are used extensively in Stages 1, 2 and 3a; only a few such relations occur in Stage 3b; and Stage 4 is based on the almost exclusive use of parallels. (A few perspective drawings occur at Stage 4, but they are so rare that one can safely ignore them.)

The simplest explanation for the drawings in Stages 1 and 2 is that children are representing the two-dimensional shape of each face without foreshortening. Even when the shape of some faces is distorted at Stage 3a, the perpendiculars and parallels remain. Alternatively, it could be argued that Stages 1 to 3a show the same primitive tendency to represent perpendiculars as is shown in Figure 16.4(a): the depiction of parallels can be seen as the inevitable but unintentional consequence of the perpendiculars. (In the task illustrated in Figure 16.4, children's drawings often show three sets of nearly parallel telegraph poles, but a 'correct' drawing results only when all the poles are deliberately drawn parallel to the single direction representing the vertical.) Stage 3b may then be seen as the result of a transition, from an emphasis on perpendiculars up to Stage 3a, to an emphasis on parallels in Stage 4: many lines are drawn in a direction which is intermediate between parallel to an opposite edge and perpendicular to an adjacent edge.

This explanation essentially consists of a claim that perpendiculars in the object are more salient than parallels. But why should this be so? One possibility is that children realise that adjacent edges of a cube or cuboid are perpendicular, but do not realise that the opposite edges of the faces are parallel. A second possibility is that children do not notice the parallel edges, and a third is that they notice them but do not realise their significance for their drawings. The following experiment was designed to investigate these possibilities.

A group of 32 English children aged 9 years 6 months (± 7 months) who drew a cuboid at Stage 3a or 3b was randomly divided into two sub-groups. One sub-group was taught to recognise 'friendly' (parallel) edges on three-dimensional models, and the effect of this knowledge on their drawings was investigated. After training on 12 examples of pairs of parallel and non-parallel lines in two dimensions (where there were 11 per cent errors), the children made only 4.5 per cent errors in identifying parallel and non-parallel edges

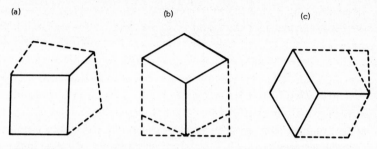

Figure 16.6 Average responses to homograph-completion tasks. Full lines represent the given lines and the broken lines the modal responses.

on a set of truncated pyramids (18 tasks); this showed clearly that the switch to three dimensions in no way made it more difficult for children to recognise parallels. The children were then presented with a sequence of four cubes (two face-on and two edge-on) and two rhomboids and a partly drawn homograph of each. To complete the homograph, the child had first to draw an oblique, vertical or horizontal line parallel to a given line and inclined at 45° or 60° to another given line (see Figure 16.6). Before making the drawing, however, children were asked to identify 'friends' of the depicted edge on the model; in the control group, this meant edges of the same colour. By the median test, there was no significant difference in the accuracy on any of the homographs between the group which first identified the parallel edges and the control group, strongly suggesting that errors were not due to failure to notice parallel edges on the stimulus objects.

Figure 16.6 attempts to summarise children's drawings. The residual effect of the earlier emphasis on perpendiculars showed itself in two different ways. At all the junctions in Figure 16.6(a), the error distributions were unimodal and skewed towards the perpendicular, looking exactly like a distribution obtained from a study of perpendicular bias in isographs. At several junctions in Figure 16.6(b) and (c), the error distributions were bimodal, with one mode corresponding to near-perpendiculars and one to near-parallels, suggesting previous 'Aha!' experiences among some of the children. The flip was in fact observed several times when children were offered a chance to change their drawing if they were dissatisfied with it. It is noticeable that the vertical and horizontal edges in Figure 16.6(b) and (c) were very accurately drawn, even in the novel and difficult rhomboid; this could have been a result of alignment with the edges of the paper. It is not at all clear why Figure 16.6(a) should show no signs of this alignment effect or of the flip-flop effect shown in the other drawings.

After completing all their drawings, children were asked to describe the strategies they had used. Despite the fact that half the subjects had identified parallels on isographs and on models just before making their homographs, none of them used any directional explanations. Apart from those few who could only say, 'I just knew where to draw the lines', all the children explained their constructions in terms of lengths. The more accurate indicated that they had drawn lines equal in length to the given lines, without being able to say how they had achieved this feat. Most of those who drew a cube in the manner of Figure 16.6(a) expressed dissatisfaction with their drawings on the basis that the opposite sides of the parallelograms were not equal, but were unable to correct their drawings to achieve the desired effect. It may be noted that the three-dimensional properties 'opposite edges of each face are parallel' and 'opposite edges of each face are equal in length' are both preserved in homographs drawn in oblique projection; but whereas the former leads to a direct procedure for completing the homograph, the latter leads at best to an iterative procedure giving successively closer approximations to the correct lines (in the absence of compasses to effect the obvious Euclidean construction). It would appear that the more accurate subjects had learned the direct procedure, probably as a result of much trial and error, but were unaware of its theoretical foundation.

Learning about parallels –
We have tended to assume that the development in graphic representation shown by the step from Stage 3b to Stage 4 results from a deepening understanding of parallels and their use in homographs. The results just presented suggest that learning may well proceed in the opposite direction: only after children have been producing Stage 3b drawings for some time may they become aware that they are drawing parallels and it may be even later that they realise that this is effective because the corresponding edges on the object depicted are also parallel. This could explain findings reported in Duthie's chapter above that children can, at a certain stage, successfully represent individual solids without being able to integrate them into a single framework.

It also seems likely that the progression demonstrated in Figure 16.4 shows a growing sensitivity to the adequacy of the representation rather than a deepening awareness of verticality; and it is even possible that trial and error in the picture plane could lead to the discovery that verticals are parallel.

The use of an oblique direction to represent the depth dimension might also result from graphic experimentation rather than visual analysis. I have many times had young children express dissatisfaction with their Stage 2 drawings on the grounds that the bottom right-hand corner (see Figure 16.5) did not adequately represent the way the faces met; after several attempts, many of them repeating exactly the same drawings, a few children have hit upon the diagonal solution and have thus produced a Stage 3a drawing. Similarly, I have observed children changing a Stage 3a to a Stage 3b drawing on the grounds that a T-junction did not adequately represent a convex corner. It would seem that when children introduce obliques into their homographs they are not trying to represent the third dimension but are merely solving local graphic problems. This too is consistent with Duthie's work.

More generally, we may argue that all development in graphic representation is driven by children's analysis of their own drawings rather than an analysis of the stimulus object or its appearance to the eye. Because different objects present different graphic problems, progress is likely to be uneven; but some solutions will surely transfer from one object to another, so we should also expect a fair correlation between the styles of drawings a child produces for various objects. This is exactly what Mitchelmore (1980a) found.

6. Summary and conclusions

Although two-dimensional and three-dimensional drawing are such different processes that we have proposed new terms to distinguish them more effectively, children's isographs and homographs show many similar error patterns. This final section is devoted to summarising the results which appear to apply to both types of drawing and to examining possible explanations.

Parallels and perpendiculars

There is overwhelming evidence that children are sensitive to parallels from as early as 4 years old and probably earlier. They can easily recognise parallels in two dimensions and three dimensions, they regard parallelism as more important than orientation, and they use parallel alignment effectively in simple placement and drawing tasks. However, it is also clear that the same children experience difficulties extracting parallel-alignment information from, or drawing parallels in, more complex figures. Furthermore, drawing children's attention to the parallels present in a two-dimensional or three-dimensional figure has no discernible effect on the size of their drawing errors. It is not until middle or late childhood that parallels are used effectively in isographs and homographs.

Although there has not been so much research into children's knowledge of perpendiculars, it seems that this concept is also present from an early age. Young children can recognise two-dimensional and probably three-dimensional perpendiculars easily and copy them accurately, and they might use them extensively in alignment tasks. Indeed, the concept is so strong that in their isographs young children tend to bias acute angles towards the perpendicular and in their homographs tend to give priority to showing the perpendiculars present in the object depicted. These effects diminish with age but are still discernible in older children and adults.

Young children therefore have available two primitives for analysing direction: parallels and perpendiculars. But the one is not used in drawing when it should be and the other is used when it should not be. Why? Since both relations are equally recognisable, an explanation has to be sought in terms of saliency. The most obvious difference is that perpendiculars meet but parallels do not; the saliency of a proximal relation is always likely to be greater than that of a distal relation (Goodnow and Friedman, 1972). Moreover, as suggested by Bremner and Taylor (1982), the perpendicular bias in isographs may be at least partly due to the strong human tendency to create symmetry; and although perpendiculars and parallels both possess symmetry, it is much more obvious in the case of perpendiculars because each line is a mirror line for the other. For a discussion of symmetry see Bremner's chapter below.

The role of drawing conventions

It has been stressed many times that children have to learn various graphic conventions before they can produce an acceptable drawing of even such a basic solid as a cube. In Western culture, this means the conventions associated with oblique projection, with perspective as an optional extra. Our results strongly suggest that children can detect parallels on rectangular objects but do not realise the significance of these parallels in the production of a homograph. Moreover, it appears as if this realisation eventually comes about as a result of trial and error in the picture plane, and not as a result of a closer analysis of the stimulus or the way it appears to the eye. At a certain stage, simply showing children that drawing parallels produces the effect they are looking for should lead to a dramatic improvement in their homographs.

What has not been sufficiently stressed in the literature is that isographs are also subject to conventions which have to be learnt. Often the copy is required to be congruent to the original so that, in addition to the general structure of the figure, all parallels, perpendiculars and other angles, and all lengths, should be preserved; in other cases, similarity and the preservation of ratios of lengths is sufficient. The cause of children's failure to copy parallels in their isographs may therefore not lie in their inability to do so but in their ignorance of isographic conventions. It seems likely that young children could produce much more accurate isographs if their attention was drawn to the metric characteristics of their responses and the need for them to match those of the stimulus. By analogy with children's use of lengths in drawing cubes, it is possible that in the parallelogram-median task discussed above, children are attempting to identify and join the mid-points of the opposite sides instead of attempting to draw parallels; an effect similar to that of the Müller-Lyer illusion could then produce the observed perpendicular bias. A child who accepts that a better isograph results when parallels are copied should be better able to resist this bias.

Comparing errors in isographs and homographs

Young children's isographs and homographs both show strong perpendicular biases. Could it be that they have the same source? It is true that there is much more involved in learning to represent a three-dimensional figure than there is in learning to copy a two-dimensional figure accurately, but after a certain stage the only problem in producing a homograph lies in drawing a line parallel to a given line and inclined at an angle to one or more other lines in the figure – exactly the same problem which occurs in isographs. Whatever causes the perpendicular bias in isographs might therefore also be responsible for the errors in homographs.

There are two empirical results which argue against a close relation between isographic and homographic errors. First, the sizes of errors do not seem to be comparable. This is a difficult matter to judge because no one appears to have attempted to use the same figure in isographic and homographic tasks. However, Mitchelmore and Freeman (1984b) obtained mean errors on isographic parallel-drawing tasks which were very similar to those shown in Figure 16.6(a), but among children three years younger. Secondly, as Figure 16.6 shows very clearly, the size and pattern of homographic errors vary wildly from one figure to another in ways which do not seem related to the factors influencing isographic errors.

A deeper problem is more theoretical: how could one design an experiment to isolate the productive aspects of isographic and homographic drawing and compare the errors? It is not sufficient to present two-dimensional and three-dimensional stimuli which appear to present identical production problems, since the stimuli will inevitably differ in other aspects. For the three-dimensional stimulus must be presented with sufficient background to ensure that it is interpreted as three-dimensional, but either this background is not presented with the two-dimensional stimulus (in which case the two stimuli are not identical) or the background is added to the two-dimensional stimulus (in which case it will appear to be three-dimensional). In particular, no deductions could be made by comparing drawings of a cube (e.g. Figure

16.6(a)) either with copies of a single parallelogram taken from its homograph or with copies of the entire homograph. Nor is it satisfactory to use as a stimulus a drawing which can be presented as either an isograph or a homograph, depending on instructions, as Freeman (personal communication) has tried to do. For there is no guarantee that subjects in the isographic condition will interpret the stimuli in the manner intended; and copying a homograph is not at all equivalent to constructing a homograph, since the stimulus supplies the solution (see Chen's chapter above for a further discussion of this question).

A further possibility is that the perpendicular bias observed in isographs is actually a homographic effect, rather than *vice versa*. Derȩgowski (personal communication) has proposed that an acute angle may be spontaneously interpreted as a representation of a perpendicular in three dimensions. Support for this position comes from a study of Kaess and Derȩgowski (1980), in which errors in estimating the length of a bar were compared under four conditions: bar alone, bar surrounded by a rectangle, bar surrounded by a parallelogram and bar embedded in one 'face' of a depicted cube. Errors in the last two conditions were not reliably different, but they were reliably greater than errors in the first two conditions. One is also reminded of the inappropriate scaling hypothesis advanced by Gregory (1963) as an explanation for certain geometrical illusions involving acute angles; perhaps his 'Pandora's box' approach, used successfully by Derȩgowski and Byth (1970), could also be used to find if children do in fact interpret an acute angle presented in the frontal plane in the same way as a perpendicular in a receding plane, and how this tendency changes with age.

ACKNOWLEDGEMENT

Most of the ideas expressed in this chapter were developed in many hours of stimulating discussion with Norman Freeman at the University of Bristol while the author was on leave from the University of the West Indies, Jamaica, and in receipt of a Commonwealth Fellowship.

REFERENCES

Abravanel, E. (1977) The figural simplicity of parallel lines. *Child Development, 48*, 708–10.
Bremner, J. G. & Taylor, A. J. (1982) Children's errors in copying angles: Perpendicular error or bisection error? *Perception, 11*, 163–71.
Bryant, P. E. (1969) Perception and memory of the orientation of visually presented lines by children. *Nature, London, 224*, 1331–2.
(1974) *Perception and understanding in young children*. London: Methuen.

Caron-Pargue, J. (1979) Étude sur les représentations du cube chez des enfants de 3 à 11 ans: La représentation et le codage des propriétés spatiales. Unpublished Ph.D. thesis, l'Université de Paris Vᵉ.

Deręgowski, J. B. & Byth, W. (1970) Hudson's pictures in Pandora's box. *Journal of Cross-Cultural Psychology*, *1*, 315–23.

Dolle, J.-M., Bataillard, C. & Guyon, J. (1973) La construction représentative de l'espace volumétrique chez l'enfant. I. Le cube. *Bulletin de Psychologie*, *27*, 578–89.

Dubery, F. & Willats, J. (1983) *Perspective and other drawing systems*. London: Herbert.

Freeman, N. H. (1980) *Strategies of representation in young children: Analysis of spatial skills and drawing processes*. London: Academic Press.

Freeman, N. H., Chen, M. J. & Hambly, M. (1984) Children's different use of alignment cues when encoding and when producing a match-to-target. *British Journal of Developmental Psychology*, *2*, 123–38.

Gaillard, F., Assel, G. & Brull, J. (1974) Etalonnages de la copie de cubes avec ou sans repères spatiaux chez l'enfant de 5 à 15 ans. *Revue Suisse de Psychologie*, *33*, 137–45.

Goodnow, J. J. & Friedman, S. (1972) Orientation in children's human figure drawings: An aspect of graphic language. *Developmental Psychology*, *7*, 10–16.

Gregory, R. L. (1963) Distortion of visual shape as inappropriate constancy scaling. *Nature, London*, *199*, 678–80.

Ibbotson, A. & Bryant, P. E. (1976) The perpendicular error and the vertical effect in children's drawing. *Perception*, *5*, 319–26.

Kaess, D. W. & Deręgowski, J. B. (1980) Depicted angle of forms and perception of line drawings. *Perception*, *9*, 23–9.

Koops, H. (1981) Zur Medienabhängigkeit des räumlichen Vorstellungsvermögens bei Schülern eines ersten Schuljahres. *Journal für Mathematik-Didaktik*, *2*, 51–82.

Leppig, M. (1978) Untersuchungen über Arbeiten mit dem Richtungsbegriff in Primarstufenalter. In H. Bauersfeld (ed.), *Fallstudien und Analysen zum Mathematikunterricht*. Hannover: Schroedel.

Mitchelmore, M. C. (1975) The perceptual development of Jamaican students. (Unpublished Ph.D. thesis, Ohio State University, 1974.) *Dissertation Abstracts International*, *35*, 7130A.

    (1978) Developmental stages in children's representation of regular solid figures. *Journal of Genetic Psychology*, *133*, 229–39.

    (1980a) Prediction of developmental stages in the representation of regular space figures. *Journal for Research in Mathematics Education*, *11*, 83–93.

    (1980b) Three-dimensional geometrical drawing in three cultures. *Educational Studies in Mathematics*, *11*, 205–16.

    (1982) Variation in spatial abilities among industrialized countries. *Cross-Cultural Psychology Bulletin*, *16(2)*, 2–3.

    (1983) Children drawing parallels. Paper read at York Conference on Graphic Representation, University of York, 6–7 April.

    (1984) Spatial ability and geometry learning in Jamaica. *Journal of Structural Learning*, *8*, 139–50.

Mitchelmore, M. C. & Freeman, N. H. (1984a) Conflict between parallel alignment and perpendicular bias in children's geometrical drawings. Manuscript in preparation.

(1984*b*) Encoding and production of parallels and perpendiculars by young children. Manuscript in preparation.

Naeli, H. & Harris, P. (1976) Orientation of the diamond and square. *Perception*, 5, 73–8.

Perkins, D. N. & Cooper, R. G. (1980) How the eye makes up what the light leaves out. In M. A. Hagen (ed.), *The perception of pictures*, Vol. II, *Dürer's devices: Beyond the projective model of pictures*. New York: Academic Press.

Phillips, W. A., Hobbs, S. B. & Pratt, F. R. (1978) Intellectual realism in children's drawings of cubes. *Cognition*, 6, 15–23.

Piaget, J. & Inhelder, B. (1956) *The child's conception of space*. London: Routledge and Kegan Paul.

17

Figural biases and young children's drawings

J. GAVIN BREMNER

1. Introduction

For those used to systematic analysis of relatively orderly data, children's drawings often appear something of a nightmare. They may be packed with information, but at the same time (they often appear chaotic and ill formed.) Clearly, this is not a problem to be dismissed lightly, but I think the chapters in this book provide adequate evidence that people are learning to live with the problem, devising ingenious techniques that repeatedly extract systematic effects from the midst of apparent disorder. Despite the fact that young children are quite severely limited by 'output problems', they can be shown to be quite sophisticated artists in other ways, varying their product to take account of changing task demands.

But despite the wealth of information now being gathered from very early drawings, one could still be forgiven for preferring to work with slightly older children whose products had gained more surface order and sophistication. However, whether you do this or devise structured tasks for younger children in order to iron out their messy products, other problems remain that do not stand out so obviously in the drawings. These become evident only occasionally as sorts of orderly perversity, such as when a child draws the chimney on a house perpendicular to the roof instead of vertical. The danger is that biases of this sort affect the product in much less obvious ways in other cases. For instance, the symmetrical arrangement of windows and doors prevalent in young children's house drawings looks like evidence of production of a 'canonical house' or at least some sort of stereotyping of the product, when in fact it might be at least partly the result of some sort of figural symmetry bias akin to those pointed out long ago by Gestalt psychologists. Whatever the child intends to portray, there may be perceptual biases that serve to distort the product either towards or away from something that looks like a better product. This chapter is about these figural distortions. The aim is to show how recent studies in the area, while important for the light they cast on the relatively limited area of figural biases, yield vital evidence for our understanding of the drawing process in general.

For two reasons, it makes sense to take a Piagetian starting point. First, much of the evidence on figural distortions has its roots in Piaget and Inhelder's (1956) book on development of spatial reference systems, in particular the work on children's understanding of horizontal and vertical coordinate reference systems. Second, Piaget and Inhelder's interpretation of young children's orientation 'errors' is a good example of the sort of explanation that we should be cautious about, since they pay little attention to the contribution of figural biases that might bear little or no relation to the child's *knowledge* of the concepts involved in the task. My claim will be that similar dangers exist when we try to interpret children's drawings in less constrained settings.

Development of the ability to organise space in terms of a coordinate reference system was seen by Piaget and Inhelder (1956) as one of the major spatial achievements of middle childhood. The notion was that a general coordinate reference system provided a container in which any set of objects could be mentally organised. Its use freed the child's thinking from specific relationships, and provided a general organising system that applied in all settings. Furthermore, they point to horizontal–vertical coordinates as an example of such a system existing ready-made in nature. But they point out that it does not follow that children should apply this system spontaneously, or indeed that they are aware of the vertical or horizontal as such. In fact, they go on to argue that it is only once children have acquired the capacity to organise space within a coordinate reference system that the meaning of vertical and horizontal becomes explicit. Consequently, Piaget and Inhelder went to some lengths to investigate young children's understanding of the vertical and horizontal, the best-known example being their water-level test, used to assess children's understanding of the horizontal. In this, children are asked to predict or copy the surface of a liquid both when the container is upright and when it is tilted. A typical method of assessing children's understanding of the vertical was to ask them to draw trees on a hillside. In both of these examples, children go through three main developmental stages. First of all, they fail to construct a linear representation of the surface altogether, usually scribbling inside or outside the container outline to indicate the liquid. Next, they represent a water surface or treetrunk as a straight line, but draw it at right angles to the outline of the glass or hillside. Finally, around the age of 7, they begin to construct an accurate horizontal or vertical line, whatever the orientation of the reference lines.

The errors made by the second-stage children become more surprising when we realise that they happen even when children have a model to copy from (a finding confirmed by Liben, 1981). Although the correct angular relationship is in front of them, they make the same errors. Taking the water-level case, children have taken the step of using a line to represent a surface, which in some ways seems a bigger step than copying the angular relationship, and yet they fail utterly on the latter part of the task. There are many cases of children failing to draw what they see in front of them, and although the present example may arise for different reasons from other cases where children may choose not to draw what they see (e.g. intellectual realism in object drawing: see Chapter 14 above by Crook), it should serve to alert us to the possibility that children may sometimes adopt other methods of portrayal because direct copying is simply something that they are quite bad at.

Piaget and Inhelder interpret the errors made by these children as evidence that they have not yet formed a Euclidean coordinate reference system based on the horizontal and vertical. In the absence of such a system, they are unable to relate the water level to anything but immediate referents, the sides or base of the glass. Even if a horizontal line representing the table top is included in the diagram, they persist in drawing the surface perpendicular to the sides of the glass, for although an appropriate perceptual referent is present in this case, children could only recognise its appropriateness if they were already capable of utilising a horizontal–vertical coordinate system. Without this system, the added line is just another line, and they rely instead on the more immediate referents presented by the base or sides of the glass.

In summary, the main point about the Piagetian argument is that the child's problem is basically conceptual; in the authors' terms it is to do with operative rather than figurative knowing (Piaget and Inhelder, 1968). It is the lack of an operational knowledge of the horizontal that produces the problem, and perceptual biases do not really come into it. The argument being developed here is that we cannot adopt such explanations until we have shown that more basic perceptual biases have no part in the phenomenon. As we shall see, in addition to it being impossible to rule such factors out, much of the explanation is probably most appropriately made at a more basic level than concepts.

Piaget and Inhelder's phenomena have been subjected to considerable investigation in recent years. However, much of the work has been rather unhelpful from the point of view of those trying to get at the mechanisms underlying the phenomena. In true neo-Piagetian style, much of the effort was directed at seeing whether correct performance could be 'trained' (Beilin, Kagan and Rabinowitz, 1966; Thomas and Jamison, 1975) or whether the underlying Piagetian concepts could be assessed in better ways (Howard, 1978; McGillicuddy-DeLisi, DeLisi and Youniss, 1978). These approaches are perfectly justified, and the studies tell their own story. On the other hand, they do not add much to the account being developed here, since they do not make a detailed analysis of the task factors that might lead to error. However, two relatively old studies mark the beginning of attention to this sort of detail.

Smedslund (1963) investigated Piaget and Inhelder's claims in a more systematic manner than their informal clinical method. In particular, he sought to test the Piagetian argument that success in the task waited on operative progress, the implication of this being that performance should not be 'trainable' in pre-operational children. Smedslund's evidence seems to fit this account. He found that children who showed no signs of appreciating the horizontal did not benefit at all from being shown a slow rotation of the bottle containing the liquid. This fits the claim that experience of the invariant orientation of the surface would be of no use unless it could be assimilated to the appropriate intellectual structure. In contrast, he found that those children showing some grip of the concept did benefit from the experience. Again, this would make sense in terms of Piagetian theory, according to which children do benefit from experience if there is already existent some primitive notion of the concept in question. However, the finding that is probably most important for the present account was that children's accuracy was relatively unaffected by response mode. They were just as bad or as good at producing the correct orientation in a drawing as they were at picking the correct picture from a set. So we can immediately rule out one possibility that is often raised in studies of drawing, that the phenomenon is due to specific production difficulties, in this case those arising from the child having to draw a horizontal line.

Secondly, a study by MacKay, Brazendale and Wilson (1972) provides some empirical support for the main issue raised in this chapter. They found that children's errors in judging the horizontal and vertical depended on the form of figures presented. In particular, errors were greater if the figure consisted of a tilted symmetrical framework (for instance, a cross-section of a deep, slanting lake) than if the tilted framework was asymmetrical. While they conclude that children's problems in these tasks may be partly conceptual, they argue that orientation errors may have part of their source in Gestalt perceptual forces towards figural simplicity. For instance, part of the reason for the water level being drawn perpendicular to the sides of the glass is that the resulting figure is symmetrical.

The notion that Gestalt perceptual factors operate within drawing tasks in a way encapsulates the thrust of this chapter. Without having to accept the rest of Gestalt theory, the point is that these biases may act outside the awareness of the child. They may be relatively automatic distortions that the child is not even aware of when faced with the product.

Having raised the possibility of effects of this sort, the next step is to see what current evidence can tell us in detail about their nature. A number of questions arise at the outset. Are we dealing with pure figural effects, or are they tied closely to the meaning of what is being drawn? Are we dealing with biases towards Gestalt 'good figures', for instance towards increased symmetry, or are the effects tied to specific angular relationships, for instance right angles? If such figural effects are common, are they independent of figure orientation or not? All these questions are important, not only in their own right, but for their implications for drawing research in general. When a child produces a free drawing of an angular object (take the house example again), all of these questions need to be asked. Basic figural effects may influence the outcome in any of these ways without there being any necessary relationship to what the child thinks about the object, or even to what s/he knows of methods of portraying the object.

Fortunately, I think we are now in the position to produce reasonable answers to many of these questions, and some others as well. However, to reach them, we must go through some fairly complicated evidence.

2. The perpendicular error

A paper by Ibbotson and Bryant (1976) marked the start of a more analytic approach to angular errors in children's drawings. Ibbotson and Bryant were concerned that a number of factors might have been responsible for children's errors in the standard Piagetian tasks. First, they were worried that children might have been 'misled' by the meaningful materials used. Glasses are normally encountered resting on horizontal surfaces, and unless you live in particularly mountainous surroundings, trees are usually more or less perpendicular to the ground. Hence, there was the possibility that children were employing a sort of intellectual realism instead of producing what was before them, creating the surface or the treetrunk in its typical orientation with respect to its immediate referents. Secondly, they pointed out that the cases involving difficulty contained both an oblique baseline (referent) and a non-perpendicular line to be copied. Consequently, there was no way of

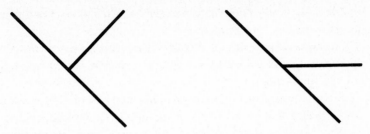

Figure 17.1 Perpendicular and non-perpendicular figures used by Ibbotson and Bryant (1976).

telling whether either or both of these factors affected the child's attempt. In a way, this immediately sets aside Piaget and Inhelder's primary question, since it is not possible to study the horizontal or vertical through these means without confounding these two factors (sadly for the experimentalist, nature is often a confounded thing). But they are certainly addressing very directly the sorts of questions that we want answers for.

Ibbotson and Bryant tackled the problems of interpretation by using line figures that were devoid of any obvious meaning. They presented two types of figure (see Figure 17.1), both of which comprised a straight baseline with a shorter line joining it at the middle. In one, this second line joined the baseline at 90°, and in the other it joined at 45°. The assumption was that use of these 'abstract' figures dealt effectively with both of their main worries at once. The original meaning of the stimuli had been abolished. Also, it was possible to present both perpendicular and non-perpendicular figures with the baseline horizontal, vertical or oblique, so the confounding of oblique baseline and non-perpendicular angular relationship was avoided.

In their first experiment, they presented 5- and 6-year-olds with a series of 24 of these figures, 2 perpendicular and 4 non-perpendicular for each of the four baseline orientations (vertical, horizontal, right oblique and left oblique). With each figure, children were supplied with a corresponding response sheet with the baseline already drawn in, so they had only to draw in the second line to make their copy look like the model.

Two measures of error were derived from children's products. *Overall errors* were measured simply as the amount by which the produced angle deviated from the correct angle. This is a measure of general accuracy, and the prediction from past work is that by this measure, copies of perpendiculars should be more accurate than copies of non-perpendiculars, and it is sufficient to note here that this prediction was confirmed. But children in Piaget and Inhelder's work were not just inaccurate at orienting the water level in the tilted glass; they systematically biased it so that it was more or less perpendicular to the sides of the glass. Hence, in the case of non-perpendicular figures, Ibbotson and Bryant also wanted to know the amount by which children's products strayed towards the perpendicular. For the sake of simplicity, I shall concentrate on these *directional errors*, since they are of primary importance.

Ibbotson and Bryant found that errors were in the direction of the perpendicular for all baseline orientations, so straight away there was evidence that clear angular distortions occur even in copies of abstract two-dimensional figures. Also, similar errors occurred whether the line being drawn should have been vertical, horizontal or oblique, so they seemed to be unrelated to line orientation *per se*. On the other hand, errors were significantly lower in the case of figures with the baseline vertical, so there was some sort of orientation effect tied to the orientation of the baseline rather than to the orientation of the drawn line.

Ibbotson and Bryant went on to repeat their study with 3- as well as 5-year-olds. This time, instead of asking children to draw the second line, they provided them with a wire that they could place so as to represent the second line in its relation to the baseline. This allowed them to test 3-year-olds, whose drawing attempts had been too haphazard to score with any accuracy. Although younger children made larger errors than older ones, the same pattern emerged for both age groups. Perpendicular errors occurred in all baseline orientations (generally more so for younger children), but were significantly lower when copying figures with a vertical baseline.

Their conclusion is that this perpendicular error results from a general tendency to distort angular relationships, a configuration effect that bears no clear relation to children's orientation judgements. They suggest that it may arise through experience of the carpentered world, in which right angles abound. But they admit that it is not so easy to explain what they call the 'vertical effect', the reduced perpendicular error when working from a vertical baseline. Their tentative suggestion is that it has something to do with the vertical having primacy over other natural dimensions, with the result that children can use it more accurately as a referent for constructing angles.

Although subsequent studies replicated the general finding of a perpendicular error, not all have replicated the vertical effect. Instead, a variety of baseline-orientation effects have cropped up between different studies, creating an annoying source of variation for which there is not always a clear explanation. For instance, using similar figures, Bayraktar (1979) obtained Ibbotson and Bryant's vertical effect. However, Freeman and Kelham (1981) obtained the largest directional errors with vertical baselines, while Heard (1978, cited by Freeman, 1980) and Bremner and Taylor (1982)

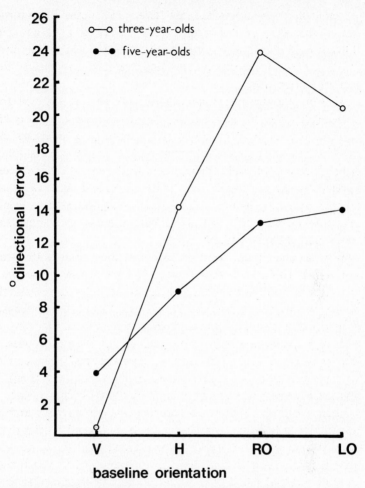

Figure 17.2 Ibbotson and Bryant's (1976) Experiment 2: mean directional errors by 3- and 5-year-olds for the four baseline orientations.

obtained lower errors for vertical *and* horizontal baselines. Also there is the hint that Ibbotson and Bryant may not have been dealing with a totally consistent vertical effect either. Although they found only a vertical effect in their second experiment (see Figure 17.2), the mean error made by 5-year-olds with horizontal baseline figures was exactly midway between the error for vertical figures and the errors for left obliques. Hence, for this age group a reliable difference between means for vertical and horizontal baselines would have meant a reliable difference between means for horizontals and left obliques. Maybe there was a more complex effect here that was lost in the overall analysis, since the pattern is not quite the same for 4-year-olds. On the other hand, in a final study in which a rectangular frame was used instead of the simple baseline, a straightforward vertical effect appeared again.

While there is only the suggestion of a different pattern within Ibbotson and Bryant's study, the differences in orientation effects obtained by different workers are quite clear and require explanation. One possibility is that the pattern obtained depends upon the response mode employed. As we shall see in the next section, a rod-alignment task presented to 5-year-olds yielded reduced errors for vertical and horizontal baselines (Bremner and Taylor, 1982). This is the same effect as Heard obtained, also using a rod-alignment task, and the pattern of means was strikingly similar to that obtained by Ibbotson and Bryant in their second experiment, in which rod alignment was also the response mode. The really convincing vertical effects were obtained in their first and third experiments, in which children drew the line, so possibly the pure vertical effect arises only when the drawing response mode is used.

3. A symmetry interpretation

Ibbotson and Bryant's results could be interpreted in quite a different way. In their figures, a shift towards the perpendicular also involved a shift towards a more symmetrical figure, so adopting MacKay, Brazendale and Wilson's (1972) argument that what appears to be a bias towards the perpendicular might in fact be a bias towards a greater symmetry, either in the local angular relationship or in the figure as a whole. There is plenty of evidence of symmetry effects in children's perception, with sensitivity to symmetry extending even to infancy. For instance, Bornstein, Ferdinandsen and Gross (1981) showed that 4-month-olds habituate more quickly to symmetrical patterns than to asymmetrical ones, and that a preference for symmetry emerges somewhere between 4 and 12 months. There is also evidence on sensitivity to symmetry in childhood. Boswell (1976) showed that children between the ages of 5 and 9 years reproduced symmetrical dot patterns more accurately than asymmetrical patterns. In addition, Paraskevopoulos (1968) found an increasing sensitivity to symmetry with age, and Chipman and Mendelson (1975) found that 5- to 9-year-olds judged symmetrical patterns as more simple than asymmetrical ones. Although Boswell did not find evidence of children introducing symmetry to asymmetrical patterns, the conditions may not have been optimal for obtaining this sort of evidence. Also Pomerantz (1977) suggests that adults may exhibit a response bias towards selecting more symmetrical figures in choice-reaction-time tasks. So there is enough evidence to make a symmetry interpretation of the present effects a possibility worth pursuing.

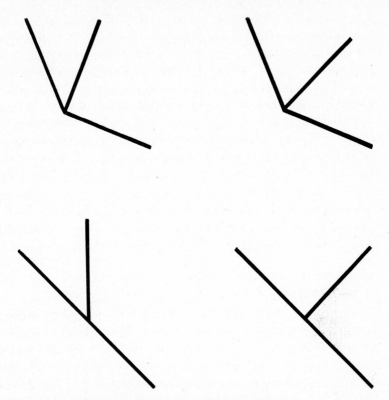

Figure 17.3 Figures used by Bremner and Taylor (1982):
non-bisection/non-perpendicular to the left, bisection/perpendicular to the right.

We set about evaluating this interpretation by comparing children's copying performance on the figures used by Ibbotson and Bryant with figures that avoided the confounding of perpendicularity with symmetry (Figure 17.3). All figures consisted of a 135° 'dog-leg' baseline with a red line intersecting the angle, and were presented in two configurations: bisection, in which the red line bisected the 135° angle, and non-bisection, in which the red line made an angle of 90° to one leg and 45° to the other. On a symmetry measure, these two configurations were the equivalents of Ibbotson and Bryant's perpendicular and non-perpendicular configurations, and the same number of figures are generated across the four baseline orientations. Figure 17.3 shows a sub-set, there being two bisection and four non-bisection figures in each of four orientations.

The point of using these figures is that instead of confounding perpendicularity and symmetry, they set them in opposition. The logic was that if we were dealing with a perpendicular tendency, children would copy the non-bisection figures accurately, since they already contained a right angle, but should make larger errors with bisection figures, tending to create a perpendicular relationship. In contrast, if we were dealing with a symmetry or bisection effect, children would copy the bisection figures accurately, but would make large errors with non-bisection figures, distorting them towards bisection. At this stage, we left open the question of whether any such effect would operate on the figure as a whole, or on the local angular relationship. The first possibility is more in line with Gestalt assumptions, but the second is also a viable possibility, particularly in a production task where the child may be focusing on the immediate relationship. So, in this section, the terms 'bisection' and 'symmetry' are used interchangeably.

Forty 5-year-olds took part in the study, 20 producing copies of the straight baseline figures, and 20 making copies of the angled baseline set. Both overall and directional errors were measured, in the same way as in Ibbotson and Bryant's study. By the overall error measure, children performed similarly on the straight and angled baseline figures, making smaller errors on symmetrical figures of both types. So one condition of the symmetry hypothesis was satisfied. But the major support for the hypothesis arose from the directional-error analysis (Figure 17.4). Non-bisection angled baseline figures yielded errors towards bisection, and consequently away from the perpendicular. This was true only for oblique presentations, but orientation and figure type did not interact in the analysis, so the baseline-orientation effect was common to both straight and angled baseline figures. The only difference to emerge between angled and straight baseline figures was a simple main effect, with directional errors greater for the straight baseline figures. This was to be expected, however, since the scope for error was greater with these figures (the maximum directional error; that is, the error resulting from an exact bisection, was $45°$ for straight baseline figures, but $22.5°$ for angled baseline figures). Thus, we felt that we had good evidence in support of the bisection explanation. Children copied non-bisection figures so that they were more symmetrical than they should have been, even when this involved a shift *away* from an existing perpendicular in the model figure.

The next question was whether the baseline-orientation effects could also be interpreted through what we know of symmetry effects from other sources. The infancy work (Bornstein, Ferdinandsen and Gross, 1981; Fisher, Ferdinandsen and Bornstein, 1981) shows that the sensitivity is limited to symmetry about the vertical axis, and this difference between vertical and horizontal symmetry lasts up to around the age of 10 years (Derȩgowski, 1971). Although only vertical and horizontal symmetry was investigated in these studies, Mendelson and Lee (1981) included figures with oblique-plane

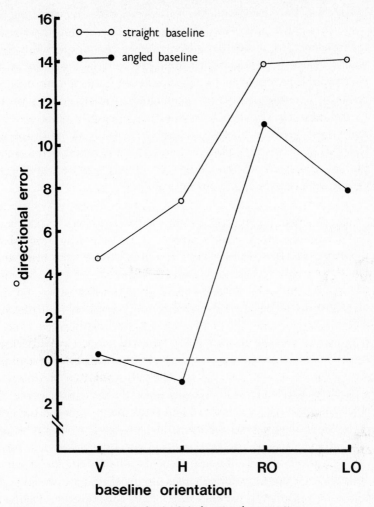

Figure 17.4 Bremner and Taylor (1982): directional-error pattern.

symmetry in an investigation of the effects of figural organisation on a matching-to-sample task. Testing 5-, 6- and 8-year-olds, they found that horizontal and vertical symmetry in the figure led to improved matching performance at all ages, but that oblique-plane symmetry became effective only at 6 years. In addition to this matching-accuracy difference with 5-year-olds, there is evidence that adults detect oblique-plane symmetry more slowly than horizontal or vertical symmetry (Palmer and Hemenway, 1978), so it looks as if children should find oblique symmetry least easy to detect.

At first sight, there seems little hope of showing a link between these effects and the baseline-orientation effects produced in our reproduction task, since the two seem to be almost complete opposites. However, further thought about the task structure shows that this is what we might expect. When symmetry is easily detected, presumably asymmetry is as well. It seems quite likely that children will be less likely to distort a figure towards symmetry when it is obviously asymmetrical. Thus, when children are faced with vertically and horizontally oriented asymmetrical figures, they may resist the tendency to make them symmetrical, since they are so obviously not so. By this argument, the baseline-orientation effects obtained in these completion tasks should be the exact opposite of the orientation effects obtained in the symmetry detection studies, and that is what emerges.

4. Some complicating evidence

Despite the fact that clear evidence for a bisection tendency had emerged, and that there seemed to be a reasonable interpretation of the baseline-orientation effects in relation to orientation effects in other parts of the symmetry literature, the possibility still remained that the errors obtained with the two different types of figure (straight versus angled baselines) arose for different reasons. It is hard to see how the errors with angled baseline figures could be explained other than in terms of some sort of local or configurational symmetry effect, but this did not altogether rule out the possibility of a separate perpendicular bias. A strong test of this possibility was to investigate children's attempts at constructing a single-angle figure. If the intersection point was fixed at the end of the baseline, any bias towards the perpendicular could not be explained in terms of angle bisection or figural symmetry.

Consequently, in what I hoped would be a final study to make the case for symmetry, children's performance on the usual straight-baseline figures was compared with their performance on figures with the intersection at the end of the baseline (Figure 17.5). To ensure that they constructed the angle at the very end of the baseline, a response method used by Freeman and Kelham (1981) was adopted. Children were provided with a response board with the baseline drawn on, and a rod that was fixed so that it pivoted around the end of the baseline. They could then complete their copy by rotating the rod until they thought their figure matched the model.

Use of these figures allowed for investigation of another factor. Ibbotson and Bryant's non-perpendicular figures obtained both an acute and an obtuse angle, and there was no way of saying whether the bias acted equally on both angles. If some sort of perpendicular bias did exist, its mechanism might be revealed in an unequal effect on different types of angle. For instance, it might

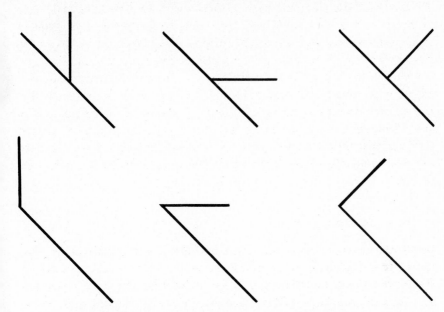

Figure 17.5 Figures used by Bremner (1984): 'middle' figures above, 'end' figures below.

turn out to be an angular overestimation effect applying to acute angles alone. Investigation of this sort of possibility was allowed for by inclusion of both acute-angle and obtuse-angle figures.

The main question was whether perpendicular errors occurred with 'end' figures. The answer is that they did – rather a disappointment to anyone seeking a simple interpretation of the phenomena. However, while 'middle' figures yielded much the usual baseline-orientation effect, 'end' figures yielded an effect related to the orientation of the constructed line (Figure 17.6). Although it was not at all clear how this orientation effect was to be interpreted, it was a consistent effect, and it is at least clear that the orientation effects differ greatly between 'end' and 'middle' figures.

So we are left with a paradox. A perpendicular error still occurs with 'end' figures, but in this case the strength of the error depends on the orientation of the added line instead of the orientation of the baseline. This suggests that we are dealing with a different phenomenon, at least to the extent that the influences on it differ between the two types of figure. With 'middle' figures, we seem to be dealing with a configuration effect that varies with the orientation of the figure, whereas with 'end' figures, we seem to have an effect that is influenced more directly by surrounding-framework cues or some other

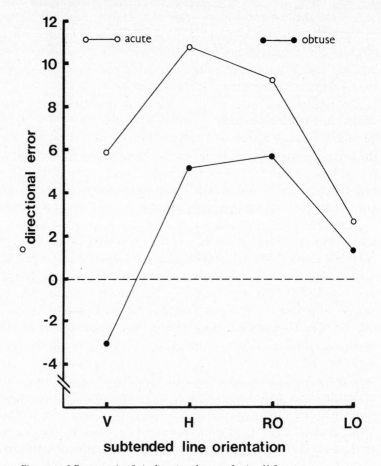

Figure 17.6 Bremner (1984): directional errors for 'end' figures.

external frame of reference (there was also evidence of framework effects in the pattern of absolute errors in 'end' figures). This suggests a striking difference between the processes underlying the two phenomena, since perpendicular errors with Ibbotson and Bryant-type figures have turned out to be remarkably resistant to effects of imposed frameworks. Manipulating a surrounding framework produces only very subtle effects on construction of these figures (Freeman and Kelham, 1981), and the effects become marked only when the baseline is reduced to about a quarter of its usual length (Bayraktar, 1979, or see Chapter 18 below). My prediction is that children's constructions of 'end' figures would be much more sensitive to manipulation of a surrounding frame.

It seems unlikely that all the results obtained in this study can be explained in terms of the action of just one type of bias. First, it is difficult to see why the same bias should be sensitive to orientation in such different ways for 'middle' *versus* 'end' figures. Secondly, we cannot easily explain Bremner and Taylor's results in terms of a perpendicular effect. We might go some way in this direction, using the evidence of stronger directional error with acute figures relative to obtuse ones to argue that a perpendicular bias would operate more strongly to increase the 45° angle than to maintain the 90° one, because the former is more acute. However, even this elaborate extension of the account cannot deal with the fact that bisection figures were so accurately copied despite the lack of perpendicular angles. The perpendicular-bias account could only deal with this if it was assumed that opposing biases cancel out, resulting in relational equilibrium.

This points to a way of maybe reconciling the perpendicular and symmetry interpretations. Although there seems no questioning the fact that a perpendicular bias exists with single angles, there is no saying whether this bias is still towards an absolute angle when two angles are involved. There is good evidence that children rely heavily on relational coding (Bryant, 1974), so maybe the absolute–relative coding question can be applied productively to this sort of problem as well. Although it seems that an absolute perpendicular bias exists, children may be more strongly affected by relational biases. Thus, when two adjacent angles are present, the bias may be to overestimate the smaller angle and underestimate the larger one, that is, towards the relation of equality. So, to put this back into the context of the present results, children's judgements may be influenced by two classes of relational effects. With 'middle' figures, internal relative forces act to produce a strong configurational distortion, so external relational forces (see Freeman and Kelham, 1981) are not directly effective. However, with 'end' figures, internal relative forces are absent, so external relational forces have a strong effect on the unstable absolute bias.

When it comes down to it, talking about an internal relative bias is probably just another way of describing a bisection or symmetry effect. Certainly, the notion of forces towards balance is very much in keeping with Gestalt theory. So it may well be that when a figure offers the possibility of balance or symmetry, such biases operate. As already argued, baseline-orientation effects obtained with middle figures can be related to orientation effects occurring in other parts of the symmetry literature. So the tentative conclusion to be drawn from all this is that a perpendicular bias does exist as such, but that it is replaced by, or converts to, a relative bias when two adjacent angles are involved.

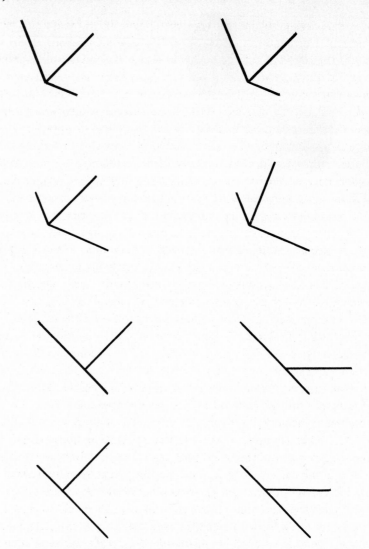

Figure 17.7 Figures used by Perrett and Bremner (1983).

— 5. Further questions

Whether we call the effect with 'middle' figures a symmetry effect or a bias towards relational equilibrium, an important question remains. As previously noted, we have to ask whether the bias acts locally, on the immediate angular relationship, or whether it is an overall configurational bias. One way of testing this is to see what happens if figures are used for which there is no way of distorting the angular relationship in order to produce a symmetrical figure. We adopted such a method (Perrett and Bremner, 1983), simply shortening one end of the baseline of the straight and angled figures used by Bremner and Taylor, so that even with the angles equated, the figures were asymmetrical (Figure 17.7). The expectation was that if the equalisation bias was an overall configurational effect, no clear bias would be obtained in this case. On the other hand, if we were dealing with a local angular bias, it would appear just as usual.

The main suggestion is that the bias operates locally. Very much the same results emerged with the modified figures as did in the previous study, with clear evidence for a bias towards bisection. This evidence is in keeping with Young and Deręgowski's (1982) claim that the children deal with figures in a piecemeal fashion, failing to integrate the elements to form a detailed representation of the figure as a whole. However, there was also some evidence of an overall figural effect, arising from an additional measure derived from the straight-baseline figures. With these, we measured the amount by which the produced bisection point departed from the intersection point in the model, and found that there was a clear shift towards the middle of the baseline. So whatever was happening to the angular relationship, there seemed to be an overall figural-symmetry effect operating as well.

Following up on this result, we found that young children made quite clear 'symmetry errors' in two other tasks (Bremner and Nisbet, 1983). The figures used are shown in Figure 17.8. The rectangular outlines were subdivided by a red line in the ratio 1:1 (symmetry), 2:1 or 3:1 (asymmetry). Children were provided with a response sheet with the rectangle on it and placed a red rod to correspond to the red line. Young 4-year-olds showed a clear symmetry bias with the asymmetrical figures, and copied the symmetrical figures very much more accurately. Older 4-year-olds showed the same biases but to a slightly lesser extent. These biases appeared for oblique and vertical presentations of the figures, and to a slightly lesser extent for horizontal presentations. In the case of the second set of stimuli, the child's task was to complete a response sheet containing all but one of the discs, by placing a counter. Again, clear symmetry effects appeared for both types of figure, although slightly less strongly in the figures in which the axis of symmetry was specified directly by a line than when it was indirectly specified by a square outline.

Thus there seem to be clear indications that configurational-symmetry effects occur: further evidence of overall biases as well as local angular ones. Returning to Young and Deręgowski's point, while children's strategies for inspecting figures may be limited to focusing on elements without integrating them into a whole, it may well be that there are other influences on perception

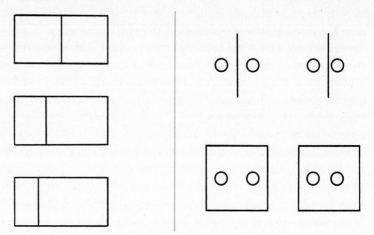

Figure 17.8 Figures used by Bremner and Nisbet (1983): those for Experiment 1 are to the left, those for Experiment 2 to the right.

or production, operating at the level of the whole figure. Freeman (1980) has obtained evidence suggesting that framework effects operate mainly at the production stage in an angular-alignment task, but there is no saying yet whether this is also true of configurational effects like those discussed above. They may for instance turn out to have a relatively automatic effect operating on perception of model and copy, and may be quite distinct from biases arising from use of a particular strategy that might be expected to appear mainly at the production stage.

6. Conclusion

This series of studies has taken us a long way from Piaget and Inhelder's original questions. Sceptics would criticise such a path of research for losing sight of the interesting issues in the pursuit of methodological innovation, and often there is a danger of this happening. However, in this case I believe that new and interesting ideas have emerged in the process, ideas that may act back to modify our future approaches to the questions that prompted the original work. All these new findings do not really bear on Piaget and Inhelder's question about the child's understanding of the horizontal and vertical, but it may be that they indicate that the errors obtained in the original studies arose because other factors dominated. The child may have been aware of the horizontal, but may not have produced it accurately as a result of powerful antagonistic effects. But if nothing else, this work points to the need to look more closely at just what is involved in the task.

There are a number of other questions that we must ask about the original task. For instance, one of the major concerns in current drawing research is the problem faced by the child converting three-dimensional reality to the two-dimensional page (see Chapters 10 and 13 above), and this is something that Piaget and Inhelder probably worried too little about in their studies of the horizontal and vertical. It is possible that the child has quite a good knowledge of the horizontal or vertical, but does not know how to represent it on the page, particularly when the latter is usually presented horizontally. The fact that Ibbotson and Bryant found no difference between same-plane and different-plane arrangements of stimulus and response figures might suggest that this factor would not be important. However, what appears unimportant in a task involving translation between one two-dimensional figure and another may be important as part of a task involving translation of three-dimensional reality to a two-dimensional representation. It turns out that the simple move of allowing the child to draw on a vertical sheet produces a marked reduction in errors on conventional tests of the horizontal and vertical (Flude and Bremner, 1983). This should come as no surprise, really, since artists presumably do not use easels for nothing. The differential obtained with this task suggests that children do have some grip of vertical and horizontal planes and are better able to show this grip if the conditions pose fewer translation problems. It now seems even more probable that the normal product is a balance between an attempt to produce the correct orientation and various other factors acting in opposition, and the problem is now one of establishing what the balance is. Are local and global configurational biases sufficiently strong to produce error in tests of the horizontal or vertical despite a clear understanding of these planes on the part of the child, or do such biases have an effect only when the child's understanding or perception of the horizontal and vertical is still poor? At present we do not have the data to answer this question.

The research reported in this chapter also has a very direct bearing on how we set about studying children's drawings more generally. In the past, there has been a tendency to develop attractive theory about the motives underlying children's drawings, with perhaps too little regard given to the range of perceptual and production factors that undoubtedly operate as well (for a comprehensive discussion of this, see Freeman, 1980). Although children's products are doubtless determined in large part by what they intend to put on paper, the final product is likely to be modified in many other ways that bear no real relation to what the child was trying to portray. Fortunately, I think that we can now say more about the forms these modifications are likely to take. This may not make the study of children's drawing any easier, since these effects are likely to be subtle as well as complex. But I would argue that we must pay more attention to the contribution of these biases to the drawing process in more everyday settings. The point can be made by returning once more to the case of a child drawing a house. As I indicated right at the beginning, the obvious bias appears in the way the chimney is often added at right angles to the sloping roof. However, according to the arguments developed later in the chapter, there are probably a number of other instances of biases operating within the same task. If we can generalise from the work with abstract figures, all the different types of effect covered in this chapter may well operate at different points in the production of a typical house drawing.

At least one form of bias should actually help to make the house look right. When the child constructs the first angle in the outline of the building, a perpendicular bias may help to make the angle 90°. The child may not *know* that the angle should be 90°; it may simply come out that way. But note that this single angle effect seemed to be sensitive to framework effects, so the prediction is that if the child was asked to draw a tilted house, even a right angle would be less accurate (this was actually found with the 'end' figures in Bremner, 1984).

Once later parts of the outline are constructed, however, we could well be in a position in which a figural-symmetry effect would start to contribute, so that the final figure would be 'biased' towards whatever symmetry could result given the size of the initial angles. Positioning of windows and doors would also be influenced by symmetry effects (see Bremner and Nisbet, 1983), and this could at least partly explain the development of a stereotype house drawing, in which even children living in terraced houses with door to one side and windows to the other often draw their own house with door in the middle and windows to each side. In the Gestalt sense, the latter is a 'better' house. (Note that I am talking about the *formation* of a stereotype here. Once formed, it is probably run off relatively automatically.)

Finally, what of the chimney? It is usually added at or near the end of the drawing, and is often a feature that interferes with the overall symmetry of the product, since it is put on one pitch of the roof rather than in the centre. In this case, it seems likely that we are dealing with a local angular-equalisation effect, since this seemed to be dominant when there were two angles at the intersection. Additionally, it should be most marked in this case, since the roof presents an oblique baseline. Tilt the house, however, and the somewhat paradoxical prediction is that the chimney's angular relationship to the rest of the house should be more accurately constructed, since the baseline (roof) would then be horizontal or vertical.

This has been a speculative analysis, but the intention has been to point out the complex interplay of different effects that we can expect to operate in drawing tasks in general. It seems likely that whenever a child draws an angle or line, or places one feature in relation to another, both local bias and overall figural or extra-figural biases have a potential role in the formation of the product. But the dominance of one over the other is determined by their relative strength. When an angle is drawn, the product will be affected in a way that depends on the relative strengths of the local bias *versus* figural effects (for instance, symmetry) *versus* extra-figural effects (e.g. framework, edge of paper, etc.). At the moment we can only guess at these relative strengths in the more complex setting of free drawing. My expectation is that by taking this sort of analysis to the case of children's free drawing, we will reach a better understanding of the process through being able to see more clearly which aspects of drawings are there as a result of the child's intention to portray particular features, and which are there because of more basic geometric biases.

REFERENCES

Bayraktar, R. (1979) An analysis of various copying errors in young children. Unpublished D.Phil. thesis, University of Sussex.

Beilin, H., Kagan, J. & Rabinowitz, R. (1966) Effects of verbal and perceptual training on water level representation. *Child Development*, *37*, 317–29.

Bornstein, M. H., Ferdinandsen, K. & Gross, C. G. (1981) Perception of symmetry in infancy. *Developmental Psychology*, *17*, 82–6.

Boswell, S. L. (1976) Young children's processing of symmetrical and asymmetrical patterns. *Journal of Experimental Child Psychology*, *22*, 309–18.

Bremner, J. G. (1984) Errors towards the perpendicular in children's copies of angular figures: A test of the bisection interpretation. *Perception*, *13*, 117–28.

Bremner, J. G. & Nisbet, S. (1983) Symmetry bias in young children's copies of two dimensional figures. Paper submitted for publication.

Bremner, J. G. & Taylor, A. J. (1982) Children's errors in copying angles: Perpendicular error or bisection error? *Perception*, *11*, 163–71.

Bryant, P. E. (1974) *Perception and understanding in young children.* London: Methuen.

Chipman, S. F. & Mendelson, M. J. (1975) The development of sensitivity to visual structure. *Journal of Experimental Child Psychology*, *20*, 411–29.

Deręgowski, J. B. (1971) Symmetry, Gestalt and information theory. *Quarterly Journal of Experimental Psychology*, *23*, 381–5.

Fisher, C. B., Ferdinandsen, K. & Bornstein, M. H. (1981) The role of symmetry in infant form discrimination. *Child Development*, *52*, 457–62.

Flude, B. & Bremner, J. G. (1983) Children's errors on Piagetian tests of the horizontal and vertical are reduced through use of a vertical response plane. Paper submitted for publication.

Freeman, N. H. (1980) *Strategies of representation in young children: Analysis of spatial skills and drawing processes.* London: Academic Press.

Freeman, N. H. & Kelham, S. E. (1981) The interference of a baseline with children's orientation judgement need not entirely mask their contextual responsiveness. *Quarterly Journal of Experimental Psychology, 33,* 145–54.

Howard, I. (1978) Recognition and knowledge of the water level principle. *Perception, 7,* 151–60.

Ibbotson, A. & Bryant, P. E. (1976) The perpendicular error and the vertical effect in children's drawing. *Perception, 5,* 319–26.

Liben, L. S. (1981) Copying and reproducing pictures in relation to subjects' operative levels. *Developmental Psychology, 17,* 357–63.

MacKay, C. K., Brazendale, A. H. & Wilson, L. F. (1972) Concepts of horizontal and vertical: A methodological note. *Developmental Psychology, 7,* 232–7.

McGillicuddy-DeLisi, A. V., DeLisi, R. & Youniss, J. (1978) Representation of the horizontal coordinate with and without liquid. *Merrill-Palmer Quarterly of Behavior and Development, 24,* 199–208.

Mendelson, M. J. & Lee, S. P. (1981) The effects of symmetry and contour on recognition memory in children. *Journal of Experimental Child Psychology, 32,* 373–88.

Palmer, S. E. & Hemenway, K. (1978) Orientation and symmetry: Effects of multiple, rotational and near symmetries. *Journal of Experimental Psychology: Human Perception and Performance, 4,* 691–702.

Paraskevopoulos, I. (1968) Symmetry, recall, and preference in relation to chronological age. *Journal of Experimental Child Psychology, 6,* 254–64.

Perrett, M. & Bremner, J. G. (1983) Bisection effects in children's copies of angular figures: Local bisection effect or overall symmetry effect? Unpublished manuscript, University of Lancaster.

Piaget, J. & Inhelder, B. (1956) *The child's conception of space.* London: Routledge and Kegan Paul.

(1968) *Memory and intelligence.* London: Routledge and Kegan Paul.

Pomerantz, J. R. (1977) Pattern goodness and speed of encoding. *Memory and Cognition, 5,* 235–41.

Smedslund, J. (1963) The effect of observation on children's representation of the spatial orientation of a water surface. *Journal of Genetic Psychology, 102,* 195–201.

Thomas, H. & Jamison, W. (1975) On the acquisition of understanding that still water is horizontal. *Merrill-Palmer Quarterly of Behavior and Development, 21,* 31–44.

Young, A. W. & Deręgowski, J. B. (1982) Learning to see the impossible. *Perception, 10,* 91–105.

18

Cross-cultural analysis of drawing errors

RÜVIDE BAYRAKTAR

1. Introduction

Many psychologists have concerned themselves with the way young children handle information about orientation. It has been shown that when children make judgements about linear inclination, they are strongly affected by the direction of the contours in the surrounding visual field. As Mitchelmore stresses in his chapter in this volume, they are very sensitive to relations of parallelism (Bryant, 1974; Berman, 1976; Naeli and Harris, 1976; Bayraktar, 1979; Freeman, 1980).

Bryant (1974) explains such findings by arguing that, on the standard rectangular paper used for various tasks, vertical and horizontal lines 'match' different sides of the paper and this relationship can easily be perceived. Oblique lines, however, produce a mismatch signal with all sides of the paper and therefore their precise orientation is not easily perceived. Thus children's failure in many drawing tasks may often be attributed to the child's reference system, which is bound by display landmarks.

Important support for the Bryant-type account comes from my previous finding (Bayraktar, 1979) that this ability to use contextual cues is not restricted to children who have been reared in a 'developed' urban culture, but is also present in rural children who have had very limited experience with drawing activities. The young children in my studies were able to use a contextual-matching rule and to take their cue from a parallel element in the immediate context.

But we then come across a clear contradiction of these results. Ibbotson and Bryant (1976) showed that when copying a line projecting at an angle of 45° from a longer pre-drawn baseline, children lose the ability to benefit from contextual parallelism cues: they copy acute angles consistently closer to 90°. This Ibbotson and Bryant call the 'perpendicular error'.

In the Ibbotson–Bryant experiment, baselines having various orientations were used; and they found that the perpendicular error was relatively smaller when the baseline was vertical than when it was horizontal or oblique: the 'vertical effect'. Thus, the perpendicular error, or perpendicular bias as I shall call it, can be partly overridden by the vertical effect. The lack of significant effect of the external frame of reference, which, though providing a parallel cue (the edge of the paper) for the target line, failed to improve the child's performance, is in contrast with Bryant's earlier findings (1969 and 1974).

In their experiment, Ibbotson and Bryant asked children to match a line (by drawing or setting down a wire) to a vertical target line set upon an oblique baseline. The square paper used gave vertical and horizontal orientation cues. The vertical target line not only coincides with an internal framework (postural) but parallels the edge of the paper (contextual cue). This is shown in Figure 18.1, condition SO, later to be discussed. Yet the children generally produce an oblique line (relative to the paper) when attempting to match the vertical target line, often in an almost perpendicular relationship with the baseline.

The researcher is, then, presented with a problem: whereas children seem to find a vertical line quite easy to match when it is isolated in the stimulus array, they are all but unable to do so when it is set upon an oblique baseline.

Analogous problems had shown up also in the work of earlier researchers. Piaget and Inhelder (1948/1956) obtained distortions of the same sort in their work on children's understanding of spatial coordinate systems. For instance they found that when faced with a tilted glass containing some liquid, young children would often not draw a water level inside a tilted bottle as paralleling the ground. Why not, if the studies showing their great sensitivity to context are right? For that matter, why will they not draw trees upright (vis-à-vis the edge of the paper) on a mountainside? Thus far, it appears that young children, when drawing a line projecting from another, tend willy-nilly to draw towards a perpendicular.

The formal similarity between Ibbotson and Bryant's and Piaget and Inhelder's paradigms is striking; the child who draws a vertical target line as perpendicular to its oblique baseline may be making the same mistake as the child who draws a tree as perpendicular to a mountainside. Piaget and Inhelder attributed this error to a problem of logic, whereas Ibbotson and Bryant attribute it to a bias in drawing, maintaining that the child uses the bottom of the bottle as a parallel cue.

In the light of the research reviewed here, the Ibbotson–Bryant and Piaget–Inhelder findings all indicate an unexpected breakdown in performance.

How can these results be reconciled with the Bryant account mentioned at the outset?

There was one essential difference between the paradigms of these studies which may perhaps explain the inconsistencies. In the one type, where contextual responsiveness was elicited, subjects merely placed a figure within the confines of a piece of paper, while Ibbotson and Bryant required them to make their responses in relation to pre-drawn baselines. In the case where the baseline is provided, the child may have two cues potentially available which she/he would not have in the other paradigm. One cue would be the angle between the baseline and the target line, the second the parallelism of the target line to one or other edge of the paper. In the case of two available cues, Piaget and Inhelder argue that young children are highly liable to 'centration' effects whereby they attend to only a small region of a figure at a time. One would therefore expect them to be guided only by the immediate local cue of the angular relation between baseline and target line and be unable to decentre and attend either to cues available from the edges of the paper or to their own internal coordinate system. Granted that the children may have been influenced by centration, the question remains as to why they drew the water level not in a random orientation, but specifically at right angles to the sides of the bottle. Whereas randomly incorrect orientations might have been adequately explained in Piagetian terms by some such concept as 'lack of horizontality concept', persistence of the perpendicular bias would mean that another explanation must be sought. It was this that motivated me to explore the effect of context in relation to the perpendicular bias. Could it be the case that a drawing task which induces a perpendicular bias actually hinders the basic relational coding of parallelism?

The experiments reported here were undertaken to investigate the effectiveness of contextual cues, and the generality and reliability of both the perpendicular bias and the vertical effect, in different copying and matching tasks. In other words I was interested in studying the effect of contextual cues; I did this essentially by modifying the Ibbotson–Bryant task.

The standard test for relational coding with linear inclination is to ask children to perform with rectangular paper set (i.e. oriented) normally to the line of the sight. By combining that task with the Ibbotson–Bryant one, I was able to modify both the *baseline orientation* (proximal cue) and *the shape of the paper* (distal cues). Thereby I tried to tease out the relative influence of these different contextual cues on children's drawings.

2. Experiment I (The standard paradigm)

The experiment was done with 84 children (42 girls and 42 boys), half of whom were from Turkish rural areas and half from Turkish urban areas. There were three age groups, whose mean ages were almost exactly 4, 5 and 6 years.

The tasks they were asked to perform were simple: to look at and copy a line which stuck out at 45° from the centre of a longer baseline. The baseline was already provided on the piece of paper given to them, so all they were being asked to do was add the target line in order to reproduce the model they were looking at. There were three baseline orientations: vertical, horizontal and left oblique (45°). Each baseline was drawn on circular, square and triangular pieces of paper, yielding a total of nine models. These are shown in Figure 18.1.

Each child was tested alone facing the experimenter. A hardboard square, triangle or circle was placed on the child's lap along with a smaller response paper of the same shape which had a pre-drawn baseline. The shape of the response paper and the pre-drawn baseline corresponded to the stimulus model in front of the child throughout the time. The child was told, 'Draw the little line like the one in the picture, making sure your line goes the same way.' When the child had completed one drawing, the task was repeated in turn with the other two baselines using the same shaped frame (i.e. if the child were first presented with, say, a triangle she/he would be given the other two triangles); then a new shape (frame) was presented and the process repeated with each of the three baselines within the new shape. Thus each child performed each of the nine tasks shown in Figure 18.1, with order of presentation (of both frames and baseline orientation) randomised.

The lines that the children drew were measured for size of angle, not for direction. Shaky lines were straightened by the author using a consistent procedure. The data were then put through ANOVA, and any reliable effects were then tracked down by the use of paired comparisons.

There was a reliable Baseline-Orientation Effect $(F(2.576) = 12.21$; $p < 0.001)$; as had been expected, the perpendicular bias was relatively less when the baseline was vertical than when it was horizontal or oblique: the vertical effect $(F(1.576) = 24.1$; $p < 0.001)$. So far the results confirm the Ibbotson–Bryant findings.

There was, however, a difference between the urban and rural children $(F(1.72) = 19.65$; $p < 0.001)$ in this baseline effect, which showed up in an interaction $(F(2.576) = 3.5$; $p < 0.03)$.

Examination of Figure 18.2 shows that, when the baseline was horizontal

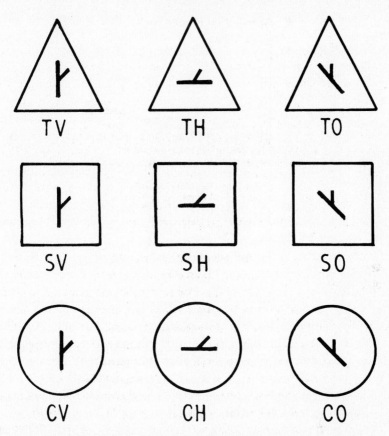

Figure 18.1 Stimuli for Experiment I. The first letter beneath each stimulus refers to the shape of the frame; the second letter refers to the orientation of the baseline.

or oblique, urban children copied the 45° angle less accurately than when it was vertical (the vertical effect), and whilst the same trend was observed among the rural subjects, the differences between the baseline orientations were less marked. A probable reason for this is that drawing tasks are so difficult for the rural children that the baseline orientation *per se* has little effect, especially for the youngest. It must be remembered that these children have no experience with using pencil or crayon as a tool in any type of drawing until the age of 7 at a minimum. It is only when you have children with some experience in drawing that the baseline orientation begins to make itself felt.

The important point to note is that no reliable effect of frame was to be found *anywhere* in the data: there was what one might call a failure to benefit

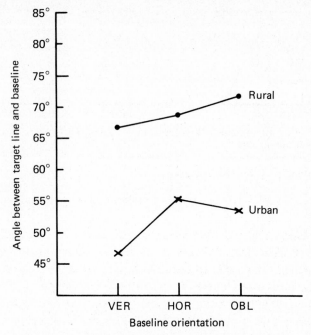

Figure 18.2 Mean angles between the baseline and the target line drawn for each baseline orientation by urban and rural children.

from the relationship of parallelism between the target line and the contextual features. An interesting complication did intrude upon this observation, in the form of a reliable interaction between Sex and Baseline-Orientation ($F(2.576) = 4.0$; $p < 0.02$), which indicated a difference in favour of males with the horizontal and oblique baselines, but no significant sex effect with the vertical. As with the Rural/Urban Effect, which also interacted with the Baseline Effect, we have here a warning that the basic phenomenon may be subject to some rather subtle influences. There is no question that the basic phenomenon exists, nor that it is impervious to the frame, but the relative strength of the vertical effect (or vertical-baseline-advantage with 45° angles, or whatever one calls it) is not constant across different samples. To focus on that aspect of the problem would have been one way to proceed, but it seemed much more of a challenge to look again at the variable which did not work: the subjects did not benefit from the relationship of parallelism between the target line and the contextual features. This does not necessarily imply that they can *never* benefit. The next step was to provide a special contextual cue for them to use if they were capable of it.

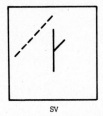 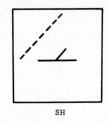 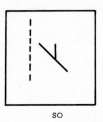

SV   SH   SO

Figure 18.3 Stimuli for Experiment IA. The dotted line represents a straight red line in the stimuli.

3. Experiment IA (The red-line cue)

Recalling the Bryant-type account of relational coding, which showed that the stimulus is affected by the presence of a visual frame of reference, the question arises as to whether the proximity of the frame determines the strength of its effect. It would seem likely that a nearer framework would be more influential than a distant one. The aim of the present experiment was to investigate this possible role of proximity in determining the frame effect. With this in mind, a more stringent test was devised combining the Ibbotson–Bryant design with the Bryant technique of providing a constant extra line, in red, which paralleled the target line. This red cue line was present on both the model and the response paper, providing what could be termed 'a constant cue condition' (Bryant, 1974, p. 74), as in Figure 18.3.

The target line which the child has to copy from the given pre-drawn baseline is parallel with a prominent feature of the framework, in this case the red line. Thus the match/mismatch hypothesis predicted that this red line would help the child in copying the target line.

Since it was the effect of this proximal cue which was being tested, only square paper was used. In every other respect the procedure was identical to that of Experiment I. Forty urban children (20 boys and 20 girls) with mean ages of almost exactly 4 and 5 were selected randomly from an upper-middle-class school.

The present results were remarkably similar to those of Experiment I. The data are shown in Figure 18.4. Again the perpendicular bias occurred unmistakeably; there was a significant Baseline-Orientation Effect ($F_{(2.76)} = 5.13$; $p < 0.008$), and the vertical effect was reliable (mean constant error 6°, 17° and 14° for the vertical, horizontal and oblique baselines respectively). There was no frame effect even with this prominent red cue. These findings imply that when the subject is presented with two orientation cues simultaneously, the proximal reference line, the baseline, is the major factor in determining copying performance.

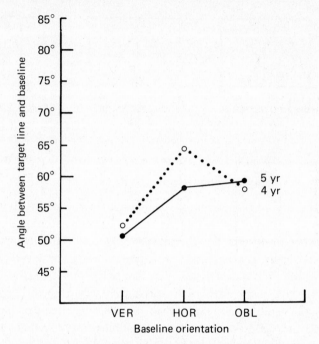

Figure 18.4 Mean angles between the baseline and the target line, as a function of baseline orientation, drawn by children at different ages.

If the orientation of the baseline is such a dominant cue that it can inhibit relational coding, it seemed appropriate to proceed by reducing it in size relative to the target in a similar experiment to see if its effect would be thus subdued. To this end, I conducted Experiment IB.

4. Experiment IB (The shortened baseline)

The standard paradigm of Experiment I was again used, and children were given the same type of materials, except that in each case the length of the baseline was reduced to a quarter that of the target line, as shown in Figure 18.5.

There are now two possibilities: either the more prominent new target line would take precedence over the shorter baseline, enabling the children to pick up the parallel cue provided by the edges of the paper; or the tendency towards making a perpendicular angle on a given baseline would prove to be so strong that despite the reduction of the latter, the children would still be unable to make use of the external frame of reference.

This time there were again 20 children, 10 boys and 10 girls, from a

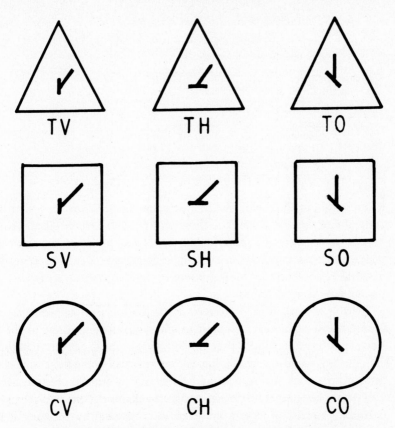

Figure 18.5 Stimuli for Experiment IB. The first letter beneath each stimulus refers to the shape of the frame; the second letter refers to the orientation of the baseline.

Turkish upper-middle-class urban school, with a mean age of about $4\frac{1}{2}$ years. The results again showed a significant main effect for Baseline-Orientation $(F (2.152) = 12.30; p < 0.001)$; the baseline kept a strong effect on the child's performance even when shortened. Both the perpendicular bias and vertical effect were found. Thus, if the baseline was vertical, the perpendicular bias was relatively less. But now, finally, a significant Frame Effect *did* appear $(F (2.152) = 5.05; p < 0.007)$. Overall, the perpendicular bias was smallest when a square frame was provided, somewhat greater with a circular frame and largest of all when the triangular frame was used (see Table 18.1).

More important, however, than the frame effect, there was a reliable Baseline-by-Frame interaction $(F (4.152) = 2.94; p < 0.02)$. As shown in Table 18.1, the oblique baseline was the most difficult to draw from, and for

Table 18.1. *Mean constant error in drawing an acute angle; data rounded to the nearest whole degree*

Frame	Baseline			Mean error
	|	—	\\	
Square	2	8	19	9
Triangle	11	24	17	17
Circle	9	14	19	14
Mean error	7	15	18	

this orientation there was almost no frame effect. However, with both the vertical and horizontal baseline there was a reliable frame effect. When the frames were square or circular, fewer errors were made on the vertical than on the horizontal baseline, with the highest error rate occurring on the oblique baseline. However, when the frame was triangular, errors were greatest when the baseline was horizontal.

There is a vertical effect as seen in the bottom row of the table, and a square-frame advantage, as seen in the right-hand column of the table. However, the main point is that providing a *potentially helpful cue* in the form of the triangular frame, which has one side parallel to the target line, *worsens* performance with the vertical and horizontal baselines, precisely where it might have been expected to help, as does no alignment cue at all (the neutral, circular, frame). The effects are even more dramatic with the horizontal baseline, where the triangular frame gives decidedly worse results than the neutral frame. By the time we get to an oblique baseline, the children are, of course, doing terribly anyway, and here is the usual lack of frame effect that we have come to expect.

This may be considered a counter-frame effect, since it was expected that the parallel cues would be helpful; and the problem of interpretation begins to make itself felt even more insistently than before.

5. Experiment IC (Two quadrants)

Although it is too early to draw definite conclusions about the mechanism behind the perpendicular bias, certain possibilities are beginning to suggest themselves. Perhaps Naeli and Harris (1978) were right in arguing that 'the child seeks to orient his reproduction so it appears "upright" relative to the framework'. This is an important claim which may well be relevant to the interpretation of various copying errors including perpendicular bias.

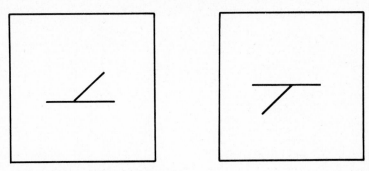

Figure 18.6 Stimuli for Experiment IC.

Hypothesising that 'uprightness' rather than perpendicularity *per se* is what the child seeks relative to the most dominant framework, which in our tests has turned out to be the baseline, Naeli and Harris later went on to predict that the perpendicular bias would be less marked if the target line was to be drawn below a horizontal line rather than above it. Experiment IC was conducted with this prediction in mind. Sixty children (30 boys, 30 girls) with mean ages of 3 years 9 months, 5 years and 7 years 9 months were drawn from Turkish middle-class urban kindergarten and primary schools.

This time there was only one shape of paper, square, with a horizontal baseline, and the target line to be copied was given in only two positions: 45° clockwise from the vertical (in the first quadrant) and 225° clockwise from the vertical (in the third quadrant). This put the target line above the baseline in one position and below it in the other position, as shown in Figure 18.6. The position had no effect on the perpendicular bias regardless of age, and the children simply performed better the older they were ($F (2.60) = 7.51$; $p < 0.001$). It will be noticed that I did not check the effects of all four quadrants of the paper space, and in the past one has sometimes been caught out by selective sampling. It so happens that Fisher's (1969) work on adults tells us that the first and third quadrants, precisely the ones for which we tested, may differ radically from the other two. In the next experiment I decided to explore the effect of all four quadrants, but also the possible interaction of the baseline orientations on the quadrants.

6. Experiment ID (Four quadrants)

This time I gave 16 copying tasks: four baseline orientations (vertical, horizontal, right oblique and left oblique), and target lines in the four quadrants of space relative to the baseline; see Figure 18.7.

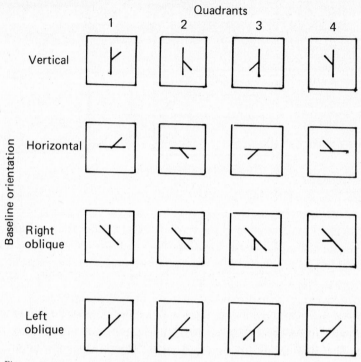

Figure 18.7 Stimuli for Experiment ID.

There were 60 children, an equal number of boys and girls, from Turkish middle-class kindergartens and primary schools, their mean ages being 4 years 1 month, 5 years and 5 years 8 months.

The results showed quite clearly that the quadrant was unimportant. It was the orientation of the Baseline (again!) which could affect performance reliably (F (3.162) = 40.00; $p < 0.01$), errors being fewer when the baseline was vertical than in any of the other cases. Ability to copy improved with Age (F (2.54) = 16.00; $p < 0.01$), but more importantly there was a significant interaction between Age and Baseline (F (6.162) = 4.25; $p < 0.01$). As shown in Figure 18.8, at the age of 4, vertical and horizontal orientation made no difference, nor did left and right oblique, but both vertical and horizontal baselines produced more accurate copying than the oblique figures.

At the age of 5, vertical baselines led to more accurate copying than the other orientations, which did not differ from one another (Tukey, $p < 0.05$). At the age of 6, all comparisons among baseline orientations were reliable (Tukey, $p < 0.01$). Vertical gave the best results, followed by horizontal, right oblique and left oblique in that order. That is, the vertical effect becomes more

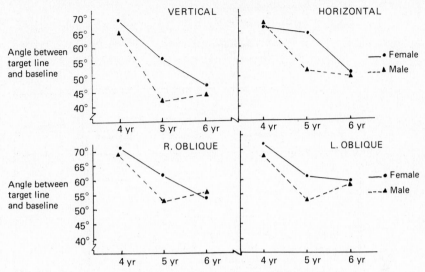

Figure 18.8 Angles drawn by boys and girls of different ages.

obvious with age, but also performance becomes more differentiated with respect to baseline orientation. The data of Olson (1975) also support my present findings. In his study with adults there was an interesting hint that verticals are recognised faster than horizontals, and right obliques than left obliques.

There was a very minor sex effect, but only at the ages of 4 and 5. In the 6-year-old age group, sex differences were absent, suggesting that by this age whatever minor sex differences exist have disappeared. This experiment has recently been replicated on British children with findings that confirm mine (M. Hansford, private communication). The quadrant, then, is a negligible factor in children's drawing, and our search must be carried further, with an alteration in strategy.

7. Experiment II (Drawing the angle from scratch: matching-to-sample)

The copying tasks in the previous experiments have required the children to make angles by simply drawing a line in the middle of a pre-drawn baseline, and overall a surprising robustness was exhibited. Findings were consistent throughout, with perpendicular bias and vertical effect wherever one looked.

It was the purpose of this present experiment to test further the generality of the findings by significantly altering the task. Instead of merely adding a line to a given pre-drawn baseline, what would the children's performance

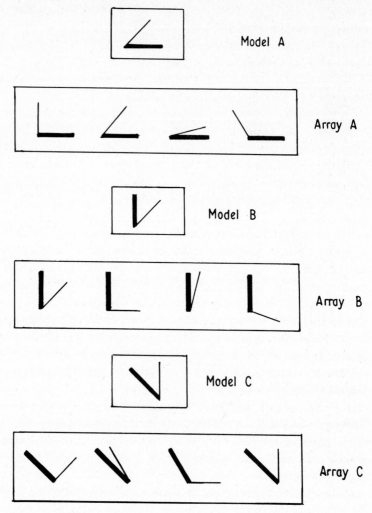

Figure 18.9 Stimuli for Experiment II.

be like if they were asked to reproduce the entire angle at different orientations? Would the same effects crop up again?

Of course before children can reasonably be asked to copy a figure such as an angle, one first has to be sure that they perceive it correctly, as stressed by Maccoby and Bee (1965) and Piaget and Inhelder (1948/1956). To rule out problems of discrimination a matching-to-sample task was added.

Eighty children from the Turkish urban community, half boys and half girls, participated in the study. There were four age groups, whose mean ages were 4, 5, 5 years 8 months and 7. Each child was asked to perform two types of tasks: matching-to-sample and copying.

There were three 45° models, each in a different orientation, as shown in Figure 18.9. In the first task, the child was asked to match each angle to an identical one in an array of four angles. The four angles in the array had values of 15°, 45°, 90° and 120° (see Figure 18.9), with the 45° angle oriented exactly like the one in the model being presented. The order of presentation of the models was randomised among the children. After the matching task, each child was given a piece of paper similar in shape and size to the model in front of him with instructions to 'Draw the same picture on your paper, making sure that your picture is exactly the same.' In this manner the children drew all the 45° angles.

Each child, then, both matched the samples of three angles and drew the same three angles. Scoring here for the matching task was merely the number of correct choices. For the drawing task the figure was scored correct if rotation from the desired angle was not more than 5°, or incorrect if the rotation exceeded 5°. I found that almost all the children except in the youngest group were able to match the samples correctly, but even so they were unable to copy them correctly. There was a definite tendency to expand the angles to 90°, again the tendency towards the perpendicular, which was greatest in the youngest group and decreased with age (F (3.76) = 5.94; $p < 0.01$). In other words, this is additional evidence of the perpendicular bias generalised to a situation in which the child has complete control over the reproduction of the target figure rather than having to draw from a pre-drawn baseline. It should, however, be noted that in the previous experiments, where the reconstruction takes place at the middle of the baseline, the distortions of angle size were greater than they were in this experiment where the entire angle was copied.

Although the perpendicular bias reared its head again, the vertical effect did not appear with its former reliability. When copying the angles at different orientations the percentages correct were 70, 65 and 50 for angles oriented horizontally, vertically and obliquely, in that order. It is immediately clear that although the vertical was not favoured, accuracy of reproduction was definitely influenced by the orientation of the model, even though the children were quite accurate in discriminating these orientations in the matching test (see Table 18.2).

Freeman and Kelham (1981) confirmed these results with a slightly modified design. They in fact replicated one of my earlier studies (Bayraktar, 1979) to explore a context effect, and found, as I did, that the responses to the horizontally oriented figures were more accurate than to the other

Table 18.2. *Mean percentages of correct recognition, of reproduction at correct angular orientation, and mean sizes of angle in reproductions, for subjects of different ages*

Age	Matching task	Copying task	
	% recognition success	% correct figural orientation	Angle size (in degrees)
7 years	100	91.7	46.9
5 years 8 months	100	83.3	46.0
5 years	97	60.0	44.6
4 years	85	11.7	59.5

orientations, although in their case the oblique gave better results than the vertical.

It is clear that there is not a perfect match with the previous experimental results, where the vertical rather than the horizontal was favoured and the perpendicular bias was greater. This implies that interpretation will not be a simple task; still, two conclusions do suggest themselves. The first is that the recognition of simple geometric forms is far simpler than the task of copying them. This finding is also congruent with those of Piaget and Inhelder (1948/1956) and Maccoby and Bee (1965), and with Olson's (1969) theoretical account that young children can make perceptual distinctions long before they can incorporate these distinctions into their copying behaviour. The second conclusion is that the problem of drawing angles is not something which can simply be put into a model with a cut-and-dried order-of-difficulty factor: as the drawing becomes freer, the order of difficulty may change (becoming greater or lesser). It would also seem to be evident that further research must focus on doing careful work of this sort for *every* type of drawing problem if we are to understand how difficult the labour of production can be. Only then can we usefully take up problems of the Piagetian water-level sort.

8. General conclusion and discussion

Contextual responsiveness
In attempting to come to terms with these findings, it would be well to recall the stages through which our understanding of children's responsiveness to context has gone. The traditional view was that they were unable to respond

to context when performing discrimination, placement and copying tasks (Piaget and Inhelder, 1948/1956). Then the work of Bryant (1969 and 1974) and Naeli and Harris (1976), as well as my own experiments (Bayraktar, 1979) on copying within frames which were shaped like the target figure, demonstrated that children did indeed have the ability to use a contextual-matching rule and take their cue from a parallel in the immediate context. Furthermore, this was shown to be true not only for children who had been reared in a 'developed' urban culture, but for rural children as well.

In support of those conclusions, which to some may seem to be based on the provision of particularly obvious cues (a triangular frame when the child is to draw a triangle, a square frame for a square, etc.), one can cite the 'rotated face' study of Freeman (1980, pp. 189–204), which showed that children used the edge of the paper as a cue to complete a drawing of a human figure parallel to it, in the absence, moreover, of a model showing the relationship of parallelism.

Then, just when this contextual responsiveness seemed clearly established, came evidence which showed that in certain circumstances – specifically when there was a baseline to work from and not simply a surrounding frame – children were far from being perfectly capable of reproducing lines at an angle in a desired orientation. Their ability to do so seemed to depend less (if at all) on the shape of the surrounding frame than on the orientation of the baseline with which they were provided, and the tendency in any case was to produce a target line more or less perpendicular to the baseline.

Perpendicular bias

This perpendicular bias persisted, let it once again be emphasised, even when the children had available to them the potential cues of the edge of the paper, or of a prominent thick red line staring them in the face parallel to the target line. Despite the decisively proven framework effect in the absence of a baseline, the experiments in these latter cases showed that children did not seem able to use the relation of parallelism between the target line and salient features in its context as a means of escaping from the perpendicular bias.

There was one what might be called ironical exception in Experiment IB (short baseline, long target line) where the surrounding frame provided by the edges of the paper did have an effect on children's reproductions, but the effect ran counter to expectations. I have therefore termed it an 'anti-frame' effect, although there should be no implication of any perverseness on the children's part: it is simply that the more potentially helpful a frame promised to be, in terms of available parallel cues, the less helpful it actually proved to be – again, in terms of the task the (adult) experimenter had assigned. No doubt the children were using it to help them do something that felt more sensible or 'right'.

At any rate, in this experiment the perpendicular bias was less with a square frame than with a circular one, with a triangular frame giving rise to the largest deviation toward perpendicularity (*vis-à-vis* the baseline), even though it provides a parallel-edge cue for the target line.

Thinking that the child's 'sensible' solution might be in the direction of 'uprightness', quadrant experiments were carried out, but they had no effect on the perpendicular bias. Of course it may be that 'uprightness' also translates as 'downrightness' but Experiment ID showed that the perpendicular bias is equally strong in all quadrants.

Finally, I found that the perpendicular bias generalised to a situation in which the child was responsible for the complete reproduction of the whole angle (i.e. where she/he started with a 'clean slate') and did not have to cope with a potentially 'misleading' baseline provided at the outset.

Possible sources of the perpendicular bias

Why do children have this bias? The answer is far from clear. Several explanations have been offered. One has been given in terms of Piagetian theory: in this model, young children have not yet formed a Euclidean frame of reference by which to coordinate directions extended in space, and tend to centre on the relation of perpendicularity. Like Piaget, Arnheim (1969) and Goodnow and Friedman (1972) believe that the young child 'centres' on the lines of a proximate spatial framework (a single baseline, for example) and is unable to utilise other, more distant, sources of spatial reference (the edges of the paper, the walls of the room, etc.). The child fails the 'water-level' test by giving a 'local solution to a spatial problem'.

This is all well and good, but it leaves glaringly undealt-with the question as to why the water level is almost always drawn perpendicular to the edge of the bottle – that is, why the child selects this among the infinitely many 'wrong' solutions available.

My earlier results, discussed in the Introduction and above, would make an argument for contextual insensitivity in orientation suspect from the beginning, and the later experiments produced data to indicate some responsiveness to the larger framework. In Experiment IB it is apparent that the target line is more accurately drawn (i.e. closer to 45°) from a short baseline when the square rather than the circular frame is provided. As noted previously (Experiment IB), the vertical edges of the square paper provide an external vertical cue which coincides with the internal vertical given by the child's body. Their combined effect is presumably to draw the child's attention strongly to the vertical coordinate and to relate the target line to this coordinate. So, contrary to Piaget and Inhelder's (1948/1956) theoretical formulation that the 'vertical and horizontal lines are not regarded as a reference frame', this finding implies that young children are able to and in fact do, under certain circumstances, use the vertical edges of the paper as a reference frame. But this was a special case and seems related to the parallelism of the baseline, rather than of the target line, to the frame.

Piaget claims that his tasks were designed to tap the deductive use of a contextual-reference axis. However, children in the present experiment were unable to use as a cue a reference line that was proximal and prominent (the thick red line). They still showed the perpendicular bias. This perhaps argues against the idea that 'intra-stimulus' alignment takes precedence over 'stimulus-context alignment' (Goodnow and Friedman, 1972). Rather, as Freeman (1980) suggests, this dominance of the proximal is specific to the perpendicular bias, and the children are capable of using both proximal and distal cues when the perpendicular bias is not a confounding factor.

Freeman and Kelham (1981), by replicating Experiment I with a slight modification, could not find an overall frame effect but found an interaction among sex, baseline orientation and frame. The frame effect was quite subtle and occurred only with girls. An 'anti-frame' effect occurred with the boys, whereby a cue which paralleled the target increased the perpendicular bias. As in Experiment IB here, relational coding did not really work. It seems clear now that the perpendicular bias is resistant to the introduction of parallel-framework cues. With Piagetian tasks, we cannot rule out the confounding effect of the perpendicular bias.

Recently, the attempts at explanation of the perpendicular bias have been complicated by references to 'bisection tendencies' and 'the pursuit of symmetry' (Bremner, 1983). Evidence has been obtained suggesting a bias which might be a special case of a bisection tendency (Bremner and Taylor, 1982). This notion is that when children copy a line intersecting a baseline at its mid-point, as was the case in most of our experiments, they tend to equalise the angles on each side of the baseline; hence when attempting to copy a $45°$ angle, they produce something that is more like a right angle. In other words, children have a tendency to make figures which are symmetrical either in terms of the local angular relationship or in terms of the figure as a whole. When the 'intersection' is abolished by placing the target line at the end of the baseline, Bremner and Taylor still found a perpendicular bias. The work is discussed in Bremner's chapter in this volume. Similarly, when children produced the whole angle at different orientations (Experiment II), they could not escape the perpendicular bias. It should again be noted here that this particular bias occurred even though in a discrimination task they readily matched all figures correctly regardless of the orientation.

A tendency towards making things upright has also been regarded as a characteristic preference of the child: in Braine's terms, 'the distinction between the perception of uprightness and non-uprightness can be seen as a kind of aesthetic judgement' (Braine, 1978, p. 21). Such a preference for uprightness might produce a perpendicular bias. But the failure in my studies to find a quadrant effect, that is, any effect related to position or direction of the target line in relation to the baseline, rules out this idea of a tendency towards uprightness as an explanation for the perpendicular bias.

As yet there is no satisfactory explanation of the perpendicular bias. Even Ibbotson and Bryant's explanation does not seem entirely adequate. Their idea is that because children live in environments surrounded by right angles these probably very quickly become important 'markers' for them and for that reason there is a bias towards drawing the perpendicular. But the findings show that children from very differently carpentered environments, such as English urban compared to Turkish urban and Turkish urban compared to Turkish rural, still show the same perpendicular bias. Therefore, it seems unlikely that carpentry is a significant explanation for the perpendicular bias. For the same reason other explanations based on familiarity with the external world would seem to fall short of the mark as well.

The perpendicular bias decreases with age, disappearing about the age of 6 or 7. Some differences were noted in favour of males as borne out by the findings of many other workers. Girls tended to make more perpendicular bias on horizontals and obliques, contrary to Freeman and Kelham's findings. But this superiority of the boys disappears at about the age of 6.

Vertical effect
Young children's copying was affected by the orientation of a baseline within a given frame. Overall, the size of errors was consistently less when the baseline was vertical than when horizontal or oblique. This 'vertical effect' shows indirectly that at least when dealing with 45° angles young children are indeed sensitive to the orientation of figures. There is considerable evidence here that the child first acquires the vertical-upright axis and then, soon after, the horizontal followed by the oblique inclinations. The findings from the quadrant experiment do not in any way change these overall conclusions; rather they verify the strength of the vertical effect.

However, there are instances when this vertical effect breaks down. One is when drawings are made in a triangular frame. Then the oblique and

factors would play a major role in a copying task of simple figures such as a circle or a square. Here it is reasonable to assume that the bad drawer has difficulties in one of the perceptual–motor processes underlying the motor skill of drawing. As the focal issue of this chapter is the motor aspect of drawing, the perceptual–motor processes will be described, and the contribution of these processes to the successful drawing performance analysed within a developmental framework.

2. Drawing skill considered within the closed-loop theory of perceptual–motor function

The processes underlying the control of the skill of drawing, or indeed any perceptual–motor skill, can be analysed within the framework of closed-loop theory. A number of closed-loop models of movement control are available in the literature (Anokhin, 1969; Bernstein, 1967; Laszlo and Bairstow, 1971; Pew, 1974). In the present chapter the modified Laszlo and Bairstow Model (1985) is used to examine the task of copying simple figures. Essentially, four interconnected components compose a closed-loop model: input, central processing units, output and feedback loops.

Input relates to the information the subject receives before starting the movement. He observes the drawing equipment he is to use, looking at the paper and pencil or pen, or blackboard and chalk. He could also touch the paper and pencil to feel the degree of smoothness of their surfaces. He needs to examine the model of the figures he is asked to copy. That is, he gathers relevant information about the environment. In addition, he monitors the position of his body and limbs through kinaesthetic input. Kinaesthesis is the sense of movement and position (Laszlo and Bairstow, 1983) which enables the subject to become aware of his own posture before he starts the drawing task; and taking this information into consideration, he is able to assume the correct drawing position (Marsden, Merton and Morton, 1981; Nashner and Cordo, 1981; Cordo and Nashner, 1982). Instructions form an important part of total input. They influence the way the movement is programmed (Evarts and Granit, 1976; Evarts and Tanji, 1976; Tanji and Evarts, 1976), the particular aspect of the task the subject pays most attention to (Keele, 1973) and whether speed or accuracy of his performance is of primary importance (Kay, 1970; Pew, 1969). In the task of copying a simple figure, the instructions should include information about the necessity of reproducing the model figure in size and/or shape, and whether the subject should concentrate on accuracy or aim for speed of performance. In general one expects that accuracy would be sacrificed for speed. Where a time constraint is not imposed, accuracy of performance would be higher than in a situation where rapid reproduction is demanded (speed–accuracy trade-off). Overall, instructions define the goal the subject is expected to aim for.

All input information is received by the Standard, which is the first central processing component. The Standard, besides processing information, also recalls stored memory traces of previous drawing attempts, and evaluates the level of motivation accorded to the task. Based on all this information the Standard is instrumental in forming the plan of action (Marteniuk, 1976). The plan includes, for the drawing task, the starting point of the movement, the direction in which the movement should proceed, the point where sudden changes in direction should take place, the force exerted on the pencil and pressure of the pencil on the paper, as well as the speed of the drawing movement. Throughout the progress of the drawing the Standard receives and monitors information delivered by the feedback loops.

Once the plan of action is constructed, the Standard instructs the Motor Programming Unit, the second component of the central processing system, to activate the necessary motor units (Basmajian, 1962). The motor units are the building blocks of the motor system. They consist of one motor nerve and the muscle fibres which are connected to it. Through the selection of the appropriate motor units, the motor unit activation pattern, the direction and extent, velocity and force of the movement are controlled (Brooks, 1981; Desmedt and Godaux, 1978 and 1979; Evarts, Fromm, Kroller and Jennings, 1983; Fetz and Cheney, 1980; Freund, 1983; Georgopoulos, Kalaska and Massey, 1981). In drawing, the two hands perform different actions, hence different motor programmes are generated for each hand.

The output of the closed loop is the drawing movement itself. Two feedback loops complete the closed-loop system; both carry information to the Standard. The central feedback loop or corollary discharge (Gandevia and McCloskey, 1976; Hulliger and Vallbo, 1979; Hulliger, Nordh and Vallbo, 1982; Vallbo, Hagbarth, Torebjork and Wallin, 1979; Wiesendanger, 1969) is a copy of the commands sent to the muscles, which provides a template or memory trace of the ongoing motor programme (Laszlo and Ward, 1978). Subjectively, active and passive movements (e.g. 'I moved my arm' versus 'My arm was moved') can be differentiated clearly: the difference is due to the presence of corollary discharge in active movement which is absent in passive movements.

At the same time the ongoing movement itself generates sensory information, which is monitored by the Standard. This is a multimodal channel, with kinaesthetic information forming the most important component. Kinaesthetic information is continuously generated from receptors situated in muscles

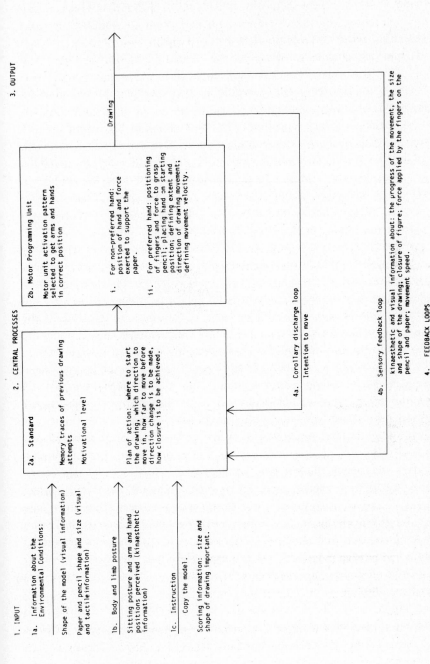

Figure 19.1 Copying simple figures from visually presented models.

(Matthews, 1972), joints (Schaible and Schmidt, 1983) and tendons (Crago, Houk and Rymer, 1982) of the head, body and limbs. The channel transmits information about static position, movement extent and direction, velocity and force. Supplementary to the kinaesthetic modality are vision, audition and touch. Their role depends on task characteristics, that is in paper–pencil skills it is vision, and in violin-playing, audition, which carry important and useful information about the ongoing performance.

The sensory feedback loop carries information about the progress of the movement. Kinaesthesis is the primary channel in detecting any discrepancy between the movement and the goal set for the task (Laszlo and Bairstow, 1971; Bairstow and Laszlo, 1979a). Visual feedback aids kinaesthesis in error detection (Laszlo and Baker, 1972).

Why is there a need for continuous error detection? Why can't we programme the movement to produce a perfect copy of the figure? There are three possible reasons for inaccuracy of the motor performance. First, there might be insufficient information stored in the Standard relevant to the task. Memory traces of previous attempts at the task, or related tasks, are stored in terms of the kinaesthetic information generated during the attempt (Bairstow and Laszlo, 1978 and 1979b). These traces are recalled by the Standard and used in instructing the Motor Programming Unit. If traces are unavailable due to absence of previous attempts at the task, or to lack of kinaesthetic coding as in young children, the Motor Programme generated is imperfect. The second reason for inaccuracy of motor performance could be found in programming ability. The efficient selection of appropriate motor units develops with age and with practice at the task; for example, the 5-year-old child often shows unnecessary force in holding the pencil and pushing the pencil against the paper, as well as moving his legs and head – an over-inclusive, inefficient programme. Finally, the environmental conditions might differ from those predicted, or might change during the movement, such as the pencil being harder than the one used previously, thus more force needing to be applied to make a visible line on the paper. Whatever the reason for error, once it is detected the Standard can instruct the Motor Programming Unit to generate error-corrective programmes. Thus the success of error-corrective programming depends on the ability of error detection and on fine programming.

In Figure 19.1 the closed-loop model of perceptual–motor function is summarised in a flow chart as it relates to the task of copying simple figures.

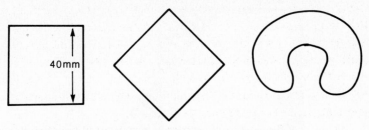

Figure 19.2 Test figures. The three figures enclose the same area.

3. A study of perceptual–motor development in drawing

Children can recognise and discriminate between various geometric figures at a very early age, i.e. 1 to 2 years (Bee and Walker, 1968; Maccoby and Bee, 1965). It is suggested that there is a time lag between this stage and the time a child can copy these figures. It has been established that a child can normally copy a recognisable circle at 3 years of age, a square at 4, a triangle at 5 and a diamond at 7 (Arnheim, 1954; Cratty, 1970; Piaget and Inhelder, 1956). Research has been carried out on non-motor aspects of figure reproduction, such as the effect of alignment cues (for a detailed review see Freeman, 1980). Placement of models in congruent frames is more accurate than in noncongruent frames even at the age of 7 years (Freeman and Kelham, 1981). Connolly (1968) showed that 5-to 6-year-old children can construct geometric figures with matchsticks, although they could not copy the figures accurately when drawing. The issue of the use of the geometry of alignment is dealt with in the chapters by Mitchelmore and Bayraktar above.

The central issue of the present chapter is the development of the motor aspects of figure reproduction from 5 years of age onwards. Most of the work up to now which has examined the motor aspect of drawing was focused on the difference between horizontal–vertical and oblique line-drawings. It was concluded that the drawing of obliques is more difficult and that the skill develops later than that of drawing horizontal–vertical lines (Berman, Cunningham and Harkulich, 1974; Goldstein and Wicklund, 1973; Olson, 1970).

There is scant evidence of systematic investigation of the developmental progression in the broader perceptual–motor aspects of drawing skills. As was shown in the previous section, drawing depends on a large number of interconnected perceptual–motor processes. The study to be reported here

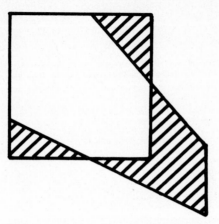

Figure 19.3 Scoring of area error: shading denotes error.

aims at elucidating the development of these processes, in isolation from cognitive factors, memory and image-formation.

Copying simple figures from visually presented models is an appropriate task for this experiment. Cognitive demands are confined to understanding simple instructions and memory. Mental imagery of the figures is 'eliminated' by allowing the subject to look at the model while she is reproducing it.

Three figures were selected: a square, a diamond (the square reorientated) and a horseshoe – labelled 'the sausage' by the children. These figures are shown in Figure 19.2. The square and diamond were chosen further to investigate the relative difficulty of drawing horizontal–vertical *versus* oblique lines in 5-year-old to adult subjects. The horseshoe was included to compare the drawing of straight lines with curved ones. A number of other criteria used in the selection of the three figures were: each figure should be easily discriminated by 5-year-olds; objective scoring should be possible; and the task should not be forbiddingly difficult for the young child, yet challenging for adults.

The area enclosed by the outlines of the figures was the same, as were the perimeters of the square and diamond, though not the horseshoe. The error-score of the drawings was measured in units of area discrepancy, as shown in Figure 19.3, by superimposing the model over the drawing, maximising the area of overlap between them and scoring the sum of the non-overlapping areas as error. This is a clear case of what is termed an isographic criterion in Mitchelmore's chapter.

Four hundred and ninety-one children, aged 5 to 12 years, and 20 adults, were tested. The task was presented to the subjects by placing the drawing

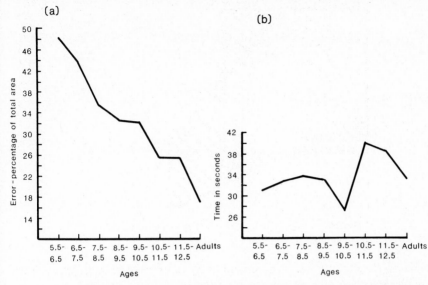

Figure 19.4 Developmental trends in: (a) drawing error, percentage of total area (combined score for three figures); (b) time taken to complete the three figures.

sheet in front of them (Figure 19.2) and providing them with a soft (2B) pencil. The subject was told to copy each model in the place provided (pointing to it). She was to draw each figure, attempting to copy it exactly in shape and size. She was asked not to hurry, to take the time she needed to copy the figures as accurately as she could, both in shape and size.

Time taken for completion of each figure was also recorded, though the subject was unaware of this. The time score was included as it was hypothesised that difficulty of the figures would be reflected by the time it took to draw them. To avoid possible inaccuracy in drawing by the introduction of a speed–accuracy trade-off, the digital stop-clock was kept under the table.

Improvement in accuracy, for the three figures combined, was found over the entire age range, as is shown in Figure 19.4a. Mean per cent area error improved from 48 per cent at age 5 to 15 per cent for adults, while the time taken to complete the figures was relatively constant over all age groups (Figure 19.4b).

What are the reasons which could account for the improvement in drawing accuracy? An examination of the flow chart presented in Figure 19.1 underlines the interdependence of all perceptual and motor processes which underlie the performance of the copying task. Proficiency at the task is possible only if, or when, these processes have reached adequate functional level. The developmental progression of each process cannot be described in

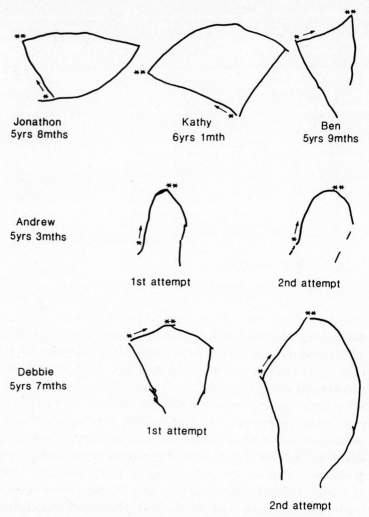

Figure 19.5 Examples of drawing the diamond. *→ denotes start and direction; ** denotes first angle drawn.

detail in this chapter (for details see Laszlo and Bairstow, 1985), but use will be made of the findings to explain present results.

Apparently the 5- and 6-year-old children have not developed perceptual–motor abilities sufficiently to copy the figures accurately. It is valuable to consider the comments the children volunteered during testing, as one can gain insight into the difficulties as they are perceived by them. Many of the children drew the square with confidence, albeit inaccurately, but when they

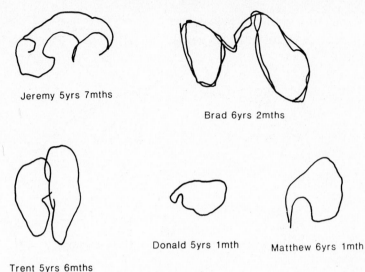

Jeremy 5yrs 7mths

Brad 6yrs 2mths

Trent 5yrs 6mths

Donald 5yrs 1mth

Matthew 6yrs 1mth

Figure 19.6 Examples of horseshoe drawings.

looked at the diamond and the sausage they announced that these were very difficult to draw. Their copying attempts proved their predictions. For the diamond the first angle was usually drawn as a sharp change in direction, though not necessarily a 90° angle. Children started at different points of the diamond, and it appeared that no one starting point was easier than any other. Thus the accuracy of the drawing did not depend on the order of the component movements. Once the first angle was drawn the difficulties seemed to increase – neither the direction of the lines nor the corners would 'turn out right', as is seen in Figure 19.5, top drawings. Closure of the figure presented a problem for some of the 5- and 6-year-old children. After completing one angle they kept extending the sides of the figure by adding bits of lines, alternating from side to side with great deliberation, until putting down the pencil and announcing that 'It doesn't work.' Apparently they knew that even if they continued their efforts, the drawing would not resemble a diamond. Occasionally we asked a child to try again, giving her another drawing sheet. The second resembled the first attempt; they couldn't improve on it. Two of these repeated diamonds are shown in Figure 19.5.

The horseshoe was also inaccurately copied by many children, who often described their 'sausage' as 'too fat' or 'too skinny'. The figures were asymmetrical and closure was not always achieved. Examples of horseshoe drawings are shown in Figure 19.6.

It was obvious from the verbal reports that the children were aware that

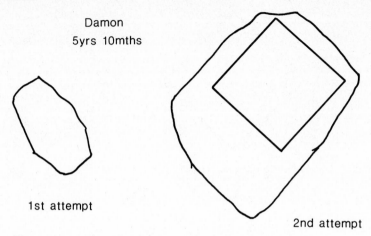

Damon
5yrs 10mths

1st attempt

2nd attempt

Figure 19.7 A 5-year-old's solution to diamond-drawing.

their drawings were inaccurate, and many of them found their efforts rather funny. One exceptionally bright 5-year-old solved the problem of diamond-drawing in a novel way. After battling unsuccessfully with the problem of producing a diamond, he quickly drew a creditable diamond around the model – Figure 19.7. By using the model as a guide he reduced the planning demands of the task and achieved success to his satisfaction.

Identical movements are necessary to copy or trace a figure, while planning of the movement is minimised in tracing compared to copying. In order to clarify whether planning of movement production was responsible for the difficulties found in drawing, all children were asked to trace over the lines of the three model figures after they finished copying them. All 5- and 6-year-olds could complete the tracing task, although many made extensive errors, deviating from the set lines by as much as 3–4 mm, staying off the line over considerable distances, as is shown in Figure 19.8.

The fact that all three figures could be traced implicates *planning* of action as one source of difficulty – this age group has not developed planning ability sufficiently to complete the drawing task. On the other hand, the extensive errors implicate error-detection and/or error-corrective programming as another possible source of difficulty.

It was shown that, in general, kinaesthetic sensitivity was not developed sufficiently in 5- and 6-year-old children to enable them to perform finely graded perceptual–motor skills, and that 33 per cent of children in this age group have only developed kinaesthetic information-processing to a rudimentary level (Laszlo and Bairstow, 1980; Bairstow and Laszlo, 1981).

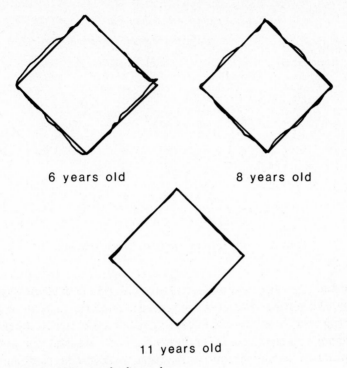

6 years old   8 years old

11 years old

Figure 19.8 Tracing the diamond.

Kinaesthetic sensitivity is necessary to discriminate displacement of the hand from the correct position, and to monitor the direction and extent of the movement in progress. In the absence of useful kinaesthetic information, errors in the movement cannot be detected and consequently error correction cannot be programmed, resulting in inaccurate performance. It could be argued that vision would be a useful source of error information here. However, the pencil line appears as a result of the movement, i.e. visual information is available only after the movement has been made, and hence error detection is delayed compared to kinaesthetic information, which is generated during the movement. To disadvantage the visual channel further, young children often assume a 'ham-fisted' pencil hold, covering a large extent of the working surface.

     The accuracy of the drawing performance improved rapidly as the children grew older. From 7 years onward, closure of the diamond and horseshoe figures was always achieved and children did not report specific difficulties. Evidence is available which shows (Laszlo and Bairstow, 1985) that along with steady improvement in kinaesthetic sensitivity, programming abilities

Table 19.1. *Results of copying a square and a diamond*

Age in years	Mean error (percentage of total area)		Error difference		Correlation of errors	Mean time in seconds		Time difference		Correlation of time
	□	◇	t	p<	r=	□	◇	t	p<	r=
5.5–6.5	34.2	56.1	5.16	0.001	0.32	7.6	9.6	1.97	n.s.	0.36
6.5–7.5	18.1	46.4	5.93	0.001	0.20	12.7	14.0	1.21	n.s.	0.64
7.5–8.5	17.4	57.4	8.07	0.001	0.13	15.1	10.6	3.75	0.01	0.60
8.5–9.5	19.9	41.1	4.37	0.001	0.25	10.4	10.6	1.27	n.s.	0.75
9.5–10.5	17.4	40.5	5.13	0.001	0.07	10.4	8.1	3.93	0.001	0.82
10.5–11.5	14.0	35.3	7.62	0.001	0.59	14.7	11.9	2.25	0.05	0.90
11.5–12.5	14.2	31.4	5.57	0.001	0.36	16.1	11.7	3.25	0.01	0.90
Adults	9.9	19.2	3.34	0.01	0.39	10.8	11.3	0.95	n.s.	0.90

also develop, and that by the age of 11, planning of action is also well established. The improvement in both drawing and tracing accuracy reflects the steady development in perceptual motor abilities (Figures 19.4 and 19.8).

A brief comparison between the square and diamond is warranted (Table 19.1). Diamonds proved more difficult to draw at all ages, including adults. The correlation between the accuracy scores for the two figures was low, again across all age groups. This would indicate that different abilities underlie the production of diamonds and squares. An odd finding indeed.

The time scores did not conform to expectations either. While diamonds were more difficult to draw, they took less time to complete than the easier square, at most stages of development, and significantly so at four ages (see Table 19.1). A tentative explanation could be offered, *post hoc*. For reasons we cannot as yet define, planning the diamond is more difficult than planning the square. Perhaps error criteria are set at a less stringent level for the more difficult task. Monitoring of error information and consequent error-corrective programming is time-consuming: the more finely the error limits are set, the more detailed is the information-processing, necessitating finer error-corrective programming and a slower movement. In the tracing task, where the planning of movement was minimal, differences in the time taken to complete the two figures were not observed. This supports the argument that planning of movement is an important factor in the observed difference in time scores when drawing the figure.

Without doubt an extensive, detailed research project needs to be undertaken before the reasons for the differences found between squares and diamonds can be explained satisfactorily.

The improvement in drawing accuracy with age was explained by considering the development of the underlying processes which contribute to the

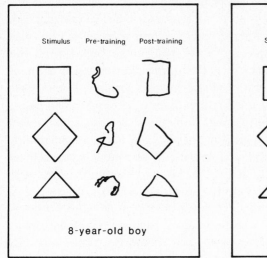
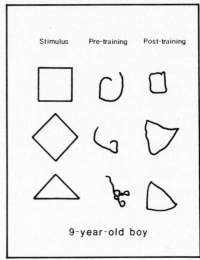

Figure 19.9 Kinaesthetic training and its effect on copying.

performance of the task (Figure 19.1). Could these processes or abilities account for individual differences in drawing skills within age groups?

4. Individual differences

Kinaesthetic sensitivity is one factor which was extensively investigated as it affects paper–pencil skills in children (Laszlo and Bairstow, 1983). Children who were diagnosed as clumsy were tested on the Kinaesthetic Sensitivity Test (Bairstow and Laszlo, 1981; Laszlo and Bairstow, 1985). Seventy-four per cent of the clumsy children were diagnosed as suffering from dyskinaesthesia, i.e. their kinaesthetic processing ability was very poor. Most clumsy children find writing and drawing difficult, some even impossible. The children who were diagnosed as having difficulty in kinaesthetic perception were trained in kinaesthetic sensitivity (Laszlo and Bairstow, 1983 and 1985). The training was completed in five 15-minute sessions, teaching the children to become aware of the information which they had ignored prior to training. Improvement in paper–pencil skills was observed immediately after training – examples are given in Figure 19.9 – and further marked improvement was observed over five months, resulting in attainment of very efficient, tidy writing skill.

Training in other abilities, such as programming, is being investigated at present.

It is obviously reasonable to suppose that individual differences at the lower end of the performance scale could be due to deficient development of one or more of the perceptual–motor abilities necessary for efficient drawing skill; it is more difficult to explain the difference between average and excellent drawing performance. The question was posed at the beginning of this chapter: what is the difference between the average drawer and Modigliani? Nearing the end of this examination of drawing as a perceptual–motor skill, we are no closer to answering this question than we were when first posing it. A more detailed knowledge of the contribution of perceptual and motor processes to the drawing skill might prove helpful here, but more importantly the interaction among cognitive, conceptual and perceptual–motor abilities needs to be considered. That is, to find the reasons which underlie the large individual differences from bad drawer to artistic performance, drawing must be studied as a complex but unique skill, not dependent on either cognition or imagery or perceptual–motor processes, but a balanced combination of all of these.

5. Concluding remarks

In this chapter we made an attempt to relate our present knowledge of perceptual–motor development to the development of drawing skill. What are the conclusions which can be reached from this perceptual–motor-orientated analysis? It was shown that the 5- and 6-year-old children lack the necessary developmental level in both perceptual and motor abilities accurately to copy simple figures. It follows that they would not be better equipped to put to paper the internal representations they build of their world. Consequently, accepting a child's drawing as a faithful representation of his mental images would lead us to underestimate his mental processes. Most adults would produce inadequate drawings of the room they are sitting in, even though they can see it clearly, and even though their perceptual–motor abilities are fully developed. The link between the adult's internal representation of the room and his drawing of it are certainly not direct. How much further removed is the young child's drawing from what he sees when he is at the very beginning of fine perceptual–motor development? The astounding thing is that the child can draw at all, not that he draws inaccurately!

REFERENCES

Anokhin, P. K. (1969) Cybernetics and the integrative activity of the brain. In M. Cole & I. Maltzman (eds.), *A handbook of contemporary psychology*. New York: Sendon.
Arnheim, R. (1954) *Art and visual perception*. Berkeley: University of California Press.

Bairstow, P. J. & Laszlo, J. I. (1978) Perception of movement patterns: Recall of movement. *Perceptual and Motor Skills, 47,* 287–305.

(1979 a) Perception of movement patterns: Tracking of movement. *Journal of Motor Behavior, 11,* 35–8.

(1979 b) Perception of size of movement patterns. *Journal of Motor Behavior, 11,* 167–78.

(1981) Kinaesthetic sensitivity to passive movements and its relationship to motor development and control. *Developmental Medicine and Child Neurology, 22,* 454–64.

Basmajian, J. V. (1962) *Muscles alive: Their functions revealed by electromyography.* Baltimore: Williams and Wilkins.

Bee, H. L. & Walker, R. S. (1968) Experimental modification of the lag between perceiving and performing. *Psychonomic Science, 11,* 127–8.

Berman, P. W., Cunningham, J. G. & Harkulich, J. (1974) Construction of the horizontal, vertical and oblique by young children: Failure to find the 'oblique effect'. *Child Development, 45,* 474–8.

Bernstein, N. (1967) *The co-ordination and regulation of movements.* Oxford: Pergamon.

Brooks, V. B. (1981) Task related cell assemblies. In O. Pompeiano & C. A. Marsan (eds.), *Brain mechanisms and perceptual awareness.* New York: Raven.

Connolly, K. J. (1968) Some mechanisms involved in the development of motor skills. *Aspects of Education, 7,* 82–100.

Cordo, P. J. & Nashner, L. M. (1982) Properties of postural adjustments associated with rapid arm movements. *Journal of Neurophysiology, 47,* 287–302.

Crago, P. E., Houk, S. C. & Rymer, W. Z. (1982) Sampling of total force by tendon organs. *Journal of Neurophysiology, 47,* 1069–83.

Cratty, B. J. (ed.) (1970) *Perceptual and motor development in infants and young children.* New York: Macmillan.

Desmedt, J. D. & Godaux, E. (1978) Ballistic contractions in fast and slow human muscles: Discharge patterns of simple motor units. *Journal of Physiology, 285,* 185–96.

(1979) Voluntary motor commands in human ballistic movements. *Annals of Neurology, 5,* 415–21.

Evarts, E. V., Fromm, C., Kroller, J. & Jennings, van A. (1983) Motor cortex control of finely graded forces. *Journal of Neurophysiology, 49,* 1199–215.

Evarts, E. V. & Granit, R. (1976) Relations of reflexes and intended movements. *Progress in Brain Research,* S. Homma (ed.), *Understanding the Stretch Reflex,* pp. 1–14.

Evarts, E. V. & Tanji, S. (1976) Reflex and intended responses in motor cortex pyramidal tract neurons of monkey. *Journal of Neurophysiology, 39,* 1069–80.

Fetz, E. E. & Cheney, P. D. (1980) Postspike facilitation of forelimb muscle activity by primate corticomotoneuronal cells. *Journal of Neurophysiology, 44,* 751–72.

Freeman, N. H. (1980) *Strategies of representation in young children: Analysis of spatial skills and drawing processes.* London: Academic Press.

Freeman, N. H. & Kelham, S. E. (1981) The interference of a baseline with children's orientation judgement need not entirely mask their contextual responsiveness. *Quarterly Journal of Experimental Psychology, 33A,* 145–54.

Freund, H.-J. (1983) Motor unit and muscle activity in voluntary motor control. *Physiological Review, 63,* 387–436.

Gandevia, S. C. & McCloskey, D. I. (1976) Perceived heaviness of lifted objects and effects of sensory inputs from related non-lifting parts. *Brain Research*, *109*, 399–401.

Georgopoulos, A. P., Kalaska, J. F. & Massey, J. E. (1981) Spatial trajectories and reaction time of aimed movements: Effects of practice, uncertainty and change in target location. *Journal of Neurophysiology*, *46*, 725–43.

Goldstein, D. M. & Wicklund, D. A. (1973) The acquisition of the diagonal concept. *Child Development*, *44*, 210–13.

Hulliger, M., Nordh, E. & Vallbo, A. B. (1982) The absence of position response in spindle afferent units from human finger muscles during accurate position holding. *Journal of Physiology*, *322*, 167–79.

Hulliger, M. & Vallbo, A. B. (1979) The responses of muscle spindle efferents during voluntary tracking movements in man. Load dependent servo assistance? *Brain Research*, *166*, 401–4.

Kay, H. (1970) Analysing motor skill performance. In K. Connolly (ed.), *Mechanisms of skill development*. London: Academic Press.

Keele, S. W. (1973) *Attention and human performance*. Pacific Palisades, Calif.: Goodyear.

Laszlo, J. I. & Bairstow, P. J. (1971) Accuracy of movement, peripheral feedback and efference copy. *Journal of Motor Behavior*, *3*, 241–52.

(1980) The measurement of kinaesthetic sensitivity in children and adults. *Developmental Medicine and Child Neurology*, *22*, 454–64.

(1983) Kinaesthesis: Its measurement, training and relationship to motor control. *Quarterly Journal of Experimental Psychology*, *35*A, 411–21.

(1985) *Perceptual–motor behaviour: Developmental assessment and therapy*. London: Holt, Rinehart and Winston.

Laszlo, J. I. & Baker, J. E. (1972) The role of visual cues in movement control and motor memory. *Journal of Motor Behavior*, *4*, 71–7.

Laszlo, J. I. & Ward, G. R. (1978) Vision, proprioception and corollary discharge in a movement recall task. *Acta Psychologica*, *42*, 477–93.

Maccoby, E. E. & Bee, H. L. (1965) Some speculation concerning the lag between perceiving and performing. *Child Development*, *36*, 367–77.

Marsden, C. D., Merton, P. A. & Morton, H. B. (1981) Human postural responses. *Brain*, *104*, 513–34.

Marteniuk, R. G. (1976) *Information processing in motor skills*. New York: Holt, Rinehart and Winston.

Matthews, P. B. C. (1972) *Mammalian muscle receptors and their central actions*. London: Edward Arnold.

Nashner, L. M. & Cordo, P. J. (1981) Relation of automatic postural responses and reaction-time voluntary movements of human leg muscles. *Experimental Brain Research*, *43*, 395–405.

Olson, D. R. (1970) *Cognitive development: The child's acquisition of diagonality*. New York: Academic Press.

Pew, R. W. (1969) The speed–accuracy operating characteristics. *Acta Psychologica*, *30*, W. G. Korter (ed.), *Attention and performance*, *11*, 16–26.

(1974) Human perceptual–motor performance. In B. H. Kantowitz (ed.), *Human information processing: Tutorials in performance and cognition.* Hillsdale, N.J.: Laurence Erlbaum.

Piaget, J. & Inhelder, B. (1956) *The child's conception of space.* (Translated from the French by F. J. Lungdon & J. L. Lunzer.) London: Routledge and Kegan Paul.

Schaible, H.-G. & Schmidt, R. F. (1983) Responses of fine medial articular nerve afferents to passive movements of knee joints. *Journal of Neurophysiology,* 49, 1118–26.

Tanji, J. & Evarts, E. V. (1976) Anticipatory activity of motor cortex neurons in relation to direction of an intended movement. *Journal of Neurophysiology,* 39, 1062–8.

Vallbo, A. B., Hagbarth, K.-E., Torebjork, H. E. & Wallin, B. G. (1979) Somatosensory, proprioceptive and sympathetic activity in human peripheral nerves. *Physiological Reviews,* 59, 919–57.

Wiesendanger, M. (1969) The pyramidal tract: Recent investigations on its morphology and function. *Ergebnisse der Physiologie, Biologischen Chemie und experimentellen Pharmacologie,* 61, 72–136.

20

The transition from construction to sketching in children's drawings

LARRY FENSON

1. Introduction

What is it about young children's drawings that makes them look so unmistakeably childlike? Of course, children's drawings are dominated by such familiar subjects as people, houses, trees, animals, suns, clouds, flowers and grass. But adult artists also frequently depict these same subjects in clearly non-childlike fashion. Freeman (1980) discusses a number of features of children's drawings identified by previous writers. Chief among these are the formula-like character of their drawings (Gridley, 1938), the segregation of elements into non-overlapping spatial bounds (Goodnow, 1977), inappropriate relative positioning of elements within a scene (Arnheim, 1954), and depiction of subjects as they are rather than as they look to the observer, for example, transparent or X-ray drawings (Gardner, 1980). There is little dispute as to the accuracy of these characterisations, though, as Freeman (1980) points out, these are descriptive accounts rather than explanatory constructs. This paper focuses on still another feature of children's drawings which has perhaps been underemphasised in past literature, one which has implications for the manner in which drawings change from the pre-school to the early school years. This feature concerns the way in which children construct their drawings from a limited pool of sub-units. Some typical pre-school drawings are shown in Figures 1, 2 and 3. What all these drawings have in common is a similar compositional foundation. All are constructed from simple geometric-like forms. Compare these with the striking drawings produced by Nadia, the autistic child with extraordinary drawing ability described by Selfe (this volume and 1977). What makes Nadia's drawings so dramatically different from those of the young child is her radically different compositional style. Nadia did not build her drawings from simple geometric forms. Rather, she sketched her compositions in a broad outlined fashion.

374

1   2   3

4   5   6

Nowhere in Nadia's drawings does one see the individual components present in the drawings shown in Figures 1–3. Figures 4–6 show human-figure drawings produced by two 6-year-olds and one 9-year-old. Though not on a par with Nadia's efforts, each drawing contains at least a partially outlined form, what Goodnow (1977) has called 'threading'. Most of the elements in these drawings are contoured forms, not geometric components.

How does the child make this journey from a constructional approach to sketching and what are its consequences? Some clues are provided by the work of a single child whose graphic development I followed for a three-and-a-half-year period. The record of the child's drawings is unusually complete in that it begins with his first productions at 3 years 5 months and includes virtually all of his graphic efforts from that point until his interest finally subsided at about age 7 years. During this span of time, the child, whose name is Randy, produced over 1,200 drawings, all of which were dated and many of which, especially in the early phases, were witnessed by the author, who is the child's father. The combination of the author's familiarity with the context in which many of the drawings were produced, along with his on-line observation of the actual production of many of the early drawings, presented an uncommon opportunity for longitudinal analysis of the structure and content of the child's early graphic development. An extended account of the child's graphic art across this entire time span is in preparation. The present report deals specifically with the issue raised above, i.e. the development of

7   8   9

a constructional approach to drawing and the beginnings of a subsequent shift to a sketching style of drawing. The account will first describe the development of the constructional style which emerged in Randy's first half-year of graphic experience and will establish his inability to sketch during these months. Some progressive steps towards sketching will then be described and some researchable questions will be posed, the solutions to which should shed light on the riddle of the transition from construction to sketching.

2. Early drawings (3 years 5 months to 4 years)

During these first seven months, Randy completed 205 drawings. His first recorded drawing occurred one evening when, at my instigation, we sat at a table with an assortment of magic markers and paper. This activity proved to be a popular one and continued on a frequent if irregular basis for some months. Most of Randy's early drawings were produced in this setting. Figure 7 is one of the first drawings Randy completed in the initial drawing episode at 3 years 5 months. It is indistinguishable from the type of drawings termed 'scribbling', often cited as the earliest stage of graphic production in young children. However, Randy completed fewer than a dozen of these relatively formless drawings over a period of several weeks before beginning to explore in a more or less systematic fashion a small number of geometric forms and compositional strategies. Frequently, most or all of the drawings completed on a given day or over a period of several days would focus on exploration of a single drawing unit such as squares, ovals or some other simple pattern.

The first forms to be explored in this way were squares and rectangles (e.g. Figure 8). Figure 9 shows a collage Randy made out of felt pieces at pre-school during this same time period, which seemingly reflects exploration of a similar form in a constructional rather than a graphic medium. Circular and oval forms were also practised on numerous occasions (e.g. Figure 10). Another

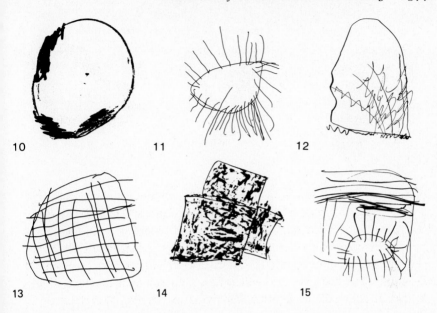

10   11   12

13   14   15

simple form prominent in Randy's productions was a sunburst, which first appeared at 3 years 7 months (e.g. Figure 11).

In addition to exploring these basic forms, Randy also exhibited several different strategies for structuring his early drawings. The first strategy to appear was 'filling in' and consisted of colouring in all enclosed forms (e.g. Figure 14). In another strategy, termed 'enclosure', Randy would form a perimeter, usually oval-shaped, then place elements within it. He seemed intrigued by the fact that it was within his power to create inside and outside relations with a few strokes of a marker. Figure 12 shows a flower garden within an enclosure. This strategy also played a prominent role for a time in the depiction of human figures. In still another strategy, termed 'partitioning', Randy would divide an enclosure into sections by drawing horizontal and vertical lines (e.g. Figure 13). Finally, a strategy termed 'chunking' consisted of the successive attachment of similar forms to one another (e.g. Figure 14).

In the months preceding his fourth birthday, Randy often combined these various elemental forms (drawing units) with his various strategies to produce composites. For example, Figure 15 shows a sunburst within an enclosure. Figure 16 shows a filled-in sunburst and Figure 17 shows a partitioned and filled-in sunburst.

Randy's gradual acquisition of a set of drawing units which he combined in various ways is consistent with the observations of Kellogg (1970). She noted the prevalence of simple geometric forms in children's drawings around

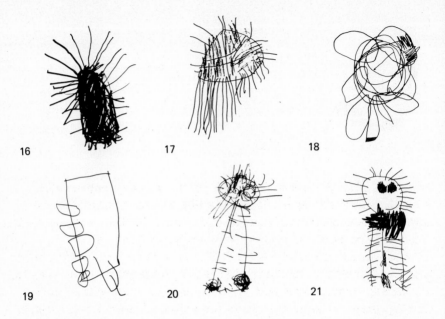

the world and detailed a number of ways in which five or six of the simplest forms or 'diagrams' could be combined in pairs to produce some 66 'combines' or combined in sets of three or more to produce an unlimited number of 'aggregates'. In the next section, we will see how Randy combined the various drawing units and strategies in his repertoire to produce pictures.

3. Picture construction

Most of the pictorial themes which Randy produced during his first half-year of drawing and in the year following were constructed from combinations of these simple drawing units with a rectangular or oval form as the core element. Examples include the flower shown in Figure 18 and the train shown in Figure 19. Thus, the child develops a repertoire of drawing units which serve as the building blocks for his graphic productions. Some of the human forms drawn by Randy during this early period provide particularly clear examples of how the elements were selected from those already present in his drawing repertoire. Figure 20, drawn at 3 years 9 months, is one of Randy's first human figures. This classic 'tadpole' person with angular legs extending from the head indeed appears to be a composite of various components already present in Randy's arsenal of drawing units. The head is composed of a sunburst pattern, the facial features and feet are scribbly circles and the hatchmarks on the legs are very much like a train-track pattern

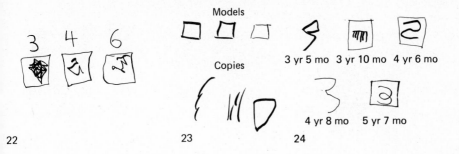

Models

Copies

3 yr 5 mo   3 yr 10 mo   4 yr 6 mo

4 yr 8 mo   5 yr 7 mo

3   4   6

22   23   24

Randy had drawn on several occasions. Figure 21, drawn one month later, is a strikingly similar figure, except that the legs are parallel rather than angular. As Randy drew the head, he said, 'This is the sun', a common use of the sunburst pattern in his prior and subsequent drawings.

We see then that Randy constructed his drawings somewhat the way a young child builds a structure with blocks. Construction in drawing is considerably more difficult (and occurs later in development) because, in drawing, the child must first create the individual units which must be structured into a progressively complete whole as he works. This requires creation of the components in the correct sequential order, because, unlike blocks (or clay), the components, once drawn, cannot be shifted around or reordered. (The reader is referred to Golomb (1974) for an elegant discussion of the effects of the medium on the child's artistic efforts.) Proper sequencing in the creation of elements in turn requires the child to plan his drawings (see Freeman, 1977) to a far greater extent than is required in block or clay construction.

Skill in the creation of simple closed forms becomes an essential first step in picture construction. Some insights into the creation of component forms may be gained by studying Randy's attempts to copy various modelled forms.

4. Copying simple forms

Periodically, I assessed Randy's skill at copying simple forms and numbers. In his earliest copying attempts, Randy experienced great difficulty in reproducing both open forms (such as the numbers 3, 4 and 6) and closed forms (such as rectangles and ovals), as is evident in Figures 22 and 23. His copies of closed forms improved rapidly over the next few months, probably as a consequence of considerable experience in drawing these types of forms, though many more months would pass before Randy evidenced ability routinely to draw geometrically symmetric closed forms with clean lines and

25   26   27

precise corners. His ability to copy open forms progressed much more slowly; for example, Figure 24 shows progressive attempts to copy the number 3 over a three-year period. It was not until age 4 years 8 months that Randy was able to reproduce the number 3 with any degree of accuracy. Even then, his ability to reproduce numbers likely reflected experience in number-writing exercises in school. It was not until Randy approached age 6 years that he was able to reproduce an open 'nonsense form' with reasonable accuracy.

5. A hypothesis about copying

Two weeks following the completion of Figure 20, a most interesting copying episode occurred. Figure 25 was drawn by Randy's older brother Brett, at age 6 years 9 months. The next morning, Randy picked it up, added the wavy hair and then proceeded to draw Figure 26, carefully studying Brett's model before drawing each component. This surprising effort is in a sense well beyond Randy's developmental level, as judged from his prior and subsequent figure drawings. It is in fact a semi-copy.

I believe the reason Randy was able to copy Figure 25 with reasonable fidelity is that he was able to analyse, or decode, the drawing in terms of components or drawing units present in his own repertoire. Randy was able to use the model not only as a guide for reproducing the components in the correct order but also for preserving the spatial relations between the components. Notice, however, that true to the classic tadpole form, the arms in Randy's drawing emanate from the head rather than from the body, as in the model (Freeman, 1980).

Randy's success in copying his brother's drawing led to the working hypothesis that copying is in part dependent on the child's ability to analyse the model *in terms of components present in the child's drawing repertoire.* A weaker form of this hypothesis linking the child's success in copying a model to the ease of identifying its component parts is described by Maccoby (1968).

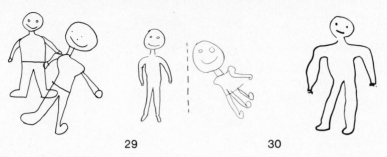

28   29   30

Both forms of this hypothesis lead to the prediction that reproducing a form segmented into components should prove easier to copy than an outlined, non-segmented form. When first invited, at 4 years 6 months, to copy the mostly segmented form shown on the left side of Figure 27, Randy experienced considerable difficulty, as is shown by his copy to the right side of the model. Though this may seem surprising given his success in copying his brother's model at 3 years 9 months, comparison of the two models reveals that Figure 27 is a more complex and less 'childlike' drawing than Figure 25. Figure 25 has a much larger head, no neck and less complex legs. Randy was next asked to replicate a segmented human at 5 years 7 months. The model is shown on the left side of Figure 28 and his copy is shown to the right of the model. This time his copy is quite a good one. It should be noted that, by 5 years 7 months, Randy had accumulated considerable practice in drawing human figures, complete with bodies, legs and other features, including necks. In completing this figure, Randy followed his usual top-down sequence, proceeding from the head to the body and legs, and finally the arms. Randy was then asked to copy the outlined form shown on the left side of Figure 29. The reader need only try to replicate this model to discover that it is not an easy task. Though the skills required in such a task have, to my knowledge, not been fully explicated, spatial planning as well as the ability to initiate and modify pen movements based on visually mediated feedback would seem to be crucial factors (see the chapter by Laszlo and Broderick, this volume). Randy's attempt to copy this outlined model is shown on the right side of Figure 29. As predicted, he clearly encountered difficulties. Moreover, analysis of his actions implicates factors beyond those suggested above. Randy attempted to follow his standard sequential strategy for spontaneous human-figure drawings (head–body–legs–arms). This strategy, which had proved successful for Figure 28, did not work in this case. Interestingly, the child artist who drew Figure 5 appears to have made a similar error on the left side on that figure. After finding his usual strategy unsuccessful on the figure's right

31   32   33

side, Randy adopted the necessary strategy on the opposite side, but gave up after completing the arm. Randy added the centre and left legs when I encouraged him to complete the drawing.

Another probe with an outlined human figure was carried out at 5 years 11 months. The model is shown in Figure 30 and Randy's copy appears in Figure 31. This time, Randy avoided his standard sequence and produced a near-perfect, completely outlined replica of the model. Copy tasks, then, also require attention to sequential order and, at least in the case of a frequently drawn subject, inhibition of familiar drawing sequences incompatible with task requirements. Assessment of the roles of the various factors which facilitate and impede performance in copy tasks is clearly open to experimental assessment. Developmental studies along these lines might prove especially fruitful.

We have seen, then, that children find it very difficult to create and to copy forms which are not composed of simple, well-practised geometric units. However, as children move toward the primary school years, they increasingly show a tendency in their drawings to fuse units into a more contoured whole (as seen, e.g., in Figure 6). What motivates the child to partially abandon a constructional approach to drawing? We consider some relevant factors in the next section.

6. Spurs toward outlining

In the four months ensuing between Randy's failed strategy shown in Figure 29 and his successful strategy shown in Figure 31, he spontaneously drew several partially and completely outlined forms; for example, Figure 32 depicts 'Mommy' in a running position. Randy's new-found willingness to attempt outlines was also apparent in several other spontaneous drawings completed between 5 years 6 months and 6 years. His first known spontaneous attempt at outlining, which occurred at 5 years 5 months, depicts a dolphin (Figure 33). Outlined forms, though still accounting for well under half of

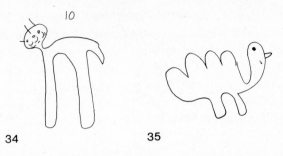

Randy's drawings, became increasingly common between 6 and 7 years. Examples include the cat shown in Figure 34, drawn at 6 years 1 month, and the turkey shown in Figure 35, drawn at 6 years 6 months.

What, then, are the factors which propel the child towards outlining? At least two factors are indicated in Randy's case. First, as was stated at the outset, the absence of outlining plays a prominent role in the childlike appearance of young children's drawings. Consequently, one of the incentives toward contoured drawings might be the striving for realism which emerges in the work of the young school-age child (Gardner, 1980). Realism requires that the child abandon a constructional style, because component parts are not ordinarily apparent in the real world of objects or in realistic paintings of it. Second, the child becomes increasingly interested in depicting humans, animals and other entities in other than full-face positions (e.g. profiles) or engaged in various forms of action (e.g. running). The child's increasingly ambitious desires to depict animate objects in an action-filled world require more flexible modes of representation.

The partial abandonment of a constructional style in the pursuit of new graphic objectives, both structural and content-related, creates new possibilities but also generates some significant new problems. It is as if the child's new aims outpace his emerging new skills, sometimes resulting in anomalous-appearing drawings not at all congruent with the child's increasing interest in realistic depiction. If the child's new ambitions are, on the whole, matched in time with the as yet largely unspecified skills which permit greater adeptness in sketching, the child may be in a position to advance toward more sophisticated forms of graphic depiction. That is, the merging of the child's new graphic objectives with the development of new graphic competencies, as a result of a convenient co-occurrence in time, natural talent or drawing instruction, may permit a continued advance toward artistic achievement. However, what appears to occur more often is a mismatch between skills and standards. The child's products do not live up to his expectations and he therefore stops drawing.

In any event, if Randy's course of graphic development is at all typical, a fundamental shift occurs between 3 and 7 years of age in the structure of the child's drawings, from a constructional style to contoured forms. Though the factors that impel and modulate this shift are not well understood, it appears to be motivated by a search for realism, mediated by increasingly skilled visually controlled actions, and facilitated by a developing ability to plan spatial arrangements and execute actions in proper sequential order.

REFERENCES

Arnheim, R. (1954) *Art and visual perception*. Berkeley: University of California Press.
Freeman, N. H. (1977) How young children try to plan drawings. In G. E. Butterworth (ed.), *The child's representation of the world*. New York: Plenum.
  (1980) *Strategies of representation in young children*. London: Academic Press.
Gardner, H. (1980) *Artful scribbles*. New York: Basic Books.
Golomb, C. (1974) *Young children's sculpture and drawing*. Cambridge, Mass.: Harvard University Press.
Goodnow, J. J. (1977) *Children drawing*. Cambridge, Mass.: Harvard University Press.
Gridley, P. F. (1938) Graphic representation of a man by four-year-old children in nine prescribed drawing situations. *Genetic Psychology Monographs, 20*, 183–350.
Kellogg, R. (1970) *Analyzing children's art*. Palo Alto, Calif.: Mayfield.
Maccoby, E. E. (1968) What copying requires. *Ontario Journal of Educational Research, 10*, 163–70.
Selfe, L. (1977) *Nadia: A case of extraordinary drawing ability in an autistic child*. London: Academic Press.

Conclusions

N. H. FREEMAN and M. V. COX

It is clear that the study of depiction is no longer a sedate pursuit. A new level of analysing and classifying depictions is being established. The study of drawing systems and denotation systems seems to give the requisite degree of formalism. There is also a rapid advance in our ideas about what it is that develops in our theories of representational development. Too often, researchers have been content with unearthing age-sensitive changes in depictive practices. Yet it is now uncontroversial to say that any useful developmental theory must involve at least two further advances. One is the drawing up of a balance-sheet of what it is that changes with age and what does not. The other is a model of the dynamic relations amongst those aspects that change. The first of these two tasks is now easier than it was even five years ago; the second is correspondingly harder.

The problem of defining what it is that develops has received different answers in the chapters. Against the background of nondevelopment at one level of projective system, the developments have been suggested to lie in artistic conventions and tricks of the trade, mental support systems such as working memory, denotation rules, perceptual–motor skills, adaptive flexibility in selecting which mode of depiction to aim for and the overcoming of fundamental biases. The task of producing a working model of such advances is going to be a long pull. Especially now that the fog of pessimism about the expertise of under-7s has lifted, a lot of the work securely established in the literature may have to be redone.

Apart from that, there is exciting new research to be carried out. It was suggested that development occurs in regulation of the relationship between projective and denotation systems. How? The importance of an understanding of the primitives of Euclidean picture-plane geometry was emphasised. Since many of the geometrical fragments studied in the relevant chapters could well arise in the early stages of producing a drawing, and since the drawing may not 'look right' in those stages, how do depictors harness their understanding of geometry to tide them over? The crucial role for visual contrasts in enhancing children's performance was repeatedly commented upon. How, precisely, does that work? Controlling the structure of a scene and its relation to a viewer but altering its appearance sometimes leads to changes in performance which are counterintuitive. How can one refine the concept of a 'visual puzzle' in order to come to grips with the phenomenon? Drawing devices are plurifunctional; thus line elimination of part of a circle's contour may be resisted with discrete objects yet welcomed with one segmented object. How do young children come to terms with that?

It is not difficult to think of general answers to these questions. It is extremely difficult to refine them so that they generate competing hypotheses. That, perhaps, is only a matter for our ingenuity. But there is also a more principled matter which is a function of the depictor's ingenuity. If we took depiction more seriously we would ask two questions. The first is why depiction should be such an important matter to young children and to adults. The second is, whenever a particular depiction characteristic appears on the page, to what problem is it a solution? In the light of the research discussed by the authors, a set of answers to the latter seems perceptibly nearer.

INDEX OF NAMES

Figures in italic type indicate illustration. Figures in bold type indicate that the name appears in a list of references.

Abravanel, E. 293, **307**
Alberti 88
Allibone, C. 224
Allik, J. 13, 147, **193**
Ames, L. B. 233, **247**
Anokhin, P. K. 357, **370**
Arnheim, R. 60, 74, 77, 96, 97, **98**, 150, **153**, 350, **354**, 361, **370**, 374, **384**
Assell, G. 300, **308**
Avons, S. E. 124, **134**

Bacharach, V. R. 158, **175**, 206, **213**, 256, **265**
Bairstow, P. J. 357, 360, 364, 366, 367, 369, **371, 372**
Baker, J. E. 360, **372**
Barnhart, E. 148, 149, **153**
Barrett, M. 8, 90, 177, 179, 185, 187, 194, 204, 215, 228, **229**, 237, 251, **264**, 289
Bartlett, F. C. 27, **28**
Basmajian, C. 358, **371**
Bassett, E. M. 233, 234, **246**, 267, **285**
Bataillard, C. 300, **308**
Bayraktar, R. 15, 86, 114, 289, 294, 316, 324, **331**, 333, 347, 349, **354**, 361
Beaumont, A. V. 8, 194, 204, 228, **229**, 237
Bechterev, V. M. 80
Bee, H. L. 346, 348, **355**, 361, **371, 372**
Beilin, H. 313, **331**
Berman, P. W. 233, 237, **246**, 246, 333, 353, **354**, 361, **371**
Bernstein, N. 357, **371**
Blake, V. 42, **57**
Bornstein, M. H. 318, 320, **331**
Boswell, S. L. 318, **331**

Braine, L. G. 352, **354**
Brazendale, A. H. 313, 318, **332**
Bremner, J. G. 15, 86, 289, 294, 305, **307**, 316, 318, 319, 321, 323, 324, 325, 326, 327, 328, 329, 330, 331, **332**, 351, 353, **354**
Bridson, A. 179, **187**, 251, **264**
Broderick, P. A. 16, 86, 291, **381**
Brooks, V. B. 358, **371**
Brown, J. 227, **230**
Brull, J. 300, **308**
Bruner, J. 150, **153**
Bryant, P. E. 86, **99**, 262, **265**, 292–3, 294, 307, **308**, 314, **315**, 316, 317, 317, 318, 319, 320, 322, 325, **331, 332**, 333, 334, 335, 336, 339, 349, 352, 353, **354, 355**
Buhler, K. 249, **264**
Butterworth, G. 353
Byth, W. 307, **308**

Campbell, F. W. 50, **57**
Caron-Pargue, J. 300, **308**
Carter 270
Cézanne 43
Chen, M. J. 7, 44, 114, 157, 160, 163, 164, 174, 289, 293, 307, **308**
Cheney, P. D. 358, **371**
Chipman, S. F. 318, **331**
Chomsky, N. 84
Clark, A. B. 79, **98**, 188, 200, 250, 258, 259, **264**
Clowes, M. B. 88, **99**
Connolly, K. 136, **153**, 361, **371**
Constable, W. G. **57**
Cook, M. L. 157, 160, 164, **174**
Cooper, R. G. 27, 29, 291, **309**

Cordo, P. J. 357, **371**, **372**
Corinth, L. 43
Costall, A. 2, 3, 5, 10, 216
Cox, M. V. 8–9, 10, 11, 90, 149, **153**, 157, 158, **174**, 179, 181, 185, **187**, 192, 193, 194, 195, 196, 197, 199, **200**, 203, 209, 210, **213**, 216, 227, **229**, 231, 233, 237, 246, **246**, 259, 272, 283, 289
Crago, P. E. 360, **371**
Cratty, B. J. 361, **371**
Crook, C. 6, 7, 8, 11, 12, 215, 228, 251, 262, **264**, 283, 289, 294, 312, 353, **355**
Cunningham, J. G. 353, **354**, 361, **371**

Davis, A. 9–10, 11, 48, 90, 157, 158, **174**, 177, **187**, 204, 205–6, 207, 209–10, 211, **213**, 217, 224, 234, **246**, 256, 263, 267, 289
DeLisi, R. 313, **332**
Derȩgowski, J. B. 86, **99**, 158, 161, **174**, 307, **308**, 320, 327, **331**, **332**
Desmedt, J. D. 358, **371**
Doerner, M. 52, **57**
Dolle, J.-M. 300, **308**
Donaldson, M. 194, **201**
Dubery, F. 28, **28**, 78–9, 81, **99**, 291, **308**
Duthie, H. 101
Duthie, R. K. 4, 5, 7, 8, 12, 13, 15, 98, 101, 289, 304

Edwards, B. 52, **57**, 264, **264**
Eiser, C. 149, **153**, 157, **174**, 181, **187**, 191, **201**, 216, 227, **229**, 231, **247**, 272, 283, **285**
Eliefja, C. 84, **99**
Elliott, J. 136, **153**
Eng, H. 69, **77**
Euclid 88, 232, 289, 299, 303, 312, 350, 385
Evarts, E. V. 357, 358, **371**, 373

Fenson, L. 13–14, 16
Ferdinandsen, K. 318, 320, **331**
Fetz, E. E. 358, **371**
Fisher, C. B. 320, **331**
Fisher, G. H. 343, **355**
Flavell, E. R. 194, **200**
Flavell, J. H. 194, **200**
Flude, B. 329, **331**
Ford 270
Forrester, S. 22
Freeman, N. H. 70, 73, **77**, 80, 81, 83, 92, 93, 95, 97, 98, **99**, **100**, 136, 142, 147, 148, 149, **153**, 157, 158, 164, 173,

174, 177, 181, **187**, 188, 191, 193, 194, 197, **200**–1, 202, 203, 204, 206, 209, **213**, 215, 216, 217, 218, 227, **229**, 231, 233, 234, 235, 245, 246, **247**, 249, 250, 253, 262, **264**, **265**, 266, 267, 270, 271, 272, 277, 283, **285**, 293, 294, 296, 297, 298, 299, 306, **308**–9, 316, 322, 324, 325, 328, 329, **332**, 333, 347, 349, 351, 352, 353, 354, **355**, 356, 361, **371**, 374, 379, 380, **384**
Freund, H.-J. 358, **371**
Friedman, S. 87, **99**, 305, **308**, 350, 351, **355**
Frisby, J. P. 23, **28**
Fromm, C. 358, **371**

Gaillard, F. 300, **308**
Gallistel, C. R. 38, **57**
Gandevia, S. C. 358, **372**
Gardner, H. 43, **57**, 85, **99**, 374, **384**, **384**
Georgopolous, A. P. 358, **372**
Gessell, A. 233, **247**
Gibson, J. 2, 3, 17, 18, 22–3, 24–8, **28**–9, 31, 32, 33, 34, 36, 44, 55, **57**, 73–4, 77, 95–6, **99**, 121, 149, **153**
Gilchrist, A. L. 46, **57**
Godaux, E. 358, **371**
Goldstein, D. M. 361, **372**
Golomb, C. 277, **285**, 279, **384**
Gombrich, E. H. 18, **29**, 44, 53, **57**, 248, **265**
Goodenough, F. 135, 136, 142, **153**
Goodman, N. 21, **29**
Goodnow, J. J. 87, **99**, 254, **265**, 266, 267, 271, **285**, 305, **308**, 350, 351, **355**, 374, 375, **384**
Granit, R. 357, **371**
Green, F. L. 194, **200**
Greenfield, P. **153**
Gregory, R. L. 39, **57**, 307, **308**
Gridley, P. F. 270, **285**, 374, **384**
Griffiths, K. 164, **174**
Gross, C. G. 318, 320, **331**
Guyon, J. 300, **308**
Guzman, A. 88, **99**

Haber, R. N. 159, **174**
Hagbarth, K.-E. 358, **373**
Hagen, M. A. 3, 5, 7, 27, 28, **29**, 30, 62, 77, 81, 192, **201**
Halliday, M. S. 132, **134**
Hambly, M. 293, **308**
Hammond, J. H. 21, **29**
Hansford, M. 345
Hargreaves, S. 267, **285**
Harkulich, J. 353, **354**, 361, **371**

Harris, D. B. 94, 95, 96, **99**, 135–6, 148, 153, **285**
Harris, H. 271, 282, **286**
Harris, P. 293, **309**, 333, 342, 343, 349, 355
Hartley, J. L. 84, **99**
Hayes, J. 86, **99**
Hayton, C. 73, 77, 158
Heard, P. 316
Hebb, D. O. 55, **57**
Heldmeyer, K. H. 86, **99**
Hemenway, K. 321, 332
Hermelin, B. 151–2, **153**
Hillary, E. 17
Hinton, G. E. 124, **134**
Hitch, G. J. 132, **134**
Hobbs, S. B. 49, 52, **57**, 86, 100, 124, **134**, 136, **154**, 157, 158, 172, 173, **175**, 183, 187, 300, **309**
Hochberg, J. 215, **229**
Houk, S. C. 360, 371
Houseworth, M. 267, **286**
Howard, I. 313, **332**
Huffman, D. A. 87, 88, **99**
Hughes, M. 194, **201**
Hulliger, M. 358, **372**
Humphreys, J. 149, **153**, 157, **174**, 177, 181, **187**, 197, **201**, 202, 209, **213**, 217, 221, 224, 226, 228, **229**, 233, 247
Huygens 21

Ibbotson, A. 86, **99**, 262, **265**, 292, 294, **308**, 314, 315, 316, 317, 317, 318, 319, 320, 322, **332**, 333, 334, 335, 336, 339, 352, 353, **355**
Inall, M. 5, 6, 7, 8, 85, 251
Ingram, N. A. 11, 12, 189, 197, 198, **201**, 231, 235, **247**, 289
Inhelder, B. 86, 91, **100**, 148, 149, **154**, 189, **201**, 202, **213**, 232, **247**, 263, **265**, 266, **286**, 292, 299, **309**, 311, 312, 313, 315, 328, 329, **332**, 334, 335, 346, 348, 349, 351, 354, **355**, 361, **373**
Ives, S. W. 267, **286**

Jahoda, G. 81, 82, 85, **99**
Jamison, W. 313, **332**
Janikoun, R. 157, **174**, 177, **187**, 202, 203, 204, 206, **213**, 234, 235, **247**, 249, **265**, 267, **285**
Jennett, M. S. 8, 194, 204, 228, **229**, 237
Jennings, van A. 358, 371
Jensen, D. von C. 84, **99**
Johnson, S. C. 276, 280, **286**
Jonckheere, A. R. 238, 240, 242

Jones, R. K. 25, 27, **29**, 30

Kaess, D. W. 307, **308**
Kagan, J. 313, **331**
Kalaska, J. F. 358, **372**
Kaptynska 294
Kay, H. 357, **372**
Keele, S. W. 357, **372**
Kelham, S. E. 316, 322, 324, 325, **332**, 347, 351, 352, 353, **355**, 361, 371
Kellogg, R. 69, 77, 267, 271, **286**, 377, **384**
Kennedy, J. M. 86, 88, **99**
Klein, J. 86, **99**
Koops, H. 300, **308**
Kosslyn, S. M. 86, **99**, 253, **265**
Kroller, J. 358, 371

Laak, T. 13, **147**, 193, 271, 277, 278, **286**
Lance, G. N. 276, **286**
Lark-Horowitz, B. 69, 77, 135, 141, 148, 153
Laszlo, J. I. 16, 86, 291, 357, 358, 360, 364, 366, 367, 369, 371, 372, 381
Lauder, E. 5, 6, 7, 8, 85, 251
Lazarev, V. N. 269, **286**
Lee, S. P. 320, **332**
Lefebvre-Pinard, M. 228, **229**
Leggett 269, 270, 281, **286**
Leonardo da Vinci 20, 20, 21, 25, 85
Leppig, M. 293, 298, **308**
Lewis, H. P. 69, 77, 79, **99**, 135, 141, 148, 149, **153**
Liben, L. S. 312, **332**
Light, P. 10, 11, 90, 149, **153**, 157, **174**, 177, 181, 185, **187**, 197, **201**, 202, 203, 206, 209, 210, **213**, 215, 216, 217, 218, 220, 220, 221, 224, 226, 228, **229**, 231, 233, 244, **247**, 250, 251, 254, 255, 263, **265**, 289
Locklear, E. P. 86, **99**
Luca, M. 69, 77, 135, 141, 148, **153**
Luquet, G. H. 80, 189, **201**, 202, **213**, 231, 232, 234, 243, 245, 246, **247**, 248, 249, 253, 254, 264, **265**

McCarty, S. 147, **153**
Maccoby, E. E. 346, 348, **355**, 361, **372**, 380, **384**
McCloskey, D. I. 358, **372**
McGillicuddy-DeLisi, A. V. 313, **332**
MacIntosh, E. 157, **174**, 181, **187**, 206, **213**, 216, 217, 226, **229**, 231, 233, **247**, 250, 251, 255, **265**
MacKay, C. K. 313, 318, **332**
McKinney, J. P. 270, **286**
Maison, K. E. 44, **57**
Marr, D. 3, 8, **29**, 35, 39, **57**, 87, 89, 91,

Marr (*cont.*)
  92, 99, 121, 232, 247, 250, 265, 267, 286
Marsden, C. D. 357, 372
Marteniuk, R. G. 358, 372
Marx, K. 17, 29
Massey, J. E. 358, 372
Matthews, P. B. C. 360, 372
Mead 229
Mendelson, M. J. 318, 320, 331, 332
Merleau-Ponty, M. 17, 29
Merton, P. A. 357, 372
Millar, S. 87, 100
Minsky, M. 39, 57, 86, 100
Mitchelmore, M. C. 4, 7, 12, 14, 24, 86, 114, 161, 164, 174, 183, 187, 293, 294, 295, 296, 297, 298, 299, 300, 304, 306, 308–9, 333, 361, 362
Modigliani 365, 370
Monet 41
Moore, V. 209–10, 218
Morse 28
Morton, H. B. 357, 372
Müller-Lyer 306

Naeli, H. 293, 309, 333, 342, 343, 349, 355
Nash, H. 271, 282, 286
Nashner, L. M. 357, 371, 372
Neisser, U. 32, 33, 34, 38, 57
Newson, E. 142, 153
Nicolaides 52, 57
Nisbet, S. 327, 328, 330, 331
Nishihara, H. K. 89, 91, 92, 99, 267, 286
Nix, C. 263, 265
Nordh, E. 358, 372
Noton, D. 50, 57

O'Connor, N. 151–2, 153
Olivier, F. 86, 88, 94, 96, 100
Olson, D. R. 27, 29, 345, 348, 355, 361, 372
Olver, R. 153

Paivio, A. 141, 151, 153
Palmer, S. E. 253, 265, 321, 332
Papert, S. 86, 100
Paraskevopolous, I. 318, 332
Pariser, D. 90, 100, 151, 153
Patterson, K. E. 130, 134
Perkins, D. N. 28, 29, 291, 309
Perrett, M. 326, 327, 332
Pettipher 132
Pew, R. W. 357, 372
Phillips, W. A. 5, 6, 7, 8, 35, 46, 49, 52, 57, 85, 86, 100, 124, 132, 134, 136, 154, 157, 158, 172, 173, 175, 183, 187, 251, 289, 300, 309

Piaget, J. 14, 17, 86, 91, 100, 148, 149, 154, 189, 201, 202, 213, 229, 232, 247, 248, 249, 263, 265, 266, 286, 292, 299, 309, 311, 312, 313, 314, 315, 328, 329, 332, 334, 335, 346, 348, 349, 350, 351, 354, 355, 361, 373
Picasso 89
Pirenne, M. H. 21, 29
Pomerantz, J. R. 253, 265, 318, 332
Pratt, F. R. 2, 5, 49, 50, 51, 52, 57, 60, 86, 100, 123, 124, 132, 134, 136, 154, 157, 158, 172, 173, 175, 183, 187, 264, 289, 300, 309

Rabinowitz, R. 313, 331
Raphael 67
Read, H. 253, 265
Reed, E. S. 25, 30
Renoir 43
Richardson, J. T. 151, 154
Richter, J. P. 20, 30
Robinson, E. 228–9, 230
Robinson, W. 228, 230
Rudisill, R. 28, 30
Ruskin, J. 248
Rutter, M. 142, 154
Ruutel, M. 271, 278, 286
Rymer, W. Z. 360, 371

Saenger, E. A. 82, 85, 100
Sayers, J. 149, 153, 157, 174, 181, 187, 191, 201, 216, 227, 229, 231, 247, 272, 283, 285
Schaible, H.-G. 360, 373
Scharf, A. 43, 57
Schmidt, R. F. 360, 373
Sechrest, L. 269, 286
Sedgwick, H. A. 26, 27, 30
Selfe, L. 6, 7, 8, 90, 100, 137, 147, 152, 154, 253, 374, 384
Shallice, T. 130, 134
Shider, F. 57
Simm, N. 199
Simmons, B. 181, 185, 187, 209, 210, 213, 218, 220, 220, 224, 228, 229, 233, 247
Smedslund, J. 313, 332
Smith, P. 227, 230
Somerville, S. C. 84, 99
Sontag, S. 21, 30
Spearman 280
Stapeley, A. 198
Stark, L. 50, 57
Stotijn-Egge, S. 136, 154
Suen 163
Sully, J. 80, 248, 264, 265
Sutherland, S. 23, 30

Tanji, S. 357, **371**, 373
Taylor, A. J. 294, 305, **307**, 316, 318, 319,
    321, 325, 327, **331**, 351, 353, **354**
Taylor, M. 158, **175**, 206, **213**, 256, **265**
Therkelsen, M. 164, **174**
Thomas, H. 313, **332**
Torebjork, H. E. 358, 373
Townsend, E. 136, **154**
Trevor-Roper, P. 43, **58**
Truhon, S. S. 270, **286**
Tukey 344

Vallbo, A. B. 358, **372**, 373
Vygotsky, L. 150, **154**, 229

Walker, R. S. 361, **371**
Wallace, J. 269, **286**
Wallach, M. A. 269, 270, 281, **286**
Wallin, B. G. 358, 373
Ward, G. R. 358, **372**
Wicklund, D. A. 361, **372**
Wiesendanger, M. 358, 373

Willats, J. 3, 7, 8, 13, 28, **28**, 71, 77, 78–9,
    81, 82, 83, 84, 85, 86, 89, 91, 97, **99**,
    100, 116, 124, **134**, 142, 148, **154**,
    158, 161, **175**, 189, **201**, 232, **247**,
    250, 289, 291, **308**
Williams, W. T. 276, **286**
Wilson, B. 84, 85, **100**
Wilson, J. T. L. 47, **58**
Wilson, L. 132
Wilson, L. F. 313, 318, **332**
Wilson, M. 84, 85, **100**
Wittgenstein, L. 27, 30
Woodcock, K. *19*
Woodworth, R. S. 23, 30
Wright, L. **57**
Wurtz, R. M. 50, 57

Yonas, A. 27, **29**
Youniss, J. 313, **332**
Young, A. W. 327, **332**

Zeki, S. 36, 37, **58**

SUBJECT INDEX

Abstractions 36–40
Adolescence 5, 12, 13, 15, 101–20, 148, 152
Affine projection, *see* Projection
Alignment cue, *see* Parallels
Angles 14, 15, 33, 34, 62, 63, 66, 69–70, 74, 80, 108, 150, 262, 289ff, 322–31, 333–54
Array-specific, *see under* Strategies of representation
Artists' aids 33–5, 41–53, 60, 132
Autism 6, 137, 141, 142, 143, 144, 148, 149, 150, 151, 152
Axonometric projections 78

Blindness 152

Camera 20, 21, 23, 27, 106
'Camera', human 2, 73
Camera lucida 43
Camera obscura 21, 43
Canonicality 9, 10, 74, 104, 148, 202–13, 215, 233–5, 245, 249–50, 263, 267, 284, 310
Caricatures 25
Cartoon 19, 43–4
Closed-loop theory of perceptual–motor function 357–60
Clumsiness 369–70
Colour 21, 35, 36, 37, 38, 45, 46, 52, 53, 105, 377
Communication, pictorial 25–8, 250
Communication game 10, 209–13, 218–29
Context 10, 125, 133, 200, 204–13, 224, 227, 263–4, 333, 335, 348, 354
Contours 3, 7, 13, 89, 90, 150, 151, 257, 375, 382–3
Contrast effects 196, 199, 204–7, 210, 224–5, 227–8
Convention 27–8, 216, 269–71, 305–6

Copying 4, 14, 15, 16, 21, 44, 50–1, 115, 157–74, 193–4, 262, 290, 348, 357–70, 379–84
Corners 44, 56, 69, 75
Cross-cultural evidence 1, 18, 27, 59–60, 63, 75–6, 82–3, 84–5, 333–54
Cube, *see under* Forms
Cubism 59, 69
Cup, *see under* Forms

Denotation systems 3, 87–98
Depiction, theory of 53–6
Depth 4, 7, 12, 13, 18, 21, 22, 79, 101–7, 114, 116, 148, 157–8, 165ff, 181–6, 232, 235, 262
Descriptions 5, 6, 8, 9, 12, 39, 40, 41, 55, 86, 122–34, 231, 253, 260, 267
Diagrams 56, 378
Diamonds 41, 362
Dimetric projections 78
Divergent projections 70
Draw-a-man Test 135–6
Drawing devices 8, 11, 12, 13, 14, 142, 144, 149, 155, 160–74, 195, 252, 267, 273, 278, 283, 288
    enclosure 13, 206–7, 217, 255–6, 267, 377
    interposition, *see* Transparencies
    line elimination 8, 9, 10, 12, 13, 137, 149, 155, 182, 185, 188, 190, 191–2, 216–17, 227, 232, 244, 255, 267, 272, 283
    occlusion 8, 13, 50, 89–90, 142, 149, 157–9, 182–6, 188–200, 219, 244, 256
    segregation 8, 12, 13, 14, 155, 190–3, 217, 219, 226, 231, 254, 256–8, 267, 283
Drawing systems, *see* Projection
Dual-coding hypothesis 151

Ecological law 28
Ecological optics 27–8
Edges 3, 26, 27, 37, 41, 44, 45, 62, 69–70,
    75, 80ff, 126, 150, 151, 176, 291,
    301ff, 340ff
Egocentrism 229, 263
Enclosure, *see under* Drawing devices
Eye(s) 20, 21, 23, 33, 34, 42, 46, 54, 62,
    66, 73–5, 79, 81, 92–6, 106
Eye axis 39, 79

Figure-ground 35, 37, 46
Foreshortening 69
Form credibility 102–4, 107–9, 112
Forms
    ball 90, 259–61
    cube 4, 5, 12, 41, 47–9, 50, 51, 55, 56,
        60, 73, 79, 83, 110, 111, 113–15,
        123, 125–30, 158, 161–70, 183–4,
        197, 221–4, 235–46, 300–3, 306–7
    cup 9, 10, 48, 157–8, 202–12, 234–5,
        263
    cylinder 116–19, 162–70, 172
    diamond 41, 362
    doll 235–46
    furniture 79, 81, 110, 116
    glass 205–7, 211–12, 217, 255–6
    house 69–73, 179–81, 216, 257–8, 330
    human, *see* Human-figure drawing
    pyramid 5, 102–4, 107, 108, 111–12,
        125–6
    stick 259–61
    square 41, 104, 169, 293, 336–49, 353,
        362
    triangle 104, 107, 336–7, 341–2, 349
Foveal vision 46
Fragmentation 46
Frame of reference 39, 40, 44–5, 282, 318,
    336–54
Framework, external 15, 323ff
Frontal plane 13, 60, 292

Geometry 3, 4, 6, 14, 15, 31, 59, 60–9, 84,
    86, 121, 232, 289, 297, 331, 361,
    374, 376, 379, 385; primary 80, 81;
    secondary 80, 81
Giftedness 135, 141, 142

Hidden-line elimination 8, 9, 10, 12, 13,
    137, 149, 155, 182, 185, 188, 190,
    191–2, 216–17, 227, 232, 244, 255,
    267, 272, 283
Hiding game 194–200
Historical comparison 59, 68–9, 84
Holography 21, 109
Homography 4, 7, 12, 16, 290, 300–7
Human-figure drawing 13, 39, 84, 87,

92–8, 147–8, 193, 245, 267–85, 357,
378–84

Image 20, 21, 24, 25, 43, 45, 46, 52,
    60–2, 63, 74, 80, 109, 111, 113
Intellectual realism 23, 41, 56, 189, 202,
    215, 231–46, 248–64, 287, 314
Invariants 22–7, 62, 66, 74, 149, 150
Isography 4, 7, 16, 290–307
Isometric projections 78, 86, 87, 109, 111,
    114

Junctions 189
Junction points 232

Kinaesthetic sensitivity 16, 369

Language 84, 138, 140, 142, 143, 150
Line-drawing 7, 25, 88, 89–91, 122,
    158–74
Line of sight 8, 61, 78, 108, 110–11, 232
Looking behaviour 50ff, 198

Magic lantern 43
Manual dexterity 136, 137
Memory 6, 35, 36, 40, 41, 47, 50–1,
    123–4, 132–3, 137, 142, 152, 287
Mental model 12, 17, 155, 253, 258
Mental retardation 135–7, 141, 142
Mirror 43
Motor control 76, 86, 122, 124
Motor development 140
Motor skill 76, 133, 136, 268
Motor units 358

Object-centred, *see under* Strategies of
    representation
Oblique lines 12, 14, 79, 80, 81, 86, 131,
    292, 314, 334
Oblique projections 78, 80ff
Occlusion, *see under* Drawing devices
Optic array 22, 23, 25, 26, 149, 150, 151
Optic image 21
Optical continuity 26, 27
Optical devices 20, 21
Optical equivalence 18–20, 21
Optical flow 25
Optical illusion 102
Optical infinity 60
Optical systems 43, 106
Orientation 14, 15, 35, 39, 50, 107,
    109–10, 176, 203, 207, 233, 237–8,
    262, 293, 316–31, 333–54
Orthogonal projection 61–2, 63, 66–76
Orthographic projection 78, 79, 80, 111,
    176
Overlap 13, 105, 191–2

Painting(s) 21, 44, 45, 48, 59–60, 248
Pantograph 45
Parallels 4, 14, 61–2, 63, 66, 69–70, 74, 75, 8off, 105, 151, 253, 262, 289–94, 295–307, 333–54
Perception: picture 2, 17, 22, 24–5, 27, 28; theory of 18, 24–5, 26, 31
Perceptual constancies 23
Perceptual habits 5, 6, 46
Perceptual learning 54–5
Perceptual–motor skill 356–70, 385
Perceptual systems 2, 42, 44, 46, 55
Perpendicular bias 15, 86, 262, 294, 296–8, 306–7, 314–31, 333–54
Perpendiculars 4, 63, 262, 289, 294–307, 312
Perspective, *see under* Projection
Perspective-frame 33–5, 43, 45, 60
Perspective-taking tasks 263
Perspectograph 20
Photographic realism 2, 7, 8, 18, 21–3, 27, 28, 43, 56, 71, 73–5, 78, 137, 141, 142, 147–8, 149, 151, 152, 157–74
Picture primitives 4, 35, 89, 91–4, 121
Picture theory of natural perception 17, 18, 24
Plumbline 45
Plummet 45
Production problems 119, 148, 216, 261–2
Projection
    affine 61–2, 63, 66–76
    axonometric 78
    dimetric 78
    divergent 70
    horizontal oblique 79–87
    isometric 78, 86, 87, 109, 111, 114
    oblique 79–87, 109, 110–12, 123
    orthogonal 61–2, 63, 66–76
    orthographic 78, 79, 80, 111, 176
    perspective: artificial 79; inverted 79; linear 1, 2, 3, 4, 7, 18, 20, 21, 52, 53, 62, 71–3, 74, 78–87, 101, 105–7, 142, 148, 149, 152, 176, 179, 184; naïve 79; natural 62, 66, 73, 75, 79; single point 111; synthetic 79; true 79
    perspective projections 21, 81, 87
    true 79
    similarity 61–2, 66
    trimetric 78
    vertical oblique 79–87
Projection devices 8, 142
Projection rays 78–9, 80
Projection systems 3, 4, 5, 61–3, 66–76, 78–98, 109, 111, 142, 148, 158, 232, 385
Pyramid, *see under* Forms

Retinal image 23, 24, 104, 106, 114, 159
Retinal snapshots 73
Rules 17, 27, 78, 80, 191, 232, 255–6

Scene primitives 89
Schema 39, 41, 50–2, 53, 136, 141, 150
Scribbling 108, 142, 378
Scripts 17
Secondary geometry 80
Secondary model 33, 43
Segregation, *see under* Drawing devices
Selection tasks 109, 111–12, 193–4
Separation, *see* segregation *under* Drawing devices
Sequencing 11, 124–5, 133, 237–46, 267–8, 288, 381–2
Similarity projection 61–2, 66
Size scaling 62, 75, 82, 149, 176, 269–71, 281ff
Sketch 20, 42, 43–4, 45
Slide projector 43
Snapshot vision 34
Social behaviour 6, 10, 142, 150
Spatial relationships 11, 111, 116, 119–20, 192, 217, 232, 235, 250, 254, 380
Square, *see under* Forms
Stage, developmental 5, 69, 82, 148, 150, 161, 246, 311–12
Stage, intellectual realism 9, 23, 41, 56, 189, 202, 215, 231–46, 248–64, 287, 314
Station point 3, 21, 60, 63, 68, 75, 78, 291
Strategies of representation
    content/structure 160, 170, 171–2, 174
    flexibility of 185–6, 220, 224, 227, 228, 246, 287
    viewer-centred/object-centred 8, 9, 10, 35, 189, 203–13, 214–29, 232, 250, 256, 267, 287
    view-specific/array-specific 35, 40, 49, 55, 56, 188–200, 214, 218, 219, 221–2, 225–7, 233, 244, 250–1, 256, 263–4, 287
Symbolic code/system 25, 88, 150, 231, 287
Symmetry 15, 39, 289, 314, 318–31, 351, 379

Tadpole figures 92–7, 238–45, 378, 380
Task-specific schemes 41, 52
Tests: Draw-a-man 135–6; kinaesthetic sensitivity 369
Texture 105, 107, 159
Topology 86, 232, 299
Training 16, 125–30
Transformations 26, 73, 86, 256

Transparencies 105, 149, 214, 217, 258–61, 374
Triangle, *see under* Forms
Trimetric projections 78
Trompe l'œil 20

Vanishing point 81
Variance cycles 47–9, 54
Verbal instruction 71–3, 178–86, 195–6
Viewer-centred *see under* Strategies of representation
Viewing position 49–50
Viewpoint, fixed/single 6, 51, 60, 74, 83, 105ff, 142, 148, 149, 150–1, 152, 189, 203, 232, 234

View-specific *see under* Strategies of representation
Visual angle 60, 78
Visual constrast 9, 10, 11, 205–13, 263
Visual field 52, 96
Visual realism 23, 24, 73, 182–6, 189, 202, 234
Visual world 148
Visuo-tactile realism 56

Water-level task 14, 292, 311–16, 328–9, 334–5, 350, 354
Writing 88